Laura Hunsberger

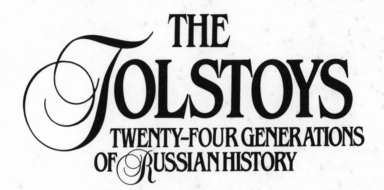

THE TOLSTOYS
TWENTY-FOUR GENERATIONS OF RUSSIAN HISTORY

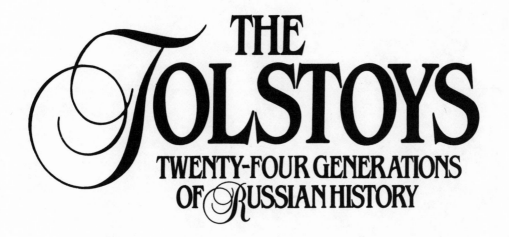

THE TOLSTOYS
TWENTY-FOUR GENERATIONS OF RUSSIAN HISTORY

NIKOLAI TOLSTOY

Quill
William Morrow
New York

For

Alexandra, Anastasia, Dmitri
and Xenia Tolstoy-Miloslavsky

Library of Congress Cataloging-in-Publication Data

Tolstoy, Nikolai.
  The Tolstoys: twenty-four generations of Russian history.

  Includes bibliographical references and index.
  1. Tolstoy family.   I. Title.
DK37.8.T64T65   1986   947'.009'92 [B]   86-12456
ISBN 0-688-06674-7

Printed in the United States of America

First Quill Edition

1 2 3 4 5 6 7 8 9 10

BOOK DESIGN BY CRAIG DODD

CONTENTS

Author's Preface

*L*ike thousands of Russians in the present century, I was born and brought up in another country and was only able to enter the land of my ancestors as a visitor in later years. It was nevertheless a very Russian upbringing, one which impressed on me the unusual nature of my inheritance. I was baptized in the Russian Orthodox Church and I worshipped in it. I prayed at night the familiar words of *Oche nash*, attended parties where little Russian boys and girls spoke a mixture of languages, and felt myself to be by origin and temperament different from my English friends. I think I was most consciously affected by those melancholy and evocative Russian homes where my elders, for the most part people of great charm and eccentricity, lived surrounded by the relics – ikons, Easter eggs, portraits of Tsar and Tsaritsa, family photographs, and émigré newspapers – of that mysterious, far-off land of wolves, boyars and snow-forests of Ivan Bilibin's famous illustrations to Russian fairy-tales. Somewhere there was a real Russian land to which we all belonged, but it was shut away over distant seas and space of years.

I knew nothing of the terrible upheaval which had brought about this strange state of affairs until I was about eight years old. My parents never spoke to me about the Revolution or the Red Terror: of this I am certain, since I distinctly remember one of my school-friends explaining the whole business to me at the age of eight. Before that I had joined with everyone else in rejoicing over the Red Army's victories which we heard of on the wireless. Now, thanks to Bill Sowry's exposition, I knew there were Red Russians and White Russians, and that I belonged to the latter.

It was well before this time, when I cannot have been more than five years old, that I had a terrible dream. I was standing by a first-floor window of the big house next to my grandparents' home in North Devon. Suddenly I was aware that all the inhabitants of Bideford had left their homes and were swarming in a dense mob along the Instow road. I knew without explanation that they were coming for me, and that no escape was possible. Of course there may be a matter-of-fact explanation for this experience, but my conviction, overwhelmingly vivid, is that my subconscious mind was experiencing the appalling cataclysm through which my father had lived at the same age, and which had been somehow implanted also into my psyche.

Be that as it may, my impression after immersing myself in recent years in the activities of my ancestors is that we are consciously aware of only a small portion of those inherited characteristics, qualities and experiences we receive from our forefathers. Time and again I recognized aspects of long-dead Tolstoys which have re-emerged in the present generation, and will doubtless surface again in the next. An advantage of studying a family, so many of whose members were writers or artists, introspective and analytical, is that one knows so much about their mental processes. Characters and attitudes recur again and again.

The Tolstoys, like any other family, are not a collection of disparate individuals united only by the same surname, but in many respects comprise a supra-individual unity, through which a common consciousness ebbs and flows. It is said that certain qualities are borne by the male genes. I am not qualified to tell whether or not this is so; but I am persuaded that, though the identification of family traits is not readily susceptible to scientific analysis, it is so strikingly self-evident as to provide testimony in itself of the influence of heredity.

I have singled out common factors which distinguish our family from an early period. Professor Marc Raeff has remarked on conditions peculiar to Russian history which made noble families exceptionally close-knit, even over periods of generations, and across quite distant cousinhood bearing the same name and origin: "circumstances explain the role played by the family – or clan, to give the literal translation of the Russian term *rod* – in Muscovite Russia. . . . The family was the only institution that could counteract the individual's sense of isolation in space and his insecurity with respect to his neighbours and to his political overlord (be he a Mongol Khan or a Russian grand duke). Family solidarity also waxed strong as a means of countering the individual nobleman's complete dependence on the prince's favour and the splintering tendencies of the inheritance system. It was also used to perpetuate, or at least safeguard, for more than one generation the gains and advantages acquired by a single individual or generation. How else could status, wealth, and privilege acquired through service be preserved and transmitted to successive generations?" The peculiar Muscovite system of *mestnichestvo*, whereby no member of a family should be subordinate to someone whose ancestor had served under one of his forefathers, greatly accentuated the stress on family solidarity.[1] Examples of this abound in the family's history. The brothers Ivan and Peter Tolstoy, isolated by Peter the Great's suspicions, were solaced by an exceptionally close friendship, unaffected by the vast distance separating them. When Leo Tolstoy had his house searched by the police in 1862, it was to his cousin Alexei Constantinovich Tolstoy, whom he scarcely knew, that he turned for help at Court.[2]

From a very early period the Tolstoys were singled out as a *rod* with strong identifying marks of unity. First, Tolstoys all possess their own patron saint, who on one occasion intervened to save the life of a member of the family. This is St. Spyridon, a Cypriot bishop who took part in the Council of Nicaea in AD 325, and whose remains were transferred ultimately to Corfu, where they are ceremonially paraded twice a year.[3]

Secondly, the entire family has been blighted by a curious malediction. It was Peter.Andreevich Tolstoy who arranged in 1718, at Peter the Great's instruction, the secret death of the Tsarevich Alexei. A family tradition recorded that in the hour of his agony the wretched Tsarevich "cursed Tolstoy and all his house to the twenty-fifth generation, and foretold that each of those generations would produce men of pre-eminent ability – but also mad and witless individuals". It is significant that a version of the curse, recorded only eight years after the Tsarevich's death, was addressed to Peter Tolstoy's *nephew*: "the death of the Tsarevich will be avenged on you, your uncle and the whole family". Clearly *all* Tolstoys were regarded as sharing complicity, even those not directly descended from Peter Andreevich.[4]

Personal characteristics remarked upon as recurring among the Tolstoys include their longevity,[5] family pride (noted by Gogol),[6] and intellectual vigour. The great nineteenth-century historian Klyuchevsky observed once that "nearly all the noble families which rose to prominence in the times of Peter the Great and Catherine II have degenerated. The Tolstoys constitute an exception. That family has exhibited remarkable vitality."[7] They were also well-known for their love of the opposite sex.[8] Also remarkable is the frequent occurrence of members possessing exceptional physical strength. Herzen was struck by the extraordinary physical energy which irradiated from Feodor Ivanovich Tolstoy like an electric force. The poet Alexei Constantinovich could straighten horseshoes and drive nails into walls with his bare hand, and his cousin Leo, the great novelist, also displayed exceptional athletic prowess. He could lift 180 lb. with one hand and, lying on his back, would straighten out his arms under a 13-stone man. At 82 he tested his strength by heaving a wardrobe onto his back![9]

Finally, one may note a strain of wildness and eccentricity, especially manifest in Feodor Ivanovich "the American", General Osterman-Tolstoy, Alexei Constantinovich, and the uninhibited Leo. Some may see in this the shadow of the Tsarevich's curse. Much may be inherited from the Miloslavsky family: Ilya Danilovich Miloslavsky was as eccentric and Herculean in build as any Tolstoy, and his cousin Ivan Mihailovich ("the old Achitophel") was the most astute politician of his age.

Pursuing a family history is a strange experience. How much does our present existence depend on a multitude of long-past chance events? Had Indris succumbed to the Black Death in Chernigov in 1353, had the Naryshkins triumphed over the Miloslavskys in 1682, or Bulavin's Cossacks stormed Azov in 1708 – I should not be here to write these lines. And, but for the bravery of an English nanny and the charity of an English chaplain in 1920, I should have been born, not in happy England, but almost certainly as one of that generation of 1935 whose brief lives began and ended in socialist corrective labour camps north of the Arctic Circle.

Nikolai Tolstoy-Miloslavsky
Berkshire, 1982.

1
Family Origins

*L*ike other European aristocracies, the Russian nobility regarded splendour of ancestry as a pre-eminent quality of rank. Indeed, during the late feudal period it was so important as ultimately to override both common-sense and the state's interest. Under an antiquated system known as *mestnichestvo*, the aristocratic officers of state determined seniority in government service by a calculation of the rôles played by themselves and their ancestors in relation to those of their colleagues. Not unnaturally, ferocious squabbles and lawsuits recurred, in which personal merit had no legal relevance.

A nobleman whose "family was equal or more honourable than another, and in state service or at table had not previously sat below that other family, nevertheless is compelled by the Tsar to sit in such a place. Then he refuses, insults and swears at the rival nobleman, and even though they compel him will not sit there, but gets up from the table. He is not allowed to pass and is told he should not be disobedient and anger the Tsar, but he continues shouting even when the Tsar orders his head to be cut off. He just will not sit where he is told, and gets under the table. Then the Tsar orders him to be carted off to gaol or refuses to admit him into his presence. This disobedience deprives them of their noble status, and they have to earn again their old position by state service."[1]

This undignified procedure should not however be judged by the more refined standards of the courts of Western Europe. It is necessary to remember, first, that the system of *mestnichestvo* was in fact a primitive check on the autocratic power of the Tsar to promote whom he chose; and, secondly, that it was not just the boyar's own office that was at stake, but the status, power and wealth of his entire family. Generations yet unborn might curse him should he weakly consent to sit in the wrong place at a Kremlin dinner. Finally, the system was frequently waived in time of crisis, such as war.

Such a ridiculously rigid system could only hamper the burgeoning power of the Russian state, and in 1682 Tsar Feodor Alexeevich abolished *mestnichestvo*.[2] The records on which claims for precedence were based were ordered to be burned in order to prevent further quarrels, and the nobility were required to deposit instead plain accounts of their ancestry in the archives preserved at the Kremlin. The Tolstoys' account of their origin ran as follows: In 1353 Indris, "a man of distinguished ancestry" (described as a "Count" in one version), came from the Holy Roman Empire to Chernigov, accompanied by his sons Litvinos and Zimonten and a force of 3,000 men. All three were baptized under the names Leonti, Constantine and Feodor respectively. A pedigree traced the Tolstoys back to Indris, through his elder son Constantine.[3]

In 1686 Andrei Vasilievich Tolstoy declared that this account had been extracted from a mediaeval Chernigov chronicle. Its sparse outline can be supplemented by evidence from the entry itself. The name "Indris" is the Russian equivalent of the German "Heinrich" (Henry), which suits well his stated origin in the Holy Roman Empire.[4] His first son's name "Litvinos" is in fact an epithet meaning "Lithuanian", and it seems likely therefore that some early redactor misinterpreted a reference to "Constantine *Litvinos*", *i.e.* "Constantine the Lithuanian". The second son's name "Zimonten" is equivalent to "Sigismund", a name of Polish origin. From this it seems reasonable to deduce that a noble or knightly Heinrich came from some part of the Holy Roman Empire to take service in Lithuania,

Previous page: the Tolstoy coat of arms

The burning of the Books of Nobility, 1682

then closely connected with Poland. There his two sons were born; and later, after an unspecified stay, they accompanied him further east to Chernigov in Russia.

There are good historical reasons for believing this account to be authentic. First, the strong likelihood that the original chronicle entry was misinterpreted in this way implies that it had been in existence long enough to have been miscopied well before 1686. Secondly, the historical circumstances of the mid-fourteenth century, when Indris is said to have arrived in Russia, corroborate remarkably the account implicit in the family record.

The Russia to which Indris and his followers came in 1353 was a land assailed on every side by menace. It would be hard to conceive of a less propitious moment for a man to think of establishing his family fortunes in that unhappy country. To the south and east lay the huge empire of the Tartars of the Golden Horde. To sit on a Russian throne a Russian prince had to sail down the rivers to the Great Khan's capital at Sarai on the Volga. There, with deep humility, he received the *yarlyk* which alone gave him authority to rule over his ancestral domains. It was an authority exercised within extremely restricted limits: let a Great Prince contemplate exercising his own foreign policy or even be tardy in paying tribute (*yasak*), and fire and sword would sweep yet again over the Russian land as Tartar armies sent their raiding-parties (*yartawl*) to their westernmost bounds.

The most powerful of the Russian principalities was Moscow, ruled over by its Great Prince Semeon Ivanovich; "the Proud" as his subjects knew him – but not so proud as not to be the abjectly obedient subordinate of Khan Jani-Beg at Sarai.

As if the crushing power of the Horde were not enough, Moscow was being hemmed in also from the west by another great empire, that of Lithuania. In the first half of the fourteenth century her brilliant ruler Guedimine had greatly expanded Lithuanian territory eastwards. His son and successor Olgerd continued

13

this policy, less by direct conquest than by ensuring that Russian princes accepted a Lithuanian presence and pursued Lithuanian interests. By chance it happened that all three of Russia's principal rulers, Olgerd of Lithuania, Semeon of Moscow, and Jani-Beg of the Horde succeeded to their respective thrones in 1340–41.

A great diplomatic game was in progress, in which Moscow was merely a pawn. Jani-Beg's policy was to weaken Moscow's hold over the lesser Russian principalities whilst conceding her just enough strength to act as a buttress against Lithuanian expansion.[5] It was a delicate juggling act, performed with great skill. If Moscow became too strong she might shake off her dependence on the Horde; if too weak, then Lithuania could expand eastwards at her expense.

This Olgerd was determined to do. His emissaries in Russian principalities arranged the promotion of pro-Lithuanian bishops and officers of state. He made an alliance with the ruler of Smolensk, and signed a treaty with Moscow in 1349. In 1352 war with the Poles and Hungarians caused a temporary setback, but in the following year Lithuanian power was in its apogee. In the west Olgerd made peace with Poland and defeated the Prussians. He deposed his brother and co-prince, making himself supreme ruler. Finally in the east the plague fortuitously removed Semeon of Moscow together with important members of his family and entourage. In the north Novgorod turned against Moscow, and opportunities for Lithuanian expansion presented themselves on a broad front.[6]

To the south-west of Moscow, on the borders of the Lithuanian empire, lay the principality of Chernigov. Ruled by native princes,[7] it had already come under Lithuanian suzerainty in the reign of Olgerd's father. Now, at some point in the third quarter of the century, Olgerd moved forward and absorbed Chernigov completely, appointing one of his sons as its Great Prince.[8]

It will be seen at once how aptly the arrival of a Lithuanian military commander (*voevod*) at Chernigov in 1353 tallies with these events. It was Olgerd's policy to establish a Lithuanian presence in neighbouring Russian states. In contemporary Prussian annals we are told that Olgerd acquired "many strongholds" in Russia, where he established powerful nobles whose forces joined him on his campaigns.[9] A Lithuanian presence was seen by many Russians as a welcome counter-balance to Tartar hegemony.

It is clear that Indris was just such a Lithuanian governor, or *voevod*. Profiting by the death of the Great Prince of Moscow in 1353 and the generally favourable concurrence of events, Olgerd despatched him with a military force to establish a presence in the inviting frontier region of Chernigov. Shortly afterwards Olgerd asserted direct rule there, retaining his *voevod* and garrison, just as he had done earlier at Pskov. In 1463 a Livonian "princeling", by coincidence named Indrik and described as "a German", was sent by the Grand Master of the Teutonic Knights to arrange a peace treaty with Pskov.[10] Indris himself was presumably a man of some substance and military experience to be entrusted with such a key rôle, and the command of a large body of troops. A likely conjecture is that Heinrich, ancestor of the Tolstoys, was a former knight of the Teutonic Order, with whom Lithuania had signed a treaty in November 1338.[11]

The Chernigov into which Indris rode at the head of his *druzhina* (war-band) was a once-glorious but now backward province of ancient Rus. Its towns were small and scattered, lying chiefly along the rivers Desna and Seim. The town of Chernigov was placed at a strategic point by the right bank of the Desna, above its confluence with the mighty Dnieper. It possessed a fortress (Kremlin), the Cathedral of the Transfiguration, and the ancient church of Saints Boris and Gleb. Below the hill on which these imposing buildings stood lay a large suburb of wooden houses, surrounded by a timbered rampart.[12] Outside the walls to the north stretched forests and marshes, thousands of versts, past Smolensk, Moscow, Novgorod, until in the darkness of the north the land ended by the Frozen Sea, where witches and sorcerers dwelt.

As the moon rode out over Russia's vast darkness, pinpoints of light indicating human habitation were few and faint, a pathetic contrast to the glittering iridescence of the heavens above. A whole army could be swallowed up once it left the few recognizable landmarks. In 1316 a large military force withdrawing from an attack on Novgorod "lost the way among the lakes and swamps, and began to die of hunger. They even ate horse flesh, and others tearing off the leather of their shields ate it. They burned and threw away their belongings and arms, having suffered no little harm."

Mankind stood on the defensive against nature, and nature seemed rarely to relent. For a large part of the year the Russian land lay under thick snow. Travel was impossible except on the frozen rivers, and men lived cooped up in tiny groups in town, monastery or peasant's hut. Time and again the elements struck. In 1326 Novgorod was ravaged by fire. In 1337 "the whole of Moscow was burnt down; and then there came heavy rain and flooded everything. . . . The same year Toropets was burned down and flooded." In 1340 rebuilt Novgorod was burned to the ground; the flames raged so fiercely that they leaped the river and destroyed the quarter across the Volkhov. "The whole of Smolensk was burnt down in the same year. . . ." Two years later Novgorod was destroyed again. What fire spared the floods devoured, and ice-floes grinding in the rivers carried off bridges and boats.[13]

When the snow had melted and the rivers subsided, Russia's human adversaries took their place. In the west the Poles, Lithuanians or Teutonic Knights were on the march, to the north the Swedes. Worst of all, of course, were the Tartars, spreading like a plague over young Russia's tortured carcase. Finally, in 1352, the year before Olgerd despatched Indris to Chernigov, the plague itself entered the country. It was the so-called Black Death, which was ravaging all Europe and is estimated to have destroyed a quarter or third of the entire Continental population. This terrible infliction was received with typically Russian fatalism: "it came on us by God's loving kindness, and in His righteous judgment, death came upon people, painful and sudden, it began from Lady Day till Easter; a countless number of good people died then. These were the symptoms of that death: a man would spit blood and after three days he was dead . . . this death . . . passed over the face of all the land; and whomever God commanded, that man died, and whomever he saved, him he admonished and punished, that the rest of our days we may live in the Lord virtuously and sinlessly."

Not for the first or last time it must have seemed the Russian people might be extinguished from the face of the earth. It was a land where even the ikons wept.[14] The Great Prince of Moscow died, as did his two sons, the Metropolitan, and hosts of the Prince's subjects of every rank. The traveller arriving in Russia passed through a desolate landscape, where only the raven croaked desultorily above, and the fox and wolf barked in the thicket. Clouds of wild geese and enchanted swans rose from the rivers, but of human habitation there was scarcely a sign.[15]

15

But survival is perhaps the Russian's most enduring quality. Whilst the Tartars, the Lithuanians and the plague swept over the land, the sound of the axe still rang out in forest clearings, and the two-tined peasant plough prepared ground for the winter rye. If the climate was fiercely hostile, the land was rich in timber for building and fuel, the forests teemed with game, honey, wild berries, mushrooms and herbs, and by the weirs fish gleamed in shoals. When the Tartar came riding and a black pall hung over town and village, the survivors moved deeper into inaccessible woods and began the work again. When the plague struck there was magic, medicine, herbs and, above all, the Church to protect Christ's suffering people.[16]

Russia would come through her testing time, and a resilient, toughened people was approaching its destiny, a destiny in which the descendants of Indris would play no insignificant part. Of Indris himself nothing more is known than the circumstances of his arrival. He must inevitably have been granted an estate (*votchina*) by the ruler of Chernigov as a means of sustaining himself and his war-band. To maintain his exceptionally large military following, he would have required a number of rich manors – possibly the property of boyars recently removed by the plague. When not on the Prince's service or attending his court, Indris would pass from one manor to another, living with his family and followers off the products of the land.

These estates could be very rich. Two centuries earlier a princely estate in Chernigov is described as possessing 700 slaves and great cellars containing hundreds of barrels of wine. Each estate was a self-contained community. A fifteenth-century example had living within its bounds two armourers, three tailors, two carpenters, four cooks, two bakers, three firemen, two archers, one clerk, six gardeners, two huntsmen, one fisherman, four millers, three falconers, one poultryman, one kitchen gardener, two stokers and one master silversmith. The estates themselves were each managed by a steward (*ognishchanin*), whose duty it was to supply his lord when in residence, and provide a specified income, mostly in kind.[17]

At times Indris would have attended at the court (*dvor*) of the Chernigov Kremlin. There was hunting and hawking, riding and military exercises, councils of peace and war, and attendance by the newly-converted Indris in the Cathedral of the Transfiguration, where Bishop Grigory presided over the majestic ritual that burned undimmed throughout the night of Tartar domination.

Then came the winters, when travel was only possible on ski or sledge, giant snowdrifts blocked the narrow streets between stockaded town houses, and the boyar was confined for weeks or months on end with his family and following in the manor on his estate, or at the Prince's court. The eighteenth-century Prince Mihail Shcherbatov looked back nostalgically to the simple life enjoyed by the richest of his ancestors. Life had been wonderfully tedious in those far-off days: "there was no variety of literature written for entertainment, and no regular social life, so that people were induced by sheer boredom to read the Holy Scriptures and thus to retain their belief."[18] But, whatever the ennobling virtues of boredom, it is probable that life was by no means so dull as it might appear with hindsight.

It is true there was no literature as we know it except for the Bible which, despite Prince Shcherbatov, required no impetus of boredom to enjoy and really constituted a complete literature in itself. There was also an astonishingly rich oral literature, of which only part has survived. As the feast was cleared away and the buffoons and jugglers (*skomorokhi*) jumped off the tables, travelling singers were ushered into the hall. Accompanying themselves frequently on a sort of recumbent harp, the *gusli*, they sang the tales of Giant Svyatogor, and of Mykula Selyaninovich and Volga Svyatoslavovich's rout of the Tsar of the Golden Horde. There were the adventures of mighty Ilya Muromets, and others recalling Chernigov's former days of glory, when Vladimir I ruled in Kiev. Vladimir's nephew Ivan Godinovich had travelled to Chernigov to woo Nastasia, the rich merchant's daughter. Blood and horror greeted them as they returned, and repetition cannot have dimmed the excitement of the tale.

Just outside the warm, joyous hall lay the dark eternal forest whose wolves, bears, and stranger denizens occupied the wastes beyond the stout fir palisade. Above the spark of glowing light was the freezing cowl of heaven, with its hundred thousand glittering stars: "There is inscribed a writing on blue velvet, and to read that writing is given neither to priests nor to deacons, nor to wise muzhiks," as the riddle ran.

After the dark night of winter came the thaw, the floods, and finally the pale spring sun, young green leaves, flowers, horse bells jingling behind the plough; and preparations for war as Prince Dmitri Olgerdovich raised the crowned eagle banner of Chernigov above his host. Perhaps the sons of Indris fought at the great field of Kulikovo in 1380, when a Russian army for the first time showed it could defeat the Tartar Horde on open ground. For two brothers of Prince Dmitri played a prominent part in the action, and the contemporary epic *Zadonshchina* tells how the Lithuanian princes eagerly set out with trumpets, lances and helms to do battle with Khan Mamai: "30 Lithuanian nobles" were killed in the victory.[19]

The Tolstoy coat-of-arms bears a sword, a key and an arrow surmounted by an angel's wing. It was described as ancient in the early eighteenth century, but how far back these symbols originate in the mediaeval period is unknown.[20] A family legend tells of an imprisoned ancestor rescued by an angel, who provided him with a key and weapons to escape. There is no means of telling whether there is any vestige of truth in this account, whether it refers to Indris himself or a descendant, or whether it is mere aetiological speculation.

After Indris's arrival in 1353 there is a period of obscurity, due doubtless to the fact that the family declined in importance during the fifteenth and early sixteenth centuries. This probably resulted from the early Russian system of aristocratic inheritance of land, whereby the landowner could bequeath his estate in any manner he chose, subject only to the family's consent. Frequently this resulted in the division of the property among several male heirs. As Jerome Blum points out, "the successive splintering of the patrimony that resulted from this practice could lead easily to the ultimate impoverishment of a family. Members of each successive generation inherited ever smaller and often scattered parcels."[21]

The descendants of Indris also followed another course widespread at the time. According to the deposition made by the family in 1686, Andrei Kharitonovich, great-grandson of Indris, migrated from Chernigov to Moscow during the reign of the Great Prince Vasily the Blind (1425–62). Depleted wealth was one motive, and the opportunities for advancement provided by the increasingly powerful Muscovite state formed another. Descendants of reduced nobility and even royalty were regularly taking service in Moscow at this time.[22]

The Great Prince Vasily evidently had high regard for Andrei, and in 1686 there was said to exist a charter testifying as much. He was also said to have bestowed on his new servitor a silver cross, passed down ever since in the senior line of the family and still, after more than five centuries, held by the head of the family with this tale traditionally attached to it. A more questionable compliment was the bestowal on Andrei of the royal nickname *"tolstoy"*, meaning "fat".[23] It was in this way that the heirs of Indris became known by the surname Tolstoy.[24]

Apart from the rôle played by Indris in the Lithuanian absorption of Chernigov in the mid-fourteenth century, the Tolstoys did not make any significant impact on the history of Russia until the second half of the sixteenth century, when the records testify to their increasing prominence in the greatly expanded Russia of Ivan the Terrible (1544–84).[25] Much had changed since the time of Indris, two centuries earlier. The small and largely helpless Principality of Moscow had expanded to a great state, stretching north to the Barents Sea and east to the Urals. The power of the Tartars was still great (their armies carried off thousands of Russians annually as slaves, and sacked Moscow in 1571), but now the Tsar of Muscovy had long firmly asserted his independence of the Khan and fought with him on equal terms. In the west the Kingdom of Poland had replaced Guedimine's Lithuania as the great power.

During this time, and the confused Time of the Troubles which followed, members of the Tolstoy family were prominent in positions of trust and daring. They appeared among the officers of successive Tsars' armies, received grants of extensive estates and numbers of serfs, and fought with distinction against foreign and internal enemies of the state. They were active in the Swedish campaign of 1589–90, and in Boris Godunov's struggle to defeat the False Dmitri in 1604. Sylvester Tolstoy, after a distinguished diplomatic and military career, was killed in 1612, during the fierce fighting required to drive the Polish conquerors from Moscow.[26] After their long descent in wealth and power since the days of Indris, the family was reascending. It was included by the great historian Klyuchevsky among those newly powerful families which, though of ancient but untitled Muscovite noble descent, had been little heard of in the sixteenth century. Where previously Tuchkov, Saburov or Godunov had been names to conjure with, it was now Naryshkins, Miloslavskys and Tolstoys who stood high in the public eye beside the throne of the newly-elected Romanov dynasty.[27] The two latter families, Tolstoy and Miloslavsky, were on the point of drawing together in an alliance whose outcome was to alter the course of Russian history. To understand the subsequent prominence and character of the Tolstoys, it is necessary to turn for a moment to their kinsmen the Miloslavskys.

2
The Tolstoys and the Miloslavskys

*W*hen Ivan the Terrible died in 1584 he was succeeded by his son Feodor II, a weakling who left the real direction of Muscovite government to his brother-in-law Boris Godunov. When Feodor in turn died in 1598, Boris persuaded a *Zemsky Sobor* (National Assembly) to choose him as Tsar. With limited success Boris attempted to restore the prestige and strength of Tsar Ivan's monarchy. But Russia was racked by increasing unrest and division, and his reign ended in those terrible upheavals so memorably dramatized in Pushkin's and Alexei Tolstoy's plays and in Moussorgsky's famous opera. Boris was accused of murdering his predecessor's heir, the Tsarevich Dmitri; and in 1604 a pretender, the "false Dmitri", marched on Moscow with Cossack and Polish allies. Tsar Boris died in the midst of the crisis and the false Dmitri was crowned in Moscow, but murdered a year later in a popular uprising.

A powerful boyar, Vasily Shuisky, now took the throne, only to succumb to ever-increasing convulsions that were plunging the country into chaos. He was deposed in 1610, and the Time of Troubles (as this period is known) developed into three disastrous years of civil war and foreign invasion. The son of the Polish King Sigismund was crowned Tsar in Moscow, a new false Dmitri raised the Cossacks and peasants in rebellion, and it was not until 1612 that the Muscovite serving nobility managed to raise an army and drive the Poles from Moscow. On 21 February a newly-convened *Zemsky Sobor* elected the sixteen-year-old Michael Romanov to the throne. During the next three hundred years his descendants were to transform Russia from an embattled principality on the edge of Asia into that enormous Empire which was to straddle three continents.

In 1913 the tercentenary of the accession of the first Romanov was celebrated with appropriate splendour by the ill-fated Emperor Nicholas II. Great enthusiasm for the times of the first Romanovs excited society, and the climax of the festivities was a magnificent ball held in the Winter Palace, at which the Emperor, Empress and principal nobility appeared in the gorgeous furred, embroidered and be-jewelled robes their ancestors had worn at the court of Michael Romanov.

Most of the great names of the seventeenth century were still borne by promi-nent members of Nicholas II's twentieth-century court, with one notable ex-ception. In the seventeenth century the House of Miloslavsky had gained almost unequalled prominence, notorious as well as glorious, only to disappear, meteor-like, in the following century. The male line had become extinct by the reign of Catherine the Great,[1] and the family was represented through female descent by the senior line of the Tolstoys. Following a representation by the head of the family, Pavel Sergeevich Tolstoy, Chamberlain at the Court, the Emperor Nicholas II conferred in 1910 the additional surname of Miloslavsky on the elder branch of the Tolstoys.[2] "And how is my friend Tolstoy-Miloslavsky?" the Tsar enquired shortly before the grant was officially announced. Courtiers were momentarily baffled until the Tsar smilingly made the position clear. But to understand why the name of Miloslavsky bears such a resonance in Russian history, and its particular significance in the history of the Tolstoys, it is necessary to return to the mid-seventeenth century.

At daybreak on 16 January 1648 the bells of Moscow began to toll. First a single clear stroke rang out from below the Uspensky Cathedral. The great

Previous page: Maria Ilinichna Miloslavsky

bell of the Cathedral tower responded sonorously, followed by the clangour of lesser bells. The groaning cadences increased, picked up by new chimes from the Blagoveshchensky and Rozhdestvensky cathedrals, the clustered cupolas of the Cathedral of Vasily the Blessed, and from the holy city's monasteries and convents, until reverberations from Moscow's two thousand churches and chapels filled and shook the clear cold air. Above the gathering clamour could be heard the deep groaning of the giant bell of Boris Godunov in its tower by the Kremlin Square. Twenty-four men hauled on ropes to set its 356-hundredweight mass in motion. A foreign visitor who had heard many Moscow bell-ringings wrote that: "Nothing used to affect me so much as the united clang of all the bells on these evenings. The earth shook with their vibrations, and the drone of their voice, like thunder, ascended to the skies."[3]

Tsar Alexei Mihailovich

For miles around, in monasteries, noblemen's seats and villages half buried in snow, men and women rose and began dressing in holiday finery. For on this joyful day was to be the wedding of the man who wielded virtually unlimited power over the millions of faithful Orthodox inhabiting the Russian land: "the Great Sovereign Tsar and Grand Prince Alexei Mihailovich of all Great and Little Russia, Autocrat of Moscow, Kiev, Vladimir, and Novgorod, Tsar of Kazan, Tsar of Astrakhan, Tsar of Siberia, Lord of Pskov, and Grand Prince of Tver, Ingra, Perm, Viatka, Bolgaria, and others; Lord and Grand Prince of Nizhni Novgorod, Chernigov, Riazan, Rostov, Iaroslavl, Beloozero, Udora, Obdorsk, Kondinsk, and all the northern lands; Lord of the Iversk country, of the Karlalinsk and Georgian kings, of the Kabardian land, of the Cherkass and Gorsk princes, and Sovereign and Lord of many other eastern, western and northern states and lands, to the father, grandfather, and heir" – titles not to be lightly uttered, since to omit even one could earn an unwary clerk a severe beating.[4]

The occasion was one of particular pleasure to the Tsar's subjects, or "slaves", as they proudly styled themselves in correspondence. The first Tsar of the Romanov dynasty, Michael Feodorovich, had ruled over an obedient and ex-panding Russia for thirty-three years. It was universally agreed that his had been the most beneficent rule in memory, but times were still unsettled and dangerous. His son and successor, the present Tsar, was now eighteen years old, had been on the throne for two and a half years, and showed every promise of being as devoted a ruler as his father. The extinction of the dynasty and a disputed succession appeared the most threatening menaces to Russia's progress, but they were now to become unlikely events with the wedding of the young, handsome and vigorous Tsar Alexei.

Amidst the din and waking bustle the Tsar accompanied by courtiers descended the Red Staircase from the Faceted Palace in the Kremlin, and passed along a plank pathway laid across the snowy Cathedral Square between ranks of Streltsi guards bearing enormous poleaxes. He entered the Uspensky Cathedral, where the Patriarch Iosif blessed him with the holy cross and sprinkled holy water on him. The Tsar moved slowly about the cathedral, kissing the ikons and praying for God's blessing on the union before the relics of the saints. The sovereign then emerged again into the square and crossed to the Cathedral of the Archangel Michael. There his father and previous Tsars of Muscovy lay buried, and a solemn requiem mass was held for the souls of the departed autocrats. Alexei Mihailovich was remarkable for his piety even in Holy Russia, and prayed long and fervently that he might be worthy of his inheritance.

As the majestic strains of the cathedral choir filled its dark painted vaultings and the bright clangour of the bells outside rang on, Moscow prepared itself for the glorious day. The city never failed to strike visitors with its astonishing beauty. The gold cupolas of the Kremlin church shone over a wintry landscape, arousing comparisons with Jerusalem and Constantinople. But Moscow's glories were made more striking by the breath-taking contrast of her clustered golden domes gleaming over the endless white plain around.[5]

In January the cold was unbelievably ferocious. Huge falls of snow had success-ively covered the land, "till, from the thickness and universal spread of the ice, the roads become impassable on foot, presenting everywhere the appearance of a mass of polished marble; and the fields, from the depth of the snow lying on them, here and there to several heights of man, are rendered altogether impervious."

To visitors unaccustomed to the frozen North it scarcely seemed possible that life could continue. Every river and stream froze over, "all the moist provisions, in the houses, cellars, and shops, froze also; and the oil which we bought during this weather was like manna or candied sugar. As for honey, it became hard as stone; and so did every egg, too hard to be broken. The fish were no sooner caught from the river than they froze, and rattled against each other like dry wood. . . ." Water brought up from holes in the ice at once froze in the barrel and had to be thawed out. Plates being washed up stuck together and congealed into a solid cylinder, and cabbages were rigid to the core. Beards and moustaches became white with hoar-frost, which had to be melted off before a fire. Nostrils were frozen internally and blocked the air passage. Spit rattled on the ground in rock-hard globules, and urine turned to ice as it hit the wall. A curious sight was that of slaughtered pigs being brought to market; they stood stiff and upright as in life on sledges passing through the streets. Fourteen years earlier the earth itself had cracked open with the cold, and a huge 140-foot fissure opened up in the Kremlin market-place. At night sharp reports like gunshots reverberated from the timbers of wooden houses crackling in the dreadful cold.

Indoors boyars and peasants alike could only survive by heaping logs into great stoves that formed the salient feature of every room. Despite this, and an internal heat comparable to that of a bath-house, white crystals of unscathed ice gleamed on every lock and doornail. In unheated rooms sheets of ice hung on the walls, despite their massive breadth of brick and stone. Windows became opaque with incrustations of marbled ice, and in one public building sheets of ice were substituted for panels of glass. As for the interminable church services, during which it was not permitted to sit, the visitor from milder climes might be excused for regarding them as a prelude for Hell itself.

Muscovites appeared quite inured to the terrible climate, and were "prepared to withstand the cold; for they are all clothed, both men, women, and children, in long close dresses with sleeves, well lined, both inside and out, with black fur, fitted to the shapes of their bodies. From their hands they never take off a kind of large cuff made of knitted wool, fur, or leather, as warm as fire in winter, with which they do all their work. . . ."[6]

Despite the evidence of these exceptional precautions, one is left with the impression that the Russians had over the generations acquired a high degree of resistance to pain and discomfort of any sort. An English envoy, shivering at the sight of little children playing in the snow dressed only in shirts, decided that the Muscovites were "so hardened and accustomed to both Heat and Cold, that their Custome seems to be turned into Nature." This, and the generally brutal treatment accorded the common people, made them extraordinarily hardy and "unquestionably . . . very proper for the Wars."[7]

The barbarous climate would not deter the citizens of Moscow on this happy day. In any case, His Majesty was deeply in love with his bride and would brook no postponement. Along frozen rivers skimmed the magnificent sleighs of the boyars towards the capital. The city gates were open and welcoming, and the normally truculent Streltsi leaned pacifically on axes or sat astride cannon, watching the crowds pass through the Kremlin's five heavily-fortified gates. Rich and poor mingled indiscriminately, for on occasions like this the Autocrat liked to be close to his faithful people. Hucksters and traders reopened their booths after the recent Christmas fair and, their mouths full of loose change, haggled with customers; tumblers and puppeteers vied for audiences; performing bears growled and danced; above all, the inns plied a roaring trade. The nightly collection of corpses had been removed from before the *Zemsky Dvor*, but the victims of drunken fights or exposure in the snow would soon replace them.

From time to time the beating of a small drum set the citizens crowding off the street, as the servants and guards of a great lord cleared the streets for his passage. High on his large sleigh sat the proud boyar, in his tall black fox-fur hat and furred caftan, with its sleeves dangling well below the wearer's idle hands. A beautiful white bearskin, large as that of a buffalo, was draped over the back of the sledge, emblematic of aristocratic wealth and luxury. His lady, the boyarine, came behind even more splendidly conveyed in a coach mounted on sleigh-runners, with hangings of scarlet and pink cloth trailing to the snow, and drawn by magnificent Persian horses. Behind the glass windows were close-drawn curtains, for a Russian boyarine must never be glimpsed by the outside world.[8]

The sledge of a Russian boyar

Meanwhile the Tsar had returned to the Faceted Palace, where he was being arrayed in imperial magnificence. What he may have lacked in the elegance and taste of his contemporaries Charles II and Louis XIV was made up in sheer splendour; a splendour of brocades covered with giant pearls and precious gems which dazzled and awed the loftiest Western visitors. In another chamber the boyars and high officers of state were being similarly arrayed in gorgeous golden robes, many of them borrowed from the royal wardrobe. From time to time a messenger prostrated himself before the Tsar and reported on the speed with which the boyars were dressing. The Tsar, who for some time had abandoned interest in everything save the wedding, decreed that his bride should be dressed as if for a coronation except that as yet she should not wear the crown. The bridal dress was that worn by the Tsar's mother at her wedding. Her attendants wove her long hair into the bridal plait. Eventually all was ready, and the Tsar with his gilded following joined her to proceed to the Cathedral. Slowly they descended the Red staircase in full view of the vast crowd, who were held back with difficulty by long ranks of Streltsi. As the royal pair entered their respective sleighs (the bride's was ceremonially hung about with long foxtails) the boyars mounted their Persian steeds to escort them with fitting pomp. Amongst their imposing ranks were men bearing the greatest names in Russian history – names in several cases far older and more resounding than that of the newly established Romanov dynasty.

There was Prince Vasily Andreevich Galitzine, Prince Feodor Nikitich Odoevsky, Prince Ivan Araslanovich Cherkaskoy, Vasily Ivanovich Sheremietev, Peter Petrovich Pushkin, and further highborn heirs of Rurik, Guedimine, and other progenitors of the great aristocracy. There too, with unconcealed exultation, rode the bride's close relatives Semeon Iurievich, Ivan Andreevich, Feodor and Grigory Iakovlevich, and the future military hero Ivan Bogdanovich – all scions of the House of Miloslavsky, who foresaw a golden age arising for all of their name. It was to be a golden age indeed, but one ending in bloodstained tragedy.

Amidst the joyful dancing of the bells and the acclamations of the crowd the golden procession rounded the corner of the Faceted Palace and flowed into the Cathedral of the Assumption (Uspensky Sobor). The interior formed a sombre contrast to the snow-covered square outside, but thousands of candles burning in chandeliers, flickering before the ikons, and held by the congregation cast a shifting glow on the great columns and walls arching up to the shadowy roof. As the nobles filed in and filled the nave they appeared joined in communion by the hundreds of saints, martyrs and tsars from Russia's past whose images glittered in gold, green, red and blue on every surface above and below. The face of Christ gazed from frescoes and ikons, gentle, suffering, threatening. A heavy scent of incense hung on the cold air, while the deep voices of a hidden choir intoned the liturgy.

Then the Patriarch and priests began the long solemn service. When all had been done, the couple were blessed and sprinkled with holy water and kissed the ikons. Then the new Tsaritsa was unveiled, and turned up to her husband a face as beautiful, modest and innocent as that of the Madonna in the Ustyug Annunciation. The happy couple took the communion wine, their bridal crowns were removed, and Alexei received on his head the historic Crown of Monomakh. The priest delivered a lengthy exhortation as to how they should live as man and wife. The Tsaritsa was bound to practise absolute obedience to her husband, who stood in relation to her as Christ does to the Church. If she offended he was entitled to beat her gently with a stick. However, they should try not to be angry with each other. More to the point, it was essential to avoid sexual activities on Mondays, Wednesdays and Fridays and to fast on all fast days. Then too they were not to commit sins on Dominical feast days or days commemorating apostles, evangelists and other sacred occasions.

Eventually the priest's homily came to an end, and he took Maria Ilinichna by the hand, presented her to her husband and told them to kiss each other. After that the Tsaritsa hid again behind her veil as all the congregation came forward to congratulate the young couple. The procession emerged into bright daylight to the sound once again of the great bells clanging over Moscow's ancient fortress. Back at the Faceted Palace a great feast was held in magnificent state. The Master of Ceremonies made a speech, the bride was presented by the boyarines with ceremonial fringed satin handkerchiefs, a choir of boys and girls sang a very obscene song, toasts were drunk in rich Hungarian wine, and the excessive formality of the occasion relaxed. Soon the time came for the Tsar and Tsaritsa to retire and, accompanied by the bride's parents and other distinguished figures, they repaired to their sleeping-quarters.

Maria Ilinichna entered the bedroom first, accompanied by a swarm of ladies and maid-servants. Many curious measures had been adopted in order to ensure the fertility of the union and to ward off the malicious intentions of the witches and imps whose malign task was to ensure that things went amiss. Beneath the marriage bed were forty interlaced sheaves of rye, whilst nearby were vessels of wheat, barley and oats, symbolic also of fertility. The ikons were covered lest the holy images should witness the night's carnal work. Maria quickly undressed down to her shift and got into bed. Soon afterwards the Tsar came to the door, and she sprang out, donned a sable-lined dressing-gown, and welcomed her husband. Together they sat at a little table and ate a roast chicken. The meal did not last long, and the young couple rose and went to their bed.

Meanwhile the boyars gave themselves up to unrestrained merriment at the Tsar's table. Contemporary accounts are unanimous that no such occasion could avoid the most energetic drunkenness, with ever-increasing shouting, singing, boasting, quarrelling and swearing. Slapping their mighty stomachs, the lords belched and farted in joyful abandon. But pleasures have an end, and after one hour a messenger from the Master of Ceremonies was despatched to find out if all had gone as it should in the marriage chamber. All had passed very happily indeed, and the boyars crowded through to the Tsar's room. Drinks were handed out all round and the joyful boyars, accompanied by fifes and kettle-drums, lurched off to their beds, whilst the Tsar returned to his. As an observer recalled not long after, "there never were such games and music and dancing" as at the Tsar Alexei's wedding to Maria Miloslavsky.

Tsar Alexei and Tsaritsa Maria

The bells had ceased their rolling, the last firework was discharged, and the Kremlin lay silent under the stars. Only the sound of a horse's hooves sounded out in the frozen night as the Master of the Horse, Ivan Vasilievich Morozov, performed his ritual task of riding until dawn round the palace where the sacred act was taking place, a drawn sword in his hand.[9]

During the prolonged festivities that followed, there were two great men who had occasion to feel as exultant as the happy Tsar. These were the Tsar's new father-in-law, Ilya Danilovich Miloslavsky, and the Tsar's former tutor, Boris Ivanovich Morozov. Both men saw the prospect of almost limitless power and wealth stretching before them as a result of the marriage. Though the Tsar had fallen deeply in love with his wife, and continued to love her throughout her life, the marriage had in fact been brought about by a skilful court intrigue.

Morozov had been tutor to the young Alexei Mihailovich, who at the time of his wedding was only eighteen and still considerably under his former mentor's influence. He cemented his power by inducing potential competitors such as Princes Repnin and Kurakin to accept rich governorships in distant provinces, whilst packing the court with nobles subservient to his interests. He did not feel himself sufficiently secure, however, and took a more direct measure to fix his hold on the youthful autocrat. Himself not of the first nobility, he was anxious to marry the Tsar to a maiden over whose family he could exert influence. Together with the Patriarch Iosif, he strongly urged the Tsar to wed. Alexei was compliant, and in accordance with Russian tradition large numbers of the nubile daughters of the aristocracy were invited to Moscow. They were housed under the care of his sister, the Tsarevna Tatiana Mihailovna, to be guarded closely in the Terem Palace until the ritual choice was made. The fearful rivalry brought about by this competition may be imagined, and a tragedy resulted.

The Tsar selected one attractive young girl, Euphemia Vsevolozhsky, and gave her a handkerchief and ring as confirmation. Her delighted parents dressed her in the state robes in which she was to be formally presented to the Tsar, but envious rivals managed to ensure that the wedding did not take place. When Euphemia appeared before Alexei she suddenly fainted away. Fearful that this might be a symptom of epilepsy, the Tsar called off the marriage. In fact the would-be bride had been maliciously interfered with; according to some her headdress had deliberately been fastened too tightly, whilst others believed poison had been administered. The Tsar was extremely upset, and when the truth was revealed felt that such bitterness and envy might make marriage impossible. But Boris Morozov had other ideas.

He was a frequent visitor to the ancestral home of the nobleman Ilya Danilovich Miloslavsky at Kirzhach, near the town of Alexandrov. Miloslavsky had three daughters, the two elder of whom were striking beauties. Miloslavsky was an exceedingly ambitious and avaricious man, and it was not long before he and Morozov arrived at an understanding. Back at the Kremlin Morozov never lost an opportunity of extolling the loveliness of the Miloslavsky girls. Alexei soon began to display interest, and Morozov arranged that on a given day the two young noblewomen should attend divine service in the Uspensky Cathedral in Moscow. From the obscurity of his magnificent covered pew the Tsar observed the visitors, and was immediately struck by the sweet and gentle beauty of the elder girl, Maria. After the service she was summoned to the Kremlin Palace, where Alexei found she was as good, kind and pious as her radiant good looks testified. He was soon deeply in love.

Morozov set in motion the next part of his plan. He was soon engaged to the second daughter, Anna (in seventeenth-century Muscovy a daughter simply accepted her father's choice of groom). Eleven days after the Tsar's wedding, on 26 January 1648, Morozov married Anna Miloslavsky. However, though Morozov continued for a while as virtual Prime Minister, the marriage brought him small happiness. As the Tsar's English doctor noticed, "the Lady was not so well pleas'd with him being an old Widdower, [he had married his previous wife in 1617!] and she a succulent black [-haired] young lass; so instead of children jealousies were got. . . ." Amongst those suspected of enjoying the luscious Anna's favours was an Englishman named William Barnsley.[10]

Meanwhile, the Tsar's new father-in-law was luxuriating in the sun of royal favour. Ilya Danilovich Miloslavsky was certainly one of the most remarkable and powerful characters in seventeenth-century Russia. Born on 3 July 1594, he came of an old and illustrious noble family which had already afforded great services to the country. Like the Tolstoys, they originated from the West, and their ancestor is said to have arrived in Muscovy in 1390 in the train of the Princess Sophia of Lithuania, who came to Moscow to marry the Great Prince Vasily Dmitrievich.[11] At the monastery of St. Sergei on the ancestral estate of Kirzhach there existed twelve tombs with inscriptions commemorating Miloslavskys, the earliest dated 1492, and other inscribed slabs were preserved before the altar of the church of St. Nicholas in Moscow.[12] In the sixteenth and seventeenth centuries they appeared regularly in high office in the register of military commanders (*Razryadnaia kniga*), and were frequently appointed as governors (*voevod*) of provinces. When the Papal Nuncio visited Russia in 1581 he was entertained at a splendid banquet by Ivan the Terrible, whom he found sitting with Feodor and Vasily Ivanovich Miloslavsky.[13]

Despite the grandeur of his name and origins, Ilya Danilovich Miloslavsky had not always lived at the summit of Muscovite society. According to the Englishman Collins, whose position as physician to the Tsar enabled him to learn much of court scandals, he was "of obscure Gentility, rais'd by the death of his Uncle *Grammatine* the Chancellor of the Embassadors Office, to whom he filled wine in his minority, . . . *Eliah* the present Emperours Father in law was of so mean account, that within this twenty years he drew wine to some English men, and his daughter gather'd *Mushrooms*, and sold them in the Market."[14] The Holstein envoy says simply that "he was not especially wealthy", which appears more in accord with the facts.[14] For it was state service which brought wealth to Muscovite nobles, and Ilya Danilovich had held distinguished offices years before Tsar Alexei set eyes on his beautiful daughter. In 1643 he had travelled as Ambassador to Constantinople.[15] The mission was full of dramatic incident, and Miloslavsky returned to Moscow only on 1 September 1644.[16] It was presumably as a result of this that he was chosen to manage the next stage in the Tsar's diplomatic strategy. In the following year he headed a similarly important embassy to the Netherlands. The Turks being stalled in the south, Miloslavsky was principally commissioned to recruit Dutch officers for service in the campaign being prepared against Poland.[17]

Not only were both embassies highly successful, but both involved large-scale financial transactions. In view of the *moeurs* of the time and Miloslavsky's notoriously acquisitive nature it seems incredible that he should not have aquired large sums along the way.

Be all this as it may, there is no question but that his daughter's happy marriage altered his financial and political position beyond recognition. Even before the wedding the Tsar sent him money and rich goods to enable him to play his part with expected credit. He was presented with a house in the Kremlin near the Tsar's palace, which he at once had torn down and rebuilt as a magnificent stone palace. Next to it he constructed a splendid church, triumphantly dedicated on 1 September 1652 to Saints Alexei and Maria, namesakes of his daughter and son-in-law.[18] Outside Moscow he and his relatives maintained vast estates, and it was a common sight to see the boyar Miloslavsky setting out in his carriage, pulled by a team of white horses and surrounded by a host of servitors and guards, for his nearby country house at Kuntsovo.[19] (Three centuries later Joseph Stalin owned a favourite country mansion on the same site.) There were many other such houses, where the Miloslavskys entertained lavishly, hunted, hawked and supervised manorial farms and forests in the beautiful Moscow countryside.[20]

The Kremlin palace of Ilya Miloslavsky

With all their faults, the Miloslavskys were on the whole men of taste and advanced culture, with a sophisticated interest in the arts and sciences that anticipated Peter the Great's enforced enlightenment. Ilya Danilovich himself had lived in Holland and maintained close liaison with the many Dutch, German and Scotch military specialists who flocked to Moscow after his recruiting mission of 1645. He was fond of books, and had his portrait painted at a time when excommunication was the fate of anyone adopting that impious Western European practice. The Miloslavkys' cultural rôle continued up to the end of their ascendancy. Fedosia Ivanovna Miloslavsky married Alexander Archilovich, Tsarevich of Imeritia, a man of sensitive literary abilities who wrote several highly-praised works in their home at his wife's inherited estate of Vsekhsvyatskoe.

The Tsarevna Sophia, whose mother was a Miloslavsky, was similarly advanced for her time and took as lover the cultured and Westernized Prince Vasily Galitzine.[21]

So great was the love of the Tsar for his Tsaritsa that it seemed there was scarcely any limit to the privileges and wealth he showered on his fortunate father-in-law and other Miloslavsky relatives. Unfortunately Ilya's appetite was commensurate with his fortune, and his name became a byword for greed and rapacity. "The old courtiers one by one had to go, and in their place were installed Miloslavsky's relations; who, since they had themselves all known want, revealed themselves very voracious, avaricious and greedy."[22] These qualities were ultimately to prove the family's downfall.

Ilya Danilovich himself was a curious compound of genuine ability, cunning and buffoonery. Tall and handsome, he was described by one who knew him as having the limbs and muscles of a Hercules. He possessed a brilliant memory and strong organizational powers, but at times made himself ridiculous by his naïve utterances. At the embassy in Holland he ostentatiously declined the epicurean dishes offered him at dinner, preferring to gorge himself on slabs of salted turbot. When asked what he thought of the finest Dutch chamber music, he replied gruffly that the beggars' laments in Russia were preferable.

Back in Moscow he behaved no more sensibly. Amongst other things he was head of the "Ministry of Health" (*Aptekarskoy prikaz*). It was reported to him in this capacity that a distinguished Lithuanian prisoner-of-war had been overheard by a guard plotting treason with the Tsar's Italian doctor. The prisoner, Gosievi, speaking in a foreign language, was heard to refer several times to "Crim Tartary": a power whose armies had once again taken the field against the Russians. Gosievi was hauled before Miloslavsky, who bitterly upbraided him for his treacherous conduct. Gosievi was baffled by the charge, until he recalled that the doctor had prescribed for his illness . . . cream of tartar. The boyar was convinced only with difficulty.

Only towards the Tsar himself did Ilya behave at all circumspectly. At first Alexei's youth made him quite fearful of his gigantic father-in-law. As time went by, however, familiarity bred contempt, and he treated the old man with more asperity. He referred to him only as "Ilya," and was known when impatient to punch his great body. On 10 November 1661 Tsar Alexei consulted the Duma as to the course of action to be taken to repel an invasion of the Polish army. Ilya Danilovich, sitting nearby, heaved himself up and declared sonorously that were he to be given command of the army he would return in no time with the Polish King a prisoner. This boastful nonsense was more than enough for the Tsar, who bawled out: "What, you born idiot! Have you the face to boast of your military expertise? When did you ever take part in war? Just tell us about your heroic actions, so we can hope you'll be able to do what you say. Old idiot, go and hang yourself!"

With which His Majesty jumped up, punched the boastful boyar and, pulling his beard, continued, "Are you trying to make fun of me, you blackguard?"

Poor Ilya was jerked from his seat and literally kicked out of the hall by his irate master.[23]

The venality and corruption practised by Miloslavsky and his son-in-law Morozov very nearly led to instant disaster. By corruptly forcing up the price of salt (which they and their creatures had cornered) they aroused ferocious discontent amongst the suffering population. Less than five months after the Tsar's wedding, on 1 June 1648, the mob rose in the streets and invaded the Kremlin, demanding the heads of Morozov, Ilya Danilovich and Ivan Mihailovich Miloslavsky, and other oppressors. Fearful scenes of confused violence took place. A large part of Moscow was burned to the ground, several of the Miloslavsky-Morozov clique's protégés being brutally murdered. Morozov escaped by the skin of his teeth, though his palace in the Kremlin was sacked and his wife only spared because, as one leader of the crowd explained, "Were you not the sister of the Tsaritsa, we would cut you in pieces!"

The popular belief, true or false, was that the Tsar had been betrayed by evil counsellors.

The Miloslavskys' newly-gained power appeared to be no sooner won than dissolved. Hatred of their rule spread to the provinces. On 9 July Mihail Vasilievich Miloslavsky, Voevod of Ustyug, was nearly lynched by an irate mob, and only escaped by the sacrifice of an unpopular underling.[24]

It is interesting to note the rebels' persistent delusion that the corruption and misrule was entirely the fault of subordinate officials – a delusion of which the Tsar was not slow to take advantage. On 3 June Morozov and Ilya Miloslavsky's administration was replaced by that of Prince Cherkaskoy, who summoned a national assembly with a view to conducting reforms. Meanwhile a number of highly-placed subordinates were sacrificed to the savagery of the mob. The Tsar was obliged to discard Morozov permanently, but courageously declined to permit him to be killed. Ilya Miloslavsky, however, with characteristic suppleness, bribed, flattered and cajoled the leadership of the rebellion, and reasserted his influence over his nineteen-year-old son-in-law, within a few weeks reappearing in public office more powerful than ever. With Morozov out of the way, Ilya Danilovich "in essence became head of state," and, as a recent historian has written of the Miloslavskys, "for the next half-century they exercised a major influence on Russia's domestic affairs and played a frequently disruptive role in Muscovite Court politics. By the end of the century, the name Miloslavskii had become feared and hated throughout Russia."[25]

Ilya Miloslavsky received all the posts formerly occupied by the favourite Morozov. He headed five separate *prikazi* (chancelleries). He was in charge of the *Inozemskoy prikaz*, which administered the foreign mercenary officers who were playing an increasingly important rôle in developing a modern Russian army. He was also head of the newly-founded (1649) *Reitarskoi prikaz* which was responsible for the maintenance of all cavalry forces in the empire. According to Dr. Collins, this made Ilya equivalent to Generalissimo of Russia's armies, and an extremely capable one at that: "He knew all the Commission Officers of an Army eighty thousand strong, where they quarter'd, and what their qualifications were."

He frequently attended musters at the Gartoly parade ground outside Moscow. His attention to detail was so great as to irritate some of the foreign officers: General Patrick Gordon, a Scotch mercenary, on his arrival at Moscow was ordered with other officers to attend a muster that afternoon.

"Being come into the field, wee found the Boyar [Ilya] there before us, who ordered us to take up pike and musquets (being there ready) and show how we could handle our armes; wherewith being surprized, I told him, that if I had knowne of this, I should have brought forth one of my boyes, who perhaps could handle armes better as I myself; adding it was the least part of an officer to know how to handle armes, conduct being the most materiall. Wherat he, takeing me up short, told me, that the best colonell comeing into this countrey must do so; to which I replyed, Seing it is the fashion, I am content. And so haveing handled the pike and musket, with all their postures, to his great satisfaction, I returned."

During his period of office Ilya Danilovich Miloslavsky continued military reforms initiated by his predecessor Morozov which, with shortcomings, largely created the new Russian army that, when taken in hand by Peter the Great, was to become so devastatingly effective a generation later. Against this achievement must be weighed the greatly increased rigours of serfdom instituted in 1649 to placate and strengthen the military service class from whom principal recruits were drawn.[26]

Ilya Miloslavsky, in addition to heading the Russian army, was as earlier noted head of the *Aptekarsky prikaz*. As such he was responsible for the (largely foreign) court physicians. They were obliged to appear at the *prikaz* office and beat their heads before the Boyar to learn their daily duties. Finally, he headed two other important chancelleries, the *Bolshoi kazni prikaz* and the *Kazennoi prikaz*. These, to the great satisfaction of the greedy Ilya, controlled most of Muscovy's wealth, from the treasure-stores of the Kremlin to the controls and licensing of merchants and traders. The wealth that poured into his coffers from these offices was vast, and his corruption was so notorious that the Tsar could not fail to be aware of it. But scandal had it that he was not displeased: Ilya had no sons, consequently one day his royal son-in-law would inherit all.[27]

Perhaps the worst of Ilya Danilovich's malfeasances was his experiment with counterfeiting. From 1654 onwards he minted some 120,000 roubles' worth of bogus copper coinage. The suffering caused by this debasement of the currency was so great that once again the people's patience snapped, and a mob several thousand strong marched out of Moscow on 4 August 1662 to ask justice of the bright eyes of their most gentle sovereign at his palace of Kolomenskoe. In particular they demanded the heads of Ilya Miloslavsky and his cousin Ivan Andreevich Miloslavsky, the Minister of Posts. But the Tsar had been forewarned, and Ilya (who was present) was quickly hidden in the Tsaritsa's apartments. The Tsaritsa Maria was also there, and witnessed the Tsar's presence of mind. He promised to dispense firm justice and persuaded the rebels to return to Moscow. Within a few days a force of Streltsi had attacked the mob, killed large numbers, and strung up some five hundred on gibbets as an effective warning to the remainder.[28] The terrified Tsaritsa was ill for a year after; but the debauched Ilya had escaped retribution yet again: as Dr. Collins suggested, "the Czaritsa alwaies kept up his Interest."

So the old villain continued to flourish. At court he adjudicated over minute points of etiquette and was always close to the Tsar, whether feasting in the Kremlin or hawking at Kolomenskoe. Prominent too among the ladies of the Tsaritsa Maria Ilinichna's household were her mother and, subsequently, step-mother (Ilya's wives), and her blackhaired and flighty sister Anna. Amongst the boyars most prominent at court were several cousins, two at least of whom were of exceptional ability.

But even as Ilya gorged himself his hour drew near. Not content with his unprecedented career of peculation and corruption, he turned to buggery as a pastime. This did not please the pious Alexei Mihailovich, who "at last perceiv-

Tsar Alexei receives a foreign embassy

ing Eliah too kind to some of his handsome Tartar and Polish slaves, he urged him
(being an old Widdower) either to marry or refrain the Court. For the Russians
highly extoll marriage, partly to people their Territories, and partly to prevent
Sodomy and Buggery, to which they are naturally inclined, nor is it punished
there with Death. A lusty Fellow about eight years since being at this beastly
sport with a Cow, cry'd to one that saw him *Ne Mishcay*, do not interrupt me; and
now he is known by no other name over all *Muscovy*, than *Ne Mischcai*." So wrote
the disapproving Dr. Collins.

Poor Ilya was soon past the pleasures of coining and buggery. He suffered a
severe stroke, which left him physically helpless and incapable even of recognizing
visitors. On 19 May 1668 he died at the age of seventy-four, and was buried in his
father's tomb. His Falstaffian personality was not forgotten, however, and he was
portrayed as a character in a 'Comedy' staged before the Tsar in the former

33

Tsaritsa Maria Ilinichna in procession at court

Miloslavsky palace. One may imagine that the actor made play of the old reprobate's mien and manners.[29]

Ilya had chosen the right moment to depart the stage. Within less than a year his daughter the Tsaritsa was also carried off. Without her protection his latter-day excesses might have overstretched the patience of the goodnatured Tsar, who at her side had survived wars and rebellions, plague and fire, and who was grief-stricken at her death and arranged suitably grandiose obsequies.[30]

Contemporary accounts unite in extolling her beauty, dignity and piety. The latter quality verged on the censorious, as she banished the buffoons, plays and other secular entertainments that had lightened her predecessors' solemn round. We learn that she and her consort slept in separate chambers but came to each other when they wished to be together at night. These occasions were not rare, and she bore him thirteen children during their twenty-one years of marriage. Two succeeded her husband as Tsars of Russia, a third was Regent for seven turbulent years, and Tsars with Miloslavsky blood in their veins reigned at intervals up to 1741.

The Miloslavsky family was in a justifiable state of apprehension. For how much longer could their hold on Russian public life continue? Ilya was dead and, much worse from the family's point of view, their gentle protector at the Tsar's side was no more. In the following year, however, the honour of the Miloslavskys burned with a lustre that outshone all old Ilya's disreputable triumphs and helped to postpone briefly the family's inevitable decline.

In his famous historical novel, *Yuri Miloslavsky* (1829), the author Zagoskin makes a character remind the eponymous hero of a popular saying that "the Miloslavskys always stood stoutly for the faith and Holy Russia." Such a motto could certainly have been adopted by Ivan Bogdanovich Miloslavsky, who in 1670 played a key rôle in saving Muscovy from overthrow and destruction at the hands of the famous Cossack rebel, Stenka Razin. Between Razin's hordes and the key city of Kazan stood the lightly fortified town of Simbirsk, whose governor (*voevod*) was Ivan Bogdanovich Miloslavsky. Miloslavsky withdrew what forces he had into the town's citadel. Swearing to "die before I yield to this robber", he fortified the citadel as best he could. On 4 September Stenka Razin's army arrived before the town and made vigorous preparations for a siege. The Cossacks speedily succeeded in occupying most of the town itself, and it was in the citadel

(Kremlin) alone that Ivan Bogdanovich's motley band held out for perilous weeks. It was not until exactly a month later that an advance unit of the Tsar's army, commanded by Prince Yuri Bariatinsky, came to Miloslavsky's relief. Stenka Razin was actually in the process of launching his fourth and most dangerous attack. The rebels fought with ferocious bravery, Stenka himself being twice wounded in the mêlée. But by the evening he realized the tide was turning and made his escape under cover of night. Bariatinsky and Miloslavsky then fell upon his disorganized followers and routed them utterly. Eight hundred of the survivors soon swung from gallows, and the Cossack host retreated southwards.

In April 1671 Stenka Razin fell into the hands of the Tsar's troops and was executed in Moscow after suffering the most appalling tortures. Meanwhile Ivan Miloslavsky advanced with an army and flotilla down the Volga to the surviving Cossack stronghold at Astrakhan. On 27 November 1671 the city finally fell, and Miloslavsky entered in triumph at the head of his troops. It is gratifying to record that he treated the defeated enemy with a clemency uncharacteristic of Muscovite armies of the period.[31]

Ivan Bogdanovich had long glittered prominently among that constellation of Miloslavsky cousins who dominated the last age of pre-Petrine Russia.[32] Most prominent posts at court and in government were occupied by men of their name, or by their protégés and connexions by marriage.[33] Increasingly significant among the latter were the Tolstoys, whose history is inextricably bound up with that of the Miloslavskys. It was noted in the previous chapter that the Tolstoy family, though ranking as nobles, were by no means so distinguished in the sixteenth century as they had been in the fourteenth. Reasons peculiar to Russian society made such a decline a not unusual occurrence. However, a revival of the family fortunes coincided with the establishment of the Romanovs on the throne. Three generations were headed by men of exceptional ability. Vasily Kharp Ivanovich Tolstoy played a distinguished part in the defence of Moscow against the Poles in 1618, and was rewarded in the customary manner with broad hereditary estates (*votchina*). Honours and rewards were heaped upon his shoulders, he became increasingly prominent in embassies and on the battlefield and he founded the town of Khotmyzhsk.[34]

About 1642 he was shrewd or lucky enough to marry his son Andrei to Sol-

omonida, daughter of the boyar Mihail Mihailovich Miloslavsky. At the time the match was not an unequal one, but within seven years Maria Miloslavsky became Tsaritsa and her family entered on its half-century of pre-eminence. The fortunes of the Tolstoys rose proportionately, though an early mark of the family's identification with the regime of Ilya Danilovich was the Moscow mob's destruction of Vasily Tolstoy's mansion in 1649. Vasily died in the following year, but his son Andrei soon proved that it was not just his Miloslavsky wife that earned him distinction. In 1669 he defended Chernigov (where his ancestors had settled three centuries earlier) with great gallantry against a Cossack assault, and was registered as a noble at the Duma.

It was the year the Tsaritsa Maria Ilinichna died and the Miloslavsky interest declined swiftly. The Tsar decided within the year that he would marry again, and in accordance with tradition suitable aristocratic maidens were invited to court, amongst whom he would make his choice. They included Andrei Tolstoy's relatives Anastasia, Matriona and Maria Tolstoy.[35] The parade of Russian beauties was, however, only a parade. The Tsar had already made up his mind.

Early in 1671 the Tsar Alexei Mihailovich married Natalia Naryshkin, the lively and pretty twenty-year-old daughter of a minor noble family. She had been brought up in the household of one of the Tsar's ablest advisers, Artamon Matveev, a man of relatively humble origin but outstanding abilities. His wife was a Scotswoman, and his home a remarkable enclave of Western culture. Whilst the Tsaritsa Maria and her father lived, he accommodated himself discreetly to the Miloslavsky interest (a portrait of his patron Ilya Danilovich hung in his hall). But with his young protégée sharing the throne of the Romanovs he seized the opportunity to repeat the rôle enjoyed by Boris Morozov over two decades earlier. A swarm of Naryshkin relatives parcelled out lucrative posts at court while in the provinces, often at the expense of Miloslavsky occupants, Matveev received continuing marks of favour and power from a gratefully uxorious Tsar.

An even greater blow to the Miloslavsky interest was the birth of a son to the new Tsaritsa. On 30 May 1672 the Tsar was overjoyed to receive a strong healthy boy. For three days Moscow's bells tolled joyfully and guns thundered from the Kremlin's walls: a cannonade whose reverberations would one day echo through all Russia. A month later the child was christened Peter amidst further public festivities, and the proud Tsar ordered a medal struck whose inscription idealised the child as Russia's "hope for a great future".

The Miloslavskys watched all these rejoicings in sullen anger. Did not the Tsar already have two sons ready to inherit the ivory throne of Ivan the Terrible? These were the Tsareviches, Feodor and Ivan, born in 1661 and 1666 respectively. When they succeeded their father the Miloslavsky interest should be stronger still, since neither of the boys was vigorous in character or body and inevitably power would fall largely into the hands of their mother's relations. Now the Tsar had resigned himself to the likelihood that neither of his two sickly elder sons was likely to be fit to succeed, and was grooming the Naryshkin boy to be his successor. The boy Peter shewed signs of disturbing precocity, learning to walk at seven months, absorbed with toy soldiers, guns and swords, and clearly the delight of his kind-hearted father. Meanwhile Peter's half-brothers remained pathetic invalids, scarcely fit to rule and indeed unlikely to survive to do so.

Astrakhan at the time of Stenka Razin's uprising, 1671

Then, as happened so frequently in Muscovite politics, the pendulum swung again. On 8 February 1676 the vigorous Tsar, only forty-seven years old, un-expectedly caught a severe chill and died. This was a turn neither of the two jealous factions of Miloslavsky and Naryshkin had expected. Alexei Mihailovich left behind him a name as the noblest man to grace the Russian throne. Majestic in appearance, he was pious, hardworking, and generally benign to those who graced his "bright eyes". In all this he took after his mild father, the Tsar Michael. At times, however, he showed himself the father of the future Peter the Great. When angered he could punch and kick offending courtiers, as the burly Ilya Miloslavsky could testify. He would play robust practical jokes, ducking his huge-bellied boyars in an ice-cold pond, or kicking them playfully up the backside. (He would incidentally have earned the approval of the modern medical profession: smoking in Russia during his reign was punishable by death.)[36] Above all he was single-minded in pursuing the goal of Russia's greatness, recapturing Smolensk from the Poles, attacking the Swedes on the Baltic, and crushing with merciless brutality the uprising of Stenka Razin. But though he practised the cruelty of the age as an instrument of state policy, he was no bloodthirsty tyrant. In general, as an historian has pointed out, "the ferocious penalties of Muscovite law were rarely carried out"; and it was Alexei himself, responding to a proposal to execute some deserters, who observed humanely that "it is hard to do that, for God has not given courage to all men alike."[37]

Now the Most-Gentle Tsar was dead, and his over-mighty subjects could prosecute their feuds without check. For the moment the Miloslavskys were triumphant. The fourteen-year-old Tsarevich Feodor, against all expectations, was crowned as Tsar Feodor III in the Uspensky Cathedral. The poor young man was so enfeebled with his congenital ailment that he had to be carried to his throne, but more vigorous relatives were advancing exulting from the wings. The leader of the Miloslavsky clan was now Ivan Mihailovich Miloslavsky, an energetic, cunning and unscrupulous forty-seven-year-old cousin of old Ilya. When the Tsar died he was in far-off Astrakhan, captured from the Cossacks by his cousin Ivan Bogdanovich five years earlier. But the Governorship of Astrakhan was in fact a form of exile, designed by Artamon Matveev to keep the most dangerous of his enemies far from Moscow.

Ivan Mihailovich Miloslavsky posted to Moscow and swiftly seized the real reins of power. Matveev and two of the Naryshkin brothers were packed off into exile on trumped-up charges, and Miloslavskys once again dominated the state. The new Tsar fell at first under their sway, but inheriting his father's benign nature, he declined to allow Matveev or the Naryshkins to be put to death.[38] It seemed the Miloslavskys had finally triumphed, a triumph consummated by yet another victorious campaign against Russia's enemies conducted by the intrepid Ivan Bogdanovich in the Ukraine in 1679.[39]

But the Miloslavskys had a tendency to overplay their hand. It was clear that neither the sickly Tsar nor his brother Ivan would live long. When they died their half-brother Peter would succeed, and the star of the Naryshkins would rearise – for ever. It was essential therefore that the Tsar should marry and produce an heir. Unfortunately for this scheme the Tsar suddenly fell in love. The girl was called Agafia Grushetsky, and from the Miloslavskys' point of view was a disastrous choice. The romance had been encouraged and presided over by rival boyars, who now looked to take over power. Ivan Mihailovich Miloslavsky tried to poison

Feodor's mind against the girl, but the young Tsar was so enraged at this attack on his chosen bride that he temporarily banished Miloslavsky from a court shortly afterwards presided over by the new teenage Tsaritsa.[40]

Events now moved with increasing unpredictability. The Tsaritsa Agafia and her newly-born son died a year later in 1681, but if Ivan Miloslavsky was cheered by the event it was not for long. A bare seven months later the Tsar married for the second time. This time it was to Martha Apraxin, daughter of an old noble family. One of her godparents was none other than that Artamon Matveev whom Ivan Miloslavsky had threatened with death and driven into exile a bare five years earlier! The new Tsaritsa even before her marriage had successfully appealed to her bridegroom to restore Matveev to his estates. The Tsar consented to the extent that Matveev was ordered to come to a village some three hundred miles from Moscow, there to await further instructions.

The feelings of Ivan Miloslavsky may be imagined, as his old adversary seemed again poised to take power. But once again fate, and then Russia's turbulent politics, intervened to dash and raise the prospects of the Miloslavskys. First came the sudden but not unexpected death of the ever-ailing Tsar Feodor Alexeevich, a bare two months (27 April 1682) after his second marriage. *That* menace was thus abruptly lifted, but was at once succeeded by one potentially worse. The heir presumptive to the throne was of course Feodor's brother Ivan, but he was so pitifully enfeebled in mind and body it seemed inconceivable that he should wield the autocratic power. His half-brother Peter, on the other hand, already displayed at ten years old those astonishing physical and mental capacities that were before long to astound the world. With the Miloslavskys out of favour at court it seemed an easy matter for the Naryshkin faction to place their Tsarevich Peter on the throne, with Natalia Naryshkin as Regent and Matveev as her principal adviser. For Ivan Miloslavsky and his relatives it was not merely permanent disgrace that loomed, but the headsman's axe. What mercy could he expect, who had openly urged Matveev's death and (it was later alleged) that of the Tsarevich too?[41]

It was decided, as in 1613 when the dead Tsar's grandfather had been elected Tsar, to put the choice to a *Zemsky Sobor*, or Assembly of the Land. A crowd theoretically representative of the different estates of the Muscovite realm was assembled in the Cathedral Square. From the top of the Red Steps leading into the Faceted Palace the Patriarch put the question to the people whether Ivan or Peter should succeed. The predominating influence of the Naryshkins, the unpopularity of the Miloslavskys, and the superior abilities of Peter carried the day. Cries of "Peter Alexeevich!" grew in volume until all opposing voices were stilled.

The Naryshkins were triumphant, and messengers rode posthaste to invite Matveev to return to Moscow. The survival of the very name of Miloslavsky was at stake. It was a woman who intervened to reverse the course of events. This was incredible for seventeenth-century Muscovy, where the women of the royal family were even more closeted from public view than their subjects, and even in church remained screened apart.

The Tsarevna Sophia Alexeevna was the fourth daughter of the late Tsar Alexei, and in 1682 was only twenty-five years old. If no beauty, she possessed quite extraordinary presence of mind. Determined that nothing should permit her mother's family to be laid low, she set to work urgently to reverse the decision made by the Zemsky Sobor. Time was everything, since once Matveev re-entered the capital the Naryshkins' position might well become unassailable. One card at least lay in Sophia's favour: the Regent Natalia, in common with her Naryshkin relatives, utterly lacked the Miloslavsky vigour, and remained closeted at this time in the Terem Palace.

Sophia and her fellow-conspirators set to work. The master-mind in all that followed was her fifty-three-year-old cousin, Ivan Mihailovich Miloslavsky, who since the death of the soldier Ivan Bogdanovich was regarded as head of his house. Described by a contemporary as "a man of extreme cunning and skill in deceptions", he was a master of Machiavellian intrigue. Other Miloslavsky siblings joined the plot, but Ivan Mihailovich's principal co-conspirators were his two nephews, Ivan and Peter Tolstoy.

According to a hostile account (that of Matveev's son), the brothers Ivan and Peter were men of immensely impressive appearance and intellect, but reputed also to be highly skilled in dark and underhand intrigues. They were known popularly as the 'Kharpenky', after their grandfather Vasily 'Kharp' Tolstoy.

Ivan and Peter, born in 1644 and 1645 respectively, were the sons of Andrei Tolstoy, who about 1642 married Solomonida Miloslavsky, Ivan Mihailovich's younger sister. It was this powerful alliance that brought them to prominence and committed them to the Miloslavsky cause. They do not seem to have been affected by their uncle's temporary reverses before 1682, and probably their native shrewdness enabled them to maintain a precarious foothold in different camps. Ivan, the elder, had further strengthened his position by marrying Maria Apraxin, sister of Feodor III's widowed Tsaritsa Martha. The marriages of father and son had raised the Tolstoys to a position of great eminence, which in seventeenth-century Muscovy meant also a position of great danger.

Throughout the weeks which followed the election of Tsar Peter, Ivan Miloslavsky was confined to his Moscow house, reputedly too ill to emerge. But the Tolstoy brothers were frequently closeted with "the old Achitophel" and messengers passed in and out of the gates at all hours. In particular they rode to the suburb of the Streltsi, the turbulent praetorian guard of the Tsars. Amongst the Streltsi at this time there was great discontent, as their officers had become increasingly corrupt and authoritarian. However, the Naryshkins were as aware as anyone of the potential threat afforded by the ill-disciplined regiments, and had distributed pay and other sweeteners to ensure their loyalty to the new Tsar. This was well so far as it went, but unfortunately for them the Naryshkin party combined a singular political ineptness with a supreme and tactless arrogance.

All these factors were weighed in Ivan Miloslavsky's ice-cold mind. Large sums of Miloslavsky money found their way to the Streltsi settlement, followed by disturbing rumours about the Naryshkins' conduct and ambitions. It was said that the twenty-three-year-old Ivan Naryshkin had impudently sat on the royal throne, donned the crown, and pushed aside the Tsarevna Sophia when she remonstrated with him. Darker hints told of a Naryshkin plot to massacre all heirs to the throne and seize it for their own. At the same time approaches had been made to Prince Ivan Khovansky, a vain, foolish and ambitious officer, who was extremely popular with the Streltsi. Khovansky responded with enthusiasm, and the skeins of the conspiracy began to draw together.

Meanwhile the event which presaged triumph for the Naryshkins and disaster for the Miloslavskys drew near. Artamon Matveev was at last returning from exile to take office beside the Regent Natalia. At first a little apprehensive of reports of the Streltsi unrest, he was reassured by memories of his earlier popularity with the soldiery and the increasingly impressive reception accorded him as he approached the capital's golden cupolas. At last, on the evening of 12 May 1682, a fortnight after Tsar Feodor's death, he entered Moscow in a state carriage escorted by the flower of the Naryshkins. He spent the first night for six years in his old home. For three days a stream of visitors poured in at his gates, bearing gifts and congratulations. The Naryshkins were jubilant; the great statesman would guide the Regency through troubled days ahead. Only one man of note failed to call on

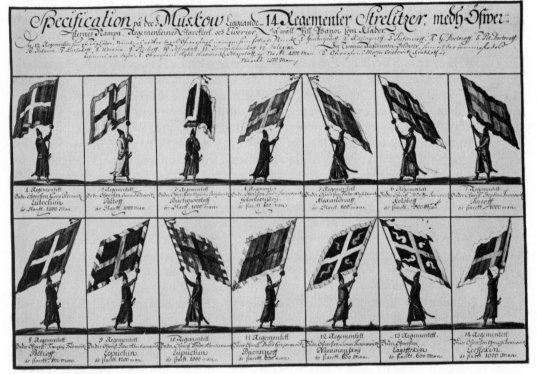

Banners of Streltsi

the returned minister, and that was Ivan Miloslavsky. But then he was "sick in bed". To a placatory message from Matveev, he merely rejoined cryptically that he would wait and see what happened.

On 15 May, after the weekend, Matveev took his seat as chief minister in the boyars' Duma. Moscow seemed calm, the Streltsi were in their homes, and the veteran statesman prepared to resume command. He had reckoned without Ivan Miloslavsky. Early that morning two horsemen had swept into the Streltsi quarter, shouting to all they encountered that "the Naryshkins have strangled the Tsarevich Ivan!" They were Peter Tolstoy and his cousin Alexander Miloslavsky (son of Ivan Bogdanovich). The excitable veterans flocking from their houses were ordered peremptorily to march on the Kremlin and avenge the murder. Prepared for some such contingency by the whispering campaign of Ivan Miloslavsky and Prince Khovansky, the men flew to arms and assembled in regiments.

The glittering columns began to defile, with colours waving and drums beating, along the Moscow streets and into the Kremlin Square. Inside the Faceted Palace the Regent Natalia and Matveev learned of the advance too late to order the closure of the Kremlin gates. From below came threatening chants from the incensed soldiers.

"The Naryshkins have murdered the Tsarevich Ivan! Punish the traitors! To arms!"

The boyars, who had crowded into the banqueting hall, gazed at each other with pallid faces. Eventually Matveev advised the Tsaritsa to display the Tsarevich to the crowd and convince them he was alive. Trembling with fear, she emerged at the head of the Red Staircase, the Tsar and Tsarevich clutching her hands.

Some soldiers scrambled up to examine the young princes. Ivan confirmed that he was alive, and the men returned to their ranks with the news. The regiments wavered; then voices began to shout in unison that the traitors in the palace must be given up to them. From a list supplied by Peter Tolstoy they chanted a string of names, headed by Artamon Matveev and eight of the principal Naryshkins. But it was noticeable that only a minority joined the shouting, and when Matveev himself and the Patriarch appeared at the head of the staircase to reason with the mob it looked as if they were inclined to disperse.

Then one of the generals of the Streltsi, Prince Dolgoruky, whose name had appeared on the rebels' list, emerged from the Palace and uttered violent threats of punishment unless they returned home that instant. The Prince's conduct was so wildly provocative and dangerous that one cannot help speculating whether he was urged on by some enemy of the Naryshkins within the Palace – possibly Prince Khovansky, who was also a Streltsi commander. It could not at any rate have been Ivan Miloslavsky, who was feigning sickness. Prince Dolgoruky's inappropriate ranting at once aroused the rage, never long dormant, of the mob. The regiments surged furiously across the square, urged on by the same element that had called for the blood of Matveev and the Naryshkins. A group of ruffians sprang up the steps and hurled the shouting Prince down to their comrades, who impaled him on their spears.

Now their blood was up, and the mob ran screaming through the halls of the Faceted Palace until they found Artamon Matveev himself. He too was thrown down the steps and hacked to pieces by those below. Anyone who could be found of the name or interest of Naryshkin was similarly dragged out and cut up in front of a gloating crowd. For three days the hunt and the slaughter continued. The scene was one of indescribable horror; along the dark, richly carved and decorated passages raced the blood-crazed soldiery, stabbing and hacking with pikes and pole-axes at beds, curtains and tapestry hangings. Tiny, misshapen figures flitted before them: they were the terrified court dwarfs, here pointing out a victim in shrill, harsh accents, there tremblingly concealing a kindly master. Occasionally a chamber was transformed into a particularly atrocious scene of horror where, as blades glinted in the flickering light of an ikon lamp, an eager group of Streltsi crouched over the mutilated trunk of a prisoner whose agonies they were skilfully prolonging.

Old Kyrill Naryshkin, the Tsaritsa's father, together with his sons and the seventeen-year-old son of the murdered Matveev, concealed themselves in a store-room. They blocked up the windows with pillows so that the room was completely dark, but did not dare to lock the door lest that arouse the suspicions of their pursuers. Accordingly they left it slightly ajar, and crouched in the darkness behind. Minutes later footsteps approached, and a group of Streltsi looked in. They began stabbing with their pikes at the heap of pillows, but then one was heard to growl out that their comrades must already have searched the room, and they continued their hunt elsewhere. Young Matveev was subsequently helped to escape by a palace dwarf, so living to recount his escape. Ivan Naryshkin was not so lucky. At the persuasion of the Tsarevna Sophia (who with Khovansky secretly controlled the invaders), the weeping Tsaritsa was compelled to sacrifice her brother to save the lives of herself and the remaining survivors. The old man was subjected to terrible tortures, then tossed up onto the spear-points and borne out to the square. There his hands and feet were cut off and his body chopped into tiny pieces which the soldiers trampled into the mud.

By this time the Streltsi had exhausted their amusement and declared that they were now content, swearing undying loyalty to the Tsar whose uncle they had just butchered, to the Tsaritsa, the Tsarevich Ivan and the Tsarevnas. So they departed from the Kremlin, leaving the stunned survivors to gather up what was left of their relatives' remains and provide them with Christian burial. Matveev's negro servant was seen sadly bearing his master's mutilated corpse in a sheet, which he took to the church of St. Nicholas.

As the blood of the Naryshkins was mopped from the floors and walls of the Kremlin, Ivan Miloslavsky and the Tsarevna Sophia made their next move. At their secret prompting, deputations of Streltsi demanded that the Tsarevich Ivan be crowned Tsar alongside his younger half-brother Peter, and that the Tsarevna Sophia be made Regent in place of the Tsaritsa Natalia. No one dared object, and on 6 July 1682 the pathetic Ivan Alexeevich, handicapped in speech, sight and limbs, was crowned with Peter in the Uspensky Cathedral amidst customary scenes of splendour by the Patriarch Ioakim. Prominent among the great men present were Illarion Semeonovich and Matvei Bogdanovich Miloslavsky, and Andrei Vasilievich Tolstoy. It was a bare ten weeks since the death of Feodor III and the Naryshkin coup.

The virtual elimination of the Naryshkins and the assumption of the Regency by Sophia left the Miloslavskys almost without rivals in the state. One man alone appeared to threaten their security, and that was the vain and unstable Prince Khovansky. He was said to be plotting to have Ivan Miloslavsky and other leading boyars killed, make himself Tsar, and marry his son Andrei to the Regent Sophia. It may be that these rumours originated with the artful Ivan Miloslavsky, who concealed himself in his country house outside Moscow and began to draw the strings tight around Khovansky. He persuaded Sophia of the reality of the danger, and she made skilful pretexts for leaving Moscow to visit monasteries and celebrate her name's-day in the country.

Once safe from the power of the Streltsi, she gathered her own troops around her and, the moment Khovansky and his son were rash enough to venture beyond the walls, sent a body of soldiers to arrest them. Khovansky protested angrily, and declared himself ready to reveal who were the *real* instigators of the riot in the Kremlin. These words were his death-warrant. Ivan Miloslavsky reported the danger to Sophia, who at once despatched an order for the Khovanskys' execution. This was immediately put into effect, great care being taken to see that they had no chance to reveal any dark secrets. Soon afterwards the Streltsi were pacified and disciplined, and the Regent Sophia assumed unchallenged control of Russia's destinies.

As a contemporary wrote later, "that rebellion took place by the will and at the instigation of the Tsarevna Sophia Alexeevna, through the above-mentioned

Russia, c. *1700*

Miloslavsky and his aides, Tsikler and Peter Tolstoy, in order that she should receive the power of government in her hands during the [Tsars'] minority. . . . ." But the triumph had been bought at a fearful cost and was to prove short-lived. With every year that passed the energy and abilities of the Tsar Peter became more apparent. In 1689, seven years after the rampage of the Streltsi in the Kremlin, the seventeen-year-old Peter grasped the reins of power.

In 1697, that Tsikler who had been one of Miloslavsky's principal aides informed Peter the Great of a conspiracy allegedly involving the Tsarevna Sophia. The Tsar, who had never forgotten the ghastly scenes he witnessed as a ten-year-old boy in the Faceted Palace, was so enraged that he swore vengeance against the whole tribe of Miloslavsky. Ivan Mihailovich, whose ambitions (so suggested Leo Tolstoy) had been influenced by the recent examples of Cromwell in England, had died in 1685 and was buried in the ancestral vault alongside Ilya Danilovich, the founder of the family's great fortunes.[42] Now his body was ordered to be dug up and dragged by swine to the foot of the place of execution. There it was strapped in such a position that the blood of beheaded criminals splashed over the corpse's skull. When, in the following year, Peter learned that the Streltsi had again risen and threatened the capital, he wrote furiously to Moscow that "this is the seed of Ivan Miloslavsky rising up again", and hastened home to suppress the rebellion in a welter of blood.[43] His vengeance on the family, living and dead, was so ferocious that the name ceased to have any further public significance.

An historian of Russia in the seventeenth century singled out the Matveevs and the Miloslavskys as "meteors", which burned with dazzling light and then vanished into the dark. It is true, too, as Professor Bruce Lincoln points out, that "no Miloslavskii ever held a high government position in Russia after 1689".[44] It has been seen, however, that the name was restored to the family's heirs in 1910. And it may well be that many of the qualities displayed by successive generations of Tolstoys were inherited from their Miloslavsky forebears. The brothers Ivan and Peter Tolstoy in particular resembled greatly their uncle Ivan Miloslavsky, "the old Achitophel", in their cunning, courage and ambition. The "seed of Miloslavsky" was a vigorous and enduring strain.[45]

3

The Curse of the Tsarevich

Only great skill and good fortune saved the Tolstoys from sharing the fate of the Miloslavskys. A shrewd calculation of the odds convinced the brothers Ivan and Peter that, despite the great abilities of the Regent Sophia and her minister-lover Vasily Galitzine, time would favour the growing Tsar Peter, who was inevitably to gather about him a "court" of ambitious men determined to profit by the change when it came. These included Feodor Matveevich Apraxin, one of whose sisters was the widow of Tsar Feodor and another of whom, Maria, had married Ivan, the elder of the Tolstoy brothers. This connexion provided the bridge across which the Tolstoys edged themselves after the death of their great patron Ivan Miloslavsky in 1685. Apraxin was indeed eager to draw two such able and influential men across to Peter's party.

By 1689, when Peter felt strong enough to move decisively against the Miloslavsky Regent Sophia, his half-sister, the Tolstoys had become his firm allies. Indeed, by the time the tide had turned against Sophia, virtually all her supporters had wisely gone over to Peter – even her lover Prince Galitzine. She was confined to a convent outside Moscow and the seventeen-year-old Peter became Tsar in reality.

What then could the brothers Ivan and Peter Tolstoy expect from their vengeful new master? Their mother, after all, was the sister of that Ivan Mihailovich Miloslavsky who, more than any other, had been responsible for the scenes of terror and cruelty in the Kremlin in 1682. And it was notorious that the Tolstoy brothers had participated in those nightly gatherings at Ivan Miloslavsky's house where, feigning sickness, the unscrupulous boyar had plotted with the Streltsi officers. At dawn on 15 May, Peter Tolstoy himself had ridden on his Crimean steed to rouse the Streltsi to their bloody task.

Tsar Peter never forgot the sinister rôle the Tolstoys had played in his childhood, and combined respect for their outstanding abilities with continuing suspicion of their integrity. As a contemporary wrote of the brothers, they were "intellectually very penetrating, and supremely able in great intrigues, dark deeds, and secret conceptions". Long after Peter Tolstoy had proved his new loyalty by a series of extraordinary achievements, Peter the Great was heard to remark darkly of him: "Ah, head, head, were you not so clever I should have had you cut off long ago". And a few weeks before his death, when drunk and discoursing of his ministers' qualities, he was heard to say that "Peter Andreevich [Tolstoy] is in every way a very able man, but it is just as well when you have dealings with him to keep a stone in your pocket to break his teeth in case he decides to bite you!" Tolstoy was nearly eighty at the time, but within a month or so was to show that his capacity for intrigue was undimmed.

Another anecdote tells of his reaction to a similar gibe at one of the Tsar's notorious bacchanalian evening gatherings. Tolstoy himself disliked drinking to excess, but sat down before the fireside, doffed his wig, nodded his head and pretended to be sound asleep. In fact he was listening intently to the muttered conversation of the Tsar and his companions. Tsar Peter, walking up and down the room, suddenly noticed the bald head inclining back in the chair, smacked it twice and said, "Dissimulating, master Tolstoy!" Then a moment later he remarked again sombrely, with a clear allusion to Tolstoy's dead patron Miloslavsky: "This head, which acted first under another head, was drooping: I fear it may tumble

Previous page: Peter Andreevich Tolstoy (I. G. Tannauer, 1719)

from its shoulders." Tolstoy, affecting to awake, looked up at the Tsar and replied swiftly: "Don't worry, Your Majesty, it is quite firm on me and true to you; what happened before was not and will not be repeated". "Look at that!" exclaimed the Tsar, "he was not drunk, but pretending! Bring him three glasses of good *flin* [Warm beer, containing a liberal infusion of brandy and lemon juice], so that he will be friendly to us and join our gossiping".[1]

In fact the Tolstoy brothers were precisely the sort of men to whom Peter looked for service.[2] After serving in the Tsar's Semeonovsky and Preobrazhensky Guards, Peter Tolstoy was rewarded in 1693 with the Voevodship of Ustyug (where his grandfather Mihail had nearly been drowned by the mob during the uprising of 1648), and there on 12 May his sovereign entered the town to salvoes of cannon and dined with "the cunning Tolstoy", as contemporary accounts invariably name him.[3] But Peter was well aware of the Tsar's persistent suspicions and fortunately had an early opportunity of establishing his *bona fides*.

The Tsar, as is well known, was devoted to the aim of establishing a Russian presence on the Baltic and Black Sea littorals, and to the creation of a powerful Russian fleet. On 20 March 1697 Peter set out on his famous journey to Holland and England, where he was to study ship-building and other sophisticated Western techniques of military and civil engineering. At the same time he was anxious to have trained Russians capable of serving as officers in the new fleet. Four weeks before his departure Peter notified the Doge of Venice that he was despatching a group of Russian nobles "who intend to study, eagerly and assiduously, the new military arts and methods" and whom he trusted the Venetians would protect and assist. Specifically, as their commission laid down, they were "to learn the maps, instruments, and other guides to seafaring, to handle a ship and to know her rigging, equipment, and structure, and if possible, to participate in naval combat and, upon their return, to convey to others the specific naval skills acquired in Europe".[4]

It was suggested then and since that Peter Tolstoy, who was already fifty-two years old with a wife and children, volunteered to join the band of nobles in order to allay the Tsar's suspicions of his loyalty. It is perhaps more likely that the Tsar feared to leave Peter Tolstoy in Russia at a time when he himself would be abroad.[5]

On 30 January 1697 Peter Tolstoy received formal instructions to depart. Within less than a month he had packed and bade farewell to his wife Solomonida Timofeevna and sons Ivan and Peter. Taking his own horse and accompanied by a horde of household servants, he set out on 28 February. His progress was slow and stately as his train of sledges moved along the frozen rivers to Europe. At Smolensk, just before the Polish frontier, he despatched home the majority of his following but took the horses on as far as Silesia. Travel was slow in seventeenth-century Europe. Tolstoy arrived at Vienna only on 22 May, stayed there a week and finally arrived in Venice on 11 June. There he spent the winter and, in March 1698, travelled down hot, dusty roads to the south of Italy. He also went on two voyages in the Mediterranean, visiting Malta and returning to Venice *via* Rome in June.

The official purpose of his trip was studiously accomplished. With his comrades, Tolstoy studied the arts of navigation under a Venetian naval officer, Captain Marko Martinovič. The instruction took place at Martinovič's home port of Boka

Kotorska, in what is now Yugoslavia. A contemporary painting shows Martinovič seated at a table with an astrolabe, chart and compass, whilst his moustachioed noble pupils eagerly discuss their lesson. Most of the teaching was, however, of a practical nature. Tolstoy threw himself into it all with enthusiasm, interrogating Turkish corsairs, arguing with his captain about map-readings, and becoming familiar with all the abstruse terminology of the sea. He vividly recorded times of storm, when the ship was heaved high up on gigantic billows, but neither these nor other grim perils daunted him.

Peter Tolstoy and his companions study naval science

Peter Tolstoy's stay in Italy is remarkable for the detailed diary he kept throughout. This provides a rare glimpse of an intelligent Russian's view of Western European civilization on the eve of the Petrine reforms. Everything he encountered excited Tolstoy's interest. His observations reveal the extraordinary gulf between early Romanov Russia and enlightened Europe. Though Tolstoy was overcome with enthusiasm for all he experienced, he remained inevitably in part a child of his society. He was intensely interested in all aspects of religion, comparing the different faiths, their churches, practices and beliefs, contrasting them with the "devout Greek faith" of the Orthodox. But he attended Catholic services and gazed with pious credulity on saints' relics he found preserved there. At the town of Borisov in Poland he had been shown an ikon, originally Orthodox but now in the possession of the Catholics. "From that time," Tolstoy reported with satisfaction, "a black spot as big as a kopek appeared on the ikon which the Catholics could not paint out however hard they tried; in fact it increased!" On his return journey he was impressed to learn that the spot had reappeared many times.

He visited academies where one could study "the high arts", participate in debates, and browse in libraries. He learned much of that classical art and mythology with which the new enlightenment was imbued. He was quite bowled over by the unbelievable beauty and magnificence of public buildings in Vienna, Venice, Naples and Rome, but despite this overpowering enthusiasm soon learned to distinguish between styles, periods and qualities. One difficulty facing the diarist was simply the paucity of the Russian language in face of such wonders. Again and again he is reduced to exclaiming that such a painting or cathedral is an "astonishing" or "wonderful" masterpiece, an "amazing piece of work" or even "passable" or "respectable" (*izriadnaia*): words bearing a much higher significance in the limited vocabulary of the time than later. But the reality of his emotional response at the glories of Italy bursts even through Tolstoy's linguistic shackles, and one can almost sense the frustration of this gifted and sensitive man when trying to record something of that which had flooded his imagination. Confessing the inadequacy of vocabulary he simply writes of "that marvellous work, which no-one could describe fully", or of a "masterpiece which the human tongue simply cannot portray". But even he could on occasion find a phrase that told of his delight. Before Milan Cathedral he gazed and found it "quite wonderful and glorious in all the world". Elsewhere he saw horses "carved in the white stone with such marvellous skill as though alive".

Music too he loved, and attended operas and plays, preferring the former. Much of the most beautiful music was to be heard in church, and the impressionable nobleman heard in a Venetian convent singing "so fine, that in the whole world such sweet singing and harmony never was known, as wonderful as that of angels". Church organs he found less sublime, though. "Their notes are so loud that they shake the entire church", he noted.

Tolstoy soon became proficient in the Italian language; so much so that he was able to declare that the Roman dialect was the clearest he had heard, and that the Florentines' speech was superior to that of the Bolognese. Other provincial variations attracted his notice. In Venice the ladies "always enjoy strolling and amusing themselves, and are extremely frail in matters concerning sins of the flesh". From what is known of Peter Tolstoy's character it is safe to presume that he had some personal knowledge of this matter. In Naples "women and girls have modest ways and are hidden in the Muscovite manner". The comparisons with Moscow life throw an interesting light on the polarity of Tolstoy's experience. In Naples again, he observed, the nobility "do not live a solitary existence when they and their wives drive around in their carriages, and willingly take foot passengers, just as in Moscow", and the nobles' houses reminded him of those at home. Similar, too, were the clerks penning petitions by the square of San Marco in Venice, but generally things were very different.

Great buildings five storeys high; hospitals caring for a thousand patients; the canals of Venice; the carnivals, when crowds in fancy dress flocked the streets. Then, too, there were the street lights of Venice, which kept the whole city ablaze with light all night. More significant than these visible marks of a cheerful, confident, cultured existence were other indications. Tolstoy noted that any citizen could, in the course of his business, freely approach a Venetian magnate – a stark contrast with the fate of a Russian petitioner who is said to have been accidentally killed by Tsar Alexei Mihailovich when approaching too near the royal person. In Venetian courtrooms people talked calmly and politely "without shrieking" – as presumably they did in some other country Tolstoy had in mind! Similarly, Venice was remarkable for the absence of public drunkenness; altogether her inhabitants lived a life of contentment, "always cheerful, never blackguarding each other, and with nothing to fear from each other; each one does as he likes according to his wishes. There has always been this freedom in Venice, and Venetians always live without fear, without offence and without burdensome taxes". Obviously an idealized picture, but it is not hard to see the comparison he is making.

Peter Tolstoy's idyllic life was about to draw to a close, however. On 25 October 1698 he received an official letter from the boyar F.A. Golovin requiring him to return. With what was then regarded as commendable speed he arrived home three months later "by the grace of God in good health". He never ceased expatiating at court on the unforgettable glories of Venice, Naples and Rome, until one day the irritable Tsar could stand no more and compelled the abstemious aristocrat to down a brimming bumper of wine as a penalty.[6]

Nothing, however, could drown the impressions Tolstoy and other Russian travellers in the West brought back with them at this time.

Peter Tolstoy's trip abroad had coincided with that of his master the Tsar, who was also ecstatic about the superiority of Western European culture and technology over that of backward Russia. In Holland, where old Ilya Miloslavsky had been Ambassador half-a-century earlier, he had studied ship-building, drunk enormously, and to his irritation found himself Holland's greatest tourist attraction. From there he moved to England, where he watched a review of the fleet at Spithead, ruined Mr. Evelyn's house and garden at Deptford by his "right nasty" habits, and had a prolonged affair with an actress.

The Tsar's single-minded purpose in all this, as he explained in a letter to the Patriarch, was to learn navigation, "so that, having mastered it thoroughly, we can, when we return, be victors over the enemies of Jesus Christ [the Turks], and liberators of the Christians who live under them, which I shall not cease to wish for until my latest breath". He was continually recruiting English, Dutch, Danish and Swedish ship-wrights, naval officers, surgeons and the like, and despatching them to Russia ahead of his return.

By June Peter had reached Vienna, where he met privately the Emperor Leopold. Leopold promised not to make peace with Turkey without the Tsar's consent and, greatly satisfied, Peter prepared to continue his journey south. It was at this moment that he received a month-old letter from Prince Romodanovsky in Moscow, in which he was informed that some Streltsi regiments had again revolted and were marching on Moscow. In England Bishop Burnet had noted that Peter "seemed apprehensive still of his sister's intrigues", and now the Tsar was convinced that once again the seeds of Miloslavsky had sprouted. Without waiting to find out more he returned swiftly home, arriving on 4 September to find the rebellion already crushed by loyal troops.

All that was left for Peter to do was to interrogate the culprits and execute large numbers after the most barbaric tortures. No connexion was proved between the rebels and the ex-Regent Sophia, who was nevertheless kept under close guard and compelled to become a nun.

With the Tsar's return the old ways, cautiously criticised at this time by Peter Tolstoy in his diary, could no longer survive. The very day after his arrival, the Tsar witnessed scissors and razor at work on the beards, sleeves and coat-skirts of his boyars. When Peter Tolstoy returned home three months' later in January 1699, clean-shaven, wearing Western clothing and enthusing over the freedom of life under a Mediterranean sun, he found all these characteristics had overnight fallen into fashion. The change had indeed been extraordinarily sudden: even the New Year had, for the first time, started on 1 January instead of the previous 1 September. Years were henceforward dated from the birth of Christ, instead of from the Creation, 7208 years previously. Only the Gregorian calendar remained distinct.

However, Peter Tolstoy undoubtedly knew himself to be a very fortunate man. His absence abroad had saved him, for had he been in Moscow when "the seed of Miloslavsky" was sprouting, it is conceivable to say the least that the Tsar would have regarded him with the utmost suspicion. Indeed, it cannot be asserted with confidence that Peter Tolstoy would not have been tempted to fish in troubled waters, though more likely his shrewd brain must have perceived where power lay.

Desperate to prove himself and achieve the position to which his intelligence entitled him, he paid a lavish bribe of 200,000 gold ducats to the Minister for Foreign Affairs, the boyar F.A. Golovin. In return he received a post commensurate even with his abilities, that of Ambassador to Constantinople. His elder brother Ivan had already held this office in 1701[7] after the signing of the Russo-Turkish peace treaty, but now Peter Tolstoy was to travel out as resident Ambassador for an indefinite period, at a time when the survival of Russia quite certainly depended on the maintenance of good relations between the two empires. Though the bribe provided Golovin with the impetus to overcome Tsar Peter's misgivings, there was no doubt that Tolstoy was supremely well-qualified for the rôle. Italian, one of the languages he spoke fluently, was the language of diplomacy at the Sultan's court and he was a man of culture, polished manners and extreme intelligence who would be at home in any company or exigency.

Meanwhile Peter's elder brother Ivan had also achieved high office, being appointed Governor of Azov. The fortress was the key to the whole of the Tsar's southern strategy. Peter the Great had captured it after a fierce siege (at which Peter Tolstoy had been present) in 1696.[8] Now that it was in Russian hands, Russian warships could descend the Don from the shipyards of Voronezh and enter the Sea of Azov at will. In 1700 Turkey and Russia had signed a thirty-year truce, but the Turks made no secret of the fact that they regarded the Black Sea as a Turkish lake. So long as Azov remained Russian it was endangered, and Ivan Tolstoy's governorship was unlikely to be a sinecure. It fell to the Tolstoy brothers to sustain Russia's vulnerable southern flank during the crucial first decade of the eighteenth century, one Tolstoy on the military and the other on the diplomatic front.

It may have been the outbreak of the Great Northern War with Charles XII of

Sweden that caused the Tsar to reconsider his attitude towards the Tolstoy brothers. Charles XII had invaded Poland and overthrown Peter the Great's ally and friend King Augustus the Strong. Marshal Sheremietev gained striking victories for Russian arms by the Baltic, but the real war had scarcely begun. The Tsar decided to kill two birds with one stone. Leaving the conspiratorial brothers kicking their heels in Russia was a recipe for trouble, and their presence with the army in Poland might prove equally dangerous. There was, however, one field where their talents could be safely employed to the full. The Turkish "front" was crucial, for Russia could not survive war with the Sultan as well as Charles XII. If the Turks were to be held to the thirty-year truce, men of extreme tact, skill and boldness would be required to treat with them. At the same time, the Tolstoys would be far from any opportunity for dangerous intrigues.

In February 1703 Tsar Peter visited his naval base at Voronezh, where he conferred with Ivan Tolstoy and others. On 15 May Ivan Tolstoy sailed down the Don to his new governorship at Azov. A week later his brother-in-law, Admiral Apraxin, reported to the Tsar: "The Voevod of Azov, my liege, travelled there on 15 May, and the soldiers which were in Voronezh . . . have been sent on. To Azov, my liege, I sent two letters urging them to live on permanent 'qui vive', and I have supplied them lavishly with cannon, cannonballs and bombs." The new Governor threw himself energetically into repairing and extending fortifications, exercising the garrison and building up great reserves of stores and ammunition. On 11 October Ivan Tolstoy himself reported to Tsar Peter that Azov had been made secure and that the prying eyes of the Turkish Ambassador (who was travelling through southern Russia) would find out nothing.[9]

Meanwhile Ivan's younger brother Peter had set out on his arduous mission. The Tsar provided him with elaborate instructions: he was to preserve peace with Turkey, persuade her to prevent the Khan of the Crimea from waging war in southern Russia, and do everything he could to prevent the Turks from fortifying the Straits of Kerch. The last instruction revealed the extent of Peter's ambitions: he had his hands more than full with the Swedes, but his mind was still looking forward to the day when his fleet at Azov would sail freely past the Straits into the Black Sea. Finally, Tolstoy was required to furnish maximum intelligence of everything that passed in the Ottoman court and empire. Daunting tasks, even for the cleverest head in Russia. For, as Tolstoy was to experience, the Turks were by no means meticulous in the observance of diplomatic niceties when a foreign envoy gave offence.[10]

As Peter Tolstoy made his protracted land journey to Constantinople, he wrote continually to his brother Ivan at Azov. Some of these letters have survived and not only provide fascinating glimpses of his life at Adrianople, but also reveal him as an unexpectedly affectionate family man. The continuing suspicions of Peter the Great towards the brothers had perhaps isolated them to some extent and drawn them close together.

"My dearest little father, lord brother Ivan Andreevich, greetings my lord; may you live many years with your household, wife and children!" begins a typical letter. "Please my brother," runs another, "do not abandon me in all my affairs, and do not forget my wife and lads". . . . "I beg you," pleads the lonely Peter, "be so kind as not to forget me, but send me news of your health, so as to get rid of my sadness; and after that don't forget to cherish my wife and boy, which through God's grace I do not doubt that you will."

He tells Ivan of his polite reception by Turkish frontier officials, where fifty finely-apparelled racehorses were brought him by a train of officials and guards. Delays followed as a result of the death of the Vizier and his replacement. The Sultan, Mustapha II, was then at Adrianople, and Peter Tolstoy spent months there before moving on to Constantinople. He was, however, able to interfere with the Crimean Khan's pressures for permission to invade Russia. Finally, on 12 October, he was granted an audience with the Vizier. He presented his credentials, explaining that the Tsar wished only to live in love and friendship with the Sultan. The Vizier replied with equally honeyed words, and the half-day's interview ended with each wily old bird satisfied he knew precisely what the other was after. Indeed Tolstoy had good reason to feel satisfied. "At this time," he replied to Ivan, "not a little of God's purposes has been fulfilled through my unworthy labours." He had sufficiently impressed the Sublime Porte with Russia's retaliatory power to persuade the Sultan to restrain his impetuous satellite the Khan of Crim Tartary.

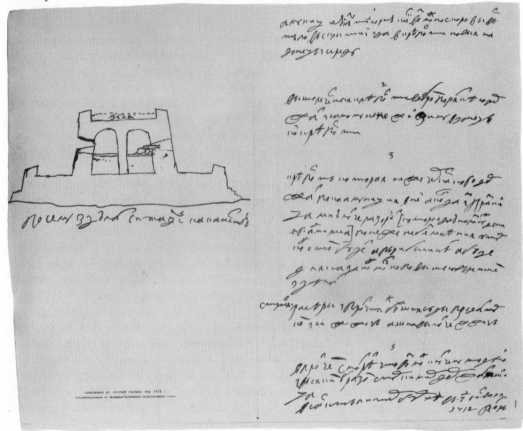

Letter of Peter the Great to Ivan Tolstoy, 3 January 1712

Intrepid Cossack messengers bore Peter Tolstoy's letters out of Turkey to Azov, and their frankness testifies to his confidence that they would not come under Turkish inspection. His worries were not confined to high matters of state, however. "Have the kindness," he urged Ivan over some domestic business, "to ask my Feodosy when he is sober; look after him kindly, but when Feodosy turns to drink I sincerely beg you to punish him sternly, so that by your grace he may be drawn from the practice."

Ivan Tolstoy in turn engaged in a voluminous correspondence with Peter the Great, who never ceased to keep an anxious eye on Azov. Ivan's first task was to settle the new frontier, which the Tsar was desperately anxious to see drawn up in such a way as not to endanger the safety of Azov and its neighbouring harbour at Taganrog. A stream of instructions poured from the pen of the worried Tsar. When a delay in reply occurred, a strong note would reach the harassed Governor:

"Sir: I received your letter about the inspection; I very much marvel that you never wrote when it went off in what condition are those places at present? The Admiral [Apraxin] has set out from us to you, and he will speak to you about it: be pleased to believe it and do it. Peter." But the temperamental Tsar would follow up with lavish praise for Ivan's efforts, providing him with a detailed account of his latest victory over the Swedes. Then, too, Peter the Great would impulsively intervene in Tolstoy's personal affairs. A hurried note (inscribed on the back in Tolstoy's handwriting, "received through my son Boris in 1706") simply read:

"Ivan Tolstoy! Your son Boris . . . asks that you be paid a thousand roubles from the Azov treasury on account of your yearly salary – take it. Peter."

During these critical years Ivan and Peter Tolstoy achieved the miracle that enabled the Tsar to harbour all his resources for the ultimate defeat of Sweden, and survive the bleakest period in Russia's history since the Poles captured Moscow a century before. The miracle was to keep Turkey, with her enormous resources in manpower and munitions, from entering the war and recovering Azov. The significance of Azov could not be disguised; it was a pistol pointed at the centuries-old condition of the Black Sea as a Turkish lake.

Russian threats and Russian weakness were well-known to the Sultan and his advisers, who were determined to restore the Sublime Porte to its former power and glory. All Russia's military strength was engaged with the Swedish enemy, and Peter Tolstoy's only weapons for preventing Turkish intervention were his native cunning and the traditional resources of bribery, Russia's "golden rain".

A year after Peter Tolstoy's arrival at Adrianople, the Sultan Mustapha II was deposed and replaced by his young brother Ahmed III. Tolstoy was now permitted to take up residence in the capital, Constantinople, where he arrived on 22 August 1703. The new Sultan was highly cultured, a painter and lover of poetry, and so swamped the city's gardens with his favourite flower that his reign became known as the "period of tulips". But he was also extremely interested in politics and, as a result of the circumstances of his brother's deposition, suspicious and cunning to a degree. A few years later the British Ambassador reported that he was "as far as we can know his character . . . exceedingly covetous, haughty and ambitious. He is hasty, violent and cruel, but variable and unsteady".[11] Tolstoy was to experience all these qualities during the years of his embassy.

His position was scarcely enviable. After his arrival, he wrote to say that the Turks "considered matters thus: it never happened before that a Muscovite ambassador lived at the Porte, and they began to take great care, especially with regard to the Black Sea, where your fleet causes them extreme dread . . . Already I have spread it abroad that I have been sent as a firm guarantor of peace."

A further cause of suspicion lay in Tolstoy's religion. The Turks believed with justice that Russia's designs included intrigues with the extensive Orthodox population of the Empire, and were determined the new Ambassador should be frustrated in this respect. "In my courtyard," Tolstoy wrote in April 1703, "Janissaries are stationed; supposedly as a mark of honour, but in reality to prevent the Christians from coming to see me. But no Janissaries guard the French, English and other ambassadors. The Christians dare not pass my portals, and since my arrival the Patriarch of Jerusalem has never been near me."

It was virtually impossible to know what was going on. Between 1702 and 1705 Sultan Ahmed changed his Vizier seven times. This was a very expensive business for the Russian Ambassador, who had no sooner bribed his way into gaining access to one Vizier, than another took his place. In September 1704 Tolstoy lamented to Golovin, "Here we are with the sixth Vizier, and he is worse than all the rest." When he too fell swiftly from office, Tolstoy was in despair. "I don't have enough to keep up with these changes of Vizier," he lamented. Once again lavish gifts had to be provided, but "as for presents for him I don't know what to do; I can't hasten to see the new Vizier because I haven't the means of sending him a present."

In fact, matters were better than they appeared. The last of this swift-changing succession of Viziers was Tchorlulu Ali Pasha, a highly capable and intelligent statesman, whose policy was to consolidate the strength of the Empire as a prerequisite to reviving Turkey's enfeebled fortunes. He began vigorous measures to improve the army, fleet and economy – measures that must ultimately threaten Russia but which, for the time being, meant that the Vizier's policy coincided with the aim of Peter Tolstoy: the preservation of peace on the frontiers.

Despite the extreme suspicion with which the Turks regarded him, and the elaborate restrictions inhibiting his movements and contacts with the citizens of Constantinople, the cunning Peter Tolstoy managed to perform valuable intelligence services for his master. Within a year of his first arrival at Adrianople he had compiled and despatched home a well-researched 166-page analysis and description of the Turkish Empire. Similarly, at the beginning of 1706, the Ministry of Foreign Affairs received a detailed account of the ports and other towns of the entire Black Sea littoral. As he had shown during his stay in Italy, the Ambassador's interests were wide-ranging. Together with details of the respective attitudes of the Christian and Moslem peasantry towards their overlords, the various methods of levying and employing troops, and the personal habits of the Sultan, came snippets of curious information which would have intrigued the inquisitive Tsar as much as his agent: "They say," wrote Tolstoy of the remote deserts of Mesopotamia, "that there are more than 20 towns constructed in ancient times, which have been deserted since their destruction by Tamerlane." These "ancient dwelling-places are still empty, inhabited not by people but only by lions and other wild beasts."

Despite all his efforts the Ambassador found life in the Moslem capital dull, unrewarding, and even dangerous. Nothing could be gained without the expenditure of vast sums of money, which at the same time could be hard to account for. He had arrived with a sum of 200,000 gold ducats and a consignment of costly sables with which to bribe officials, but the succession of changing Viziers at the outset of his embassy soon exhausted even his treasury. He could trust no one, except his beloved son Ivan, who had accompanied him on his mission. Ivan had inherited his father's abilities, learned Turkish, and acted as interpreter ("in the same way he can read and write, except for the [official] letters of the Divan, with which there is great difficulty"). But Ivan returned home at the beginning of 1706, bearing messages from his father. "I am becoming more free," conceded Tolstoy, "but I still have my sentry."[12]

A revealing glimpse of the hazards under which he existed and his Draconian methods of dealing with them is provided in a characteristic despatch home. "I am in great fear of my attendants. As I have been living here for three years they have got acquainted with the Turks, and have learned the Turkish language. Since we are now in great discomfort I fear they will become impatient on account of the imprisonment, and will waver in their faith, because the Moslem faith is very attractive to simple people. If any Judas declare himself he will do great harm, because my people have seen with which of the Christians I have been intimate, and who serves the Tsar, as for example Saba, the Patriarch of Jerusalem, and others; and if anyone turn renegade and tell the Turks who has been working for the Tsar, not only will our friends suffer, but there will be harm to all Christians. I follow this with great attention, and do not know how God will turn it. I have had one affair like this. A young secretary, Timothy, having got acquainted with the Turks, thought of turning Moslem. God helped me to learn about this. I called him quietly and began to talk to him, and he declared to me frankly that he wished to become a Moslem. Then I shut him up in his bedroom till night, and at night he drank a glass of wine and quickly died. Thus God kept him from such wickedness."[13]

Without his son Ivan, and in the face of endless insuperable frustration, Tolstoy felt he could continue no longer. To Count Golovin he wrote despairingly: "I beg you to have mercy on me in my loneliness, for the love of the Son of God and His Blessed Mother; of your goodness, plead for me in my wretchedness that our Sovereign order me to be transferred." The reply came in the Tsar's own hand: "At present, before God, you must suffer a bit more, as it is necessary for you to stay on still. God will not forget our labours, and we can never abandon them."

The "bit more" promised by the Tsar was to continue longer than either of them could have expected. Turkey had to be kept quiet: the tireless Charles XII had led his invincible Swedish troops to victory after victory over the Tsar's Polish and Saxon allies, and the real reckoning could not be far off. No-one except Peter Tolstoy could manage the Turks. He had built up a complex intelligence network with threads extending across the Empire. The Orthodox Church, which looked to the Tsar as its future deliverer, provided a ready-made organization of which he made skilful use. Tolstoy was able to do much more than merely transmit information, and the Turkish government itself was on occasion manipulated by the Ambassador.

When Daltaban Pasha, Grand Vizier in 1702, displayed an inclination to conduct a foreign policy hostile to Russia, large sums of Russian money began to circulate in court circles. The Sultan's mother suddenly developed a dislike for the Vizier, who simultaneously lost his office and his head. It really did not pay to cross the wily diplomat, who was proving himself a worthy heir of his uncle Ivan Mihailovich Miloslavsky. Though now over sixty years old and a virtual prisoner in his embassy, the representative of a country known to have every reason to appease Turkey, he controlled a web of extraordinary complexity and influence. One of history's great spymasters, he provides a remarkable example of what an effective espionage and subversion system can achieve. In 1706 he reported the melancholy but, it seems, not unexpected news that "two of the most prudent pashas have been strangled at the instigation of the Grand Vizier, who does not like capable people. God grant that all the rest may perish in the same way."

The time was swiftly approaching when his most skilful efforts would be crucial to Russia's survival. Over the winter, spring and summer of 1706–7 King Charles XII of Sweden was recruiting, re-equipping, drilling and training the most formidable army in Europe for one purpose: the destruction of the Russian Empire. More than seventy thousand men, whose arms had successively conquered the Danes, the Poles and the Saxons, lay along the frontiers from Finland to Saxony. Superbly armed and accoutred, masters of the devastating Swedish battle-drill, and supremely confident in the invincibility of the military genius who led them, it seemed that nothing could stand in their way.

The Tsar knew this too well, and after frantic but unavailing efforts to induce every power in Europe to intervene on his behalf, began to prepare for the worst. As early as January 1707 the frontiers were laid waste by squadrons of Cossacks and Kalmucks, and by June Peter was pessimistically arranging improvements to the defences of Moscow itself. Foreigners in the capital did not know which to fear most: the Swedish occupation, or a bloody uprising of the citizens against their hated government. Finally, on 27 August 1707, drums rolled, Charles XII swung into his saddle, and the Swedish army began its march to the East.

It was Peter the Great's most terrible hour since the day he witnessed the uprising of the Streltsi, a quarter of a century earlier. Not yet daring to risk his army in open battle with the Swedes, he ordered its withdrawal to Minsk, while he himself removed to his new capital at St. Petersburg, where he frantically supervised defensive preparations parallel to those being conducted at Moscow. It was precisely at this moment he learned that the Cossacks had raised the standard of revolt in the south. The uprising was indirectly connected to the Swedish threat, and could not have come at a more dangerous moment.

Among desperate efforts to raise recruits for his army, Peter had despatched a force under Prince Yuri Dolgoruky to the Don region, which was however massacred to the last man on the River Aidar by a band of Don Cossacks led by the fierce Ataman of Bakhmut, Kondraty Bulavin, who soon after proclaimed a general uprising of Cossacks, peasants and other dispossessed against the boyars and Germans who ruled under the Tsar. On 4 November 1707 Peter heard from Ivan Tolstoy that one of Prince Dolgoruky's officers had reported that "after the death of Prince Yury, the Don Cossacks took him and several soldiers out onto the steppe and held a council of war (*krug*). And they invited him and the soldiers and Cossacks to join them in the rising, and swore they would not do worse than Stenka Razin." As in Stenka Razin's time, the spark lighted on a bed of dry tinder. From the Caspian to the Dnieper Cossacks and fugitive peasants flocked to Bulavin's horse-mane standards. Tsar Peter found himself in the spring of 1708 faced by a rebellion which was shaking the throne itself. Around Tambov and even Tula, a bare hundred miles from Moscow, villages and manors burned and smoked. Far to the south Ivan Tolstoy in Azov was no longer Governor of a great port threatening the might of Turkey, but was cut off behind the uprisen Cossack horde. He was used to living isolated in a wild country, perpetually threatened by lawless Kuban Cossacks and hostile Crim Tartars.[14] Those he could afford to ignore, but now it seemed he might be engulfed.

On 14 April 1708, the Tsar received an alarming report that Bulavin "intends to carry the war from Cherkask to Azov . . . and kill the Voevod [Tolstoy], his

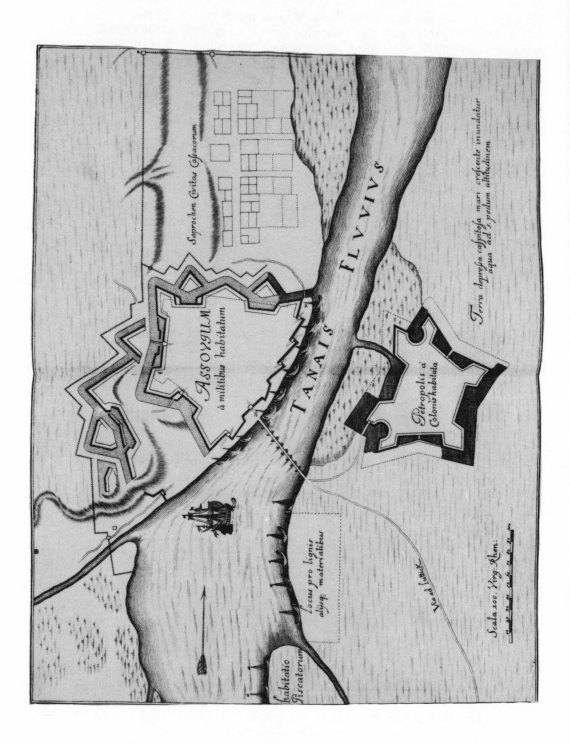

Map of Azov

principal people and the Germans, and open up the gaols".[15] The Tsar was desperately worried and, on 9 May, despatched an anguished letter to his Governor informing him that he was sending a regiment to strengthen the garrison, whilst an army of relief was being collected under Prince Vasily Dolgoruky, brother of Prince Yury whom Bulavin had killed the previous October. The real question was, however, could Tolstoy rely on his own soldiers? Peter enclosed a code, so that the Governor could get messages out to Dolgoruky. The letter came through, somehow, but the fate of Azov hung by a hair. On 10 June a letter from Tolstoy to Dolgoruky reported that he had now received a letter from "the robber Kondrashka Bulavin himself" containing threats of "his robberlike intention to seize Azov". Bulavin had already sent messengers all over the Don and Kuban countries to assemble overwhelming forces.[16] His men had seized the Don towns of Dmitrievsk and Cherkask, besieged Saratov, and now held Azov with a ring of steel.

News continued to trickle through to the capital from the beleaguered fortress. On 28 May Peter wrote again to Ivan Tolstoy: "Sir Governor! I've received your letter, in which you write what has happened at Cherkask, to which I reply that you must do everything you can to preserve your garrison from being subverted. Don't stint money, and keep yourself going somehow with God's help. I will certainly come down to you – of that I have definite hopes . . . Peter." The letter took over a month to arrive, being smuggled through by a guardsman named Igor Pashkov. The Tsar's fears of some treachery on the part of the garrison were realistic. As Bulavin's guns thundered outside the ramparts, Ivan Tolstoy uncovered a plot by rebel supporters in the citadel. They were committed to gaol, but not before a number had escaped and joined Bulavin. They were daring Zaporozhian Cossacks, who floated downstream in a number of purloined boats.

Despite the desperate danger in the south, there was no possibility of the Tsar's joining Ivan Tolstoy in Azov. The whole situation was a nightmare. Bulavin announced he was seeking the help of the Sultan in what was now open war with Muscovy. The Khan of the Crimea, whose territories bordered on the Zaporozhian Cossacks, was known to be equally eager to march against the Tsar's forces. Peter ordered the Tsarevich to fortify Moscow against the rebels.

But meanwhile, what of the most formidable enemy of all? Over the winter Charles XII had driven the Russians from Poland, placed his own candidate on the throne in Warsaw, and wintered the Swedish army in Minsk. Whatever the danger to Azov, Peter had to supervise the defence of Russia against the invasion which had now begun in earnest.

Left to himself, Ivan Tolstoy could only rely on his scanty and unreliable garrison. On 5 July 1708 Bulavin had appeared and camped before the walls of Azov with 5,000 men. At one o'clock next afternoon the besiegers launched a ferocious attack. Ivan Tolstoy's men stormed out into a suburb occupied by the rebels, but after stiff fighting were driven back. Eventually Government reinforcements managed to gain the citadel, and with concentrated artillery fire from walls and warships on the river the garrison managed to break up the siege. Bulavin's star was waning; another of his armies was defeated by Dolgoruky's relief column, and before the end of July Tolstoy reported to the government that the rebel leader, deserted by his followers, had shot himself in despair. Like Stenka Razin's rebellion, that of Bulavin disintegrated with astonishing rapidity once his Cossack followers sensed the tide was on the turn. Lacking any settled programme, Cossack rebellions swiftly degenerated into colossal orgies of plunder and destruction. The survivors were treated with customary brutality: floating gallows bore ghastly warning of the dangers of rebellion down the quiet Don, though the dangling corpses were for the most part watched only by widows and orphans huddled outside smoking villages.

Bulavin's corpse was carried into Azov, where its head was hacked off and the bloody trunk hung upside-down at the point where the main assault on the fortress had been directed. On 15 August 1708 the Governor Ivan Tolstoy received a congratulatory letter from the Tsar which, along with the rest of their correspondence, was preserved as a treasured relic among our muniments in the family home at Murzikha, near Kazan. "Sir Governor! We have received your letter . . . from which with great joy we learned of the fatal end of the evil robber Bulavin, whose purposes the Lord God through your labours suppressed. For which achievement I thank you and yours . . . ." Ivan was soon after promoted to the rank of Privy Councillor. His grateful reply of 18 October was borne to the Tsar by his son Boris Tolstoy, together with presents of saltfish, pressed caviar, and grapes from the South.

In 1710, however, Ivan Tolstoy was replaced as Governor of Azov, in an arrangement whose significance is unclear. His brother-in-law Admiral Apraxin was appointed Governor on 6 February 1710, while Tolstoy received the following edict: "1710, 9th February. The Great Sovereign and Great Prince Peter Alexeevich, Autocrat of Great, Little and White Russia, ordains that Governor Tolstoy for his true service, do take for the purchase of an estate two thousand roubles from the sale of the Bakhmutsky saltmines. This edict of the Great Sovereign confirms [the post of] Admiral Apraxin." Ivan Tolstoy, however, not only stayed on in a position of command at Azov, but confusingly continued to be known as Governor.[17]

It is a matter of family pride that the rebellion of Stenka Razin was halted by a Miloslavsky and that of Bulavin by a Tolstoy.

The destruction of Bulavin had come not a moment too soon. The month before, the Swedish army had broken camp and forced the major rivers protecting the Russian frontier. At Golovchin Charles XII routed a superior Russian force, but, finding the countryside devastated by Peter's light horse, he decided to move south. There he could gain fresh supplies and consolidate before the final thrust to Moscow. By October he was nearing the Ukraine, and on the 27th Peter received news that the Hetman of the Ukrainian Cossacks, Ivan Mazeppa, had gone over to the Swedes. Joined by his welcome new ally, Charles XII wintered in the Ukraine. As if all this were not enough, the Khan of the Crimea, Devlet Ghirey, sent emissaries to the Swedes, offering to join in the destruction of the hated Russian power. For this he needed authorization from his suzerain, the Sultan of Turkey. Messengers from Charles XII and Devlet Ghirey arrived in Constantinople, pressing the Sultan to agree. The temptation to do so was enormous, for here at last was the opportunity to recapture Azov and restore the Black Sea to its centuries-old condition as a Turkish lake. Tsar Peter, frantically collecting his forces to meet the Swedish threat, could only urge Peter Tolstoy in Constantinople to employ every resource to prevent the Porte's consent to the Tartar request.

What his brother's courage had achieved on the walls of Azov in the previous summer, Peter Tolstoy's native wit set out to emulate in the spring of 1709. The "golden rain" began to descend again on Constantinople.

The Swedish army left its winter quarters and moved south to await reinforcements from Poland. Peter the Great was struck with anxiety: what if Charles were planning a forced march to Voronezh, where he could destroy the Tsar's fleet on the Don? Nothing could then prevent a Turkish attack on Azov. The Tsar with his usual impetuous energy sailed down the Don and joined Ivan Tolstoy in Azov just after the middle of April. There he fell ill for most of May, but still managed to replenish the garrison and stage an impressive review of his fleet for the benefit of the Sultan. (All was not quite so effective as it seemed. On 24 March Peter had instructed Ivan Tolstoy that "the ships which are very bad and which were ordered to be broken up in Azov: on the contrary do not have them broken up without specific instruction. Peter.")

In Constantinople Peter Tolstoy (who had acted firmly towards the Turks during the panic caused by Bulavin in the previous year) made good use of these essentially defensive – almost despairing – moves. Rumours spread through the city that an enormously powerful Russian fleet was on the point of leaving Azov to enter the Black Sea and ravage the neighbouring provinces. The agitation grew to such a head that mobs surged angrily through the streets. The Sultan informed Peter Tolstoy that the Sublime Porte would on no account open hostilities with Russia that year; a welcome message that was swiftly passed on to the Tsar, who received "the good news" on 19 May at Azov.[18]

By 27 May the Tsar was well enough to travel and, urging Ivan Tolstoy to exert the utmost vigilance, set off to join his army, which since the beginning of the month had been defending the small town of Poltava against the Swedish army. What followed was the greatest hour of the new Russia, as the Tsar explained to Ivan Tolstoy in a letter written on the day of victory at Poltava.

"Sir Governor. I announce to you that a magnificent and unexpected victory, which our Lord God has, through the indescribable bravery of our soldiers, been pleased to give with little bloodshed in this form. On the very morning of this day the enemy attacked our cavalry with the whole of his army, horse and foot. Though they resisted with the utmost valour, they were obliged to yield after causing the enemy great loss. After that the enemy formed themselves up opposite our camp, opposite whom we ordered all the infantry from the entrenchments, who formed up under the eyes of the enemy with the cavalry on both flanks. When the enemy saw this they immediately came on to attack us, and we went to meet them in such a way that they were at once beaten from the field. Most of their colours and cannon were taken, as also were General Field-Marshal Rehnskjold and four other generals; viz. Schlippenbach, Stackelberg, Hamilton and Roos. In addition Prime Minister Count Piper with Secretaries Imerlin and Cederheilm were taken, with several thousand officers and men. I'll write about it all soon in detail (at present there is just not time); and, in a few words, the whole enemy force has met with the fall of Phaeton. (But I can't yet tell what's happened to the King, whether he's still with us or gone to dwell with his fathers.) I have sent Lieutenant Prince Galitzine and Bauer with the cavalry to smash up what's left of the enemy. I greet you with this unheard-of news. Peter."[19]

As a postscript to a similar letter sent to Ivan Tolstoy's brother-in-law Admiral Apraxin, Peter added exultantly:

"Now, with God's help, the final stone in the foundation of St. Petersburg has been laid." The victorious Tsar understandably believed that this consummation of the nine-year nightmare of the Swedish war spelled the end, for the moment at least, of his troubles. But a passing parenthesis of his triumphant letter unwittingly recorded the start of an episode even more dangerous to him and his faithful servants, the Tolstoy brothers.

King Charles XII, who had been prevented by a wound from taking part in the battle in his usual dashing manner, had not gone to rest with his fathers. Together with a small band of his followers he made for the south, to the safety of the territories of the Crimean Khan. Aided by his ally Mazeppa's Cossacks, he crossed the rivers Dnieper and Bug and found refuge with the Pasha of Ochakov, the Sultan's local governor. The fact that his army was destroyed and he a fugitive separated by all Eastern Europe from his own country did not daunt the intrepid King for a moment. Moving further into the Sultan's dominions, he and his small band of devoted followers established themselves at Bender, on the Dniester. At the same time he despatched envoys to Constantinople, urging the Sultan to join him in an alliance against Russia.

Once again all the diplomatic and other skills of Peter Tolstoy were brought into play to counter the influence of the Swedish agents. At first all seemed to be going well for the Russian cause. The King, daunted not a jot by the disaster at Poltava, carried his pride so high as to cause considerable offence to the Divan. King Charles even offended his staunchest ally, the Khan of the Crimea, by a prickly insistence upon precedence when they met, but the Tartars were so set on war that they overlooked the difference.

By this time (May 1710) Peter the Great was reaping the full fruits of the Poltava victory. He had restored his ally Augustus to the Polish throne and obtained eager recognition and offers of alliance from all Europe, and even now his armies were sweeping through Sweden's Baltic provinces. Denmark invaded southern Sweden. Charles's only belligerent ally, Mazeppa, was dead. The time could scarcely have appeared less propitious for the exile at Bender, and Tolstoy's task must have appeared proportionately straightforward. For the first time since his arrival seven years earlier the Janissaries were removed from his door and he was given "the liberty to choose his quarters where he pleased, and the same freedom which other Foreign Ministers enjoy. . . ." The delighted Ambassador at once found himself a suitable residence in Pera, on the other side of the Golden Horn.

Unfortunately, however, Tolstoy for the first time miscalculated. Having set up house in Pera, he began to press for his Embassy to have precedence over all others, in recognition of Russia's new-found power in the East. After all the humiliations he and his country had suffered, it was understandable that now he should wish the awakened giant to receive its due. He was assured by his hosts, in Oriental imagery, that "Rivulets would all flow at last into his River". But Peter Tolstoy and his master had misunderstood the Turkish character. The extra-ordinary character and achievement of Charles XII strongly appealed to the chivalrous and martial nature of the Turks. Tchorlulu Ali Pasha, the Vizier whose policy had been peace and retrenchment, fell; he was replaced by Numan Pasha, of whom it was "little doubted but he will favour the King of Sweden more than his Predecessor did". Increasing resentment was felt by a proud nation at Russian arrogance.

Paradoxically, the victory of Poltava had increased, not allayed, Turkish desire for war. Tolstoy himself had anticipated this when he first received news of the battle. "Although I have great faith in the Mufti and others," he reported on 8 August 1709, "please do not wonder that at first, when the King of Sweden was at the height of his power, I reported on the Porte's peaceful intentions: but now that the Swedes are beaten, I doubt them." When Russia was weak the Turks felt confident, but now all that was changed. The peace treaty was renewed on 3 January 1710, but throughout the following year Turkey began to gather up her might. From all over the gigantic Empire troops and supplies began to pour in: Janissaries from Egypt, Albanians and Bosnians from Roumelia, Spahis from Africa and Timariots from Egypt. A hundred and twenty thousand men were moving towards the frontiers, and shipyards hummed with preparations on galleys, frigates and bomb vessels. A formal ultimatum from the Tsar that Charles XII be expelled from the Turkish dominions provided the final pretext. The Khan of the Crimea arrived in Constantinople, warning the Sultan that his throne would be in danger if he did not follow the paths of honour and national interest. The first blow fell on the Russian Ambassador. Peter Tolstoy, "going to the Audience appointed him by the Vizir, at his landing at the usual place in Constantinople was met by the Chiaux Bashi and Muxur Aga Captain of the Vizirs Guard of Janissaries, who accosting him acquainted him, that they had orders from the Vizir to carry him to the Seven Towers, after which, not suffering him to mount one of his own Horses, they put him on an Ordinary Gelding and so conducted him thro' the Town to the place of his confinement." This was the Turkish method of declaring war, a move confirmed immediately afterwards at a formal session of the Divan.[20]

The war that followed was very nearly as disastrous for Peter the Great as his previous campaign had been triumphant. Marching his army eagerly into the Turkish Balkans, where he hoped for support from the Orthodox Christian population, the Tsar was surrounded by superior Turkish forces on the River Pruth. Defeated in the ensuing battle and hopelessly outnumbered, Peter was compelled on 12 July 1711 to sign a treaty. Russian troops were to evacuate Poland and all Turkish territory gained in 1696 and 1700, the Black Sea fleet was to be broken up, and peace was to be made with a restored Charles XII. Humiliated, the Tsar and his army returned home.

The terms of the treaty included clauses directly affecting the fortunes of the two Tolstoy brothers. No longer would the Tsar be permitted to maintain a permanent ambassador in Constantinople, and Azov was to be surrendered. Peter Tolstoy's life was now grim indeed. The Tsar sent a new envoy, Shafirov, to negotiate the peace settlement, the execution of which he was instructed to postpone as long as possible. Meanwhile the original Ambassador continued to languish in gaol.

"When the Turks imprisoned me," Peter Tolstoy wrote afterwards, "then my house was completely pillaged and all my things pilfered. They sent a few things with me to the prison, though they had all been ransacked. As for me, I was brought to the stronghold of the Seven Towers and I was incarcerated in a deep underground dungeon, under a tower. It was very dark and stinking; but eventually I was released from this and locked up in a little hut for 17 months, of which I lay sick for seven months in unbearable pain. I could not ask them even once to send a doctor to look at me, but was left without any care. What at last kept me going was my managing secretly to buy medicine through many people. Moreover, every day they menaced me with tortures and torments, asking how much money I gave to which Ministers for the maintenance of peace."

The last enquiries probably stemmed from court attempts to get up a case of treason against the deposed Grand Vizier Tchorlulu. Despite these threatening enquiries, Tolstoy managed to maintain continual contact with his network of secret agents, countering the influence of the Turkish war party.[21]

Tolstoy's sufferings can scarcely have been exaggerated, considering that he was sixty-seven years old at the time of his incarceration. But to the single-minded Tsar delay was essential to Russian recovery. His anguish over the agreement to surrender Azov was extreme. Instructions were given, first, not to destroy the fortifications; and then to destroy them, but preserving the foundations and plans of the defences. When Ivan Tolstoy was summoned by the Turks to hand over his charge in fulfilment of the Treaty, he "laughed at the Orders, and returned their answer by the mouth of their Canon". By November the Sultan had lost patience, and once again declared war, swearing "if it please God to march next Spring in person with Grandeur and Magnificence together with my victorious army. . . ."

Peter was reluctantly obliged to fulfil his commitments, and in the beginning of 1712, Azov was finally given up. A letter formerly in our family archive at Murzikha contained details of the exchange. The Turkish representative, Achmed Pasha, requested that Ivan Tolstoy himself come to the Turkish camp. His brother-in-law Admiral Count Apraxin, presumably considering Peter Tolstoy's current sufferings, wrote anxiously urging him not to take the risk. But Ivan declined to be inhibited by any fear of personal danger, and boldly appeared before the Pasha.[22] Azov was once again a Turkish stronghold, and a year later (25 August 1713) its former Russian Governor died at Cherkask.

From Ivan Andreevich Tolstoy is descended the senior line of the Tolstoy family, later Tolstoy-Miloslavsky. Ivan's widow, Maria, sister of Admiral Apraxin and the Tsarina Martha Matveevna, made out her will in the following year. It is a document full of interest, both for the light it throws on Ivan Tolstoy and the life-style of a Russian noble of the period. Maria Tolstoy left estates and Moscow houses to the eldest son Boris. To his younger brother Andrei and Andrei's son Ivan were left valuable ikons with gold and silver facings, first in the inventory and obviously most precious. Then followed quantities of plate and glass: "a chased cup, gilt in places, surmounted by a small swan", "teapot with gilt bottom and gilt handle", "chased goblet with lid, gilt inside and out", etc. . . . "The above plate weighs forty pounds." Only a small amount of furniture is itemized: "mirror with white carved frame; another mirror in black frame . . . twelve chairs and armchairs covered with silk blue cloth".

A number of articles were obviously relics of Ivan Tolstoy's embassy to Constantinople in 1700. There were two Turkish horse-cloths, a Turkish tent, a steel Turkish sword with a silver mounting, a Circassian bridle mounted in silver, and a Turkish goblet. We can almost picture the Governor as he set out from his residence in Azov to welcome Tsar Peter or Admiral Apraxin at the gates. He wore, like all the nobility of that period, European clothing. Perhaps he was wearing the French coat, made of "red cloth, with gold and silver cuffs on a blue background . . . buttons and buttonholes trimmed with gold" and matching breeches. Other coats were lined with sable and beaver and yet another was "trimmed with gold and lined with cornflower-blue satin". Across this flamboyant dress hung an elk-leather sword-belt inlaid with gold braid, bearing a sword with silver-mounted lizard-skin scabbard. As he descends the steps, a groom brings out his war-horse, with the German saddle, red horsecloth (*shabrack*) and pistol-holsters. Or maybe his coach comes rattling up from the stables. There was one painted red and black; another more cheerfully was "lined with blue cloth, decorated with nut trees and birds painted on the sides".[23]

With Azov in their hands at last, the Turks made peace. Peter Tolstoy was released, along with his fellow-diplomats, from the Seven Towers, and at once despatched a piteous appeal to the Chancellor Golovkin, "with tears of blood, prostrating myself at your feet, I implore you: be so kind as to request of our all-gracious Sovereign, that he have mercy on me and direct me to be freed from this infernal Tartarus after my ten years' torment." He explained that he could be of little further use anyway, as the Turks regarded him with such unremitting suspicion. Peter approved Tolstoy's request, but the poor man's sufferings were not yet at an end. Achmet Aga, incited by Charles XII, reported to the Porte that Russian troops were still in Poland, in contravention of the treaty. Turkey for the third time began warlike preparations, and once again the unfortunate Tolstoy was cast into the Seven Towers, together with his fellow-diplomats and a large number of Embassy servants and hangers-on.[24] Their quarters were restricted to a single tower and couple of huts "and they keep us in such confinement that we must surely die within a few days from the putrid exhalations". But Peter Tolstoy was a survivor, and somehow kept going through this last and most unpleasant imprisonment.

In April the prisoners were transferred to Adrianople. On 18 October 1713 the belligerent powers ratified the Treaty of Adrianople and made peace. Tolstoy and his companions were released from confinement, but squabbles over frontier delineations caused their departure to be held up for nearly a year, and it was not until September 1714 that Peter Tolstoy returned home.[25]

The Russia of 1714 had changed dramatically from the country Peter Tolstoy had left twelve years before. A new capital, St. Petersburg, had risen miraculously from the swamps of the Neva. His elder brother was dead. Surrounding the Tsar were new faces, many of very different background from men like Tolstoy and Apraxin. The Tsar's two favourite companions and advisers were Prince Menshikov, reputed to have started life as apprentice to a pastry-cook, and the Tsarina Catherine, a Lithuanian peasant-girl captured by Sheremietev in the campaign of 1702. The Chancellor Golovin, whose patronage had advanced Tolstoy on his return from Italy in 1699, was dead and his place taken by Gavril Golovkin.

Tolstoy's earliest biographer, the French Consul Villardeau, alleged that the returned diplomat bribed Menshikov with twenty thousand roubles to provide him with high office, and that the Tsar accordingly was persuaded to appoint him to the Privy Council.[26] But, as the historian Pavlov-Silvansky pointed out, this appears to be nothing more than a piece of malicious gossip, circulating at the time. For Tolstoy's great services in Constantinople had fully earned him the Tsar's gratitude and any position to which he might reasonably have aspired. A bribe may perhaps have changed hands, but the promotion was a logical step.

In any case, Peter Tolstoy's diplomatic abilities were once again in demand. Charles XII, whom Tolstoy in Constantinople had planned to kidnap with a party of light horse, now made a dramatic flight from Turkish territory, where he had been a virtual prisoner for five and a half years. The signing at last of the Russo-Turkish peace Treaty of Adrianople, which brought about the return of Peter Tolstoy to Russia, simultaneously removed any further motive for the

Swedish King to linger in Turkey. No further help could be forthcoming from the Sultan, and in sixteen days he made a dramatic ride across eastern Europe, travelling disguised with a single servant. On 22 November 1714 he appeared in Stralsund, Sweden's remaining foothold on the south coast of the Baltic. It was clear that the war between Russia and Sweden, until then lingering on in a half-hearted way, was to be resumed with all the vigour of which the dynamic young King was capable. But the position was no longer what it had been before 1709. Russia was now a great power, with powerful allies. Swedish territory on German soil was looked upon as an anomaly by Denmark and the north German princes, and a Northern Alliance had come into being which now moved to check the eruption Charles's presence portended.

Peter Tolstoy was closely involved in delicate negotiations resulting in a Russo-Danish Convention, whereby a combined Russian and Danish army occupied the Swedish island of Rügen, off Stralsund. The city fell soon afterwards in December 1715, and Charles XII was obliged to escape to Sweden in a small boat.

On 24 January 1716 Peter himself set out for Copenhagen in an effort to persuade the dilatory King Frederick of Denmark to join in an invasion of the Swedish mainland. With him travelled his principal diplomatic advisers, Golovkin, Shafirov and Tolstoy.

The second, related, purpose of Peter's journey into Europe was to attend the wedding of his niece the Tsarevna Catherine Ivanovna (granddaughter of Maria Miloslavsky) to the Duke of Mecklenburg. The wedding took place in Danzig, and there the Tsar's party arrived on 18 February. The Tsar was no longer as wild and uncouth as he had appeared during his previous stay in the West in 1697–98 and contented himself with minor excesses, such as attempting to purloin a valuable painting from the Marienkirche, or borrowing the Burgomaster's wig during a chilly church service. But the boorish character and manners of the bridegroom ensured that the happy ceremony was accompanied by buffooneries which would have raised eyebrows at Versailles or Windsor.

Peter Tolstoy was much in evidence, assuring the Mecklenburg settlement negotiators of the moderation of Russian troops on Mecklenburg territory. ("*Un poco di pane! Un poco di pane!*" – "a piece of bread!", was all they wanted.) But even he behaved without his usual polish when he decided that the ring the Duke gave him as a wedding gift did not come up to the lavish standard he had known in Constantinople. A colleague gave him *his* ring in addition, but Tolstoy's complaints continued loud and clear.

He was engaged in more professional exchanges with the Poles, whose King Augustus, despite the fact that he owed his restoration to the Tsar's victory at Poltava, had been conducting policies inimical to Russian interests. The Tsar now departed for Copenhagen to concert the invasion of Sweden, whilst in September Tolstoy and the other diplomats treated with Peter's other powerful ally King Frederick William of Prussia, in Berlin. But on 17 September the Tsar decided to postpone the invasion of Sweden until the following year, and continued his journey westwards until he arrived on 6 December in Amsterdam, where he spent the winter.

Meanwhile Tolstoy was engaged in an attempt to increase the strength to be brought to bear on the Swedes when the campaigning season of 1717 opened. On 26 November 1716 he was provided with instructions as a basis for negotiations with the Government of Hanover. Since 1714 the Elector of Hanover had also been King George I of England, and Peter hoped to induce King George to employ the Royal Navy against the Swedes in the Baltic. But Hanover was suspicious of the Russian presence in Mecklenburg, and wished to see the bear's paw withdrawn altogether from the Empire. Tolstoy stressed that the troops were only there to assist Denmark against Sweden, and, as the event proved, this was in fact the truth. But Britain and Hanover continued sceptical of Russian professions of good faith and evaded bringing the discussions to a satisfactory conclusion. The Tsar hoped to break through the impasse by consultation with George I and sent Tolstoy and another diplomat to call on the King as he passed through Holland. But they found he had already departed on his yacht for England.[27]

Having had no luck with Britain, Tsar Peter began to respond favourably to suggestions coming from France that the two powers arrange an alliance to their mutual advantage. Greatly enticed by the thought of a visit to the centre of civilization itself, he announced to the French Ambassador at the Hague on 30 March 1717 that he intended to travel personally to Paris and consult with the Regent of France. The French made elaborate preparations to receive their Muscovite visitor.

The Tsar and his train arrived at Dunkirk, where they were greeted by a gentleman of King Louis's household. Among Peter's companions, the Frenchman noted in a report to his master that "the councillor Tolstoy is in his [Peter's] confidence, is very polite, and speaks Italian". It was also remarked that he was the only one to speak good French, and when on 20 June Peter left Paris, Tolstoy stayed behind with Shafirov to negotiate a treaty of friendship, which was however a mere formal expression of goodwill.[28] They then followed in their master's tracks to join him at Spa, near Liège, where Peter was staying to take the waters.

It was here that the Tsar entered into deep conference with Tolstoy concerning a matter which had for months occupied his mind with increasing intensity. It was known now to everyone that Peter's son and heir, the Tsarevich Alexei, had fled from his father's control at the end of the previous year and gone into hiding. It was a business personally shameful to the Tsar and dangerous to Russia. What had happened was this.

The twenty-seven-year-old Tsarevich was Peter's son by his first marriage to the Tsarina Eudoxia. Under the frighteningly erratic and largely loveless upbringing inflicted on him by his father and the great favourite Menshikov, Alexei grew up pious, sensitive, drunken, and absolutely terrified of his awesome parent. He was married, as a matter of state, to Princess Charlotte of Wolfenbüttel, who bore him a daughter Natalya in 1714. But about this time Alexei took up with a Finnish peasant girl, Afrosinya, with whom he became infatuated and whom he openly installed as his mistress. Princess Charlotte then gave birth to a son, Peter, in 1715 but died in childbirth. As time went by Alexei had found his father's expectations and demands ever more daunting, and his consequent cringing failures made the disappointed Tsar still more harsh in his treatment.

At last Peter delivered an ultimatum. On 11 October 1715, immediately after the Tsarevna Charlotte's funeral, he wrote to his son threatening him that unless he displayed a much greater proclivity for the military life, "I will deprive you of the succession, as one would cut off a gangrenous limb." Alexei replied, eagerly accepting and volunteering to abdicate all his rights. This was not the reply Peter had expected or wanted. Soon afterwards he fell ill and nearly died, and this impressed on him still further the importance of securing the succession. To shake his son into more profitable ways he presented him with a much harsher choice: pull yourself together, or enter a monastery. On 20 January 1716 Alexei agreed to take the cowl. This further rebuff aroused Peter's anger and suspicion. Could anyone so readily abandon such a magnificent inheritance? And could his son so lightly take a step which would deprive him of his mistress, with whom he was known to be obsessed? There was something wrong here; the Tsar gave his son six months to reflect seriously before committing himself to a decision.

Two days later the Tsar left for his journey to Copenhagen, Amsterdam and Paris. On 26 August, seven months having passed without a satisfactory reply, Peter wrote from Copenhagen, ordering his son to explain by return of post what was his decision. If he did wish to remain Tsarevich, he must set out at once to join his father in the planned invasion of Sweden. The roads were bad and post slow, and it was not until 21 October that the delighted Tsar, travelling from Copenhagen to Lübeck, was overtaken by a courier who informed him that the Tsarevich had left Russia and was on his way to join him. But Peter's joy faded as weeks passed without any sign of his unpredictable son. On 9 December he wrote from Amsterdam to General Weide, commanding Russian troops in Mecklenburg, asking him if he had any news of the Tsarevich. German-speaking officers sent out by Weide failed to discover the missing heir, but found indications that he might have gone to Vienna.

Meanwhile Peter summoned to him his diplomatic resident in Vienna, Avram Veselovsky, ordered him too to trace the fugitive, and gave him a formal request for extradition addressed to the Emperor Charles VI. Veselovsky returned to Vienna and at once despatched agents to pick up the trail. Through discreet enquiries at inns and examination of town registration of visitors for the previous October, the spies established that a small party of travellers including a self-styled "merchant from the Russian army" had passed from Danzig to Breslau, and had been seen leaving the latter city "on the Vienna road". Veselovsky himself now took up the trail, and tracked down the "merchant", who had now become "the Polish chevalier Kremenetsky", to the Black Eagle hostelry in Vienna, where he had arrived on 23 November. Whilst there he had bought a coffee-coloured outfit for his "wife", who thenceforward dressed as a man. A postmaster outside Vienna had received an enquiry from such an "officer" concerning the journey to Rome, but for the moment the trail ran cold at Vienna.

Veselovsky was following up word that the Unknown might have travelled on to the Tyrol, when on 19 March he was joined by a fresh emissary from the Tsar. This was a hulking, muscular Guards Captain named Alexander Rumyantsov, who had been sent for the specific purpose of abducting the Tsarevich and returning him to Mecklenburg. Veselovsky now learned from a bribed official that the stranger whose movements he had traced was held under the Emperor's protection at a remote castle called Ehrenberg in the Tyrol. He immediately despatched Rumyantsov to spy on the castle. The Captain returned ten days later to report that the stranger was indeed the Tsarevich, and that he had been at Ehrenberg since January. Armed at last with this identification, Veselovsky obtained an audience with the Emperor, explained that the Tsarevich's whereabouts were known, and presented the Tsar's official request for his return. The Emperor skilfully avoided admitting any knowledge of the matter, but promised to look into it. Veselovsky continued to press the matter in response to Peter's ever more peremptory demands; but on 2 June he wrote to his master (who was by then in

Castle of Ehrenberg, Tyrol

Paris) to report that the vigilant Rumyantsov had now trailed the fugitive to Naples, whither he had fled from Ehrenberg. Veselovsky now feared to make a further official approach at court, as it seemed more than likely that the Emperor would remove him to an even more remote asylum once he knew the present one had been detected. Rumyantsov himself rode post-haste to the Tsar with this awkward news.

This was the dilemma which faced Peter at Spa in July 1717. Already, in Paris the previous month, Peter Tolstoy had offered to seek out the Tsarevich, and it was to him that the Tsar now turned. Tolstoy was seventy-two, but his extraordinary resource, cunning and flair for intelligence work had already been displayed during his fourteen years' embassy in Turkey. In addition he spoke fluent Italian and knew the city of Naples well. Peter gave Tolstoy an elaborate set of instructions together with a personal request to the Emperor for his son's extradition. Charles VI, however, had a personal reason for protecting the Tsarevich: the Empress was sister to the Tsarevich's late wife.

On 26 July Tolstoy and Rumyantsov arrived in Vienna, and on the 29th they appeared with Veselovsky before the Emperor. His Majesty listened attentively to Tolstoy's persuasive plea and read his fellow-sovereign's letter, which contained mingled pleas and threats. The Emperor gave a non-committal reply, but promised to reply to the letter. This appeared unpropitious, and next day Tolstoy called on the Princess of Wolfenbüttel, mother of the Tsarevich's late wife. To her he explained earnestly that if the Tsarevich failed to reconcile himself with his father,

71

not only he but his children would be deprived of the succession. She could not wish to see her grandchildren disinherited, and could she not speak to her daughter the Empress about the matter? The Princess was impressed by the argument.

On 18 August a Secret Council of Ministers met to advise the Emperor on his reply. The Ministers were apprehensive that a refusal to comply might lead the unpredictable Tsar to march his armies in Poland and Silesia into Bohemia. But they advised their master that, grave though the danger was, it would be far worse to violate the laws of nations by surrendering their uninvited guest to what might well be a harsh fate. What His Majesty could do, however, was to explain to the Tsar that the Tsarevich was in no way a prisoner, and that Tolstoy was free to visit him to see for himself. The Emperor agreed with the recommendations, and the same day one of the Ministers, Count Sinzendorff, received the three Russian envoys and explained the decision. Tolstoy argued his sovereign's case at length, but without avail. He was content at length with permission to visit his prey. Before his departure he called again on the Princess of Wolfenbüttel, asking her to back his plea to the Tsarevich.

"I know the Tsarevich's character," she replied. "His father is striving in vain to fit him for military service: he would rather have rosary beads in his hands than pistols, but it would be a great grief to me if the Tsar were antagonized and my grandchildren suffered."

At a third interview, she agreed to write to the Tsarevich urging his return, pausing only to ask Tolstoy whether he believed in the Tsar's promise to allow his son to live where he liked if he obeyed? Tolstoy replied that in his opinion "there would be no difficulty, if the Tsarevich went with him".

On 21 August Tolstoy and Rumyantsov set out from Vienna, but did not arrive at Naples until 24 September, on account of severe flooding in Italy. Two days later they met the terrified Tsarevich. Tolstoy, gentle and charming, handed him a letter from the Tsar, in which he solemnly swore before God not to harm his son if he did his duty and returned with Tolstoy. Alexei trembled so much he could hardly speak: it was the menacing figure of Rumyantsov that appalled him. But old Peter Tolstoy spoke to him in soothing tones, and eventually the poor youth stammered out that he needed time to reflect. They met again at the Viceroy's Palace two days later. The Tsarevich told them he was afraid of what might happen if he returned, and that he would continue to invoke the Emperor's protection. Darting a terrible look at him from under his thick eyebrows, Tolstoy hissed menacingly that in that case the Tsar would declare him a traitor, and take him alive or dead. "I have instructions not to leave here without you, and if you go elsewhere, I shall follow you."

The Tsarevich was so terrified he fled to the next room, where he asked the Viceroy whether it was true his father could take him by force if he wished. The Viceroy informed him that the Emperor, while wishing for a reconciliation, would not abandon him and was quite powerful enough to look after those under his protection. Encouraged, the Tsarevich returned to Tolstoy and vowed never to fall into his father's hands. Tolstoy, all appearance of rage vanished, replied smoothly that this could not be his final answer, and that he must have time to reflect. On 1 October the parties met again, only to reach a similar impasse. The situation might well have appeared intractable, but the wily diplomat had now had time to make a full appraisal. It was clear that the Emperor had decided to stand very firm on the question of principle, and that the Viceroy had received strict instructions to prevent a physical abduction of the fugitive heir. It was not the giant strength of Rumyantsov that was needed here, but the Machiavellian sublety of Tolstoy. As a virtual prisoner in Constantinople he had engineered the downfall of three all-powerful Viziers, and would surely now be able to deal with this one feeble youth.

Appraising the situation, he saw that the Tsarevich possessed two weak points. The first was the mortal terror with which he regarded his fearsome father, a terror which could virtually unman him. The second was his obsessive love for his mistress: whilst she in turn possessed a vulnerable weakness of her own, her native simplicity and ignorance. Cowardice, love and stupidity were not weaknesses to which the old intriguer was at all prone, and he resolved to make the fullest use of them.

Turning to the Viceroy, Count Daun, Tolstoy urged him to press Alexei to agree to return home, pointing out the enormous pressure the Tsar could bring to bear on the Emperor, and how much better it would be to avoid an unnecessary rupture by acceding in the first place. Daun was inclined to agree, but qualified his support always by referring to the Emperor's instructions. Something more positive than this was required. As Tolstoy explained in a report home, "Afterwards I got to work on the Viceroy's secretary, who has been useful in all correspondence and is an extremely understanding fellow, to repeat to the Tsarevich as if in confidence the same words which I had advised the Viceroy to explain to the Tsarevich. I gave that secretary 160 gold ducats, promising him more to come. . . ."

The secretary immediately confided this friendly advice to the Tsarevich, who was so alarmed that he at once despatched a note by him to Tolstoy: "Peter Andreevich! Could you call on me today by yourself, and bring the letter from my Sovereign-Father with you which you mentioned yesterday: I badly need to talk to you about something which could be useful." Tolstoy deliberately delayed responding, affecting lack of interest. Finally he arrived, and spoke earnestly and at length to the Tsarevich. He had not actually brought the Tsar's letter with him, but was able to quote at length from memory. The Tsar was gathering his armies together in Poland and would shortly pay a visit in person to Italy: urgent preparations were under way already. These menaces, coupled with the secretary's confidential warning, were too much for the trembling youth. "Come and see me tomorrow with Captain Rumyantsov," he blurted, "and I will give you a definite reply."

The net was closing, but Tolstoy was leaving nothing to chance. Panic could as easily drive the fugitive to refuse as accept. His strategy is best explained in his own words.

"I at once went straight to the Viceroy, to whom I explained what was needed. I asked him to send a message quickly to him [the Tsarevich] to say that he was sending the girl away: which he [the Viceroy] did. It appeared to me from his [the Tsarevich's] words that he feared returning to his father above all because it would mean a separation from his girl. That's why I asked the Viceroy: so that suddenly from three directions threatening news might reach him. That is, the above-mentioned secretary removed any hope of the Emperor's protection by explaining to him that his father would soon be on his way, my telling him of his father's imminent arrival, and finally the Viceroy's separating him from the girl. . . ."

The Tsarevich begged successfully to be allowed to keep Afrosinya with him that night, but even this concession the resourceful Tolstoy contrived to turn to his advantage. Getting the girl on one side, the old gentleman earnestly impressed on her the enormous advantages a return to Russia would confer on the Tsarevich and herself. He is even said to have sworn to arrange a marriage between her and his younger son Peter, the dowry being a thousand serf households. The girl, who is described as being "pretty enough, lively, and full of ambition", was swiftly won over; that night she worked on her lover by methods even more persuasive than those of the benign old gentleman.

Next day (30 October) Tolstoy and Rumyantsov once again met with Alexei: Afrosinya was also present, disguised as a boy. The Tsarevich at once announced his intention of returning with the envoys, provided his father promised to be merciful and to allow him to marry Afrosinya before their arrival at St. Petersburg. Tolstoy accepted with pleasure, pointing out in a report home that "it is worth consenting, firstly because it will prove to the whole world that he ran away not because of any injury but purely for his girl; secondly it will greatly upset the Emperor, who will no longer believe in him." It was the same policy Tolstoy had pursued in Turkey, and which he had seen his uncle Ivan Miloslavsky apply to Matveev and Khovansky all those years ago at the time of the Streltsi uprising. Assist your victim to dig his own grave, and then choose the perfect moment to give him a gentle push.

The Viceroy was amazed and a little incredulous when he learned of the Tsarevich's abrupt change of mind, but all appeared above board. Alexei wrote at once to his father, entreating him to confirm the two conditions for his return; and also to the Emperor, requesting the opportunity to call on His Majesty in Vienna to convey his thanks in person. Then at last, on 14 October, the Tsarevich, his young lady, and his escorts left Naples, not for the North, but eastwards to Bari on the Adriatic. Tolstoy wrote to the Tsar that day, urging His Majesty to write swiftly conceding the promises requested by his son, "so that we can tell him about them. At present he is making excuses about seeing Rome, Venice and other places, though in fact what he wants is to linger on the journey so as to make sure of receiving your instructions concerning his marriage before he reaches home." Tolstoy was also apprehensive about the Tsarevich's plan to call on the Emperor, and prepared to take every precaution possible in order to avoid such a dangerous meeting.

The Tsar wrote to his son on 17 November, agreeing to his son's conditions. The letter must have arrived somewhere *en route*, as the little group of travellers made their leisurely way through Italy, held up by heavy rains and the Tsarevich's desire to pay his respects at religious shrines. His Afrosinya, who was now four months pregnant, followed behind, greeted at every major halt by anxious letters from her adoring lover. On 21 October Tolstoy's party was at Rome, but by 15 November they had only reached Bologna. Ten days later, however, they had crossed the mountains to Innsbruck. Ever more fearful of what might yet go wrong should the Tsarevich meet the Emperor, Tolstoy arranged with Veselovsky in Vienna that they should pass hastily through the Imperial city at night. What excuses were made to the Tsarevich (who had expressed anxiety to pay his respects to the Emperor), is not known, but within two days he had been hurried on northwards without any contact being made with Charles VI or his ministers. On the evening of 8 December they arrived at Brünn in Moravia, where Tolstoy must have felt he could breathe again. But that same night an official arrived from

Count Colloredo, the Imperial Governor, to explain that a courier had just ridden in from Vienna with orders to prevent the Tsarevich's departure until he had seen the Emperor. Tolstoy barred the way, explaining emphatically that the Tsarevich was in bed asleep. The official retired, but next morning before the Russians could depart the Governor himself appeared, only to be told that the Prince was not there. Count Colloredo insisted that he knew him to be there, and eventually a message came down from Tolstoy to say that that was impossible, and in any case they were setting off that minute. The Governor then tackled Tolstoy himself, demanding to be permitted to present the Emperor's compliments to His Highness. Tolstoy gave a haughty refusal, repeating that they had no time to lose, as the Tsarevich was so anxious to regain his fatherland. The Governor, despite ever angrier protests and threats, finally informed Tolstoy that they could not leave until he had received further instructions from the Emperor.

Tolstoy found he had no choice but to wait. Meanwhile he discovered that measures had been taken to prevent his sending a message to the Tsar. His anxiety increasing every hour, he had to wait two days for the next development. On the 11th a messenger at last arrived from Vienna, but it was nine in the evening and he was told the Tsarevich was asleep. Next day Tolstoy offered further evasions and refusals, until the Governor lost patience and assembled a body of troops to force an entry. At last Tolstoy consented: the Tsarevich would receive His Excellency between four and five o'clock. The reception was in the entrance hall of the inn, where Captain Rumyantsov was waiting. Tolstoy and the Tsarevich emerged from the latter's room, and the Governor presented his Imperial master's compliments, and his particular request to know whether His Highness was leaving his dominions of his own free will? Tolstoy and Rumyantsov stood listening carefully to every word, as the Tsarevich replied in a low voice, briefly and formally, thanking the Emperor and averring that it was by his own wish they were returning to Russia. He then bowed politely and, accompanied by Tolstoy (who spoke not a word), re-entered his room. The door closed behind him.

There was nothing more the Emperor felt he could do. Permission was given to depart, and the journey continued. The Emperor sent the Tsar a strong complaint about Tolstoy's rudeness, but Peter in reply threw all the blame on his son. Travelling by Breslau and Danzig, the Tsarevich's party finally reached Russian-occupied Riga on 10 January 1718. In just six months Tolstoy had fulfilled the instruction given him at Spa. The Tsar had provided no indication as to what he intended for his son on his return, beyond writing in November to inform him that he would respect his promises to allow him to marry Afrosinya and live privately in the country. On 22 January Alexei wrote from Tver (between Moscow and St. Petersburg) to his mistress to tell her all was well, and soon they would be living in domestic bliss. An accompanying letter from Peter Tolstoy was equally reassuring; they were carried to Afrosinya at Berlin by a young relative, Ivan Andreevich Tolstoy. By the middle of April she arrived in Russia and joined her delighted "husband".

It now remained for the Tsar to fulfil his written promise and allow the young couple to marry and disappear into private life. On 3 February 1718, three weeks after his return home, Alexei appeared in a solemn ceremonial before his father in the Great Audience Hall of the Moscow Kremlin. As a prisoner he bore no sword, and by his side stood the inevitable Peter Tolstoy. Before a stately array of high

75

state officials, nobles and clergy, the Tsarevich humbly confessed his undutiful behaviour in fleeing to the Emperor's protection and implored his father's pardon. Peter then delivered an indignant denunciation of all his son's wickednesses, including his relations with his mistress Afrosinya – whose origin and situation were so strikingly similar to those of his own Tsarina Catherine. Peter continued, however, by confirming his promise of pardon, provided his son renounced his inheritance and promised to reveal all accomplices in his treachery. Here was a new and startling condition; but the Tsarevich eagerly accepted, naming a couple of people whom he had informed of his purposed flight. Then he publicly and with great solemnity abjured all claim to the throne and swore that he would in due course bear allegiance to his half-brother, the little Grand Duke Peter.

All this the wretched Alexei was only too happy to do, but his real troubles were beginning, not ending. Ivan Naryshkin, of a family that had no cause to love the Tolstoys, was heard to mutter in the Tsarevich's house that "that Judas Peter Tolstoy deceived the Tsarevich". This at least was untrue, for, as has been seen, the Tsar had written to Tolstoy declaring that he would fulfil the promises conditional on his son's return. But Tolstoy was the Tsar's true servant. The day after Alexei's public renunciation of his claim to the throne, Tolstoy presented him with a set of seven written questions concerning his past conduct and the people who might have been privy to or assisted him in his disloyal imaginings. Four days later the Tsarevich replied with a long rambling statement, implicating many, including his mother, the Tsarina, from whom Peter had long been separated. Only Afrosinya was declared to have known nothing.

It was all very harmless and pathetic, but when Tolstoy brought the reply to his master the wrath and suspicion of the Tsar knew no bounds. He suffered from the dilemma of all autocrats: how, ruling over a society where any expression of dissatisfaction was punishable with extreme penalties, could a ruler identify the discontented? For if his own son, heir to an inheritance such as no Tsar had known before him, hated his sovereign so much as to flee the kingdom, what might not lesser men be thinking? Peter struck bloodily right and left. Anyone who was charged with according the slightest sympathy to the condition of the Tsarevich was subjected to the most barbaric punishments of which even Russia was capable. Nobles and bishops, officers and priests, were knouted, impaled, broken on the wheel, had stakes driven up their rectums, their tongues torn out or their noses cut off. His former wife, the Tsarina Eudoxia, was exiled to a convent in the frozen North, while an officer who confessed to being her lover was knouted, roasted on red-hot coals, pressed onto a plank studded with spikes, and finally impaled.

The Tsarevich himself at first appeared exempt from these horrifying proceedings. But the more the executions and torture appeared to confirm presentiments of treason in the Tsar's mind, the more it became inevitable that his father's promise would not be a permanent protection. In fact the treachery of subordinate figures could have little meaning unless the guilt of the principal around whom their "confessions" hung in increasing profusion were confirmed. On 12 May Afrosinya was interrogated, without torture. She provided a damning indictment: her lover had frequently complained of his father's tyranny, spoken ill-bodingly of his half-brother, and speculated cheerfully on possibilities of mutiny in the army and what he would do when Tsar to undo his father's work. Peter himself then interrogated his son at Peterhof, a scene immortalized in the dramatic paint-

Peter the Great interrogates the Tsarevich

ing by Nikolai Gay (1871). Alexei sullenly admitted that if a mutiny had broken
out, and if the troops had espoused his cause, then he would probably have joined
them.

This and other "evidence" were enough. Peter Tolstoy was given the task of
extracting every detail of the conspiracy from the terrified youth. Alexei was
placed in the Peter-Paul fortress. When his cell door was opened it was to admit
the figure of his persecutor, that terrible old man who had spoken so gently in
Naples about the advantages of return. With him were assistants whose profession
rarely lacked work in Russia before the nineteenth century, and in the twentieth
found their skills in demand on a scale that taxed even their resource. On 22 June,
in Tolstoy's presence, the heir of the Romanovs received twenty-five blows of the
knout. The knout was a thick, hard leather whip more than three feet long. Peter
Tolstoy's knoutmasters were skilled in their trade. An English resident in Russia
at that time has left a description of what was involved. The torturer applied "so
many strokes on the bare back as are appointed by the judges, first making a step

77

back and giving a spring forward at every stroke, which is laid on with such force that the blood flies at every stroke and leaves a weal behind as thick as a man's finger. And these masters as the Russians call them, are so exact in their work that they very rarely strike two strokes in the same place, but lay them on the whole length and breadth of a man's back, by the side of each other with great dexterity from the top of a man's shoulders down to the waistband of his breeches."

It may be imagined how the tall, ungainly, cowardly Alexei felt as he lay afterwards in the darkness. Those few people who had ever dropped him a word of kindness had been tortured and killed for that very offence; his mother was an exile; his father the author of all his sufferings; and the girl for whom he had given up everything had voluntarily consigned him to this fate. Two days later the bolts were drawn, and Tolstoy and his aides stood again before him. This time he received fifteen strokes, and confessed in his agony that he had wished for his father's death and would have been ready to support a foreign invasion of his country.

This was all that was needed. Peter Tolstoy hurried to the Tsar with the signed deposition, and on 24 June the High Court pronounced a death sentence on the prisoner. His crime was double parricide: designing to kill the father of his country and his natural father. The document, which set out the culprit's crimes in full, was signed by a hundred and twenty-five of Peter's principal lieutenants, prominent at the head of whose signatures appeared that of "Privy Councillor and Lifeguard Captain Peter Tolstoy". The young man's death was announced two days later under circumstances which have never been fully clarified. According to the Tsar's official account, sent to King Louis XV, his son had suffered a fatal bout of apoplexy on for the first time appreciating the full heinousness of his crimes. This is the least likely of the varied accounts that have survived.

A letter, purporting to have been written the next day by Alexander Rumyantsov, Peter Tolstoy's strong-arm man in Italy, provides a circumstantial account:

"And when the Tsarevich at that time fell ill, the sentence was not passed on to the court, but we went to him in the fortress. The Most Serene Prince Menshikov, the Chancellor Count Gavril Golovkin, Privy Councillor Tolstoy and I, went to read him the judgment. No sooner did the Tsarevich hear the death sentence than he turned very pale and reeled, so that Tolstoy and we only just managed to hold him by the arms and prevent his falling." They laid him on a bed and, on reporting the matter to the Tsar, Tolstoy, Rumyantsov and the two others were summoned to his presence at one o'clock in the morning. Peter explained at length the motives for the sentence as painful but inevitable; he concluded: "I do not want to profane the royal blood with any public punishment, but bring about the end quietly and secretly so that his coming death may appear to have arrived from natural causes." Led by Tolstoy, the group returned to the fortress and entered the Tsarevich's cell. He was asleep and a sudden qualm of conscience or fear struck the executioners, that Alexei should not be despatched to the other world without first making his peace with God.

"Reflecting on this and gathering up his resolution, Tolstoy gently poked the Tsarevich, saying, 'Your Royal Highness, get up!' He opened his eyes and, quite bewildered, sat up in bed and gazed at us, too confused to ask us what we wanted. Then Tolstoy, approaching nearer, said: 'Prince Tsarevich, by the judgement of notables of the Russian land you have been sentenced to death for many treacheries against your princely father and the fatherland. We it is, by His Majesty's com-

Peter Tolstoy. From the portrait in the Hermitage museum

mand, who have come to you to execute the sentence; for which you must prepare yourself with prayer and confession, as your term of life is drawing to its close.' As soon as he recognized Tolstoy's familiar tones, the Tsarevich burst into tears, lamenting the day he had been born with royal blood. As he continued and it became clear he was incapable of prayer, one of Tolstoy's companions muttered a quick prayer on his behalf. They then threw their victim back on the bed and pressed two cushions over his face until his flailing arms and legs fell still. As soon as all was over, Tolstoy reported to the Tsar and arranged for the disposal of the corpse."

This account, supposedly by a participant, has however been strongly condemned as a forgery, though likely to be based on stories circulating at the time. Whether the Tsarevich died from the effects of the tortures he had undergone,

79

from general shock, or was secretly executed will probably never be for certain known. All that is certain is that his end was ordained by his father and resulted from his treatment at the hands of Peter Tolstoy.[29]

It is recorded that "in the Tolstoy family a tradition is preserved, whereby the Tsarevich under the agonies of torture cursed Tolstoy and all his family unto the 25th generation; and that as a result of this there are born to each generation, alongside very remarkable figures, also witless and feeble-minded members". In Tolstoy's own lifetime the people directly accused him of the killing of the Tsarevich and said that punishment for this would fall upon the whole family. In an unpublished anonymous letter of 1726 we find the following threat, addressed to Tolstoy's nephew (Peter Mihailovich): "the Tsarevich's death will be avenged on you, your uncle and the whole tribe."[30]

It is a curious coincidence that, exactly two hundred years later almost to the day, the last reigning descendant of Peter the Great was murdered in circumstances of extreme brutality, together with his whole family. Among them was his adored only son, another Tsarevich Alexei. At the same time the Tolstoy family was deprived of its inheritance and harried over the face of the earth.

However that may be, Peter Tolstoy's immediate rewards were immense. Already in June 1717 he had been granted lucrative monopolies in luxury goods and other commercial privileges, which alone must have brought in a vast income. Then in mid-December, when he was bringing the Tsarevich home through Austria, he was nominated President of the newly-created College (Ministry) of Commerce. These were rewards for the great services he had already rendered the state, and after the successful conclusion of the affair of the Tsarevich tribute poured in. On 13 December 1718 he was designated Serving Privy Councillor and awarded estates totalling 1318 serf households, formerly the property of condemned "accomplices" of the Tsarevich. He received the star of Russia's highest order of chivalry, the St. Andrew (21 March 1722) together with 1700 serf families, and, as will be seen, was before long to be created a Count of the Russian Empire. Finally, on 12 October 1718, his second son Peter (the same whose hand he had offered to the Tsarevich's Afrosinya the year before) made a brilliant marriage, through the Tsar's influence, to the fifteen-year-old daughter of Ivan Skoropadsky, Hetman of the Ukraine since Mazeppa fled to Turkey as the ally of Charles XII.[31]

Peter Tolstoy was now one of the Tsar's closest collaborators and most trusted advisers. Along with his Presidency of the College of Commerce, he headed a permanent Chancellery of Secret Investigations, which sprang from the temporary investigation into the affair of the Tsarevich. The Secret Chancellery came closely under the eye of the Tsar himself, and all too often involved the practice of torture to extract evidence.[32]

Peter Tolstoy's energy at the age of seventy-five was remarkable. In addition to these arduous duties he continued to play a leading role in Russia's diplomacy. In 1719 a British envoy, Lord Whitworth, arrived in Berlin with the purpose of persuading Prussia to sign a treaty with Hanover and England, and make peace with Sweden. The prospect of Russia's losing her only major ally, Prussia, in this way was very dangerous to Russia. "The Tsar in alarm sent Tolstoy to Berlin, as the only man capable of dealing with the situation."[33]

In 1721 Tolstoy accompanied the Tsar to Riga during events leading up to the Peace of Nystad, which at last brought an end to the twenty-one-year-old war with Sweden. All this was as nothing to his strenuous activities in the following year. Peter, now Emperor and awarded the sobriquet of "The Great", decided to use the opportunity afforded by the conclusion of peace with Sweden to move against Persia and establish a Russian presence on the Caspian. In May 1722 the Tsar set out to join his army accompanied by the Tsarina, one of his principal companions being Peter Tolstoy, whose knowledge of Turkish and Middle Eastern politics was unrivalled. The journey to the Caspian, largely by boat down the rivers Oka and Volga, took two months, and the Imperial party arrived at Astrakhan only on 5 July. Tolstoy, who had been held up at Saratov on business connected with his wife's death, caught up with the Emperor two months later. While Peter and his army sailed slowly along the edge of the Caspian to seize and garrison Derbent, Tolstoy stayed in Astrakhan supervising the diplomatic affairs of the expedition.[34]

As energetic as his public round was the old gentleman's social life. His grateful sovereign showered rewards on him. Tolstoy writes requesting the gift of a choice estate outside Moscow: Peter replies that he needs it, otherwise "to no one other than you would I give it". But Tolstoy had already been given a mansion in St. Petersburg, another in the town of Zemlyan ("with all its buildings and internal ornaments, tables, chairs and hangings"), and an estate at Suzdal containing 277 households. In addition he already held the beautiful patrimonial estate of Znamenskoe in the province of Ryazan. Altogether he was reputed to own five or six thousand families of serfs. His vast income has already been noted, and that in turn may well have been supplemented from other sources. In March 1722 the French Minister informed his government that a sweetener of ten or twelve thousand ducats to the influential Tolstoy might not go amiss.[35]

At his St. Petersburg home he arranged splendid assemblies and dinners to entertain the Emperor. Wine flowed in abundance, despite Tolstoy's abstemiousness, and the tireless old man would dance away the night with girls young enough to be his granddaughters. On 9 December 1718, for example, he entertained Peter to festivities which lasted five days. The expense was worth it, for it was on the last day that he received the rank of Serving Privy Councillor and one of his many estates. He had become a widower in 1722, but it was years since he had had any intimate connection with his wife, which his wandering life would in any case have made impossible. When he was with the Tsar at Riga in April 1721, the Saxon Ambassador recorded this little vignette of the diplomat's private life:

"Besides, the cunning Tolstoy takes round with him everywhere his Italian angel; warm as this nymph is, the cold climate does her much good and provides him with a glow which he hasn't known for some time. I saw her and inspected her well during an entertainment which this old sinner gave and in which I played a good part – dressed in an embroidered black velvet gown . . . a perquisite which must have been put down to my 5,000 ducats." The bribe had probably been well spent, however, for the beautiful Laura (according to the French Minister) "exercised absolute power over the Count and no one could obtain anything at the College of Commerce (of which he was President) except through the agency of this woman". She apparently shared her protector's skill in diplomacy and espionage, and was on one occasion, despatched on a secret mission to Venice and Rome, supplied by the Tsar with 10,000 ducats for expenses.

In 1724, when the Duke of Holstein's betrothal to the Tsar's daughter Anna was being celebrated in St. Petersburg, Peter Tolstoy entertained the Duke on 7 December, and the Duke's aide-de-camp left an account of the meeting. "His Highness went to the Privy Councillor Tolstoy, whom he had come to know in Riga, because he went almost everywhere with the Tsar. He is a genial, pleasant fellow, speaking very good Italian. The Tsar loves him greatly. He doesn't have a wife, but he does have a mistress, whose upkeep costs him dearly. He received His Highness extremely politely and conducted him to his room. . . . His Highness immediately remarked on two completely contrasting pictures, hanging in opposite corners of the room: one represented some Russian saint, and the other a naked woman. The Privy Councillor, observing that the Duke was looking at them, laughed and said that he wondered how His Highness noticed everything so quickly when hundreds of other visitors calling on him had overlooked the nude figure, which had deliberately been placed in a dark corner."[36]

Peter Tolstoy had achieved his wealth and power through his uncanny skill in balancing on the precarious tight-rope of the Russian power-struggle. It was a taxing feat, for not only must he retain the favour of the erratic Tsar but, as time moved on, consider what move he should make in the event of the Tsar's death. Tolstoy was a generation older than his master, but Peter's wild energy had on occasion resulted in excesses that brought him to the point of death. After the death of the Tsarevich his infant half-brother the Grand Duke Peter had been declared heir. But in February 1722 Peter had radically altered the law of succession, proclaiming that the Emperor, as Autocrat, could choose his own successor, regardless of dynastic priorities. This made the country's future devastatingly insecure. Not only was there no longer any settled, legally secure heir; there also remained the question whether a successor would receive sufficient acceptance once his only source of legitimacy, the reigning Emperor, was no more. As recently as 1715 provisions laid down by Louis XIV, the greatest monarch in Christendom, had been disregarded the moment he died.

In 1722 Peter the Great had living two grandchildren (daughter and son of the murdered Tsarevich) and three children (by the Tsarina Catherine). Any of them might be nominated by the wayward autocrat, and as they ranged in age from four to fourteen the new Emperor must certainly be but the vehicle for some powerful minister's ambitions. There was however one person who would inevitably be at Peter's side when his towering figure was carried from the stage, and who would be closer to the springs of power than anyone else. This was the former Lithuanian laundry-maid, the able and goodnatured Empress Catherine.

Soon after the return of the Tsarevich, Tolstoy took steps to ingratiate himself with the Empress. His distant relative Anisia Tolstoy was Catherine's favourite lady-in-waiting,[37] and the old charmer himself found no difficulty in befriending the Emperor's thirty-four-year-old consort. In fact it was Tolstoy who arranged the most dramatic advance in her fortunes since her marriage to Peter. In November 1723 the Tsar announced that Catherine would not merely bear the titular rank of Empress, but would shortly be crowned as co-sovereign with the Tsar. The coronation took place in May next year at the Kremlin, the extraordinary magnificence of the ceremony being entirely organized by Tolstoy. He was appointed Grand Marshal, and moved at the head of the procession bearing a silver wand surmounted by the Imperial eagle. One wonders whether, when the Imperial couple made the traditional appearance at the head of the Red Staircase leading down from the Faceted Palace, the Tsar recalled a day forty-two years earlier; when as a ten-year-old boy he had seen the drunken, bearded, swirling faces of the Streltsi below, howling for his and his mother's blood – demands suggested to them by Peter Tolstoy.

The ceremonies and festivities continued for days. As a first mark of her powers as co-sovereign, Peter empowered Catherine to create Tolstoy a Count of the Russian Empire. He was able to perform an equally signal service for her sooner than either could have expected. Catherine had a handsome attendant, a German named Wilhelm Mons. Through his favoured position near the Empress, Mons was enabled to procure favours great and small to those who afforded him sufficient incentive. The corruption grew to a scale enormous even by Russian standards, and the most powerful in the land (including Menshikov and Tolstoy) became indebted to him at some point. The Tsar alone remained in ignorance of the scandal until he suddenly received incontrovertible evidence. His rage was all the more ferocious when he did discover: predictably Mons was sentenced to death and the hunt was on for accomplices, real or imaginary.

It was rumoured at the time, though most historians discount the suggestion, that Mons had been Catherine's lover. Be that as it may, the Empress's position suddenly became dangerous indeed. When Catherine plucked up courage to ask for Mons to be spared, Peter flew into a terrible rage and drove his fist through a fine mirror. "Thus," he shouted, "I can destroy the most beautiful adornment of my palace!" Catherine understood the allusion: the fates of Peter's sister, wife and son testified how light an obstruction were family bonds when his blood was up. According to the French diplomat Villardeau, "The Tsar (so many people claim) intended to make a summary example of the Tsarina his wife by executing her as well as Mons – but for the lively protests which Tolstoy dared to deliver to him at that time. He made it plain that summary punishment of his wife would not only dishonour him before the face of the world, but would also do an irreparable wrong to the children he had had by her, whom he loved tenderly – and who could have had no part in their mother's sins."[38]

Catherine and her husband were reconciled, and Tolstoy too remained the great favourite. But Peter's daemonic energy was used up. On 5 November he succumbed to a fever, caught while rescuing some sailors from the frozen Neva. He never fully recovered, and on 23 January 1725 took to his bed and received the last rites. Tolstoy, Apraxin and Golovkin came to his bedside to receive precautionary instructions for measures to be taken in case of his death, but there was no mention of an heir. On the afternoon of the 27th, when his spirit was clearly fading, he called for a slate on which he wrote the words "give all to . . ." He was unable to finish, and it was suddenly clear that the fate of Russia would no longer be decided by that giant will, which for twenty-seven years had kicked and pummelled a drowsy giant into formidable action.

That evening, as Catherine prayed by the bed of the failing Emperor, a group of nobles and senators assembled in the neighbouring Council Chamber of the Winter Palace. The majority had gathered for the purpose of ensuring the succession of the Grand Duke Peter, nine-year-old son of the late Tsarevich. He was undoubtedly the senior male heir of the Romanovs, one whose parentage was untouched by any cloud of dubiety such as inevitably attached itself to the homely Catherine and her offspring. More importantly, that sizeable section of the country which had become increasingly distressed by the effects of Peter's wars and reforms saw in the youthful heir their hope for a recovery of the values damaged by the late Emperor. The assemblage was principally composed of the leaders of this faction, who bore many of the greatest names in Russia's thousand-year-old history: Galitzines, Dolgorukys, Troubetskoys, Bariatinskys and Repnins. They nurtured the additional grievance that the late regime had seen so many people of low or foreign origin placed in positions of power: Menshikov, Osterman, Devier and the like – to say nothing of the Empress herself.

Prince Dmitri Galitzine was the principal spokesman for the Grand Duke's interest. What he proposed was an apparent compromise: Peter should succeed to the throne, with Catherine as Regent. Many voices were raised in support, and it was quite clear that the majority opinion favoured the accession of Peter II. It was, however, Peter Tolstoy who spoke next. Though nearly eighty years old, he expatiated with moving eloquence on the dangers to the Empire of rule by a child, asserting that so vast a country required above all a firm and experienced hand at the helm. Now, the Tsarina had been initiated by Peter the Great himself into the arts of government over a period of years, and had played a wise and on occasion, heroic part in sustaining her husband's stupendous achievement. But what was there to discuss? Her Majesty had actually been crowned as Empress in her own right, and so, according to Peter's edict of 1722, she was the legal heir of the Tsar. As Tolstoy concluded his argument, there was a burst of applause from a corner of the chamber. Turning, the assembled nobles noticed, to their surprise, a group of Guards officers had entered unnoticed. By what right or under whose orders they had entered no one appeared to know.

What had happened was that Tolstoy, not trusting entirely to rational argument, had taken certain diplomatic precautions. The accession of the son of the Tsarevich whose death lay at his door would have been personally disastrous, even if the aggrandisement of the Tolstoys had not aroused the resentment of the other nobles. The compromise over the Regency did not commend itself at all as protection. In 1689 Tolstoy had seen another boy Tsarevich named Peter overthrow a Regency, and on that occasion he himself had been fortunate not to lose his head. He readily persuaded Peter's great favourite Menshikov that his position would also be endangered. The Imperial treasure was now under Catherine's control, and it was arranged for money to be distributed to the Guards and the garrison of the Peter-Paul fortress. Troops were assembled in the vicinity of the palace, and sentries were doubled at the doors.

The presence of the soldiers at the Senate gathering bore a clear implication, one emphasized when Tolstoy's friend General Buturlin shouted an order out of a window. From the courtyard below came a muffled roll of drums and clatter of muskets. Field-Marshal Repnin, commander-in-chief of the army, angrily demanded to know by what right Buturlin gave his orders. "What I have done, Your Excellency," replied Buturlin confidently, "was by the express command of our Sovereign Lady the Empress Catherine, whom you and I and every faithful subject are bound to obey unconditionally."

A heated and prolonged discussion ensued. Tolstoy managed to win over Repnin, whose jealousy of Galitzine was well-known. The argument continued into the night, when at about four o'clock in the morning Tolstoy and Menshikov prevailed.

A deputation filed into the Emperor's bedchamber where Catherine was found kneeling, bathed in tears. Peter the Great had just breathed his last, and she turned pathetically to her visitors, asking them to protect her as "a widow and orphan". Very moved, all present swore to defend her, the Guards and the nobles crying out enthusiastically "Long live our beloved Empress! God grant her a happy and prosperous reign!" In 1682 Peter Tolstoy had helped engineer a change in succession, and now, forty-three years later, he had achieved a like success. On 30 January 1725 an Edict was issued by the Senate, proclaiming "the Empress Catherine Alexeevna, Autocrat of All the Russias". Among the signatories was Peter Tolstoy,[39] who now possessed power greater even than he had known in the previous reign.

The new Empress owed her succession to Tolstoy and Menshikov. On 13 February 1725 the French envoy Campredon noted that "Tolstoy appears to be Catherine's most trusted minister. He is skilful, clever, experienced. He consults with the Empress every evening. He is her right hand. He is the cleverest head in Russia. Not seeking any superiority over his colleagues, he employs all the skills of a cunning politician and secretly brings them round to everything he had already concerted with the Empress."

A year later the power of the new rulers of Russia was seemingly consolidated by the creation of a new Supreme Privy Council, to which power was effectively devolved from the Senate. It had only six members: Tolstoy, Menshikov, Admiral Apraxin, Chancellor Golovkin, Osterman and Prince Dmitri Galitzine, of whom the first two were the effective rulers of the country. Tolstoy wished for the realities of power, while Menshikov's prevailing characteristics were limitless ambition for wealth and ostentation of grandeur. Tolstoy had ineffectively tried to influence Peter the Great against his corrupt favourite[40] but, once again, it seemed possible to control what could not be removed. At the end of 1726, the forty-two-year-old Catherine suddenly fell very ill. By January 1727 she had recovered, but a *frisson* ran through Russian public life. All positions had to be urgently reconsidered in the light of the possibility that the throne might once again fall vacant. Menshikov knew himself to be widely hated, and saw how precarious was his power-base. If Catherine died his own survival rested on the succession of her daughter Anna, who had married the Duke of Holstein on 21 May 1725. But now Holstein rashly chose to quarrel with Menshikov.

It was at this vulnerable moment that the Most Serene Prince (Menshikov) was approached by the Austrian Ambassador Count Rabutin with a subtle scheme, worthy of Peter Tolstoy at his best. A family tree will make clear the circumstances more easily than pages of description.

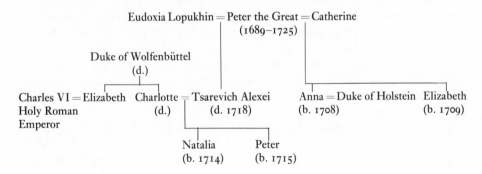

The Romanov Dynasty in 1727.

From this pedigree, it can be seen that the late Tsarevich Alexei's son Peter was also nephew of the Holy Roman Emperor Charles VI, who had done so much to help his wretched father during the flight to Naples. The Emperor was anxious to sustain his nephew's right of succession to the Russian throne, and his Ambassador had instructions to further the claim as skilfully as possible.

Shortly after Catherine's unexpected illness, Ambassador Rabutin proposed to Menshikov that he confirm his hold on power by marrying his daughter Maria to the late Tsarevich's son Peter. This dangled a far more glittering prospect before Menshikov than anything he had hitherto envisaged. To be father-in-law of the future Emperor! The Austrian Ambassador's policy triumphed: he divided Menshikov from Tolstoy, and provided the Grand Duke Peter with a powerful protector. Tolstoy's alarm can be imagined. He hurried to the Empress to explain the danger in which she was placing her children, should she consent to the marriage. The Duke and Duchess of Holstein lacked the courage to plead their own cause, but the eighty-two-year-old Peter Tolstoy was eloquent on their behalf.

"Madam," he begged, "I can already see the axe raised over your children's heads and your own. May God protect yours: I speak to you today less for myself than for you. I am over eighty and look upon myself as a man who has already finished his career, and to whom all events, good or bad, must be a matter of indifference. But you, Madam, think of yourself, avert and ward off the blow which threatens you; there is still time: soon there will not be." Catherine was alarmed, and repeated Tolstoy's words throughout the court. But Menshikov reappeared and proved swiftly capable of allaying the fears that agitated the Empress's breast, who was at the time distracted by her attraction to a handsome young Count Sapieha.

Despite his noble rhetoric before Catherine, Tolstoy was now becoming desperate. He feared with reason that the young Grand Duke Peter would not forget the part he played in his father's death, and that his "grandmother will be brought to the Palace and begin to avenge herself on him for his rudeness to her" at the Tsarevich's examination. His only hope now in view of the Duke of Holstein's feebleness, was to establish the succession of the younger of Catherine's daughters, the Grand Duchess Elizabeth. Matters were not propitious. The Grand Duke Peter's supporters included not only his original sympathizers among the great noble families and their new ally Menshikov, but also the cunning young Osterman who now decided the path to success lay with Menshikov. Tolstoy had to pick his allies from among the secondary ranks: men like energetic General Buturlin and the unscrupulous Anton Devier, a Portuguese Jew ennobled and advanced by Peter the Great. "What has happened to you?" asked Devier maliciously, "you are not of my ancestry!" But he threw himself into the plot which Tolstoy unfolded. The moment the Empress Catherine was dead her daughter Elizabeth would be proclaimed Empress, while the Grand Duke Peter would be packed off abroad "to complete his studies".

But even as Tolstoy planned to persuade Catherine to confirm this arrangement, fate struck again. The Empress fell ill once more, and Menshikov, under pretext of attending on her stood watch over her night and day, surrounding her quarters with his protégés and troops in his pay. On the pretext that Devier had misbehaved in the Palace he and another of Tolstoy's confidants were seized and put to the question. After twenty-five cuts with the knout, Devier confessed all, and Tolstoy and the others were arrested.

The old fox, brought to bay at last, displayed no signs of fear, and "with a serene and noble aspect" explained that his family would be in the utmost danger if the Grand Duke Peter were to succeed, and he was simply taking a sensible precaution in attempting to secure the succession of the daughter of Peter I, "his great benefactor". "If you believe," he addressed his examiners, "that I have acted wrongly, here is my head: have it cut off this instant and afterwards dispose of my body and my property as you see fit. I don't ask for mercy; everything in this world already appears pointless to me, and I feel I am in a happier condition than all of you."

This was on 3 May 1727. On the morning of the 6th Menshikov extracted (or claimed to have done so) Catherine's signature to an edict setting out Tolstoy's crimes, which included the holding of suspicious conversations with Devier, Buturlin and others "in order to arrange the succession of the Tsarevna Elizabeth Petrovna". He was spared the knouting and torture undergone by Devier, and was sentenced to be banished into exile.

That evening the Empress Catherine died. Peter Tolstoy's star had waned. Not all the wiles of the old intriguer had been able to prevail over a succession of unlucky chances. Had the Duke of Holstein not engaged in a petty quarrel with Menshikov; had the Empress Catherine's middle-aged heart warmed to anyone but young Count Sapieha; had she not decided on 21 January 1727 to dress more elegantly than warmly at the blessing of the Neva . . . had any of these little affairs not occurred, then old Tolstoy might well have succeeded in placing the Empress Elizabeth on the throne fourteen years earlier than her actual accession. It was almost as if a curse had come to dog his footsteps.

To his nephew Boris, son of the heroic Governor of Azov, the old conspirator wrote hurriedly: "By edict of Her Imperial Majesty my St. Andrew and sword are removed, and I am ordered to be sent this day to the Solovetsky Monastery from the [Peter-Paul] Fortress. For that reason, Boris Ivanovich, do come to say good-bye to me; but my son Ivan I expect from sadness will be unable to come, though orders have been given for you both to be admitted. And send quickly Malov and Yashka with a bed, pillows and blankets; also 200 roubles and a hundred gold pieces; also a prayer-book and small psalter, and anything else you think necessary. I cannot write more from wretchedness; send the sheepskin kaftan . . . beyond that I don't know what I need. However, I send my blessing to all my people."[41]

On the day the edict of banishment was issued, as the Empress who could have saved him lay on the very point of death, Peter Tolstoy and his son Ivan set out on the long journey northwards. Escorted by a body of ninety-five soldiers, they arrived at Archangel on the White Sea on 18 June, whence they sailed to the remote island-monastery of Solovetsky. It was a grim refuge. The low rambling buildings of the monastery are surrounded by a massive defensive wall and round flanking-towers. The monks were renowned for the degree of asceticism they practised. Nearly two centuries later Lenin was to establish one of the earliest Soviet political prison camps on the island. A prisoner there in 1924 described the peculiar harshness of this desolate spot in the Arctic waters.

"Nature herself is against the exiles. . . . The climate is severe and damp. Summer lasts only two months, or two months and a half. It is very late before the snows melt and spring comes. There are frequent gales, snowstorms, biting northerly and north-easterly winds. For three-quarters of the year the Solovetsky

Monastery is completely cut off from the outside world. The long, dark winter is most oppressive. . . . The damp from the Solovetsky marshes has an injurious effect on the health of the prisoners, worn out by hard labour."[42]

Tolstoy was confined to a dark, damp cell, from which he emerged only in fetters to attend church, or for an occasional stroll under strict guard. When the Abbot wished to provide the prisoner with a mug of beer on the occasion of Tsar Peter II's namesday, permission had to be asked of the Secret Chancellery. When an old friend wished to send him a packet of bread and fruit the request was similarly referred to the Chancellery – and refused. The bitterest blow of all was the death of his faithful companion, his son Ivan, who had been with him in those exhilarating days at Constantinople in 1703. The old man, stripped of all his titles, powers and property, and now of his favourite son, did not survive long. He died on 30 January 1729, aged eighty-three. His body was buried in a prominent space before the Preobrazhensky Cathedral on the island, and years afterwards visitors were shewn a mouldering slab on which could be read the half-defaced inscription "Count Peter . . . ."[43]

4

The General and
the Three Bears

After the deaths of the brothers Ivan and Peter Tolstoy, Peter the Great's able lieutenants, the Tolstoy family underwent a lull in its fortunes until the end of the eighteenth century. During the glorious reigns of Elizabeth and Catherine the Great they appear regularly among the lists of generals, marshals of nobility, privy councillors, *voevods* and the like, but no Tolstoy rose to any sort of pre-eminence. The turbulent and colourful reigns of the two empresses provided opportunity, however, for the family to show that neither their courage nor loyalty faltered at that time.

The arms of the descendants of Peter Andreevich Tolstoy

In May 1760 the title of Count was restored to the descendants of Peter Tolstoy by the Empress Elizabeth. When Catherine the Great seized the throne in 1762 (like Catherine I, she possessed no claim beyond being the widow of the previous ruler), there was discontent among a group of army officers who planned to replace her with the deposed Tsar Ivan VI, the last descendant of Tsar Alexei and Maria Miloslavsky. The conspiracy was discovered and revealed by Lev Vasilievich Tolstoy, a lieutenant in the Preobrazhensky Guards. He was richly rewarded by a grateful sovereign and remained her confidant and favourite. It was perhaps he to whom Catherine refers charmingly in one of her love letters to Prince Potemkin: "The Neva is still covered with ice and people walk across it. Forbid Tolstoy to do this as he has children and serves me well. I won't have him drowning."[1]

This Lev Vasilievich's elder brother Nikolai is of particular interest to me, as I was named after him. He was my great-great-great-great-great-uncle, born in 1737. A distinguished cavalry officer, he took part in the capture of the great Turkish fortress of Bender in 1770 and the conquest of the Crimea in 1771. His health compelled him to withdraw from active service after these hard-fought

Previous page: General Count Osterman-Tolstoy

90

Sergei Vasilievich Tolstoy and family

campaigns, and he retired with the rank of Colonel to his estates in the province of Kazan. His retirement was brief. In 1773 occurred the last of those anarchical Cossack upheavals, two of which (those of Stenka Razin and Bulavin) have been chronicled in previous chapters of this book. Proclaiming himself to be Tsar Peter III (Catherine the Great's late husband), Emilyan Pugachev raised the Yaik Cossacks in rebellion at a time when Russian armies were embroiled in preparations for a fresh offensive against Turkey. He laid siege to Orenburg, defeated a military expedition sent against him, and attracted large numbers of deserters from Government forces. Seriously alarmed, the Empress despatched General Bibikov to assemble forces in Kazan to crush the uprising.

Nikolai Tolstoy had already emerged from retirement to take command of a regiment of lancers raised by the nobility of the province, which was placed under Bibikov's command. His health gave way almost at once and he was reluctantly obliged to resign his command again. But when Pugachev's hordes advanced into the province, Colonel Tolstoy re-emerged from convalescence to lead an improvised mounted legion of local volunteers against the enemy. He was captured by the Cossacks, however, and cruelly tortured to death by them on 10 July 1774.

Nikolai's younger brother Lev was the ancestor of the senior line of the Tolstoys, afterwards Tolstoy-Miloslavsky. The brothers had a sister Anna who married Count Feodor Osterman, son of the talented minister Andrei Osterman who had broken with old Peter Tolstoy in 1727 to join Menshikov in placing Peter II on the throne. Despite this, the Ostermans allied themselves closely with the Tolstoys, for in addition a daughter of Andrei Osterman married Matvei Tolstoy, descendant of another branch of the family. It is their grandson who is the principal subject of this chapter, a hero whom all the family must regard with pride and affection.

General Alexander Ilich Bibikov

Alexander Ivanovich Tolstoy, great-grandson of Count Osterman and great-nephew of Lev Vasilievich Tolstoy, was born in St Petersburg in 1770. From his earliest days he was brought up in an entirely military atmosphere. His mother was the sister of that General Bibikov who commanded the forces defending Kazan against Pugachev. The Bibikovs were of ancient Tartar stock, which may account for Alexander's dark complexion. His father was a distinguished general, commanding Russian artillery in Catherine's wars against the Turks. He was by all accounts an unfeeling, even cruel, martinet. An impoverished noble, he "was harsh, gloomy, discontented with Government, and often giving vent to his bitterness on his family", as one memoirist wrote; while another refers to him as "a despot in his own family as well as over his serfs".

Ivan Tolstoy determined that his son too should be a soldier, and soon after birth the baby Alexander was registered as an under-officer in the Preobrazhensky Guards. His real service started at the age of thirteen, when he was commissioned into the Regiment as an ensign. In 1788 Catherine sent a large army under the command of her lover Prince Potemkin to attack the Turks in the Balkans, and eighteen-year-old Alexander Tolstoy fought bravely in several fierce engagements. But what he chiefly recalled in later years was the terrible cold. "Do you know," he said, "how many shirts I had when my father sent me off to one of the Turkish campaigns? Only six, and those were made from pretty coarse, homespun linen."

Next year the campaign was resumed, and Alexander was promoted to second lieutenant. It was in 1790, however, that he took his first real step on the road to a career whose success must have gladdened even his morose father. On 11 September 1790 Potemkin ordered a general advance on the line of major Turkish forts guarding the lower Danube. Tolstoy took part in the capture of Kilia on 18 October, but within a month the advance ground to a halt before the mighty stronghold of Ismail. It was well supplied and held a garrison of 35,000 troops

Agrafina, mother of Alexander Tolstoy

with 265 guns. The besiegers had only 31,000 men, and a fortnight later their generals had fared so ill as to recommend a withdrawal. Desperate for success, Potemkin replaced them with the formidable Alexander Suvorov, a brilliant commander, possessing the odd habit of crowing like a cock in moments of triumph. After a reconnaissance, Suvorov announced he would take the fort in five days' time. The assault began at dawn on 10 December, and after an unprecedently bloody battle, fought from house to house, the two-headed eagle fluttered above the ramparts.

Suvorov had sworn to have no mercy upon the Turks, and allowed his troops to loot the town. Fearful scenes of bloodshed and rapine ensued. Tolstoy, who had been in the thick of the fighting, both in naval actions fought by galley fleets on the Danube and in the storm itself, was revolted by the cruelty and, despite the distinguished part he had played in the combat, in later years remembered the campaign with disgust.

"He used to tell of his exploits, hardships and suffering in the campaign on the Danube, when he nearly died of hunger. . . . Alexander Tolstoy himself as a young man experienced the cruellest school of military experience, and witnessed horrific examples of suffering arising from war. His first step in this field was the famous siege of Ismail, when 30,000 Turks were killed; their bodies were thrown into the Danube, as a result of which the troops decided to eat no fish from the Danube for several weeks."

But the young officer's coolness in the fighting had attracted the attention of Suvorov, who selected him from the whole army to bear the glorious news of victory to the Empress Catherine. No doubt his handsome bearing played a part in the choice, and the delighted Empress received him with the greatest cordiality. He returned to the Balkans, and next year on 29 June distinguished himself once again when Prince Repnin defeated the Turks at Machin. The Turks were now exhausted, peace was signed at Galatz, and young Tolstoy returned to St. Petersburg. The Empress's favour beamed upon him more benignly than ever: he was promoted to Captain in the Guards, and two years later was a Lieutenant-Colonel. At Court he became a popular figure, possessing good looks, youth, great charm, a gallant military career, and a profound sense of chivalrous honour. All he lacked was money, and now that too was bestowed on him by a generous providence.[2]

About this time he came to know his two great-uncles, Counts Feodor and Ivan Osterman, brothers of his grandmother and sons of Peter the Great's Andrei Osterman, who had shrewdly joined Menshikov's successful bid to place Peter II on the throne in 1727, but backed the wrong horse when the Empress Elizabeth acceded in 1741 and was exiled to Siberia, where he died in 1747. All Osterman's vast property had been confiscated, but his sons' abilities gained them distinguished careers under Catherine II and the family fortunes were restored.[3]

Neither of the uncles had offspring, and they grew very fond of their promising great-nephew. With the Empress's strong approval, they decided to appoint him heir not only to their property but also their title and name. On 27 October 1796 Alexander Tolstoy, now Colonel of a Regiment of Chasseurs, was created Count Alexander Ivanovich Osterman-Tolstoy in his own right. (He came of a non-titled branch of the Tolstoy family.)[4] Still more satisfying to the impoverished young veteran was the ultimate prospect of possession of three enormous estates, in the provinces of Petersburg, Moscow and Mogilev. As the eighteenth century drew to its close, fortune smiled ever more kindly on him. In 1797 he retired from the service with the rank of Major-General and was appointed a Serving Privy Councillor at the early age of twenty-seven by the new Tsar Paul. Finally, in October 1799 he married the twenty-year-old heiress of one of the richest fortunes in Russia, Princess Elizabeth Galitzine. He now enjoyed fabulous wealth, but the lure of the service proved as strong as before, and in 1801 he rejoined the Army with his old rank.

In March 1801 Tsar Paul was assassinated, and his son Alexander I assumed the throne. Napoleon's ambitious and unscrupulous policies soon aroused the new Tsar's suspicion and hostility. Pressed into action by Britain, which had still greater reason to fear the threatening colossus, Russia prepared for war. Alliances were made with Britain, Austria and Sweden; and when Napoleon annexed Genoa to France, the Tsar angrily recalled the Russian Ambassador to Paris and arranged with the Emperor Francis for the advance of Russian troops into Austria.

On 9 September 1805 the Emperor Alexander rode from St. Petersburg to the frontier, across which two great armies under Generals Kutuzov and Buxhoevden, to be followed by a third under Bennigsen, were to advance into the heart of Europe and link up with their Austrian allies. The Allies' main thrust was to be on the Danube, but at the same time the Russian General Staff planned an extended flank attack in the north. An expeditionary force of more than 20,000 men had been assembled with exemplary speed and embarked on board a fleet at Kronstadt. They were commanded by another distinguished military Tolstoy, General Peter Alexandrovich. Senator, Inspector of the Infantry, commander of the Preobrazhensky Guards and Governor of St. Petersburg, he was a well-deserved favourite of Alexander I. Tolstoy's orders were to sail into the southern Baltic: if Prussia was found to be friendly, he was to employ his Corps in north Germany in cooperation with Russia's ally Sweden; if not, he was to land in Pomerania and combine with the fleet in blockading and harassing the Prussians. On 12 September the convoy sailed. As his second-in-command Peter Tolstoy took Alexander Osterman-Tolstoy, both men being now thirty-five years old. As members of the Tolstoy family they were distantly related, but a much closer connexion existed through the fact that they had married two Galitzine sisters.

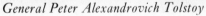

General Peter Alexandrovich Tolstoy   *Osterman-Tolstoy*

The fleet had a smooth passage at first, but after Revel they were hit by a storm, which caused the loss of several hundred men and some guns. Nevertheless they arrived safely in Swedish Pomerania, where King Gustavus Adolphus had promised troops to swell the expedition. Meanwhile the Tsar himself travelled to Berlin and persuaded the apprehensive King of Prussia to sign the Treaty of Potsdam, in which he promised to come to the Allies' aid before the end of the year. All looked highly promising. General Peter Tolstoy, who had travelled to Berlin to take part in the talks, now hastened to the King of Sweden to urge his immediate participation in a campaign against the French in Hanover, which they had occupied in 1803. But Gustavus suspected Prussia of designs on Swedish Pomerania and made excuses in order to retain his troops there. Peter Tolstoy decided not to wait for his dilatory ally, and early in November marched his troops across the Elbe into Hanover. Osterman-Tolstoy headed the Corps, whose appearance and discipline excited the Germans' admiration; they had not seen a Russian army in their country since the Seven Years' War. Many balls and splendid entertainments were provided for the officers *en route*. But there was business to be done, and the Russians pushed on to the River Weser, where on 2 December they were joined by a British army of 24,000 men commanded by Generals Don and Lord Cathcart, who placed themselves under Tolstoy's overall command; Tolstoy thus became the only Russian general in history to command a British army. Finally 12,000 Swedes made a late but welcome appearance. There was now assembled a tidy force of some 56,000 men, and it was proposed to seize Hamelin, cross the Rhine and so – on to France!

It was at this moment that news reached the army of Napoleon's crushing defeat of the main Austrian and Russian armies at Austerlitz. So the great expedition ended. The Tolstoys lingered to cover the British withdrawal, and then marched home in good order through Prussian territory.

Back home at last, Osterman-Tolstoy must have repined at having witnessed only such a backwater of the great war. The frustration had been intense, for if the Swedes and British had acted with the Tolstoys' dash, the Northern Army might have turned Napoleon's flank and saved Russia from defeat. What Suvorov would have done on such an occasion! A small consolation came in the likelihood that Prussia's belated entry into the war in 1806 stemmed in part from the good impression Tolstoy's troops made upon King Frederick William.[5]

If Osterman-Tolstoy was impatient, he was not so for long. He was soon to know warfare on a scale even Suvorov had not experienced. In September of the next year, 1806, Napoleon at Jena and Auerstädt utterly crushed that proud Prussian military caste which had jeered at Peter Tolstoy's withdrawal from Hanover. The Russian armies were compelled to withdraw as Napoleon himself at the head of 80,000 veterans of Austerlitz and Jena pushed into Poland and established themselves along the Vistula. The Tsar's armies were superior in numbers, but the supreme command was greatly inferior. "Who is the man among us who enjoys universal confidence and who combines military talents with the severity indispensable for the post of commander? I myself know of no such man!" the Tsar confided to Peter Tolstoy.[6]

But the Russians were determined to fight, and the French for the first time began to encounter serious opposition. Davout succeeded in forcing the Narew,

Battle scenes: silhouettes by Feodor Petrovich Tolstoy

but French losses were as great as Russian. Osterman-Tolstoy distinguished himself that day and was promoted to Lieutenant-General. But his major exploit was on 26 December, when he commanded the left flank at the battle of Pultusk. There the French under Lannes were driving in the Russian centre, when Tolstoy's 2nd Division marched up to their relief. It was now that he displayed that dogged courage which, in its resolute determination never to yield ground when any resistance was possible, became celebrated throughout the Russian Army. Lannes failed to break through, and it was only when Davout sent up large reinforcements that Bennigsen reluctantly withdrew the Russians from Pultusk. The battle was in reality a draw, and has been described as the first to show that Napoleon's string of victories was to have a term. For the conspicuous part he played in the battle Osterman-Tolstoy received the Order of St. George, Third Class.

But Pultusk was a mere skirmish to Eylau, fought in ice and snow with terrible losses on both sides. Osterman-Tolstoy commanded on the left flank, where Napoleon's strategy demanded his main attack should fall. Time and again Tolstoy's men beat back the fiercest onslaughts. Even when outnumbered and outflanked by Davout and St. Hilaire, Tolstoy withdrew step by step, never faltering until reinforcements under the Prussian Lestocq came to relieve him. He himself was for a while surrounded by the enemy and on the point of being captured, when he was rescued by a brave officer named Mazovsky, whose portrait he afterwards always kept hanging in his study. The Russians had to leave the battlefield, but the legend of French invincibility had gone, and 25,000 *grognards* lay on the bloodstained snow to prove it. It was not until June 1807 that Napoleon finally achieved his decisive victory at Friedland, and by then Osterman-Tolstoy had been severely wounded in the leg and obliged to retire from active service. After a spell in hospital at Memel, he returned home. He was showered with awards by his grateful sovereign: the Order of St. Anne, First Class; a gold sword, encrusted with diamonds, inscribed "for bravery"; and the command of the First Guards Division. What made him a popular hero were his modesty, high sense of personal honour, and rugged courage that nothing could daunt.[7]

By his troops he was looked up to with devotion. "As commander of an army he was strict, but his strictness consisted only in a look, in two or three minatory words, which were much more feared than a full dressing-down from another commander," recalled an officer who had served under him. "In all the time he commanded the Corps he caused no resentment, though he did have occasion to punish. He never refused anyone who needed his professional assistance; if he

helped someone it was with an open hand, and he was generally generous. . . . He could not stand devious methods or petty intrigues and disliked those who engaged in them; he never pushed forward his own interests and never asked anything for himself, nor could he tolerate flattery. But when it came to shooting, he boldly thrust himself forward. He cared for the food and health of his soldiers like a father. When the army was encamped, almost every day he did a round at meal-time to try out the troops' food, and woe betide that commander in whose regiment poor or unhealthy rations were discovered!"

Alexander Ivanovich Osterman-Tolstoy bore a highly idiosyncratic, not to say eccentric, character – unusual even by the standards of his erratic family. In appearance he was "tall and lean; his dark features were lit up by bright expressive eyes, whose kindliness shone through an expression of coldness and even severity. His most striking moral qualities were straightforwardness, candour, nobility and a deeply-engrained sense of Russianness." He had been heard to declare that Russians should "be no better acquainted with the language of foreigners than would be sufficient for communication or common courtesies." When a young officer reporting to his tent was rash enough to speak in French, the Count's brow darkened as he enquired how any patriotic Russian could use such a language. Greatly dashed, the officer withdrew, only to be summoned back again. "I am giving a ball on Friday," explained Tolstoy, with a twinkle in his eye and speaking in fluent French, "I do hope you will do me the honour of attending my little evening's entertainment."

It will be seen that the odder aspects of his behaviour became much more pronounced after his active military service was over, when he was regarded with some disfavour by staider colleagues. But even during his campaigning days there was much in his conduct to arouse comment. For example, an enormous white eagle accompanied him everywhere in his tent. More striking still was his appearance when on the march at the head of his Corps. Behind the Count and his staff travelled a carriage whose occupants aroused the utmost astonishment among honest citizens of German and Bohemian towns, who had come to witness the arrival of the Russians. From its windows leaned the amiable faces of the General's three fully-grown pet bears, who accompanied him on every campaign. Wherever he and his staff were quartered, places were laid at table for these three strange comrades. Tolstoy was a stickler for good manners, and apparently their behaviour was impeccable.

Meanwhile Russia was once again at peace. Devastated by the defeat at Friedland, and suddenly charmed by the grandiose scheme of alliance proffered by Napoleon, Tsar Alexander accepted his invitation to meet at Tilsit. There, on 30 June, the two great Emperors, masters of the world from the Atlantic to the Pacific, met on the famous raft built by the French Guard Artillery. For a week the sovereigns rode together, dined together, and planned Europe's future. Every morning Count Nikolai Alexandrovich Tolstoy, elder brother of General Peter, and Chief Marshal of the Court, appeared at Napoleon's house to enquire how his Majesty had spent the night, while Marshal Duroc appeared similarly before the Tsar. Alexander was exultant. On 7 June the Treaty of Tilsit was signed, repartitioning central Europe at the expense of Alexander's ally Frederick William of Prussia. Many Russians, however, remained immune to the atmosphere of sweetness and light. Count Nikolai Tolstoy did the honours for his Imperial friend and master, but made no bones about betraying his real feelings. He grumbled when required to arrange a banquet for the French, his friendship with the Tsar enabling him to express openly what many felt privately. A year later, when Alexander and Napoleon met again at Erfurt, and the Tsar announced his intention of bestowing on him the St. Andrew, Tolstoy in a famous *riposte* made his repugnance still more clear. Pointing contemptuously to the Legion of Honour, just bestowed on him by Napoleon, he enquired gruffly whether he "should wear our Andrew next to *Bonaparte*'s order?"[8]

Count Nikolai Alexandrovich Tolstoy

With the signing of the Treaty of Tilsit diplomatic relations were resumed between the two Empires. The Tolstoys, who appear generally to have disliked Napoleon as much in his lifetime as Leo Tolstoy did in retrospect, played their part reluctantly enough. The Chief Marshal swallowed his indignation at having to receive as French Ambassador General Savary, the former head of *gendarmerie* who had arranged the judicial murder of the Duc d'Enghien. He also overcame his brother General Peter Tolstoy's aversion to accepting the post of Ambassador in Paris, where he remained *en poste* during the crucial years of Tilsit and Erfurt, 1807 and 1808. [9]

On 23 October 1810, for reasons of health and perhaps also as a result of his annoyance at seeing Prince Barclay de Tolly appointed over his head as Governor-General of the newly-conquered Grand Duchy of Finland,[10] Osterman-Tolstoy retired from service. On 19 April 1811 Count Ivan, the last surviving Osterman brother, died and Tolstoy added their rich estates to his already vast fortune. His retirement was not to last long. War with France had only been postponed and just over a year later, on 24 June 1812, Napoleon's Grand Army began crossing the Niemen onto Russian soil, with the proclaimed intention of putting "an end to the fatal influence which Russia has exercised over Europe for the past fifty years".

Nikolai Alexandrovich Tolstoy and family

The left flank of the Russian 1st Army rested on Vilna, where Count Shuvalov commanded the 4th Corps. Shuvalov was however a sick man and requested Tsar Alexander to relieve him of his command. By a fortunate chance it was at that moment that Count Osterman-Tolstoy arrived, begging to be permitted to take part in the coming conflict. Feeling "there was not a moment to lose", the Tsar responded with enthusiasm, appointing him to the command of the 4th Corps without even consulting Barclay, the Army commander, who was at first offended at the slight. The Count, now forty-two years old, was delighted. A year before he had thought his fighting days were over, and now here he was, with 20,000 foot

Count Feodor Andreevich Osterman

under his command, ready to dare his country's foes to do their worst.[11]

For the moment Napoleon's strategy appeared to be unfolding much as the great Emperor had planned. He drove the bulk of the Grand Army forward on Barclay's heels, as the Russian commander-in-chief withdrew towards Orissa.

Murat's cavalry led the attack, moving along the Dvina in force, huge clouds of dust rising above his spurring columns. Barclay dashed off an urgent plea to Bagration to join him, and sent Osterman-Tolstoy's 4th Corps back to Ostrovno in an effort to delay Murat's advance. On 25 July Tolstoy drew up his infantry outside the town, and launched straight into an attack on the French. The battle raged all day, with Murat's two cavalry corps and one infantry regiment greatly outnumbering the Russians. The odds were hopeless, but Tolstoy's instructions were to protect the 1st Army until Bagration arrived. The fire grew so terrible that whole ranks were falling under repeated swathes of grapeshot. The hard-pressed vanguard begged the General to tell them what to do. "Do?" cried Tolstoy. "There's nothing to do – except stand and die." Barclay sent reinforcements, but the arrival on the French side of Prince Eugène Beauharnais's forces gave them overwhelming numerical superiority. Under cover of night Tolstoy made a fighting retreat out of the blazing town, and carried out a slow, battling withdrawal towards Vitebsk.

Tolstoy's 4th Corps had fought with a valour far exceeding the letter of his instructions, and this had an effect quite out of proportion to the scale of the engagement. Barclay was simply buying time, but the extraordinary toughness of the resistance convinced Napoleon that the Russian commander had fallen into his trap and was preparing to give battle. He accordingly took the risk of delaying for a day while he collected reinforcements. This gave Barclay the chance to slip away, and when Napoleon entered Vitebsk on 28 July, he found the bird had flown.[12]

Having escaped the closing jaws of Napoleon's trap, the Russian Army withdrew to Smolensk and so on to the gates of Moscow. It was there that the Russian commanders, Kutuzov and Barclay, halted and turned to fight at Borodino. The great battle and its outcome have been too frequently described (not least, of course, by Leo Tolstoy in *War and Peace*) to be set out again in more than outline. Entrenchments were thrown up and artillery emplaced, when on 24 August the Grand Army appeared and Napoleon began his assault. After fierce fighting for most of the day they succeeded in driving the Russians from their advanced Shevardino redoubt, and the next day was spent in preparing the armies and assessing enemy dispositions. Osterman-Tolstoy's 4th Corps formed part of the right flank commanded by General Miloradovich. Their position was strong, as before them lay a steeply-banked river, the Kolocha, with marshes spreading beyond. The main highroad from Smolensk passed through Borodino village and on past their immediate left, but Kutuzov had in fact miscalculated in thinking it likely the French would deliver their main thrust here. Napoleon had marked the strength of the Russian right and in any case decided against dangerously overextending his army by any long-scale flanking attacks.

The battle proper began at dawn next day, 26 August, when an exceptionally bright and golden sun beamed over the countryside, lighting up the battlefield with unusual clarity. Frail, dispersing mists hanging over the Kolocha and Semeonovko rivulets were suddenly jarred by the thunder of hundreds of guns opening up along the fronts, and replaced by accumulating thick, acrid white clouds of artillery smoke. A rattle of drums sounded a sonorous refrain, as enormous columns of French infantry debouched from the obscurity, and moved menacingly forward on the Russian centre and left. Beauharnais's leading division seized Borodino village, having crossed the Kolocha, whilst Ney and Davout grappled to force the fortified position on the left. The Russian response was ferocious, and within half an hour tens of thousands of men were locked in terrible combat. Bagration's entrenchments on the left were stormed, taken, and retaken, with appalling losses on both sides. The French General Montbrun was killed, while Davout, Ney and Rapp were wounded. The Russians withdrew from their position, but forming squares on the level ground behind, beat off wave after wave of Murat's cavalry.

In the centre General Dokhturov held the Central Redoubt, with its twenty 12-

Battle scenes: silhouettes by Feodor Petrovich Tolstoy

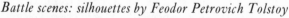

pound guns pouring deadly fire into Beauharnais's attacking division. Following the bloody stalemate on his right, Napoleon ordered Beauharnais to storm the Redoubt. With admirable dash and courage, Morand and Gerard flung themselves up the esplanade through a torrent of grapeshot and forced their way in over the ramparts. But the Russian units behind sprang forward and retook the position, the key to their whole front, after deadly hand-to-hand fighting. Beauharnais, reeling back, was obliged to content himself with directing a deadly artillery fire on the emplacement which virtually destroyed its newly-ensconsed defenders. The battle was being waged with a ferocity and resolution which surprised even the most battle-scarred veterans, and Napoleon, who that morning had half expected to discover the Russians withdrawn, now found himself faced with a battle of attrition. On both sides the losses had been appalling, and the Emperor decided that the moment had come, before the thread of battle was drawn from his hand, to launch a gigantic *coup-de-main* at the Russian centre.

On the Russian side General Barclay, who in the virtual absence of Kutuzov at his retired headquarters commanded the battle, had time to survey the carnage and prepare for what would clearly be the critical phase. His centre and left flank had been fearfully bloodied while the right, ignored by Napoleon's concentration to the south, was virtually out of the battle. Already Baggavut's Corps on the extreme right had crossed the entire rear of the army to restore the balance on the left. Osterman-Tolstoy was however still sitting his horse at the head of his 4th Corps, impatiently watching the great pall of smoke and stabbing flame swirling around the Great Redoubt.

It was midday, and under the burning sun experienced officers could detect an underlying lull, despite the continuous grumble of the guns. Napoleon was preparing for the coup-de-grace. Prince Eugène Beauharnais was assembling three divisions of infantry for a direct assault on the Great Redoubt, whilst Murat, the King of Naples, prepared his cavalry for another devastating charge like that which broke the Russian lines at Eylau.

In the Russian centre there was every reason for apprehension. There Raevsky's Corps, having borne the brunt of the fighting, including the defence of the Great Redoubt, was shattered and almost spent. Now Tolstoy received the order for which he had been waiting. An aide-de-camp from Barclay galloped up with the order to cross over and take up position behind Raevsky's 7th Corps in the centre. Orders rang out, drums rolled, and the 4th Corps marched down behind the blood-stained Great Redoubt and took up position immediately to the rear of Raevsky's torn ensigns and depleted ranks. What was left of the 7th Corps moved

back and the 4th Corps moved up to the front, its right resting to the rear of the Great Redoubt. Osterman-Tolstoy had been eager for battle, but what he now saw preparing below might have daunted even his lion's heart.

Napoleon had advanced no less than 400 guns onto the bluff opposite, which concentrated a hideous bombardment on the Redoubt and 4th Corps position. Then, at three o'clock, bugles rang out on the left and drums rolled on the right as the attack commenced.

Three divisions of infantry under Beauharnais poured across the Kolocha and swept up to the Redoubt, while the 82nd Cavalry Corps under Caulaincourt came galloping in a dense column of sabres and cuirasses, silver and gold in the sunshine, straight at what was left of Raevsky's Corps and Tolstoy's 4th Corps. Wave after wave of horsemen hurled themselves against the line: French, Saxon and Polish cuirassiers. At first the density and élan of the assault seemed irresistible. The cavalry poured over the advanced Russian positions, sabring gunners and riding down the infantry. Tolstoy's Corps poured in a murderous fire, emptying countless saddles, one of them being that of the intrepid Caulaincourt himself, but the decimated squadrons turned the rear of the Redoubt just as Beauharnais's powder-blackened and exhausted infantry poured over the ramparts and slaughtered the defenders to the last man.

Through his telescope from the Kurgan hill, Napoleon saw the tricolor flutter above the smoking stronghold, and felt his moment had come. Even as the Russian Army reeled from this wound torn in its centre, he hurled Grouchy's Corps forward into the gap. But amidst the shouting and firing, smoke and chaos, the Russian 4th Corps did not flinch despite its punishing losses. It seemed for a while as if these included the General himself, for Tolstoy was obliged to withdraw to the field hospital where he was treated for very severe bruising. Pausing only to receive a dressing, he hastened back to his hard-pressed Corps, passing a tragic scene on the way, where the mortally-wounded General Prince Peter Bagration lay surrounded by agitated surgeons.

Meanwhile, Barclay, anxious to know whether the centre would hold, despatched General Loewenstern to investigate.

"General Barclay," Loewenstern remembered afterwards, "not knowing what was happening to Count Osterman's [Tolstoy] Corps, sent me to him. That valiant General, distinguishing himself with reckless courage, had already returned from hospital. In the course of eight or ten minutes which I spent beside Count Osterman several of his entourage were killed and wounded, including his adjutant Valuev, who was killed next to me, and young Prince Michael Galitzine, wounded

by a bullet. Carefully examining the situation, I was convinced that there was nothing special to worry about, and that Count Osterman would defend his position like a lion."

Encouraged by this, Barclay ordered a massive cavalry counter-attack. The battle raged on until dusk, but the Russian line continued to hold.

Both sides claimed a victory, but both were too bloodied and exhausted to continue the struggle. Napoleon withdrew to his original positions west of the Kolocha, while Kutuzov marched off on the road to Mozhaisk.[13]

For his conspicuous gallantry Osterman-Tolstoy received the Order of St. Alexander Nevsky, which he wore alongside the ribbon of St. Anne and cross of St. George.*

On 1 September the Russian Army, still fearfully bloodied and in some disorder, halted at Fili, just west of Moscow. There, in a peasant's hut, Kutuzov held his celebrated conference, at which the question was posed: should they stand and fight – and risk losing the Army; or withdraw to fight another day – and abandon the holy city of Moscow to the enemy? In the darkened room, a lamp burning before an ikon of the Virgin and Child, gathered the great leaders of 1812: Kutuzov, Raevsky, Osterman-Tolstoy, Bennigsen, Ermolov. The scene has been immortalized by Leo Tolstoy in *War and Peace*, where he wrote with evident family pride: "In another corner, leaning his head with its bold features and flashing eyes on his broad hand, sat Count Osterman-Tolstoy, apparently sunk in his own thoughts."

Tolstoy joined Kutuzov and Barclay in favouring withdrawal; there was scant chance of his being accused of cowardice, and the risks of Bennigsen's proposal to stand and fight were self-evident. "Moscow does not comprise Russia," he pointed out; "our aim is not just the defence of the capital but of the whole fatherland, and to save that the most important object is the preservation of the Army."[15]

Tolstoy's view was that finally accepted, and Napoleon in consequence entered Moscow, whose citizens burned most of it to the ground. But the hour of vengeance was near. When the Tsar in St Petersburg failed to respond to Napoleon's peace-feelers, and the Russian armies poised round Moscow and French communications to the rear grew with every hour, the French Emperor had no choice but to retreat. The final straw had been the signal defeat of Murat at Tarutino, a battle in which Osterman-Tolstoy's Corps was once again prominent. He was in the thick of the fighting at Malo-Yaroslavets on 12 October, and marched in pursuit of the shattered Grand Army to Vilna.

By now even Tolstoy's iron constitution was flagging. Badly knocked about at Borodino and believing always in being at the point of most danger and enterprise, he had also undergone the fatigues of forced march and atrocious weather. It was on the night of 22 October, after his Corps had occupied Viazma, that the mild

---

* Many of his family had displayed similar gallantry, though in less exalted positions. They included the eccentric "American", Feodor Ivanovich Tolstoy, subject of the next chapter of this history; and my great-great-great-grandfather, Pavel Lvovich, who served in the Semeonovsky Guards at Vitebsk, Smolensk and Borodino, receiving a sword of honour and retiring through disability with the rank of Lieutenant-Colonel. Count Osterman-Tolstoy's brother-in-law General Peter Tolstoy, his former commander in Hanover in 1805 and Ambassador in Paris in 1807–8, raised no fewer than eighteen infantry and five cavalry regiments of militia;[14] it was in one of the former that "the American" served.

weather broke and snow began to fall heavily. Tolstoy's thermometer recorded eighteen degrees of frost, and the cold was cruel. One of his staff officers, Prince Nikolai Galitzine, saw terrible sights, never effaced from his memory.

"At each step we came across wretched figures, numb with cold; they began staggering like drunkards because the frost had penetrated their brains, and afterwards fell down dead. Others sat round fires, horribly frozen, not noticing that their feet which they wanted to warm had been turned into charcoal. Many from hunger devoured raw carrion. I saw how several dragged themselves over to corpses, tore at them with their teeth, and tried to stave off with this hideous food the hunger that tormented them. We were unable to help these wretches because we ourselves lacked the necessities of life, travelling on a route ravaged every day since the beginning of the campaign. For a whole week I had to content myself with plain dried crusts and corn vodka, which our sutler happened by chance to have: *my General never sat down to table throughout the whole campaign.*" (My italics.)[16]

Another awed aide recorded details of Tolstoy's legendary hardihood.

"Against the harshness of the Russian climate the Count, it appeared, supplied his own warmth: he would often inspect a regiment wearing a simple uniform jacket in a deep frost. He was made of iron: character, body and spirit. His diet was incredibly modest; at table he rarely took a sip of champagne. Refined dishes, especially pastries, he could not tolerate. He loved boiled buckwheat *kasha* . . . Once when the Corps was on the march, after a regimental inspection in a hard frost, returning to his own quarters he drank a cup of tea and set off again on his round. In the meantime a dinner table had been prepared for us in honour of the regiment by its commander Bolkhovsky, a noted *gourmand* and connoisseur of the culinary art, whose ingredients we had already smelt. I and the Corps surgeon, who accompanied the Count, were only able to enjoy the scent of those delicacies. Our curses fell freely on him! At the first dreary halt he asked us if we wanted to eat, and on receiving an emphatic affirmative, ordered up . . . *buckwheat kasha*, over which had been poured a liberal infusion of green hempseed oil. He eagerly began devouring it; through sheer hunger I swallowed a few spoonfuls, but the surgeon declined."

But even his health was now temporarily broken, and Osterman-Tolstoy was compelled to retire from the Army to effect a recovery. Over the winter of 1812 to 1813 he recuperated, but by spring the old war-horse smelt battle in the air and rode eastwards to rejoin the Army, which had pursued Napoleon into Germany and joined forces with the Prussians who had at last found the opportunity to

break out from French tutelage. But Napoleon's amazing genius had not yet deserted him. Raising new armies in France, he appeared again like a vengeful god of war in the heart of Germany. At Lützen on 2 May 1813 he defeated the Allies, and advanced to encounter them at Bautzen three weeks later. Here Tolstoy held a command on the left wing, appearing as usual heading his troops in the firing line. A bullet hit him in the left shoulder, but for three hours he continued directing the fighting. He was carried off, half dead, when the Allies fell back in defeat yet again. Once more he had to recuperate while receiving medical treatment.

Napoleon himself was recuperating too, despite his victories at Lützen and Bautzen. A brief truce was agreed with the Allies. But by August war had broken out again, this time with Austria's and Sweden's armies fighting alongside those of Russia and Prussia. Worried by an Allied thrust towards his key stronghold of Dresden, Napoleon flung himself into the Saxon capital. As the Russian and Austrian Emperors laid siege to the city from the south, they suddenly found themselves threatened in turn by the advance of 40,000 French under General Vandamme, who were marching to Napoleon's relief. Osterman-Tolstoy, who had returned to the Army, was detached with his Corps to reinforce a small force blocking Vandamme's way. But once again Napoleon snatched victory from defeat. As his troops drove back the Russians and Austrians from their positions, news came that Vandamme's numerically superior force was pushing back Tolstoy. Fearful of being caught in a closing trap, the Allied Army straggled southwards in an ignominious attempt to regain the safety of Bohemia.

Now was Napoleon's chance: Murat, Marmont, Mortier, Victor and Saint-Cyr emerged at the head of their corps and marched south from Dresden close on the heels of the fleeing Allied Army. The latter was straggling through the mountainous defiles of the Bohemian Forest in separate columns travelling on poor roads. The intention was to rendez-vous on the other side of the Forest at Teplitz, some thirty miles to the south. There, in the relative safety of Bohemia, they could expect to gather reinforcements and supplies from Prague. The French could travel no faster than they through the mountains, but there was one factor which placed the Allies in deadliest peril. To the south-east of Dresden, around Pirna, lay the Army of Vandamme, 40,000 strong. If Vandamme could reach Teplitz before the Allies, their columns would be caught in front and rear, and destroyed piecemeal as straggling columns emerged from the passes. The survival of the Allied cause hung in the balance, for they had committed the major part of their armies to the attack on Dresden. Among the dispirited columns spurring

frantically through the dripping darkness of the woods rode the disconsolate figures of the Emperors of Russia and Austria, and the King of Prussia. Vandamme had two days' start – and to Schwarzenberg and Barclay, the Allied generals, matters looked desperate indeed.

As has been seen, when the Allied sovereigns laid siege to Dresden they had only been able to spare a single corps to mask their flank from Vandamme's approach. This was the Corps of Osterman-Tolstoy, a mere 18,500 men facing Vandamme's 40,000 on the Elbe. On the night of the 27th an officer rode into Tolstoy's camp with a message from Barclay: if, as was presumably the case, his route to Bohemia was blocked by Vandamme, he was to move south-west to join the retreating Russian Army at Maxen. The order was clear, but Tolstoy was unhappy. He saw at once the appalling danger in which his beloved Sovereign and Army lay. Whilst *he* moved towards Maxen, Vandamme would disengage and make for Teplitz by forced marches that must inevitably get him there before Barclay. He saw that he, and he alone, could halt or delay Vandamme, and decided then and there to disregard Barclay's order and fight. The risk, as he saw, was tremendous. On the face of it his force, outnumbered by comfortably more than double the number of enemies, must certainly be destroyed. But his men were of very good quality, including as they did seven thousand men of the Guards Division under his old comrade Ermolov. The alternatives were to risk losing the Guard – or the Army. The Guard must be sacrificed.

At dawn on the 28th Tolstoy ordered Prince Eugen of Württemberg to deliver a feint attack on the French with the 2nd Division, while the Guards and remainder of the Corps made for Peterswald further south. Württemberg's attack was so fiery that Vandamme was convinced he had to deal with the whole Corps (whose number, he was informed by a captured Russian surgeon, exceeded 70,000 men). All day long Osterman directed the march on Peterswald, while his rearguard fought continually against the pursuing French. Württemberg's force was reduced to a mere 2,000 men, and Vandamme sent Napoleon a triumphant despatch announcing a major defeat of "the enemy". The Emperor, who was on his way to join Vandamme at Pirna, decided that matters were proceeding well enough for him to leave the destruction of the Allied Army to his subordinates, and returned to Dresden.

Next morning at five o'clock Tolstoy broke camp at Peterswald and continued his forced march to Teplitz. Prince Württemberg again commanded the rearguard, but by now Vandamme had discovered his enemy's numerical inferiority and pressed hotly forward. Fearing that his Corps would be crushed or pushed aside, Tolstoy faced about with two regiments and some guns on a rise at Nollendorf. This allowed the shattered rearguard time to catch up. At the same time he sent Ermolov on with the main force to find a suitable spot to halt and fight. This they would do whatever the odds, rather than let Vandamme reach Teplitz. Fighting in a driving Scotch mist which obscured everything around, and even soaked the priming powder of muskets before they could be fired, Tolstoy and the rearguard pulled back to where Ermolov had drawn up his men behind the village of Kulm. There the General formed up his little army, his main strength having its left on the slopes of the hills, and the cavalry on the right by the village of Priesten. They were desperately short of cartridges, the 2nd Corps having only what the soldiers

Opposite: The Battle of Kulm, 1813

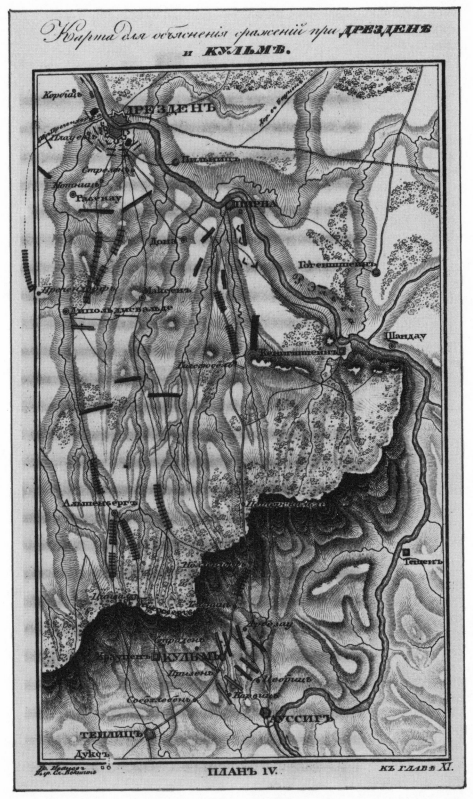

ПЛАНЪ IV.   КЪ ГЛАВѢ XI.

bore in their knapsacks. But morale was high; as Tolstoy reported to Tsar Alexander, "with distinguished commanders commanding the Guard, all ranks were burning with zeal to achieve my purpose."

As he rode up and down the lines he told the men that he was resolved not to give way a foot: they must stand or die. It was the same instruction he had given at Ostrovno at the outset of the 1812 campaign, and his words were received with a deep, confident "Hurrah!" that echoed in the forests above. Musicians, drummers and even regimental clerks begged for arms to join the struggle. At this moment an adjutant galloped up with an urgent appeal from the King of Prussia to hold out as long as possible. "The fate of the Army rests on your endeavour," he explained.

At ten o'clock came Vandamme's first assault. The attack was a portent of the ferocity with which the battle would be waged. In the houses and gardens of Priesten and Straden and among orchards and boulder-strewn meadows around, Russians and French met at the point of the bayonet. Straden changed hands, and General Khrapovitsky of the Ismailovsky Regiment was wounded. Priesten fell to the French when its defenders ran out of cartridges, and was retaken by a determined charge. Masses of men swayed this way and that, locked in deadly combat, and Vandamme decided to force the issue to a conclusion. A small stream lay between the armies and from slopes on the far side 80 French guns opened up a rapid bombardment, followed by the advance of virtually the whole of their army. The nature of the ground hindered their bringing all regiments fully into action, but the pressure of the great columns was inexorable. Tolstoy threw all his reserves in, save the Preobrazhensky Regiment, and the struggle rapidly became one of sheer physical strength, with officers playing their part with swords, pistols and fists alongside private soldiers. In such a struggle numbers had to tell, but Tolstoy and his men were spurred to Homeric efforts by the thought that *time*, not victory, was what they needed to gain to save the Tsar and the Army.

At this point King Frederick William of Prussia appeared from the mountains accompanied by a welcome battery of horse artillery and an Austrian regiment of light horse. He had admired Tolstoy's command of his troops as he passed through Prussia in 1805, and now he saw him in action. Vandamme divided his mass into two columns. The right-hand force, by sheer weight of numbers, drove the Russians out of Priesten and for a moment cut a gap in the thinning line. Only a determined charge by two regiments of lancers and dragoons drove the enemy back. General Osterman-Tolstoy swiftly threw in his only reserve, the Preobrazhensky Regiment, and was riding beside them when a cannon-ball from one of Vandamme's batteries smashed into his left arm. As he reeled back, two soldiers hauled him from the saddle and laid him gently on the ground. He tried to rise and rejoin the fighting, but was too weak. "This is my payment for the honour of commanding the Guard," he said proudly. "I am quite content!"

The regimental surgeons appeared at a run, and began the gruesome business of amputating Tolstoy's arm, which still dangled from his shoulder. Gazing up at the anxious circle of faces, he beckoned to a young doctor named Kuchkovsky. "I like your face," said the General; "cut off my arm!" As the operation proceeded (naturally without anaesthetics), he asked some soldiers standing by to sing a *Russian* song. The loss of blood was soon so great that he fainted. King Frederick William rode up and, dismounting hurriedly, knelt down weeping beside the unconscious man. Tolstoy opened his eyes and, recognizing the King, asked the question that was ever present in his mind. "Is that you, Sire?" he asked weakly; "is the Emperor my master safe?"

Thanks to Tolstoy's decision at Pirna and coolness at Kulm, the Tsar *was* safe. Ermolov took over command of the army, and next morning Prussian and Russian reinforcements began arriving on the field. Vandamme was defeated and taken prisoner, and a *Te Deum* held on the open field. Just as at Ostrovno in the previous year, Osterman-Tolstoy had by his bravery saved the Russian Army. Had Vandamme reached Teplitz in time to fortify himself there, the Allies would almost certainly have been crushed between his forces and those of Murat and the other marshals to the north, and Napoleon could have marched unopposed through Bohemia to Vienna. A tremor ran through the Allied armies, who had hitherto suffered nothing but defeats since Napoleon reappeared in Germany. "The battle of Kulm changed into a cry of joy the despair which was spreading through the valleys of Bohemia," as General Buturlin, the Tsar's aide-de-camp, put it. Napoleon himself is said to have recognized it as the significant moment, when his destiny shifted.

Congratulations and rewards were showered upon the victorious General and his army. The Tsar wrote a moving letter of thanks and bestowed on him the Cross of St. George 2nd Class, the Order of St. Vladimir 1st Class, and a magnificent Sèvres vase, bearing scenes from the battle of Kulm. The ladies of Bohemia and Hungary, who in the event of defeat would have seen their country ravaged and their castles plundered by the arrogant Vandamme, sent him a commemorative golden goblet, decorated with precious stones from each district of their country. It was accompanied by a glowing epistle, full of warm compliments which would certainly have touched his chivalrous heart. Equally warming was their husbands' gift: every year the great magnates of the two kingdoms despatched to the Count's palace at St. Petersburg a generous consignment of the finest Tokay and Rhine wines.[17]

Osterman-Tolstoy was the hero of the hour. After two operations the amputation healed successfully, and his vigorous constitution soon brought him back to normal health. He decided, however, to retire from active service and was not present at the great battle of Leipzig in October, when the armies he had saved at Kulm returned to inflict a resounding defeat on Napoleon, who was obliged to retire permanently beyond the Rhine. Tolstoy was in Vienna when the great news arrived. An Austrian lady provides a glimpse of him as he was at the summit of his glory: "the Empress, [of Austria] . . . was received with tremendous enthusiasm at a charity concert in aid of the widows of men who had fallen at Leipzig. Suddenly all attention was focused on a man wearing a simple blue overcoat who was applauding with one arm only, as the other was missing and an empty sleeve hung down. This was the victor of Kulm, this was Osterman. At once the entire audience rose to its feet, the hero's name was passed from mouth to mouth, the lovely Empress Luise spotted the Count, turned and greeted him by clapping her hands, whereupon three thousand people followed her example. Like a roll of thunder countless cheers roared out, and tears coursed down the hollow cheeks of the gallant Russian general. What a moment in the life of a warrior!"[18]

The veteran General appears to have stayed on in Germany in the following year (1814), for he was seen at Weimar, dining with two of the Tsar's sisters and the great Goethe.[19] With the complete defeat and surrender of Napoleon, the Tsar and the Russian Army returned home. Tolstoy likewise came back, and on

17 December he was appointed commander of the elite Pavlovsky Regiment. He was extremely proud of this honour, and out of his great wealth provided funds for soldiers' widows and orphans. In particular he granted pensions for life to the two grenadiers who carried him from his horse when wounded at Kulm, and the surgeon who amputated his arm. In 1817 he was appointed full General but shortly afterwards retired from service.

For the remainder of Alexander I's reign Osterman-Tolstoy lived in Russia, enjoying a life of unbelievable splendour. "Those were my glittering times," he used to recall later. Certainly fortune seemed to have showered him with every conceivable gift. He possessed almost limitless wealth, derived from his wife's inheritance and the Osterman bequest. In St. Petersburg he built a magnificent palace on the English Quay in the Admiralty Quarter, only a stone's throw from the Winter Palace, where he was a welcome visitor. A young relative who stayed there left a description of this pleasure-dome. "The windows of my drawing-room and study looked out on the English Quay and the Neva; from them could

General Osterman-Tolstoy. By George Dawe

be seen Rumyantsev Square and the first 'line' [avenue] of Vassilievsky Island, one of the grandest streets in St. Petersburg. In autumn when lamps blazed in the streets and on ships anchored in the Neva opposite our windows – the view was magnificent. In the reception room the walls and furniture were adorned with pale-blue damask, but in the study – green. The window embrasures of the house were extremely deep and sofas were set out in them. The windows (what was then extremely rare) were single panes of Bohemian plate glass (each pane cost 700 paper roubles), and had the convenient quality that whilst from the rooms all was as superbly clear as if no glass intervened, from the streets in daytime nothing could be seen that was going on in the rooms, because the plate glass reflected the outside view, shutting out any interior view. . . . Count Osterman's house in Petersburg on the English Quay was probably the most magnificently furnished building in the capital at that time. The decorations of the White Chamber alone cost 46,000 roubles. [Six silver roubles were then equivalent to a pound sterling.][20] . . . On the internal walls stood on one side in a recess a full length statue (the work of Canova) of Emperor Alexander I, before which stood two censers in the form of large vases. In the four corners of the hall on tall pedestals stood busts of Peter I (as commander), Rumyantsev, Suvorov and Kutuzov. [Tolstoy served under the three latter generals, and his cousin Matvei Tolstoy married Kutuzov's daughter and heiress Praskovia.] The walls were set off with white marble and gold trophies; the floor was of ash with huge inlaid laurel wreaths; the room was illuminated by great chandeliers. On the side opposite the Emperor's statue was a gallery for musicians and singers, and an enormous fireplace. The gallery was shut off by two transparencies illustrating the two most important and decisive moments in Russia's war with Napoleon; the Battle of Leipzig and the Allies' entry into Paris. On a huge marble slab by the hearth stood the porcelain vase of Sèvres ware with its representation of the Battle of Kulm given to Osterman by the Emperor Alexander, and the golden goblet encrusted with precious stones presented to the victor of Kulm by the Bohemian and Hungarian magnates. . . . A marble slab bore statues (with features done from the life) of those two Pavlovsky grenadiers who supported and carried Osterman from the battle . . .

"The construction and ornamentation of the ballroom, for which Osterman gave a ball after its restoration in honour of the Grand Duchess Elena Pavlovna [the Emperor's sister], cost 200,000 paper roubles [about £8,300, the sum spent by George IV on the Banqueting Room at Brighton Pavilion].[21] All the other rooms were similarly splendid, and some were quite original. Thus in one room the walls were lined with felled logs making it appear like the interior of a peasant's house. In another stood a statue by Canova of the Count's wife in a seated position; and in another was Osterman's own monument by the same artist, designed by himself. He is represented lying back with his arm resting on a drum, as he was at the time of his operation, with the amputated arm lying beside him. A clock was set in the drum, whose hands indicated the moment at which he received his dreadful wound, and bore the Latin inscription: "*Vidit horam, nescit horam!*" ("He saw the hour, but did not know it"; *i.e.* the fatal moment cannot be anticipated.)

Count Tolstoy not only preserved a marble representation of the celebrated arm, but also the limb itself. It was kept in spirit for some years, and was then in 1818 the subject of an unusual ceremony. Accompanied by a number of priests, he went to the Sapozhovsky estate, an inheritance from his Osterman uncles, and solemnly buried his arm in the Osterman family vault as a tribute to his uncles' generosity.

Altogether, Osterman-Tolstoy's wealth was extraordinary even by the standards of the great aristocracy of the day. Apart from the St. Petersburg palace just described, he owned a similarly grand place in Moscow and great country estates where he resided in the summer. All these homes were filled with valuable furniture, paintings, gold and silver ornaments, and quantities of jewellery. He was very fond of contemporary Russian literature, and the library in his St. Petersburg mansion was particularly famous. He was exempted from the censorship, and possessed a remarkable collection of works on military history and science gathered for him by the celebrated Swiss strategist, General Jomini.

Colonel Dmitri Varfolomeevich Tolstoy

The entertainments provided by the Count were as splendid and unusual as the settings. He always dined at three o'clock in the afternoon precisely; on the stroke of three the doors were shut with military precision and no one, whatever his rank, was admitted thereafter. On weekdays about thirty people generally sat down together, and on Sundays twice that number The guests were not only obliged to wear full-dress uniform, but also to keep their shakos and cocked hats on their knees throughout the meal. Despite the formality, which simply maintained a splendour in keeping with the setting, the entertainment was relaxed and very agreeable. A characteristically eccentric touch was provided by the presence in the dining-hall of live eagles, which clung to the chandeliers and occasionally swooped over the heads of the diners. Also in attendance were the tame bears, faithful companions of his campaigns and now living in honourable retirement. Splendidly dressed in the Tolstoy livery, they stood to attention behind the guests, leaning on ceremonial halberds. Once, when the Count was irritated with the nobility of a certain province, he had the bears dressed up in the official uniform of that province.

Matvei Feodorovich Tolstoy c. *1790*

Count Nikolai Alexandrovich Tolstoy

Matvei Feodorovich Tolstoy c. *1810*

115

The company was as lively and interesting as the hosts. Prominent among them were old comrades of the glorious days of Eylau and Borodino: Osten-Sacken, Miloradovich and Paskevich. General Alexei Ermolov, however, did not appear. It was he to whom Tolstoy had handed over command at Kulm, and when Tolstoy received the St. George Cross afterwards he modestly urged that Ermolov should receive it instead. But a point of punctilio had driven them apart. Just before Count Tolstoy departed with Tsar Alexander to open the Polish parliament in 1818, he received a letter from Ermolov addressed to "the Commander of the Grenadier Corps, Count Osterman-Tolstoy". But Tolstoy had by then left that command, and sent back the letter with a stiff superscription, "General Ermolov ought to know that Count Osterman no longer commands the Grenadier Corps, and for this reason his letter is returned." Such matters were of high importance to the old warriors, who no longer had the French on whom to work off their extraordinary energies.

A much-loved friend was the artillery general, Kostenetsky. Every day the Count sent a carriage to fetch him, and every day the General declined it, insisting on walking whatever the weather. The military bee in his bonnet was a scheme for the introduction of steel ramrods into the Russian Army. On a notable occasion he had saved a battery, fighting single-handed against a party of the enemy. His only weapon had been a wooden ramrod, and he was frequently heard to lament the number he had broken over the French.

Another eccentric, though illustrious regular visitor was the Grand Duchess Maria Nikolaevna, who could never be brought to remember what had happened to the Count's left arm and was often heard asking where he could have put it.

After dinner there was smoking and chatting, piano and dancing. Then some of the young people might flock over the Moika Canal to the Bolshoi Theatre, to hear Semeonova sing in *Vestalka*, see Karatigin the great tragedian, or direct an opera glass at the pretty dancer Istomina, over whose lithe body half the young Guardsmen in Petersburg were quarrelling or duelling. The Count himself rarely or never attended the theatre, but kept a box there for the use of the ladies and one of the great stuffed armchairs in the pit for the young gentlemen.[22]

It is clear that these gatherings at the *palais Tolstoï* were far from being assemblies of veterans riding their hobby-horses. The Count was fond of the company of young people, and was in turn greatly beloved by his youthful relatives. There were the dashing young Galitzine princes, Valerian and Leonid; Alexei Petrovich Tolstoy, at just over twenty a veteran of the great battles of 1813 and father of an illegitimate son; and Ivan Matveevich Tolstoy, a young diplomat, brother-in-law to old Kutuzov's daughter and future Grand Marshal of the Court and Minister of Posts. The conversation was always lively and uninhibited, even touching on major political concerns of the day. On one occasion, when affairs of state were the subject of warm discussion among the young men, a high state functionary of a type not yet passed away, stiff and conceited, asked his host why it was that today young subalterns had the temerity to speak freely about great matters of state. "I'll tell you why," growled the one-armed General, who knew the dignitary to be a great prowler after actresses; "it is because state servants don't attend to state business, and it is only subalterns who concern themselves with *decent* matters."

Anything remotely dishonourable, particularly regarding the gentler sex, aroused the Count's unrelenting ire. Perhaps this arose from memories of his mother's kindness, which had done much to soften the effects of his father's cruelty. He always wore a miniature of her round his neck, and tears would start to his eyes when he spoke of her. Though he was fond of his wife Elizabeth, she was more often than not absent on account of continuing ill-health, and they had no children. He had an illegitimate daughter, Evdokia, who from her age appears however to have been conceived before his marriage in 1799. As ladies generally played a welcome part at his gatherings, the hostess in his wife's absence was often his niece Sophia Apraxin, daughter of that General Peter Tolstoy in whose Corps Osterman-Tolstoy had served in 1805.

In 1820 the Count was fifty, but still extremely handsome and fit. Abstemious in his tastes, he possessed an iron constitution. It was not unusual to see him inspecting troops, disdaining a greatcoat in several degrees of frost, or driving in an open calèche in midwinter. The *beau idéal* of all Petersburg, he was universally regarded with awe and affection. A newly-appointed general once asked him if he were not nervous of suffering an accident if, with his single arm, he were to be accidentally pushed in a crowd. The Count gave him a grim look. "People do not push me!" he replied curtly, firmly turning his back.

In some respects a virtual widower, it would be surprising if he had not been greatly admired by the ladies. He in turn nurtured deeply romantic feelings of chivalrous devotion towards them, unusual even in the age of Walter Scott. Many people likened his passions to those of mediaeval knights-errant. He adored beauty, kindness, gentleness and wit, but no breath of scandal touched his idealized attachments. Inside his uniform coat, whose medals bore permanent witness to the glories of Eylau, Ostrovno, Borodino and Kulm, the General would carry a precious flower bestowed on him by his latest Dulcinea. The flowers and Dulcineas changed from time to time, until he encountered a magnificent Polish beauty, Princess Teresa Yablonovska. His adoration knew no bounds, and he devoted himself to being her cavalier. Everywhere he went he took a fine full-length portrait of the Princess, which was hung in the place of honour. There was no hint of scandal in all this: the Count's noble character and enthusiastic loyalties were too well known; besides, "people do not push me!"

Only occasionally did his oddities arouse hostility, and then only through unfortunate misunderstandings. It happened, for example, that he required a coachman. A man was sent to him with excellent recommendations, but who proved on arrival to have a strikingly red beard. "I should like to take you on," explained Tolstoy apologetically, "but I can't stand red hair." "I was born like this," replied the coachman stoutly; "what can I do about it?" "Well," reflected the Count as he dismissed him, "you could go to General S—, who has succeeded in turning his hair black, and ask him to teach you the secret." Unhappily, next day the coachman appeared before General S—, explaining that "Count Osterman sends respects to Your Excellency and requests a recipe for changing the colour of my hair."

An even more regrettable misunderstanding was connected with Osterman-Tolstoy's beloved bears. One day he received through the post two letters: the first from a lady of his acquaintance announcing the death of her husband, and the second from an officer with whom he had placed a bear in care, who explained likewise that it had passed away. The Count, whose handwriting was almost illegible, dictated replies to each correspondent. Unfortunately he addressed neither by name, but simply began "dear friend" and continued with appropriate expressions of condolence. He signed the letters and told his amanuensis to seal them up, providing him with the addresses. By an understandable though most unhappy mischance, the officer shortly afterwards received condolences on the loss of a worthy husband; while the lady was shocked to read deeply-felt regrets for the departure of a beloved four-legged, furry companion, whose fierce growls and shambling dances must so often have entertained her.

But, all in all, those who knew Count Osterman in Tsar Alexander's golden days recalled most vividly his concern for the well-being of the troops under his command, his kindliness to his subordinates and to the young, and his unswerving honesty and sense of *noblesse oblige*. His splendid dinners; the bears and eagles; the delightful soirées, with Ivan Matveevich Tolstoy singing his French *chansonettes* at the piano, and the tireless Danish Ambassador Blum dancing his heart out; all these, with their *bonhomie*, style and the marked character and reflected glory of their host remained indelibly fixed in the memories of the participants. Half a century later a couple of them, now grown old, recorded memories as fresh as the events themselves.

For Osterman-Tolstoy, the Golden Age finished with the death of his admired master, Tsar Alexander I. His code of pure knightly loyalty included intense devotion to his Emperor, for whom he had fought many hard battles and received so many grievous wounds. When his master died on 19 November 1825, he decided that the new more authoritarian Russia would be no place for him. It was not only the character of the departed Tsar that he missed, but the condition of Russia under his successor that he disliked. He had publicly displayed his contempt for Tsar Alexander's unpleasantly authoritarian minister Arakcheev, though loyally, if irrationally, dissociating the minister from his master. Now the new Emperor Nicholas, Alexander's brother, suppressed the Decembrist uprising with insensitive harshness and provided every indication of running Russia on the lines of one of Arakcheev's loathed military colonies on the frontier.* Osterman-Tolstoy attached great importance to discipline and order, but his authority was always exerted with sincerely paternal interest in those for whom he bore responsibility. He had experienced poverty and cruelty in his youth, and can have felt only dislike for the harsh punishments visited on young officers.

And, accordingly the following year, when he was fifty-seven, he resolved to leave a Russia that was changing fast in ways he disliked. He is said to have made no disguise of his contempt for the new rulers of his country, departing suddenly instead of appearing at a solemn state ceremony, at which as one of Russia's most honoured generals he should have played a significant part.

The next five years were spent in Italy and Germany, where the Count retained many friends from his days of convalescence after 1813. Little is known of his movements at that time, though an old friend encountered him in his travelling-carriage crossing the Vistula at Dirschau in Pomerania in October 1827.[24] There was, however, another motive for his residence abroad than that of dislike for the policies of Nicholas I. It was whispered in St. Petersburg that "a great love" had drawn him from Russia to Italy; and it is true that, like Peter Tolstoy a century earlier, he had a beautiful Italian mistress.

* General Count Peter Tolstoy, Osterman-Tolstoy's brother-in-law, it was who took command of those colonies. He did not regard them with great enthusiasm, however, and was accused of "combining an indescribable indifference to all official business with an examplary, legendary laziness."[23]

As his wife was still living, though an ever-increasing valetudinarian (she suffered from dropsy), he had to take precautions to prevent the news reaching her. This should not have been difficult, as she continued to live in Russia when he took to his travels. On one occasion, though, his secret had to be preserved by a curious subterfuge. Whilst he was still in Italy his wife paid a visit to Paris to undergo medical treatment. Just then the Count found himself also obliged to travel to Paris "for an unexpected reason of the heart". Knowing his wife to be there, he took up quarters in an obscure *quartier* under the assumed name of Ivanov, and arranged for letters to be forwarded to the Countess as if from Italy. What can be said in extenuation of this tale is that it at least implies that Tolstoy conducted a regular correspondence with his wife.

Countess Osterman-Tolstoy

The Count's relationship with his mistress was lengthy and durable. In 1831, when he was at Munich, he resolved to fulfil a long-standing ambition to visit the Middle East. Perhaps arising from his service under Rumyantsev and Suvorov in Catherine the Great's time, he retained an eager interest in the affairs of the Turkish Empire. He was a close friend of Constantine Ribopier, formerly Ambassador in Constantinople, with whom he discussed the politics of the Sublime

Porte. He wished to see Wallachia and Moldavia (later Roumania) annexed by Russia, and Egypt and, above all, Greece given their independence. Like Lord Byron, he dreamed of leading the Greeks to freedom, and spent much time in St. Petersburg studying and speaking Greek.

For three years the General, who was now in his early sixties, roamed the East. He travelled in Greece, the Balkans, Asia Minor, Syria and Egypt accompanied by the German explorer, Jakob Fallmerayer. In 1831 the warlike Ibrahim Pasha invaded the Sultan's domains in Syria with an army from Egypt, and the victor of Kulm is said to have provided him with professional advice which was instrumental in securing the victory. If so, he was acting directly contrary to the interests of the Tsar, whose policy now consisted in propping up an enfeebled Turkey as a bastion against what Nicholas I saw as British and French penetration of the region. However it is not necessary to suppose that this consideration would have greatly troubled Count Tolstoy.

In Jerusalem the Count, a devout Orthodox Christian, prostrated himself with great emotion before the tomb of Our Lord. Travelling on to Egypt, he startled the inhabitants with his unusual life-style. He hired a large boat in order to sail down the Nile, on board which he carried a library of five hundred books. On deck was a large bust of Alexander I and also a small improvised chapel containing a rich display of ikons before which lamps glowed and incense smoked. As the vessel cruised slowly down the still stream, *fellahin* working on the banks glimpsed the tall angular figure kneeling and praying before his shrine. Deeply awestruck by the floating apparition, they presumed him to be an Imam of a particularly devout sect, and described him reverently as the One-armed Slave of God.

In Constantinople Osterman-Tolstoy called to pay his respects on the Sultan Mahmud II. After an exchange of compliments, the Sultan remarked on the curious stick on which Tolstoy was leaning: it was extremely thick, heavy, and bore as its knob a realistically-carved representation of a skull. Mahmud asked what was its significance? Tolstoy was not overawed; he had after all once seen thirty thousand of the Turk's compatriots floating in the Danube. "*Hodie mihi, cras tibi,*" he replied, and translated, "today for me, tomorrow for you". Then, in case the Sultan had not received the message, he expounded further. "Although you've had a great many heads chopped off in your time, your own head will without fail one day come to resemble the top of my stick, and maybe a great deal sooner than you think."

The allusion was clearly to Mahmud's notorious massacre of his Janissaries in 1826, but the Sultan was too taken aback to take offence and ordered his distinguished visitor to be treated with the greatest courtesy.

In 1835 Osterman-Tolstoy returned to Italy and his lady-love. It was in October, soon after his arrival at his beautiful villa in Florence, that he received to his surprise a letter from the Emperor Ferdinand of Austria.

"My dear Count Osterman-Tolstoy. The Emperor my father [Francis] had resolved to dedicate a monument to the memory of the Russian Guards whose heroic resistance halted the advance of the French Corps of General Vandamme, on 29 August 1813. It has been reserved for me to fulfil my late father's intention, and you will assuredly be moved to learn that on 29 September last the Emperor, your august master, His Majesty the King of Prussia, and I laid the first stone of this monument.

"We regretted on this solemn occasion the absence of him who in that glorious fight commanded the brave Russian troops, and whose name is henceforth inseparable from the day we have just commemorated. To compensate a little for this, I am sending you the medal which I have had struck for the occasion. You will feel some pleasure in receiving this reminder of a day so glorious for you, for your brave comrades in arms, for the Sovereign whom you served at the cost of your blood. I ask you to keep it also as testimony of the feelings of high regard which my late father held for you and which I share equally. Ferdinand, Emperor."

The medal, a very fine one, bore a representation of the finished design of the monument.[25]

Tsar Nicholas had in fact invited Tolstoy to attend the ceremony, but for some reason he had declined under various pretexts. It cannot have been the length of the journey that dissuaded him, as within a month or so he returned to Russia and stayed briefly on his country estate in the province of Mogilev. There he received a much greater award; an officer arrived from St. Petersburg with an exceptionally gracious Imperial letter of congratulation and a packet containing the insignia of Russia's highest order of chivalry, the St. Andrew. According to a semi-official account, Osterman-Tolstoy was highly gratified by this mark of distinction; but another version has it that he never bothered to open the parcel.[26]

His wife Elizabeth died about the time of Tolstoy's return from the Middle East, in April 1835, and the General was able to set up a permanent home with his mistress. An engraving made in Pisa in 1827 portrays him seated on a bench with

his pipe in his hand; on his left is a cradle with a sleeping baby, and on his right two boys are playing with a lamb. An inscription below includes the words "At 55 it is time to settle down."[27]

Eventually, though, his innate sense of chivalry put a term to his well-earned domestic contentment. He became increasingly convinced that the disparity in age was making his young mistress's position dangerously vulnerable, and insisted despite great sadness of heart in bestowing her in marriage on a young, handsome Italian, together with a large dowry. He provided the children with first-class educations, and arranged generously for their future – so generously that he was obliged to fell forests on the Osterman estates near Moscow. His young friends united in attributing to him the ideal qualities of a father. "In the heart of this stern-seeming man there frequently sounded tender chords."

In 1837, perhaps withdrawing from halcyon scenes now grown painful, General Osterman-Tolstoy retired to Geneva. There he passed his last twenty years in the old Swiss town by its deep blue lake. Strategically placed on the high road from France to Italy, it attracted some thirty thousand visitors a year and a number of permanent settlers from abroad who found "among the upper classes, a very agreeable society, including many individuals distinguished for their literary and scientific acquirements."[29] Apart from a few friends of older and happier days, however, the old Count lived a solitary existence. All the Allied sovereigns he had served so well had passed away, as had their arch-enemy Napoleon. Suvorov and Kutuzov, Barclay and Bennigsen, had died long before; and when in 1850 he reached the age of eighty few among the French and English tourists who saw the old, one-armed gentleman walking slowly with the aid of his stout stick along the ramparts above the lake would have recalled the brave days of Borodino and Kulm. Another world had arrived, one which saw Russian armies under a different Tsar and new generals humiliated in the Crimea. By the citizens of Geneva, however, he was regarded with respectful and proprietary pride.

To Russian callers he appeared now to be ageing fast. But he never repined or lamented the past, and his memory (what memories!) appeared clear as ever. His study remained a shrine to his beloved Emperor, with every conceivable representation of the late Tsar Alexander – portraits, busts, medallions – covering the walls and furniture. He lived there in the past, reading over and over again the poetry of Derzhavin, favourite writer of his youth in Catherine the Great's reign. "My Bible," he always called the well-thumbed volume. He would never speak of the new Russia which had replaced the one he knew before 1825. "What do you do with yourself these days?" a visitor enquired politely. "I turn my back on Mont Blanc," grunted the veteran, who for some idiosyncratic reason generally sat in an armchair backing onto the most breath-taking view in Europe.

But his interest in young people remained. "When he lived at Geneva," wrote an old friend who had known him in the days of his glory, "his favourite company was that of the local students. His pronounced, youthful features, with their spare, old-fashioned lines and black expressive eyes under black brows, were most striking. How wonderfully handsome he used to be, for all his missing arm, in his adjutant-general's uniform at the court of the Tsar!"[30]

At the beginning of 1857 the Count, now nearly eighty-seven years old, fell very ill. It was hoped by his family and friends that his vigorous constitution would pull him through. But age and innumerable wounds had taken their toll. The Grand Duke Michael Nikolaevich called to pay his respects, but the man who had preserved his uncle's throne was already unconscious. In February 1857 he died peacefully in his daughter's arms, with his son-in-law and grandchildren weeping at the bedside. His body lies buried in Switzerland, and only his arm remains in the country of his ancestors.

5
"The American"

One of the most celebrated Russian duellists, Count de Tolstoy, having quarrelled with a naval officer, sent him a challenge, which was declined on the plea of the Count's dexterity in the use of arms. Tolstoy then proposed that they should fight with pistols muzzle to muzzle, but this also the sailor declined, and insisted upon fighting according to what he called a naval manner, which was to seize each other and jump into the water, the victory being awarded to the party that escaped drowning. The Count in his turn objected to the proposal, on the plea that he could not swim, on which his adversary accused him of cowardice, when the Count rushed upon him, seized him, and threw himself with him into the sea. They were both, however, drawn out of the water, but the naval officer was so much injured that he died a few days after".[1]

The principal in this bizarre encounter was Feodor Ivanovich Tolstoy, universally known to his contemporaries as "the American". His cousin Leo, the great author, met him as a young man and described him as "an extraordinary personality, criminal and attractive". His cousin's contradictory character fascinated him, and he introduced him into the story *Two Hussars*, and as a factor in the personality of Dolokhov in *War and Peace*.[2] Feodor's eccentricities and adventures made him a byword even in the remarkable period (the Napoleonic wars and their aftermath) in which he lived.

All contemporaries were agreed that Feodor Tolstoy was astonishingly able, and he enjoyed the friendship and respect of Pushkin, Goncharov, Viazemsky and others of that brilliant constellation of writers who crowded the early decades of the nineteenth century. One gains the impression that the elemental energy which in Leo Tolstoy outpoured itself in pure artistic genius, was in Feodor somehow obstructed so that it burst irresistibly forth in different directions.

Feodor's father, Ivan Andreevich, was born in 1747, served with distinction in the army and was Marshal of the Nobility of Kologriv. His wife Anna came of an old but modestly circumstanced family, and they led an honourable and respected existence in their province. There was certainly nothing about either of them to suggest that their son would prove to be the wildest man in the Russian Empire, and it seems that in a strong-blooded race the current can trace a regular course for a generation or so before bursting its banks or erupting in a cataract.

Feodor was born on 6 February 1782 and brought up in the free atmosphere of a country estate. As his father was away in the army, it may be suspected that he lacked discipline, though not more so than most of his fellows. A childhood anecdote is recorded alleging his revolting cruelty in torturing frogs. It is hard to know what to make of this tale. Boys can be very unfeeling, but presumably the source of the story must have been Tolstoy himself, who was prone to delight in shocking people. He was certainly very violent in later life, but not noticeably cruel.

At an early age he was entered for the St. Petersburg Naval Academy, but graduated not into the Imperial Navy but into the crack Preobrazhensky Guards. One who knew him well described him as "a dangerous madcap, because he shot superbly with a pistol, fenced as well as Severbek [a well known fencing-master of the time], and fought professionals with the sabre." With all this he was unswervingly courageous and, notwithstanding his fiery nature, self-possessed in battle or duel. He was "an eccentric, possessing that peculiar nature which is quite outside

Previous page: Sketch of Feodor Ivanovich Tolstoy, by Pushkin

normal behaviour, and at all times flew to extremes. Whatever anyone else did, he did ten times over. Then that was the mode amongst young people, but Count Tolstoy carried it to desperation." His propensity for going further than anyone else was taken quite literally; he soared above the earth with the famous balloonist Garnerin, and sailed round the world with the explorer Kruzenstern.

These extravagances began very early in his career. In September 1798, at the age of sixteen, he was commissioned as an officer in his Regiment. But six months later he was temporarily assigned to the drudgery of garrison duty in an inferior unit as a punishment for some unrecorded misdemeanour. Back with his regiment, he continued his wild existence of drinking, gambling, womanizing and extravagant exploits of every sort. The first of which any detail has survived was a duel with his commanding officer, Colonel Baron Drizen. A poem by his friend, the future partisan hero and poet Denis Davydov, provides allusions no longer clear:

> Tolstoy says nothing: is he drunk?
> Has he triggered it off again?
> No, my dear boor,
> He would have put paid to Drizen.
> I would long ago have read that Drizen
> "has been removed from the records".
> So it seems he has not received
> The attentions of Tolstoy's toothpicks,
> And it seems my Tolstoy is not drunk.[3]

One may surmise that not all the blame lay with the younger man from the fact that the Colonel agreed to the encounter, and from Tolstoy's apparent immunity from punishment. For he was still in the uniform of the Preobrazhensky Guards when shortly afterwards he took part in the adventure which was to provide him with his nickname and extend his notoriety throughout the Empire.

In 1803 the Russian-American Company, which controlled trade and settlements on the Pacific coasts of Siberia and Alaska, had suffered some severe setbacks. Natives had sacked the Russian fort on Sitka Island and massacred the garrison; the newly-built ship *St. Dmitri* had been lost off Umnak Island, and British and American traders were making dangerous inroads into the fur trade. All these misfortunes arose from the difficulties of maintaining supplies over the vast land-mass of Siberia, and the Company, with the support of Tsar Alexander I, decided to fit out two large ships in the Baltic and despatch them by sea to the Far East. The ships were bought in London: the *Leander*, rechristened the *Nadezhda*, and the *Thames*, renamed the *Neva*. The expedition was to be commanded by an experienced sea-captain, Ivan Kruzenstern.

By the spring of 1803 both ships were anchored off Kronstadt. The Tsar at this stage decided to enlarge the original aim of the voyage and despatched on board an embassy to the Japanese court, which had hitherto been chary of Russian overtures, but might by a bold stroke of this sort be persuaded to accept a mission. To ensure the emissary's prestige he was appointed a suitable suite. Amongst those it was proposed to include in this train was Feodor Ivanovich's first cousin, Feodor Petrovich Tolstoy. Feodor Petrovich was a year younger than Feodor Ivanovich, and had also studied at the Naval Academy. But he had already discovered those artistic gifts that were to raise him to the foremost rank as painter, sculptor and medallist, and declined the honour.[4] The Emperor appears to have thought that one Tolstoy would do as well as another, and Feodor Ivanovich was appointed in his stead. This proved to be a serious mistake. A further error lay in the categorization of Tolstoy as "politely educated".

The *Nadezhda* and *Neva* sailed from Kronstadt on 26 July 1803. Tolstoy, in his uniform as a Lieutenant in the Preobrazhensky Guards, sailed on board the *Nadezhda*, under Kruzenstern's own command. The ships put in successively at Helsingfors, Copenhagen and Falmouth, and then made out into the Atlantic. After a stay in the Canaries they crossed the Equator on 14 November, being the first Russian ships ever to display the flag in the Southern Hemisphere. A sailor disguised as Neptune made his appearance, but Kruzenstern forbade the other ceremonies usual on European ships for fear of encouraging indiscipline. In the event, however, it proved to be not the sailors but an officer who endangered good order on board.

Off Brazil the ships were delayed for seven weeks while the *Neva*'s damaged masts were replaced, and preparations were made for the hazardous journey round Cape Horn. It was not until 3 March 1804 that they appeared in the Pacific, having survived ferocious breakers off Patagonia and a near-collision with a school of twenty whales. In May the *Nadezhda* dropped anchor at Nuku Hiva in the Marquesas. The ship was soon surrounded by hundreds of naked islanders swimming and sporting in the waters around her hull, and holding up coconuts, bananas, and breadfruit for barter. Amongst them was an Englishman, named Roberts, naked and bronzed as the rest, who had lived for seven years on this island paradise with a native wife.

In due course the King of Nuku Hiva paid his state visit to the representative of the Tsar. He was not quite as naked as his subjects, as he sported a belt. He was a well-built, good-looking man aged about forty-five, whose whole body from head to foot was covered with intricate tattoos. Good relations were soon established with the Russians, and Kruzenstern shortly afterwards paid a visit to the King's court, where he met also his beautiful daughter. The inhabitants were polite and friendly with their unexpected visitors, but appeared to subsist in a state of permanent warfare with the neighbouring islands. More menacing in Kruzenstern's eyes was the arrival one day of more than a hundred naked girls swimming round and simulating in the most inviting way certain delights awaiting the sailors. As far as was possible the dangerous women were kept at bay, though the susceptible Tolstoy is believed to have found an opportunity of closer acquaintance.

Large numbers of sailors had themselves tattooed during their stay, and Tolstoy seized the occasion of having his body permanently inscribed with the most intricate designs. By some means he acquired an extraordinary ascendancy over the hospitable King of Nuku Hiva, whom he trained to run by his side on all fours like a dog. Shouting "Fetch, fetch!" Tolstoy would throw a piece of wood into the sea, whereupon His Majesty would dash in and come gambolling back with the trophy between his teeth.

There was a Frenchman living completely wild on the island, who was said to associate with cannibals. Though he could not have known of the recent rupture of the Peace of Amiens, he kept up the vast struggle reawakening on the other side of the globe by entertaining bitter emnity towards Roberts the Englishman, the only other European resident in Nuku Hiva.

A native of Nuku-Hiva

The two ships sailed on to the Sandwich Islands (now Hawaii), where after a brief stay they parted company. Because of the delays caused in rounding the Horn it had been decided to visit the Russian colonies first, and pay the state visit to Japan afterwards. The *Neva* made for Kodiak Island off the coast of Alaska, and engaged in the reconquest of Sitka, while the *Nadezhda* sailed direct to Kamchatka where she arrived in mid-July. They had now been nearly a year at sea, and it is clear that Tolstoy's restless spirit had chafed at the confined existence on board ship. True, he had amused himself with the King of Nuku Hiva and some of his fairer subjects, but in general his rôle as a sort of junior military escort to the Japanese embassy left him with nothing but time on his hands.

His pranks and excesses tried even the endurance of the patient Kruzenstern. There was, for example, an old priest, Father Gedeon, on board to provide spiritual solace to the ship's company. His weakness was that he was overfond of the bottle. One one occasion Tolstoy joined him in a drinking bout, which ended with the priest flat on his back and sound asleep. Tolstoy then proceeded to stick the old man's beard to the deck with a large blob of wax, on which he impressed the Captain's seal which he had purloined from his cabin. When the poor priest awoke Tolstoy warned him to take care not to break the great seal, with its official two-headed eagle, lest he commit treason. In the end it was the beard that had to be cut off and left sealed to the deck.

Feodor Tolstoy took with him on the voyage an ape, described later by a cousin as "an orang-outang, clever, agile and enterprising as a human". He was inordinately fond of this pet, and it was later alleged that it became one of his innumerable mistresses. Be that as it may, the ape was certainly highly intelligent and

127

active. When Kruzenstern was on shore, presumably at Hawaii, Tolstoy and his ape tiptoed into his cabin. There the irresponsible young nobleman took out a stack of the Captain's notebooks and other writing materials, set them on the table and placed a clean sheet on the top. This he proceeded to blot and stain with ink, then screwed it up and placed it in his pocket. The ape watched attentively, and when the Count left the cabin set to work on the remaining papers. When Kruzenstern returned he found his strange visitor had destroyed most of his valuable records.

For a time the goodnatured Captain turned a blind eye to such escapades, and other excesses of drinking and gambling. But when a devil in Tolstoy set him working up mischief between Kruzenstern and Lisiansky, Captain of the sister-ship *Neva*, patience began to run thin. And then, when he went on to develop a taste for stirring up mutiny among the men, it was clear matters had come to a head. Kruzenstern had already on a previous occasion placed Tolstoy under arrest; now he gave him a sterner warning. "You are playing a dangerous game, Count; do not forget that I enjoy absolute power on board this ship: unless you alter your ways I shall be obliged to have you thrown in the sea!"

"What of it?" replied Tolstoy placidly; "the sea is as pleasant a place to be buried as the land." He could not bring himself to stop preaching revolution to the embarrassed sailors, and the Captain summoned him yet again. "Count," he repeated, "you are disturbing the ship's company and derogating from my authority. If you do not give me your word to conduct yourself correctly I will set you down on an uninhabited island – there is one in sight."

"Well, well!" cried out Tolstoy, "it seems you're trying to scare me! Throw me in the sea, or dump me on a desert island – it's all the same to me. But I am afraid that as long as I'm on board this ship I'll just have to go on stirring up trouble against you."

There was nothing for it but to implement the threat. Kruzenstern's official account states simply that "a trifling change took place in the suite of our ambassa-dor: Count Tolstoy, lieutenant of his Imperial Majesty's guards . . . quitted the ship, and set out from hence for St. Petersburgh." The full story was more complex. According to one account a ruse had to be adopted to prevent any resistance on the part of the unruly Count. The ship's company had all disem-barked on a deserted stretch of coastline when the signal to return on board was given unexpectedly soon. Tolstoy had gone for a stroll with his friend the ape and had to watch the ship set sail without him. He raised his hat and bowed with ostentatious politeness to the departing Kruzenstern, then turned to prepare himself for his new existence. A supply of food had been left for him on the beach.

Tolstoy found his way to another island, where he lived for months in the wilds, taking up with the Tlingit natives and living as one of them. He asserted later that they tried to persuade him to become their Tsar; it was probably fortunate for them that he did not take up the offer. He accompanied the hunters of the tribe on their expeditions, and became adept with harpoon and bow as he had been with foil or sabre. It is hard to believe he led a life of celibacy, though the Tlingit women lacked the attractions of their Sandwich Islands sisters: their principal adornment was a bone sewn through the lower lip.[5] Still, there was always the ape – if he had not eaten it as he claimed on one occasion later (he denied this to another friend). At one point he was captured by hostile tribesmen who wished to sacrifice him to their idol by the nutritive process of eating him. As he was

Kruzenstern at Petropavlovsk

waiting, tied up, for the repast to begin, fierce shrieks announced the appearance of a rival tribe. Tolstoy remained a not impartial onlooker as a bloody battle ensued. Fortunately the newcomers were triumphant, though the Count's troubles were not over when he found himself this time worshipped as an idol himself; like Captain Good in *King Solomon's Mines*, on account of "his beautiful white legs".

Another incident made a strong impression on his mind. One dark night when tramping on foot alone in the wild interior, he felt himself utterly lost. Suddenly he saw before him the radiant vision of a heavenly being motioning him to turn back the way he had come. He obeyed, and in consequence his life was saved. Afterwards he noticed from his improvised calendar that it was 12 December (1804), and that the saint must therefore have been St. Spyridon, patron of all the Tolstoy family. As soon as he returned to Moscow he had an image of the saint made which he always wore on his chest. (The historic cross of the family, now held by my father as its head, is said to contain a relic of St. Spyridon. May it continue to protect us for another six hundred years!)

As the winter drew on Tolstoy tired of his primitive existence and eventually decided to return to civilization. He attracted a passing ship by lighting a bonfire on the beach, and was transported to the port of Petropavlovsk on the Kamchatka mainland. Thence he made his way on horseback, by boat, and on foot (when out of funds) across the whole length of Siberia. By June of 1805 he had reached the province of Kazan.[6]

Somewhere in the vast wastes of Siberia he encountered a drunken old man, probably a political or criminal exile, who sang doggerel verses piteously to the sound of his balalaika. Afterwards Tolstoy used to recall that "rarely in the theatre or concert-hall had he been so deeply moved as by that absurd song". One is reminded of the poet Alexei Tolstoy's similar enthusiasm for the song of a wandering Kirghiz herdsman. In the province of Kazan his arrival was recorded by an eyewitness, who recalled his amazement at encountering the wild figure, tattooed from head to foot and dressed in the weather-stained uniform of the Preobrazhensky Guards, in which apparently he had led the Tlingit on their walrus-hunts.

"He surprised us by his appearance. His head bore a crop of thick, curly black hair; his eyes, probably as a result of the heat and dust, appeared bloodshot; his rather melancholy expression appeared troubled and his very quiet manner of speaking frightened my companion. I don't understand why I didn't feel the least fear, but on the contrary a strong attraction. He stayed a little while with us, when he talked in a very normal though extremely plain manner of speech, but so intelligently that I felt disappointed that he was leaving and not going on with us. Possibly he noticed this, as he was warmer towards me than the others and on the road gave me some currant syrup, asserting that he would no longer need it now he was approaching civilization."

Feodor Tolstoy's extraordinary adventures attracted universal interest for the rest of his life, though at the moment of his return all eyes were fixed on the war raging in Central Europe where Russia's armies had gone to the aid of Austria. He delighted in memories of his life among the Alaskan savages, and his apartments were decorated with specimens of their wares and weapons. A hundred anecdotes of his relations with Kruzenstern and, above all, the ape were circulated in Petersburg drawing-rooms. One favourite story was however a little *ben trovato*, or at least distorted. It was said that on the very day of Tolstoy's return to the capital he learned that Kruzenstern was giving a ball. Clothing his tattooed body in evening dress, he appeared in the hall. Kruzenstern could scarcely believe his eyes."Count Tolstoy, can it be you?" "As you see," replied "The American" drily, "I was so happy on the island where you dumped me that I quite forgave you, and have come here to thank you." As Kruzenstern returned to Russia after Tolstoy this account cannot be accurate, though the incident may have perhaps occurred sometime after *Kruzenstern's* return in 1806 and Tolstoy's reappearance in Moscow.

As the years passed Tolstoy's own memories became a little confused. When in 1842 the newspapers were filled with accounts of friction between the British and French in the South Pacific, the old Count observed that he had reason to believe that the current Queen Pomare of Tahiti was his daughter.[7] In fact the *Nadezhda* never sailed near Tahiti.

However amused society may have been by Tolstoy's extravagances, his superiors were not. On 10 August 1805 he was posted to the St. Petersburg reserve, and soon after that despatched to garrison duty at the remote fortress of Nyslott in the Finnish lakes. For over two years he eked out a depressed existence in that beautiful but lonely spot, all his superabundant energies being directed towards escaping the dreary solitude. All overtures were however in vain, until in February 1808 Tsar Alexander, instigated by Napoleon, declared war on Sweden. The intention was to conquer Swedish Finland, thus removing the frontier from what was seen as its dangerous proximity to St. Petersburg. An old friend, General Prince Mihael Dolgorukov, was appointed commander of the military district around, and bore sufficient influence in high quarters to enable Tolstoy to be attached to his staff. The Prince was greatly tickled by "The American's" skilfully-related tales, and always dined with him, calling him "Uncle Fedya".

Tolstoy's coolness and bravery in the field proved as remarkable as that displayed in his private exploits. At the battle of Idensalm, in October 1808, the General saw a swift opportunity of seizing a bridge lying opposite the Swedish lines.

"In order not to allow them time to take the bridge, the Prince ordered his adjutant Count Tolstoy to take some Cossacks and engage the nearest Swedish dragoons," wrote a friend who was present. Behind Tolstoy doubled two companies of light infantry and one of sappers. The Cossacks galloped furiously for the bridge, arriving just in time to hold it under heavy fire long enough for the pioneers to complete the work of destruction.

Bridge at Idensalm

Soon afterwards, however, Prince Dolgorukov was struck lifeless by a cannon ball. Tolstoy and the other aides-de-camp mournfully accompanied his cortège to St. Petersburg,[8] but despite his gallantry at Idensalm, "the American" was still forbidden to stay in the capital. Immediately after the Prince's funeral he was seconded to a battalion of his old regiment, the Preobrazhensky Guards, stationed at Åbo in the southwest of Finland. There he swiftly distinguished himself once again. Prince Galitzine, his commander, ordered him to reconnoitre the Sound separating Finland from Sweden. With a small escort of Cossacks Tolstoy rode the length and breadth of the frozen straits, once again a lonely figure in a vast empty landscape. He returned with a very full report, in which he pressed his view that the passage was difficult but not impossible, and that at any rate the Swedes were certainly not expecting an attack from that direction. It was on the basis of this report that General Barclay de Tolly launched his brilliant attack across the frozen Gulf of Bothnia, capturing the Åland Islands and landing forces on the Swedish mainland which menaced the capital Stockholm. Sweden was compelled to sue for peace in the spring of 1809, and Finland passed into Russian hands.

Dolgorukov memorial at Idensalm

Tolstoy's gallantry at the victory of Idensalm and his decisive part in Barclay's feat in the Sound would have earned him reinstatement and promotion, but the wild, destructive streak in his nature reasserted itself once again. In garrison at Åbo in 1809 he fought two notorious duels, the first with a Captain Brunov, and the second with a young Life Guards officer named Alexander Naryshkin, whose ancestors had been at such bitter loggerheads with Tolstoy's Miloslavsky forebears in the seventeenth century. Accounts differ in detail, with talk of a pretty Swedish girl, slanderous rumours and the like. The most detailed version puts it down to an absurd misunderstanding over a mild pun.

A group of officers used to gather in Tolstoy's quarters to play cards of an evening, amongst whom was young Naryshkin. One night it was warm enough to encourage the players to leave off their coats. In the course of a game Naryshkin asked Tolstoy to give him an ace. Tolstoy put down his cards, rolled up his shirtsleeves and, exhibiting a knotty fist, retorted with a grin: "As you wish!" He was playing on the word *tuz*, which in Russian means either an ace or a box on the ear. Naryshkin flared up at what he took to be an insult, threw down his cards and crying "Very well then, I'll give you a punch!" flung himself out of the room. Alarmed at the implication, the others present persuaded Tolstoy to write explaining that it was all a joke, but in vain. As Naryshkin explained, if anyone else had made such a joke he would have laughed with the rest, but it was impossible to back down before Russia's most famous duellist without risking rumours of cowardice. He would fight. At the duelling-ground Naryshkin announced his intention of killing his adversary. "As for that," replied Tolstoy, as they raised their pistols, "here's for you!" Naryshkin was struck in the side and died three days later.

It cannot have been difficult for tempers to flare, given the tedium of garrison life and the strict code of honour of the period. The Government, however, strongly disapproved of duelling, and Feodor Tolstoy was arrested and incarcerated in the fortress of Viborg. An anecdote tells of his endless pleas for release, in which he fastened on every quasi-legal quibble imaginable to persuade the commandant to review his case. But it was in vain, and not until 2 October 1811 was he dismissed the service and retired to live on his estate in Kaluga. Presumably he was still forbidden to attend the capital, and very likely time hung heavy on his hands. It did not do so for many months. On 24 June 1812 the Grand Army crossed the Niemen, and Napoleon began his advance on Moscow.

Feodor Tolstoy, who was no longer a serving officer (it is not clear whether he was cashiered in 1811, though he is said to have been degraded to the ranks eleven times in all), volunteered for service in the Moscow militia. After the great battle of Borodino an old friend was standing by the central battery when "he heard that someone was looking for a certain Colonel Count Tolstoy. It appeared that it was my old friend, at that moment commander of a detachment of militia. He had gone up out of curiosity to the outposts to look at the French. . . . We only succeeded in exchanging a few words and recalled Prince Dolgorukov. Telling me where and what his command was he rushed on to his command. On the 28th [after the battle] I heard from one of the wagons the Count's voice summoning his man, who was some way off. I went up to find the Count was wounded in the leg: he offered me some Madeira."

At about the same time General Ermolov also saw Tolstoy lying in his cart, and had difficulty in recognizing him such was his condition. To prove that he really was wounded, Tolstoy ripped the bandage from his leg and allowed the blood to stream out. Ermolov was sufficiently impressed to arrange for Feodor Ivanovich to be appointed full Colonel. For his bravery in the battle he also received the Cross of St. George.[9]

After the campaign was over Tolstoy set up home in Moscow, where he was lionized by large sections of society. He was famous as a war hero, and notorious for his duelling, gambling and womanizing, for his tattooing, his ape, and his adventures in Alaska. He was in addition witty, charming and gifted with great intelligence and creativity. He was accordingly popular with both men and women, though some of the former must have shied away from his ferocious reputation as a duellist. He is credibly reported to have killed eleven men in these encounters, which must imply that the total number fought was greater still.

A great friend of these Moscow days was Peter Alexandrovich Nashchokin. The friendship began in a characteristically eccentric way. "There was a hellish deep play at the club. Eventually everyone had left excepting Tolstoy and Nashchokin, who remained at the card-table. When they came to settle accounts, Tolstoy explained that the other owed him twenty thousand roubles. 'No, I won't pay,' said Nashchokin, 'you wrote that down, but I didn't lose it.' 'Maybe that is so, but I am used to going by what is written down, as I shall prove,' replied the Count. He stood up, shut the door, placed a pistol on the table and added: 'It's loaded: are you paying or not?' 'No.' 'I'll give you ten minutes for reflexion.'

Nashchokin took his watch out of his pocket, then a pocket-book, and replied, 'The watch is worth maybe five hundred roubles, and in the pocket-book there are twenty-five paper roubles; that's all you will get if you kill me. But to the police you will have to pay not just a thousand to escape punishment. How much do you get by killing me?' 'Good fellow!' cried out Tolstoy, grasping his hand. 'At last I have found a man!'"

They embraced and henceforward became fast friends. For the rest of their lives they were almost inseparable, revelling together, joining each other for the occasional term in prison, and arranging great hunts on their estates in the country. Accompanied by hundreds of huntsmen and an enormous pack of hounds they would spend all day in the saddle. When the evening drew on all would resort to the nearest gentleman's park, set up tents on the lawns or in the courtyard, and spend all night in drunken carousals. The surprise and alarm of the landowner may be imagined.

Tolstoy carried loyalty to his friend to extravagant lengths. One night, in Tolstoy's house, playing cards and drinking hard as usual, Nashchokin broke out into a quarrel with one of the other players. Words soon threatened actions, and a duel was arranged for the next morning. Tolstoy, of course, was to be his second. Next morning at the appointed time Nashchokin came to his friend's room, to find him still in bed with a half-empty bottle of rum by his side. After taking a glass himself, he reminded the Count that they were late for their appointment. "Well, it may be you that is late," laughed Tolstoy, sitting up. "What! You are insulted under my roof and imagine I'll allow you to become involved in a duel? I alone had the right to avenge you; you arranged to meet this young fellow at eight, but I fought with him at six. He is dead."[10]

With all these anecdotes of Tolstoy "the American" it must be remembered that there are elements of exaggeration or transposition, and that Tolstoy himself delighted in outraging public opinion and shocking susceptible people. Leo Tolstoy used to recall another gambling story of his wild cousin. "Count," he was accused by another player, "you are cheating, and I shall play no more with you." "Of course I am cheating," agreed Feodor Tolstoy, amiably, "but I don't like being told so. Play on, or I'll crack your skull with this candelabrum." His opponent politely continued playing – and won.

Tolstoy was proud of his skill at cheating, and held that it was quite legitimate provided he was not detected. "Only idiots rely on luck," he used to remark confidently: and, on another occasion, "I correct Fortune's mistakes!" But to a true friend who invited him to play, he excused himself: "No, *mon cher*, I'm too fond of you for that. If we played, my instinct would oblige me to trust to something more than luck."

Feodor Ivanovich was also renowned as a gastronome. The writer Bulgarin, a close friend, noted that "He did not offer his guests an excessive number of courses, but each course was a superlative specimen of the culinary art. He always bought the food himself. Several times he took me with him, asserting that the finest mark of culture was choice of provisions, and that good food ennobled the belly's lining, from which intelligence itself springs. For instance, he only bought fish from the fishmonger's aquarium which swam strongly; that is to say the lively ones. The quality of meat he knew by the colour, etc."

His wit, as might be expected, could take a sardonic turn. Of some unfavoured character he remarked, "I see he is rather swarthy and black-haired, but by comparison with his soul he seems quite blond." At the fashionable and exclusive English Club he gazed across the dining-table, fascinated by a gentleman with an exceedingly ripe, red nose. His fascination with the protuberance grew as he noticed that the man drank only water. "There's a hypocrite!" he exclaimed; "how dare he sport such an undeserved decoration on his face?"[11]

It is tempting to judge him by the standards of our quite different age and consider him a madman, bully, and even murderer. That would not only be anachronistic, but would oblige us to ignore the testimony of many sensitive friends and acquaintances, among them the most gifted men of the age. With Prince Viazemsky, Denis Davydov and other poets and bons-vivants he founded a dining club, similar to the contemporary English Beef Steak Society, known as the Knights of the Corks. Suitable anthems were composed, with refrains such as:

> A merry din, singing and laughter,
> Swapping of bottles and talk,
> Devoting themselves just to frolic
> Our band of revelling folk!

Verses were composed for individual members, and Tolstoy's was suitably complimentary:

> And here's to our American who,
> On Borodino's glorious field
> Bravely bore your warrior's wound,
> And high your bayonet did wield!
> In memorial of which St. George
> Adorns your martial manly breast.
> In our pacific brotherly orgies
> With Denis you're one of the best!

The allusion was to Denis Davydov, also a hero of 1812.

In 1823 the playwright Griboyedov completed his celebrated work *Gore ot Uma*, or "the wretchedness of being clever". A brilliant satire on Russian intellectual life, its public performance was prohibited by censorship. The author held frequent private readings, however, at one of which those present included Pushkin and Feodor Tolstoy. At this sitting Griboyedov read aloud the whole comedy with a few omissions, and the ovation at the end was rapturous. The satire was so brilliant and apt, that all recognized to the life aspects and characters of current Russian life. A certain Zhikharev, gifted with little tact but an excellent memory, insisted on reciting a passage the author had chosen to omit. In this a character named Repetilov describes a notorious figure:

> No such head to be found in all Russia
> (No need to name it, you'll see by the likeness):
> Nocturnal bandit and duellist,
> Packed off to Kamchatka, came back by the Aleutians,
> Does not play a very straight hand;
> Clever maybe, though secretly a rogue:
> When of honesty strongly he speaks,
> You're reminded of some kind of demon:
> With bloodshot eyes and burning face,
> He weeps . . . and we're all in sobs.

The host and other guests sat aghast at this crass piece of tactless behaviour, for there among them sat "the American" himself, "a man who would kill someone as lightly as he would cheat at cards or drink a glass of wine. The position of Kokoshchkin as host was frightful; Griboyedov was silent and the guests did not know which way to look," as one related afterwards. After a pause champagne began to flow and people talked fast and nervously, trying to erase the memory of the unfortunate incident. The unwitting Zhikharev, however, remained oblivious. He proposed a toast to the character Repetilov, gushing with praise for the character's verisimilitude. Finally, still standing beside the burning-eyed "American", he turned to Griboyedov to pay him the most unwanted compliments ever received by a literary man. "Permit me, most highly respected Alexander Sergeevich, to offer you my most heartfelt thanks that you gave me, Mr. Zhikharev, this opportunity, and I hope you will now allow me to repeat that part of Repetilov's speech of which you yourself are so fond." By now the whole assembly, and Griboyedov in particular, was in an agony of apprehension. The wretched Zhikharev did his party piece again, with great emphasis, until at last he had finished and gazed proudly round at his terrified audience.

At last Griboyedov found courage to turn to Feodor Tolstoy and stammer out a lame explanation that he had never for a moment thought of him when penning those lines. Tolstoy turned his piercing gaze on the playwright. "Alexander Sergeevich," he said emphatically, "those were not mere artistic touches, but my portrait to the life. My entire biography. Once again I thank you. So long as Russia lives, so long as the Russian language is spoken, so long will your good-natured comedy live and be repeated by Russian people (as the saying goes), and so through your generosity my wicked name will live on with it!" An audible sigh of relief ran round the room. The warm-hearted Pushkin, overcome by this evidence of the tiger's soft heart, embraced Tolstoy, kissing him on both cheeks. Tolstoy must however have continued to ponder the matter, as at another meeting he accosted Griboyedov: "Why did you write about me that I 'do not play a very straight hand'?" "Well . . . you don't play cards very honestly." "Is that all? In that case you should have said so more clearly."[12]

Mention of Pushkin leads to the warm but stormy friendship which developed between the two men. It was about 1819 that they appear to have come to know each other, but exile and an unfortunate quarrel divided them within a few months. According to one account Tolstoy had mischievously suggested that Pushkin had had some degrading connexion with the Secret Chancellery. The poet had just been exiled to Southern Russia for writing political epigrams that had offended the Government. Pushkin was only twenty years old (his first poem had been published in 1814) and, possessing as passionate a nature as Tolstoy's, he flared up furiously. His revenge was taken in the most appropriate manner:

> In a life dark and despicable
> He submerged for many years,
> All courses then applicable
> With debauchery he smears . . .
> Now, forsaking all his worst crimes
> And turning a fresh new leaf,
> He is, thank God, in these times
> Merely a card-sharping thief.

The epigram was not published, but was soon repeated and circulated. For a while it was kept from the ears of the "card-sharping thief", who believed himself to be still on good terms with the exile of Kishinev. Still furious, Pushkin prepared another version for publication. Mysteriously (did the word strike a responsive chord?) the censor added the adjective "stupid" to one line. As Pushkin wrote to a friend (21 September 1821), "Why stupid? The lines refer to Tolstoy the American who is certainly not stupid – though a bit of extra abuse can do no harm."

By this time Tolstoy was aware of the attacks being made on him and responded with a spirited verse of his own, which also remained unpublished. Though no Pushkin, Feodor Tolstoy possessed considerable talents which were respected by literary figures of the day, between whom and himself passed many squibs, pasquinades and other *jeux d'esprit*.[13] Pushkin quoted with approval the lines of Prince Viazemsky, which shrewdly characterized their friend as:

Under the storms of fate an unshakeable rock –
In his own free passions, as light as a leaf.

But eventually Pushkin in the far-off Caucasus began to wonder whether it was as serious an affair as he had persuaded himself it was. "You know," he wrote to Viazemsky on 14 October, "why don't I just abandon him?"

In a further letter Pushkin wrote at length to explain his feelings. "Excuse me if I talk to you about Tolstoy . . . It seemed amusing to him to act hostilely towards me and gibe at me in correspondence with Prince Shakhovsky. I knew all about it, being already exiled and, considering revenge as one of the first Christian virtues, in my important banishment I spattered Tolstoy from afar with literary mud. A criminal accusation, in your view, exceeds the bounds of poetry; I don't agree. Where the sword of the law is inoperative, we have to make use of the whip of satire . . . You reproach me that from my remote place of banishment in Kishinev I publish an attack on a man living in Moscow. But to me there is no question but that I shall return. My intention was to go to Moscow, where alone I can clear up the matter completely . . . The fact is that I want to have things out with Tolstoy, and I don't want any more exchanges on paper. I could justify myself to you more strongly and clearly, but I respect your connexion with a man so little like you."

It is not clear how much Tolstoy was aware of or responded to all this ill-feeling. Pushkin sprang from as proud a line of nobles as the Tolstoys, and his blood was up. No doubt his natural indignation was exacerbated and sustained by the tedium of remote provincial life, but he really intended to fight the formidable Feodor Ivanovich. He engaged in continual practice with sword and pistol, strengthened his wrist by continually swinging and throwing an iron rod, and consulted a soothsayer concerning the outcome (he received, improbably, a favourable prognostication).

Meanwhile he was engaged in a further task which, ironically, was to do more to immortalize Feodor Ivanovich than any of the wild or creative actions of "the American" himself. In July 1824 he wrote to his brother to say that "Tolstoy appears to me in all his glory in the 4th book of *Onegin* . . . ." However, the poet's plans materialized differently. Tolstoy appears in palpable disguise in the 6th book of *Eugene Onegin*, and in a context that clearly relates to a later phase of the two men's relationship.

After five years' banishment Pushkin was permitted by the new Tsar Nicholas

I to return to Moscow. He arrived there on 8 September 1826 and dined that night, still in his travelling clothes, with a friend named Sobolevsky. He asked Sobolevsky to carry a challenge the very next morning to Tolstoy at his home in Moscow. Fortunately the Count happened to be away from the capital, and this afforded time for mutual friends to arrange a reconciliation, details of which have not survived. Their old friendship was swiftly restored. An exchange of notes in 1828 is still extant in which three friends, one of them Pushkin, invited Tolstoy to a friendly carousal. "Now that we know you're here, have the kindness to join us. Flushed with wine, we thirst for you." To which Tolstoy replied: "O exalted and life-giving trinity, I will appear before you, but in a half-drunk state; not from wine but from brandy, which will be a forerunner of Tolstoy."

In the following year Tolstoy and Pushkin were so close that it was the Count that acted as intermediary between the poet and his future wife, Natalia Goncharov, whose mother was averse to the match. Tolstoy's eloquence was effective, as one of Pushkin's letters to Mme. Goncharov testifies: "It is on my knees, pouring out tears of gratitude, that I am writing to you now to say that Count Tolstoy has brought me your reply: this reply is not a refusal. You allow me hope. If you have any instructions to give me, kindly address them to Count Tolstoy, who will arrange for them to reach me."[14] From chance references in Pushkin's and other friends' correspondence it is known that Tolstoy and he remained on close terms at least until the year before the poet's untimely death in a duel. Tolstoy, for example, attended Pushkin's reading of his poem *Poltava* on 3 May 1829.

In 1821 Tolstoy had married in typically eccentric fashion. It was the custom for young rakes of the time to visit gypsy encampments outside Moscow, or invite singers and dancers from them to perform at their carousals. Feodor Tolstoy became greatly taken with a gypsy girl with a beautiful singing voice named Evdokia Tugaev ("Pashenka"), and brought her to live with him at his house in Starokonyushenny Pereulok. He became devoted to her, an attachment which, it is said, was cemented after several years together through a dramatic incident at the English Club. During a particularly heavy gaming session he lost so large a sum that he found himself faced with the certainty of being posted up as having defaulted on payment. Unable to bear the thought of this disgrace, he decided to shoot himself. Evdokia noticed his depression and gently enquired as to its cause. "What is the matter, Count?" she asked anxiously; "tell me! Perhaps I can help you." "Why are you trying to interfere?" asked "the American" gloomily; "you can't do anything to help me. I shall be posted up on the black-list and I just can't live with that – I'll do away with myself." The girl said nothing, but a day or two later came to him and produced the necessary sum. "Where on earth did you get this money?" asked Tolstoy. "From you. It is what you gave me at different times. I saved it all. Please take it: it is all yours." This generosity and loyalty overwhelmed the Count, and they were married on 10 January 1821.

Evdokia was twenty-four at the time, and Feodor thirty-eight. On 20 August of the same year she gave birth to a daughter, whom they christened with the Jewish name Sarah. She inherited her father's wayward brilliance and became in time a well-known literary figure, writing with equal fluency in English, French, German and Italian. Her talents were praised by critics of the eminence of Belinsky and Herzen. It was about the time of her birth that a noticeable change developed in Tolstoy's existence. There were many drawing-rooms where the beautiful but low-born Evdokia was not received, and her sensitive husband refused to go anywhere he suspected she might not be completely welcome. Even disparaging remarks about gypsies in general annoyed him.[15] He was now too a very fond father, and in 1822 he reached the age of forty.

The first indication of the new man was his virtual abandonment of cheating in his gambling. He continued to live much of the year in Moscow, dividing the remainder of his time between spells at his country estates and visits to St. Petersburg. He read voraciously and spent much time and correspondence with those he regarded as his true friends. Previously his conduct and attitudes had been cynical and amoral,[16] but now he became devout on occasion to superstition.

He adored his children, spending much time playing with them and instructing them. However one after another of Sarah's brothers and sisters was carried off at birth or in infancy, and their father's grief acquired superstitious dread. He began to wonder if this were not divine retribution for the sins of his youth. In his pocket-book he had written the names of the eleven opponents he had killed in duels. As each child died he solemnly crossed out a name and wrote the word "quits" opposite. Eventually the terrible mortality reached the significant figure; and when a twelfth child was born, a charming and clever little girl, he crossed out the last name in his list and was heard to say: "Now, thank God, my curly-haired little gypsy maid can live!" The girl, Praskovia, duly survived and grew up as clever and spirited as her mother.

It is true that, when Praskovia was born in 1831, Sarah was still living. But Sarah had always been very sickly, and died tragically at the age of seventeen in 1838. Her continual illness, combined with the successive deaths of the intervening infants, could easily have persuaded the superstitious Tolstoy that she too was fated to an early death, the anticipation of which would have been far more terrible than the event itself.

On 12 February 1828, during this melancholy period of his existence, Feodor Ivanovich wrote to his friend Prince Gagarin in Paris. "I am living in utter boredom, sadness and drunkenness. I thank you from all my heart for thinking of my family. Only Sarah makes my unbearable life worth living; my wife for the third month has not left her sick-bed, after giving birth to my third dead son. Consequently my hope of living through an heir is buried with the last new arrival. A sorrow unknown to you, but believe me my dear friend that it is unceasingly painful. Forgive me, dear friend, for my incoherence, but I feel quite stupid. . . . P.S. In three days I am going to Mogilev. Find out, dearest friend, what sort of alphabets exist for very young children, on good paper with illustrations. Under alphabets I include historical, mythological and suchlike. It would be good if it could be in the form of cards. Don't hold back on expense: inform me beforehand and you will get the money at once."

Clearly Tolstoy wished to teach French to his seven-year-old Sarah.

It was during this subdued period, when he even became a temporary teetotaller, that Pushkin portrayed Feodor Ivanovich in the sixth book of *Eugene Onegin*, as the veteran duellist Zaretsky.

> Zaretsky, sometime king of brawls
> and hetman of the gaming-halls,
> arch-rake, pothouse tribuna-persona,
> but now grown plain and kind instead,
> paterfamilias (unwed),

unswerving friend, correct landowner,
and even honourable man:
so, if we want to change, we can!

*   *   *

The world of fashion, prone to flatter,
praised his fierce courage in its day:
true, with a pistol he could shatter
an ace a dozen yards away . . .
Time was, he'd been the wittiest ever,
so brilliantly he'd hoax the fools,
so gloriously he'd fool the clever,
using overt or covert rules.
Sometimes his tricks would earn him trouble,
or cause the bursting of his bubble,
sometimes he'd fall into a trap
himself, just like a simple chap.
But he could draw a joking moral,
return an answer, blunt or keen,
use cunning silence as a screen,
or cunningly create a quarrel,
get two young friends to pick a fight,
and put them on a paced-out site.
Or he knew how to reconcile them
so that all three went off to lunch,
then lately slyly he'd revile them
with lies and jokes that packed a punch;
sed alia tempora! The devil
(like passion's dream, that others revel)
goes out of us when youth is dead.
So my Zaretsky, as I said,
beneath bird-cherries and acacias
has found a port for his old age,
and lives, a veritable sage,
for planting cabbage, like Horatius,
and breeding ducks and geese as well,
and teaching children how to spell.
He was no fool; appreciated
by Eugene, not for his heart,
but for the effect that he created
of sense and judgment. For his part
His converse gave Onegin pleasure . . .
In duels a pedantic don
methodical by disposition,
a classicist, he'll not allow
that one be shot just anyhow
only by rule, and strict tradition
inherited from earlier days
(for which he must receive due praise).

It was scarcely surprising that so varied and extreme a character should appeal to Pushkin, whose Byronic temperament led him to admire a man who disdained convention and continued to astonish his contemporaries. He was a very striking figure, who attracted attention wherever he went. In the margin of his manuscript of *Eugene Onegin* Pushkin drew a sketch of his friend, which bears out the strong impression gained by other contemporaries. "Feodor Ivanovich was of medium height, thickset, strongly built and handsome; his face round, full and dark, his curly hair black and thick, his black eyes flashed; and when he was angry, it was terrifying to look him in the eye."

Herzen recalled later that "one look at the old man's appearance, at his brow covered with grey curls, at his sparkling eyes and athletic body, revealed what energy and strength nature had bestowed on him."[17]

Nor were his smouldering energy and physical strength the only reminders of his extraordinary life. His cousin Maria Kamensky, daughter of the great sculptor Feodor Petrovich Tolstoy, recalled meeting the notorious "American".

"In my childhood," she wrote many years later, "I had heard so many purely fabulous tales of my uncle Tolstoy the American that not surprisingly, when seated with him at my grandfather's dinner-table, I looked upon him as the eighth wonder of the world. But by then there was nothing so amazing about Feodor Ivanovich: he was a man like other men: elderly, with curly grey hair and ruddy features, and possessing large, keen black eyes . . . and he chatted and joked at table like everyone else, so that I already began to feel disappointed. But we had not quite finished eating when grandpa to my delight, clapped his nephew on the shoulder and said to him cheerfully, 'Now, American, amuse my guests; show the ladies your chest and hands, and afterwards show the rest of yourself to the gentlemen!'

"Feodor Ivanovich, it appeared, was quite happy with grandpa's request, and with a smile began to unbutton his black frockcoat. When he opened it out there could be seen hanging on his chest the large framed image of St. Spyridon, patron of all the Counts Tolstoy, which the devout American always wore. Setting it down by his side on the table, he undid his shirt-studs, and bared and swelled out his chest. Everyone at the table stood up in their places and gazed attentively at it: it was completely covered in tattoos. In the very middle sat in a ring some sort of big multi-coloured bird, rather like a parrot, in a red and blue hoop. When everyone had gazed his fill on the designs on his chest, Feodor Ivanovich Tolstoy took off his frock coat and rolled up his shirt-sleeves: both arms were likewise completely tattooed, with snakes and other wild designs entwined around them. The ladies sighed and gasped without ceasing, and asked solicitously: 'Wasn't it very painful, Count, when those savages tattooed you? How did they pick out the designs? Oh, what suffering!'

"When Feodor Ivanovich had finished with the ladies, the gentlemen took him upstairs to grandpa's snuggery, and there once again undressed him and inspected him from head to foot."[18]

It is hard to picture such a scene in the contemporary England of Queen Victoria and Prince Albert.

Maria Kamensky also described Feodor Tolstoy as devout to an extremity that verged on superstition. By his own account this dated from his spiritual experience on the north Pacific island, when St. Spyridon, tutelary protector of the Tolstoys, saved his life. His sincerity was patent and, and has been seen, the terrible mortal-

Feodor Ivanovich Tolstoy

ity of his children convinced him of the stern reality of Divine justice. One friend later recalled: "I did not hide from him my regret that those rare qualities which Heaven had bestowed on him had not been put to better employment. For my benefit he put on a surprising shew of repentance, possibly sincere, for tears actually started from his wan, inscrutable eyes."

Feodor Ivanovich loved at this time to recall the exploits of happier days. "In 1844," recalled Liprandi, an old comrade from the days of his Finnish campaigning in 1808, "being once more in Moscow and calling on A.F. Veltman, I met there an unknown old gentleman with very thick grey hair. Although his features seemed to me not unfamiliar, I was far from guessing who he was. The conversation was general. Finally our honoured host introduced us. Almost with one voice we asked each other: 'Is it you? Is it you?' And afterwards it transpired that so it was. [They talked at length about their experiences at Idensalm and Borodino.] The Count informed me that he had preserved [Prince Dolgorukov's] jacket ever since." Tolstoy invited Liprandi to dine with him: "Our conversation fastened on memories of the Prince and his death. . . . He promised to shew me that summer in the country his own notes referring to those days, which would establish the correctness of my memories. On my next trip I brought my diary, but the Count was no longer there."[19]

"He was excellently educated," recalled the writer Bulgarin: "spoke several languages, loved music and literature, read widely, and was close to artists, writers and lovers of literature and art. He was devilishly clever and wonderfully eloquent. He adored hair-splitting and paradoxes, and it was hard to contend with him in argument. He was however, as they say, a decent fellow, ready to do anything for a friend and eagerly helping his acquaintances. But he advised friends and acquaintances not to play cards with him; saying quite openly that with gaming, as in war, one recognizes neither friend nor brother; and that one had the right to win money from anyone anxious to lose it . . . I remember him as an extraordinary phenomenon even in those times, when people did not live by the calendar, nor speak as they were told, and did not stand to attention; that is to say, when a sort of unbridled knight-errantry overrode etiquette and convention."

Tolstoy's political views became, if they had not always been, thoroughly Slavophile and reactionary. It was he who said that Gogol was an enemy of Russia and should be dragged in chains to Siberia, when he staged his famous satire on the bureaucracy, *The Inspector-General*. As Tsar Nicholas himself greatly admired the play, Tolstoy appears to have been out on a reactionary limb of his own – which was doubtless his intention.[20]

Gogol knew Tolstoy, and in a letter of 22 October 1846 provided an interesting glimpse of the old gentleman. To the actor Shchepkin he explained how *The Inspector-General* should be played. "In general it would be good if all the actors behaved like some well-known personality known to them. For the rôle of Peter Petrovich the words should be declaimed in an especially orotund, distinct and gravelly manner. He should copy that person whom he knows to speak Russian best of all. It would be good if he could comport himself somewhat like Tolstoy the American." Here is indirect testimony to that marvellous eloquence on which so many contemporaries commented.[21]

But the wild man's days had drawn to a close. A few weeks after Gogol wrote these instructions in far-off Strasbourg, Tolstoy died. It was said that he was discovered prostrated before his ikons, where he passed away during his prayers.[22]

"Feodor Ivanovich died as a Christian," wrote a friend, A.A. Stakhovich; "I heard that the priest, confessing the dying man, said that his confession continued for a long time and that rarely had he encountered such repentance and such faith in God's mercy." His early days of violence were long past, and his passing was sincerely lamented by that wide circle of friends who included many of the finest intellects of the day. As the poet Zhukovsky explained to a friend: "He had many good qualities. For myself I only knew of good qualities. All the others were legendary, his heart was always with me, and he was a good friend to his friends."

It was hard for a tamer generation to appreciate what a spirit had passed. A friend tried to describe to a young lady what sort of man he was. "There aren't people like that any more," he explained. "If he loved you and you asked for a bracelet of stars out of the sky, he would fetch it for you. Nothing was impossible for him, and everything gave way to him. I assure you that you would have been as fearful as if in the presence of a lion. And today what sort of people do we have? Spineless weaklings!"

Feodor Ivanovich was survived by his widow, who died in 1861; and by his daughter Praskovia, who was unfortunately murdered by her cook in 1887. He was immortalized by the pen of his cousin Leo Tolstoy. "The American" appears unmistakably as Count Feodor Ivanovich Turbin in Tolstoy's story *Two Hussars*. Arriving by chance in a small country town at the time of the local nobles' election, Turbin is recognized by one of the assembled landowners, a retired officer, as the celebrated hussar and duellist, of whom so many tales were told. "What a fine-looking man he is!" exclaims another bystander; "he must be about twenty-five, isn't he?" "No," replied the other, "he looks that, but he's older. Do you want to know who he is? . . . He killed Sablin. He kicked Matnev out of the window, and he won three hundred thousand off Prince Nesterov. Everyone knows what a desperate madcap he is. Gamber, duellist, libertine; but a real hussar. And isn't it quite glorious for us, that's if anyone understands just what is meant by a real hussar. Ah, what times they were!"

During the Count's brief stay in the town its placid life is overturned as if by a whirlwind. He graciously borrows, but declines to return, two hundred roubles from the old officer; attends the nobles' ball, delighting all with the exquisite grace of his dancing and his dashing self-confidence; and wins the undying love of a beautiful widow. His approach to her might have been taken from the life.

"'My brother says, Count,' ventured the widow, 'that some upset occurred on your journey and you are short of money. If that's true, why can't I let you have some? It would give me such pleasure.'

"But saying this, Anna Feodorovna suddenly became frightened and blushed. In an instant the Count's face became grim.

"'Your brother is an imbecile!' he said sharply. 'You must know that when one man offends another they have to fight; but when a woman offends a man, do you know what he does?'

"Poor Anna Feodorovna blushed down to her shoulders and up to her ears in embarrassment. She looked down and did not reply.

"'He kisses the woman in front of everyone,' quietly whispered the Count, stooping to her ear. 'Permit me to kiss your hand,' he added quietly after a long silence, taking pity on his lady.

"'But not now,' ventured Anna Feodorovna, sighing deeply.

"'Then when? I'm off early tomorrow . . . but you owe this to me.'

"'Well, I fear it is just not possible,' said Anna Feodorovna, smiling.

"'I only wish you to allow me to find an opportunity to see you today in order to kiss your hand. I will find it.'

"'But how will you find me?'

"'That is not your affair. If I want to see you, see you I will . . . All right?'
"'All right.'"

But Count Turbin spent the later part of the night carousing with gypsies ("Ah, my little Count, my little pigeon, my treasure: what happiness!" whispers a shapely young gypsy girl.) After that he saves a young man ruined in gambling by the simple expedient of bursting into his creditor's room, where the money is being counted out on the table. When the gambler, Lukhnov, declined to play for the sum with Turbin, the Count's face turned deadly pale. Striking Lukhnov a fearful blow on the head, he grabbed the money and made off. Sticking his head round the door, he added, "If you want satisfaction, then I'm at your service: I shall be in my room for another half-hour." "What, do you want to get shot? Then I'm at your service!" he had likewise exclaimed to a young man who irritated him at the ball. There was still time to empty a bottle of champagne over a merchant's head, shove the retired cavalryman into a snowdrift, grab the gypsy girl in an attempt to carry her off to Moscow, and be off at dawn on his journey.

They were dashing along the snowy highway when the Count remembered Anna Feodorovna.

"'Back!' he yelled.

"The driver did not straightaway understand.

"'Turn back! Drive to the town! Look lively!' The troika returned through the gates and briskly pulled up at the wooden stairway of Mr. Zaitsov's house. The Count flew up the steps, through the hall and drawing-room and, finding the widow was still asleep, took her by the hands, lifting her up from her bed, kissed her sleepy eyes and dashed out again. Anna Feodorovna, half-awake, only licked her lips and asked 'What's happening?' The Count jumped into the sleigh, shouted to the driver and without stopping or even thinking of Lukhnov, the widow or Steshka [the gypsy girl], but only of what would happen in Moscow, departed for ever from the town of K."

Travelling once in Germany, Feodor Tolstoy had to provide an official with his particulars. When asked for a character reference he replied simply, "*lustig*".[23] The reality was more complex. To Herzen, and others since, the explanation lay largely in the deadening effect of the early nineteenth-century autocracy, which stifled all legitimate aspirations of energy and character.

"The suffocating emptiness and silence of Russian life, when in an odd way combined with a lively and even turbulent character, especially develops in us all kinds of deformity. In Suvorov's cock-crow . . . and the wild crimes of Tolstoy the American I hear a related note, known to us all, though with us in a feebler form or directed elsewhere. . . . It develops one wild passion, one bad propensity, and this is not to be wondered at: all depravities have long been permitted to us without hindrance, but for a struggle in the cause of humanity they pack you off to a garrison or Siberia at the first sign. . . ."[24] And Sergei Tolstoy concludes a biographical monograph of his relative with the words "Who knows? Perhaps with a different education and in a different milieu his energy and outstanding abilities would have been directed to other and more profitable purposes and for the service of humanity."

It is tempting to accept this explanation, which must indeed have some validity. To the abler and more energetic members of the Russian aristocracy, possessed of great talents, wealth, social prestige and indeed every advantage *except* real power and responsibility, life must at times have been unbearably frustrating. But this is not the whole story, and here I must introduce an aspect, partly of a personal nature, which I think sets the matter in a different light.

Several years ago, having completed a book and considering what to write next, a suggestion led me to undertake the biography of a sufficiently obscure figure, the second Baron Camelford (1775–1804). Apart from passing references hinting at a picaresque existence I knew at first nothing at all about him. At the same time I felt a strong personal interest in the subject which I was not able satisfactorily to explain. As Camelford proved to be a violent and disreputable figure, many friends and reviewers shared this puzzlement. But something drew me closely to him, and I even dreamed once that I met him, our natures fusing together in a mysterious and inexplicable manner.

I may say that at that time I knew nothing whatever of my relative "the American", beyond his name, epithet and a faint impression of his lively character. I was astonished, therefore, to find these two contemporaries leading uncannily parallel lives, to which some unconscious attraction had apparently drawn me. For Camelford also came of an illustrious family whose members possessed exceptional abilities and energies. He was a Pitt, cousin of the two great eighteenth-century statesmen. Like Tolstoy he was unusually athletic and unflinchingly brave, but also wildly eccentric and quarrelsome, the most notorious duellist in England, as Tolstoy was in Russia. Again, like Tolstoy, Camelford's daunting reputation masked a much more congenial personality known only to his intimates. He also possessed great creative and artistic abilities which were prevented from coming to fruition.

There are many other parallels of detail; both men possessed a similarly sardonic sense of humour, delighted in shocking the easily offended, and displayed physical and mental vigour far beyond the ordinary. Both too became bitterly conscious of having failed to put their exceptional talents to constructive use. Both passed through a phase of cynicism in religion, followed by extreme personal piety. But far more extraordinary than all this is the fact that the episode which supplied Tolstoy with his nickname "the American" echoed almost to the last detail Lord Camelford's most famous adventure. Twelve years before Feodor Tolstoy sailed with Kruzenstern to the Pacific, Camelford travelled as a midshipman on Vancouver's similar voyage of discovery. At Tahiti Camelford was punished for flirting with a beautiful native girl, and thereafter he had a series of violent quarrels with his Captain which culminated in Vancouver's abandoning him at Hawaii, and Camelford's returning home alone round the world![25]

I felt an overpowering sensation, as I studied my relative's life, that an unconscious predisposition, inherited in some mysterious way, led me to my pursuit of Lord Camelford. What is more significant, though, is the fact that a character almost identical to Feodor Tolstoy could flourish in contemporary England. For the England of George III was no autocracy, and indeed saw her great aristocracy at the height of its power. With his exceptional advantages of birth and talent Camelford could reasonably have expected to achieve any rôle his inclination seized upon with a complete sense of fulfilment. The fatal flaw in his character that prevented this cannot therefore be ascribed to the political and social environment in which he lived, but was something personal.

It may be that both families, Pitts and Tolstoys, possessed a superabundant flow of energy and talent. Where a ready outlet for this vital force existed, it manifested itself in the diplomatic skills of Peter Tolstoy, the military instinct of Osterman-Tolstoy, or the artistic genius of Feodor Petrovich, Alexei Constantinovich and Lev Nikolaevich. Where however a quirk of personality frustrated this inherited source of vigour it simply burst out with irresistible force whenever opportunity offered, however inappropriate the occasion. Feodor Tolstoy appears to have been aware of his possession of this elemental force, but incapable of controlling it. Leo Tolstoy in 1865 wrote of "that Tolstoyan wildness· that's common to us all. Not for nothing did Feodor Ivanovich have himself tattooed."[26]

146

6
"The embodiment of an entire academy"*

eodor Petrovich Tolstoy was the first cousin of Feodor Ivanovich, "the American", whose wild career was described in the previous chapter. Feodor Ivanovich's literary talents were respected by that brilliant circle of writers with whom he was associated, but it was his cousin who first displayed real artistic genius, which attained its full flowering in the next generation. The achievements of Leo Tolstoy in prose and Alexei Constantinovich in poetry are sufficiently well known in the West, but probably fewer people are aware that in painting and sculpture too Russia's heritage was enriched by the same family.

Feodor Petrovich, like others of his family at this time, grew up in circumstances of relative poverty. The celebrated Count Peter Andreevich's great wealth had been expropriated after his quarrel with Menshikov in 1727 and his exile to the White Sea, and though the title was restored to his descendants in 1760 they were reduced to the ownership of a mere 2,000 serfs between them. It was said by the Tolstoys in the eighteenth century that "in our family there are no rich; only those are wealthy who marry wealth" – an aphorism frequently confirmed in this book.

Feodor's father, another Peter Andreevich (great-grandson of the kidnapper of the Tsarevich), was born in 1746. This Peter's industry, and still more his honesty, raised him high in the military service until he became a Major General and head of the War Commissariat. Catherine the Great greatly valued his integrity and treated him as something of a character. On one occasion a fire broke out in the Commissariat building which was on the point of engulfing the strongroom. At great risk to his life Peter Tolstoy saved the large sum of money deposited there and brought it to his then superior. That gentleman looked at him quizzically, ordered everyone else from the room, and turned back to Tolstoy. "You are a fool, Count Peter Andreevich, an honest fool!" "What are you complaining about?" asked the astonished Count; "everything is here intact!" "I know, old man, that everything is there intact, but you're a fool, an arrant fool! We might have believed the fire destroyed everything. Oh, my brother, I feel sorry for you, very sorry! You will be poor all your life." He was right. Catherine II looked on her honest General with favour and affection, but he had offended her unpleasant heir by denying him money from the treasury. "Tell him he will remember this!" cried the angry Tsarevich, and when as Paul I he succeeded in 1796 poor Tolstoy was dismissed. His wife (whom he had married at Kazan, when she was only fourteen) had brought him no inheritance, providing him instead with six children, five boys and one girl. But she was artistic and intelligent, and it was a very happy family, however impoverished.

It might almost seem, though, as if the Tsarevich Alexei's terrible curse, which prophesied equal portions of genius and madness among the Tolstoys for twenty-five generations, was having its effect. Feodor, the fourth son, possessed truly remarkable talent but his elder brother Alexander (born in 1777) exhibited many of those wild traits that characterized his cousin "the American". Alexander possessed extraordinarily mobile features that a Grimaldi might have envied, and it was said could even move tufts of hair on his head in different directions. His short life was devoted to practical jokes, each more extravagant than the last. He

Previous page: Feodor Petrovich Tolstoy, 1840
* *Golos* (1873), no. 12.

served in the Semeonovsky Guards, on one occasion winning a bet by staging a convincing fit of madness in order to fulfil a threat that he would thrash his Colonel "like a dog". His face distorted in a horrible grimace and wearing only his underclothes and a hat on the side of his head, he knocked over the wretched officer's tent and beat him through the canvas, shrieking "Good luck, lads! Thanks, lads!" Placed under medical care, he staged a recovery so convincing that even the Colonel came to congratulate him. He won his crate of champagne.

He alone among the family was regarded with great favour by the Emperor Paul, whose own faculties were probably genuinely in need of medical treatment. But the favour was continued by Alexander I, on whom Alexander Tolstoy did not scruple to play a number of bizarre tricks, the most respectable of which was the mysterious daily disappearance of the Emperor's breakfast from his tent when on manoeuvres. Tolstoy had crawled under the canvas, explaining later that he was hungry. On another occasion a gigantic jasper urn arrived at the Winter Palace and was put on display. "Goodness, how huge!" exclaimed a charming young lady. "You could almost swim in it!" "Let's see!" shouted Tolstoy from the crowd, and vaulted into the vessel in his full-dress uniform. He was performing some simulated strokes, when suddenly the laughter died away and the crowd of fashionables began to clear a wide path to the vase. Tolstoy pulled his head down and lay still at the bottom. The Tsar and his suite entered the hall, and moved slowly between ranks of bowing gentlemen and curtsying ladies. His Majesty at once noticed that everyone was desperately trying to contain irrepressible laughter. Gazing around with a frown, he suddenly smiled. "It can only be Tolstoy!" he muttered and, after an inspection of the urn, moved on to the next gallery.

But poor Alexander Tolstoy really was "not normal", as my great-aunt Lily used to say, and came to an unhappy end. He suddenly decided to marry, but his wife departed within a year leaving him with a little daughter, Lisa. In 1812 he was decorated for his bravery in fighting the French, but the injuries he sustained contributed to a swift deterioration in health. Returning to live with his old father, he became a pathetic invalid and died at the age of forty-two. His niece remembered him as he was in those last years: huddled in an armchair, the retired prankster was reduced to "a pale figure in a white dressing-gown, with dreadfully emaciated features, who was forever coughing and spitting into a pretty little red copper basin with lion's legs. I was frightened of this unhappy invalid, and only gazed at him from a distance."[1]

Feodor's younger brother Vladimir was a soldier, who transferred later to the Civil Service. He never married but was, as a niece later remembered, "a great attendant on the ladies – like all Tolstoys". The third brother, Constantine (1780–1870) was the father of the great poet Alexei Tolstoy. He was a brave soldier, was accounted one of the best dancers of his day, but sadly encountered an insuperable incompatibility with his wife Anna, who left him with their infant son soon after his birth. The Countess Anna did not remarry and remained close friends with the family, particularly her brother-in-law Feodor. "Why didn't you marry me, Theodore?" she asked once light-heartedly. "I could have loved you very much. . . ." "It must be because," he replied, "before you I saw another Annette, whom I loved and married."

Feodor's fifth brother was Peter, born in 1787. Like Feodor he took up a naval career, and graduated from the Naval Academy in 1804 to begin what promised to be an adventurous existence. At his father's instigation, he was seconded to the

British Navy and, as his niece Maria remembered, served under Admiral Nelson "in his circumnavigation of the globe". This must refer to Nelson's expedition to the West Indies in 1805, which culminated in the Battle of Trafalgar. According to the same source, he became a great favourite with Lord Nelson, who advanced his fortunes. After six years' service, Peter returned to the Russian Navy as a Lieutenant. His family was thrilled at the appearance of the returned hero, bronzed and handsome. But alas, within a year he was tragically drowned, when his ship the *Pollux* went down in a terrible storm off the island of Gotland (25 October 1809).*

Peter Andreevich Tolstoy

Old Count Peter Andreevich Tolstoy's fourth son Feodor was born on 10 February 1783, when the Count was still a favourite of Catherine the Great. The baby was born in the family's living-quarters on the first floor of the War Commissariat building in St. Petersburg, next to the Yusupov Palace. Almost every day the Empress passed by on her sleigh, never failing to blow a kiss towards the Countess's window. No sooner was the babe baptized than he was appointed a Sergeant in the Preobrazhensky Guards, being graciously granted a year's leave from duty. But little Feodor showed no inclination towards the toy soldiers, wooden swords and drums stocked in most boys' nurseries. His only toys were paper, pencil, brushes and paints, with which he drew and sketched all day long. His precocious talent was evident from a very early age, and it was clear he could one day be a ready candidate for the Academy of Arts – but for the fact that at that time a nobleman could as soon have allowed his son to take up an artistic career as apprentice him to a cobbler or tailor. Matryona Efremovna, the family nurse, grieved greatly over her young charge's regrettable obsession. "Yes, little mother," she used to recall to his daughter in later years; "what we had to put up with from your father! He was still only a little chap, but . . .

* Living as I do in England I find it pleasant to think of my relatives' connexions with the country of my birth. I think of Peter Petrovich Tolstoy fighting at Trafalgar; General Peter Alexandrovich commanding a British Army in 1805; Alexei Constantinovich's stay in the Isle of Wight; Leo Tolstoy's briefly-held resolution to emigrate and make England his permanent home; and Alexei Nikolaevich's wartime visit to King George V and H. G. Wells.

He drew and drew so that he had no time for mischief. And what a clever little rascal that boy was: you could hardly blink before he had disappeared from the nursery. You looked and there he was coming solemnly back, with a napkin tied round his breeches, saying very seriously, 'Nanny, I want to play cooks.'"

Matryona never forgot this incident, and when her charge was fifty years old and she eighty, she used to ask him, "And how long have you been playing cook?"

Feodor's obsession with the arts both delighted and disturbed his parents. They would proudly exhibit examples of his precocious talent to friends and relatives, producing among other examples a skilful drawing of a page holding a

Vladimir Petrovich Tolstoy

torch executed at the tender age of *four*. At the same time they feared that this excessive interest in the graphic arts might hinder him in his military career, for which a great future was promised. In 1792 a visitor called at their Petersburg home: he was a cousin ("uncle", in Russian usage) who had already at the youthful age of twenty-four achieved high distinction in the army, and was clearly destined for a golden career. Count Peter Alexandrovich Tolstoy, afterwards a distinguished commander in the Napoleonic wars, was at that time commanding a regiment of dragoons quartered near Vilna. He offered to take the boy back with him and train him for his future career. Feodor's parents, after much perturbation of mind, reluctantly agreed for the boy's good.

At first Feodor was intensely bored in his new life, but he soon found new interests. He became an enthusiastic horseman, prancing at the age of ten before the Regiment, and learning to train unbroken horses. But his uncle did not neglect his promise to provide the boy with a first-class education. Feodor was sent to a college at Polotsk administered by Jesuits, to whom in the eighteenth century Russians were indebted for much of their best schooling.[2] Under the inspiring tutelage of the polymath College head, Father Gruber, Feodor began to discipline his natural talent in directions which were to prove satisfyingly fruitful. In particular, Gruber introduced him to old engravings, from which Feodor learned first to copy and afterwards to extract the technical principles of execution.

Meanwhile the boy was moving swiftly upwards on the ladder of promotion. At thirteen he was a Captain, and at fourteen a Major. Finally the time came for him to leave his uncle, for whom he cherished feelings of grateful, if critical, appreciation. "Peter Alexandrovich was no fool," he wrote later, "but his was not a distinguished intellect. He had not received a very good education, and spoke French badly. He imagined that he knew and did not need to know. . . . But he was very generous, truthful, and honest in the highest degree, and was ready to stand unflinchingly for the truth before anyone, whoever he was." This latter quality was to incense Napoleon, to whose Empire Count Peter was appointed Ambassador in 1807–8.

In 1800 Feodor Tolstoy, now aged seventeen and having returned to St. Petersburg, attended the Naval Academy. He sailed with the fleet from Kronstadt to Stockholm, making many sketches and keeping a diary on the voyage. But he suffered from the inconvenient handicap of seasickness, and pined for more intellectual activities. "I felt," he wrote, " that so much was missing from my life. The Academy course was designed only for straightforward, decent naval officers, but not for enlightened people; and I wanted to be enlightened, on account of which I used every opportunity to get to know people distinguished in the arts, and attended public lectures." He became acquainted with some of the most illustrious men of letters of his day, including the poet Zhukovsky, the fabulist Krylov, and the historian Karamzin. He was a regular attendant at the theatre, becoming particularly enamoured of the ballet. It was not long before his own talents gained appreciation. A beautifully-modelled wax relief portrait of Napoleon aroused great admiration.

In 1802 he graduated from the Naval Academy and enrolled for study at the Academy of Arts. The Academy had been founded by the Empress Elizabeth for the purpose of encouraging the fine arts in Russia, and had been further endowed by Catherine the Great. It occupied a magnificent classical building on the right bank of the Neva opposite the English Quay, considered by many to be the finest

St Petersburg Academy of Arts

building in the capital. It contained a fine collection of foreign and native masterpieces exhibited in light, spacious galleries, and an art school maintaining two hundred boarding students, many of whom the Government would despatch to study in Europe. As an impressed English visitor observed not long afterwards,

Feodor Petrovich Tolstoy in naval uniform

the exterior was "by far the most classical and chaste of its size in St. Petersburg", and "internally every part is a perfect model of architecture". Facilities and tuition at the Academy were generally of the highest standard, and after the philistinism of the Naval Academy Feodor Tolstoy found himself in a paradise to which he would devote the whole of his long life.[3]

He first enrolled himself in the class for medallists, an art in which his skills were ultimately to be most perfectly realized. The tutor, Shilov, as Tolstoy recalled, "taught me to prepare wax for modelling from his design, supplying various quantities of palm wood, which he shaped very skilfully, and gave me a profile of the Roman consul Caracalla to copy. From that moment I always attended the medallists' class, whenever my studies permitted." His enthusiastic absorption in this work aroused the curiosity of his professors. One of them, a distinguished sculptor named Prokofiev, stood for a long while watching as Feodor's fingers worked the wax with marvellous dexterity. Eventually Prokofiev could not help enquiring, "Tell me, why do you want to study? Are you doing it fundamentally as an artist or, like all your fellow-nobles, only for amusement?" Tolstoy replied earnestly that his only desire was to become a true artist. "Well then," replied Prokofiev to the young naval officer (who was obliged to wear uniform even at art classes),[4] "you must enrol yourself for the full Academy course." The young man needed no further urging, and flung himself deep into each branch of study.

It seemed at this point that all this glowing promise, which was already bearing fruit in some extremely skilfully executed drawings, would be frustrated. Tolstoy suddenly received orders to join the Russian fleet at Regensholm. In an agony of apprehension he saw all his hopes dashed and turned in despair to his benevolent cousin Count Peter Alexandrovich Tolstoy, who by great good fortune was now Military Governor of St. Petersburg. The General at once approached the Minister for the Navy, Admiral Chichagov, and secured Feodor's appointment as the Admiral's Adjutant on 23 July 1804. This required his attendance in the capital, enabling him to continue his studies.

Nevertheless, Feodor Tolstoy was decided, and in the same year (1804) he resigned his commission. To many it seemed he was as mad as his brother Alexander. Having offended the only source of patronage and advancement, he had thrown himself into an occupation which for a person of his background appeared ridiculous. He lacked money, influence and service, and appeared destined for an existence of Bohemian indigence. Much of society scoffed at his infatuation. "What? Count Tolstoy, a member of one of Russia's great families – an artist? He spends day and night toiling and slaving? He, who could have lived well, earning rank, fame and honour; he, our dear lunatic, an educated man, a man of the highest circle, has come down to earning his keep by the labour of his own hands?" So muttered the less charitable. But to Tolstoy there was no agony of choice: for him the world was art, or it was nothing.

At first his material existence was indeed hard. The condemnation that he would have to subsist by the labour of his two hands proved literal. He designed cameos for brooches in the antique style, then very fashionable, which his faithful nurse Matryona bore to the market for sale. When he spent what little money they gained in this way on books and artists' materials, she would tell him consolingly, "Don't worry, master; work, study, don't worry about it all: old Nanny will cook you up buckwheat *kasha* and cabbage soup – work away, with God's help!" The reward for this dedication was not slow in arriving. Tolstoy's marvellous drawings in the classical style attracted increasing attention, until they were brought to the attention of Emperor Alexander I. The Tsar was so impressed that he appointed him to a post at the Hermitage Gallery, with a salary of 1500 roubles a year.

With his new-found competence, Feodor Tolstoy installed himself and Matryona in a comfortable basement flat by the Chain Bridge near the Summer Gardens. He arranged living-quarters and studio perfectly to his liking, bought new clothes, and was content to let Matryona run the home economy in her customary auto-cratic fashion. Her ascendancy was, however, nearing its end. He was absent from the flat for ever longer and more irregular periods, until one day he returned with the news he was to be married. The bride-to-be was seventeen-year-old Anna Feodorovna Dudin, one of seven children of the widow of a Commercial Councillor living in one of the streets of Vasilievsky Island, just across the Neva. Feodor had become a regular caller at the old wooden house, with its tree-shaded garden stretching the width of the block. He fell deeply in love with Anna Feodorovna, who was as gentle and kind as she was beautiful. Her young heart was stirred equally profoundly by the handsome and talented young Count, and it was not long before vows had been exchanged and a marriage arranged.

The young couple adored each other, and it proved a love-match that lasted for her life. Only the old nurse, Matryona, who possessed a nice sense of social distinction, disapproved strongly. "Who are you?" she exclaimed indignantly when the news was broken to her; "tell me, who are you? A Count, or not? A Commercial Councillor! A merchant's wife, I hear? The merchant's wife Mrs. Dudin! It seems you couldn't find anyone worse? The world is big enough for you, isn't it? There wasn't one countess or princess left? You had to pick the Commercial Councillor! A fine bird indeed! Well, you'd better know that I won't be a servant to your merchant's wife! Nor to you! I'm going, I'm going, and I don't wish to see you either!" Feodor became angry too, and the old dame departed. Eventually, however, she returned and was before long won over by the young Countess's unfailing gentleness and kindness.

Annette Tolstoy

The wedding was touchingly simple and unceremonial. The young couple, Feodor dressed in his naval uniform and Annette (as he always called her) in a simple white dress and her hair bound up with flowers from her garden, walked to the nearby Church of the Annunciation. A small group of relations and friends attended the service. Afterwards, all returned to Anna's home for the wedding lunch. The lack of stately entertainment would have outraged old Matryona, but the newly-wed couple were no less happy as, surrounded by their delighted families, they strolled in the large garden, rowed a little dinghy on its pond, and romped in a big meadow opposite.

Within a year, on 10 August 1811, their first child, a daughter Elizabeth, was born. They were stirring times for all Russians, and little Lisa's first cry was not, to the amusement of the family, "Mama" or "Papa", but words which at that time were on every Russian tongue: "Hurrah! Victory!"

In the same year the proud father modelled a beautiful wax bas-relief (now in the Tretyakov Gallery), portraying the young family: father, mother, and baby, dressed in classical robes; beside them their pet poodle Hector looks on protectively.[5]

With a comfortable little home, respectable if modest income, and loving family, Tolstoy could now throw himself without reserve into creative work. Annette was not only an enthusiastic admirer and source of encouragement, but devoted herself to helping where she could. An excellent seamstress and something of an artist herself, she took much of the purely mechanical work off Feodor's shoulders, helping to prepare materials, cast moulds, and even conduct his correspondence in Russian and French. But above all, she was an inspiration. Fortunately it is not necessary to rely on contemporary descriptions of her charms. For her adoring husband not only modelled wax reliefs and statues of his pretty wife, but swiftly found in her general inspiration for his representation of the female form. Annette's gently classical features and gracefully rounded figure perfectly suited Tolstoy's conception of unadorned female beauty.

Every fashionable Russian drawing-room at that time contained a copy of Bogdanovich's lyric narrative poem, *Dushenka*, based on the Greek tale of the love of Cupid and Psyche. The poet had adapted his version to the Russian scene, the setting being a thinly-disguised park and palace of Tsarskoe Selo. First published in 1778, it drew Feodor Tolstoy's attention as a vehicle suitable for the sort of dreamlike evocation of an imaginary Mediterranean past which attracted him and his contemporaries. Airy, spacious villas, their pillared porticoes opening onto vistas of sun-drenched cypresses and olive-groves, were peopled by god-like youths and nymphs, their graceful limbs inhibited by the barest modicum of clothing. In the still, calm air one can almost hear the shrill hum of the cicadas and smell warm sea-breezes coming off the white-flecked Aegean. Amidst grave assemblages of goddesses, kings and courtiers, Dushenka's combination of demure beauty and innocent nakedness conjures an image irresistibly (and literally) erotic. The delightful Dushenka is in fact Feodor Tolstoy's sweet-natured Annette, whom he used as a model and inspiration during the thirteen years in which he worked on the drawings. As Tolstoy perceived, his restoration of classical themes discarded by Bogdanovich in the poem made a perfect setting for his delicious evocation of the voluptuous dreams of youth, and it is not difficult to recapture the depth of affection he cherished for his adorable young wife.

But this is to look ahead (the *Dushenka* illustrations were executed over the

Bas-relief by Feodor Petrovich Tolstoy of his family in 1811

years 1820 to 1833) to a time when the Tolstoys' affairs were prospering. For some time after their marriage the young couple lived a life, if not of privation, at least unburdened by luxuries. Tolstoy's flat being too small for a family, they moved into Annette's mother's home on Vasilievsky Island. It was further from

Annette Tolstoy as Dushenka

the city centre, but was spacious enough for their needs, and it was there that little Lisa was born. But within five years the old lady went to live with another married daughter in Kharkov, and the house was sold. Feodor and Annette moved to a little rented one-storey house in an even more remote district of Vasilievsky Island. The place seemed to be swarming with hens, ducks, geese, goats and cows; but what it gained in picturesque atmosphere did not compensate for its air of remote desolation.

The household consisted of the family trio, two young serfs from the mother-in-law's house, Ivan and Axinia, and a newly-hired cook. Wealthy relations seemed to prefer to forget about them. Feodor's father, old Count Peter Andreevich, was indeed anxious to help, but the French occupation in 1812 had damaged his estate and left him with little to spare. It was Feodor who relieved him, by inviting his sister Nadezhda to come to join their household. Afterwards, with wry amusement, Feodor would recall their days of Bohemian subsistence.

On one occasion, when he was absent at the Academy, his wife and sister were sitting at home when the door of their room opened to admit a gigantic monk of remarkably sinister appearance. Countess Anna responded tremulously to a per-emptory request for alms, but was terrified to see their visitor sit himself down and thunder out the chorus of some highly unmonastic ditty. Her sister-in-law was so frightened that she shrieked out to imaginary servants below, "Ivan, Peter, Andrei!" The monk gave a coarse laugh: "Call away, my darling! Perhaps I don't know that you only have a female cook, the lad Vanya and a girl (who is playing with baby in the yard), and that cook and Vanya are out? Call away, call away! Maybe they'll come!" And from beneath his cassock he half drew a long glittering knife. The ladies were almost dead with fright, when by a fortunate chance

Feodor happened unexpectedly to return and threw out their pious visitor.

Human oddities at that time aroused little comment on Vasilievsky Island. Every Sunday one such character would pass the Tolstoys' house. This was the poor, mad daughter of a General Glavachevsky, who had become possessed with religious mania. Professing herself a disciple of the well-known mystic, Vice-President Labzin of the Academy of Arts, it was her custom to walk weekly, summer and winter, through the streets completely naked except for a short jacket. In this unusual costume she would march the length of the island, carrying a bucket. This she filled with water from the Neva and then, singing psalms, walked to President Labzin's door, which she piously washed. Curious passers-by were informed, "It is only the General's daughter"; and the police evidently considered her father's rank sufficient licence for her conduct.

Feodor Tolstoy was so absorbed in his work that he remained almost oblivious to his surroundings. So much so, in fact, that on one occasion he too added to the eccentric atmosphere of this urban outpost. One morning, dressed only in his shirt and slippers, he was shaving at a mirror on the windowsill. Beside the mirror the Tolstoys' handsome white poodle Hector lay in contemplative mood. The Count had lathered his face and taken up his razor, when he saw a pair of hands dive through the open window, snatch up the dog, and disappear. Beside himself with rage, Tolstoy jumped out of the window and tore after the intruder. The thief was in sight, running for all he was worth, and Tolstoy gave chase. Passers-by stopped to stare at the apparition: naked but for his shirt and slippers, his face covered in foaming lather, and an open razor in his hand. The thief, glancing back, redoubled the momentum of his flight. Tolstoy too sprinted harder, until at last he caught up with the other just before the Bolshoi Prospekt, the crowded main thoroughfare of Vasilievsky Island. Grabbing the man by the collar, he gave him a punch which knocked him reeling and forced him to drop the poodle. As he picked up the ruffled Hector, Tolstoy's indignation had swiftly turned to relief – and then as quickly to the acutest embarassment. Passers-by had not found it possible to ignore the sight of the half-naked nobleman clutching a large poodle in broad daylight in one of the busiest streets in St. Petersburg. There was nothing for it but to return home, which he did with his face buried in Hector's curly fur.

But if he hoped the incident had passed unnoticed he was mistaken. His strange activity was soon talked about in polite society, which did not approve such outré behaviour – though many conceded that eccentricities of this sort were inevitable in a nobleman who had descended to becoming a professional artist. But his consequent ostracism by the *beau monde* worried him not at all. His days were fully occupied with his work, from which he would not willingly divert a minute. He worked at his employment in the Hermitage and gave instruction at the Mint (a post he had received in 1810), and every minute left was devoted to his painting and casting. But up to 1828 his total income was a mere 2,500 paper roubles (800 silver roubles); in contemporary English pounds sterling, about £130 *per annum*.[6]

Feodor Tolstoy was the last person to concern himself with scales of material wealth or to care for the opinions of vapid socialites. But he would have been less than human had he not nurtured some resentment, and it is this perhaps that explains some ungenerous reflexions on a rich relative. At the house of his uncle and benefactor, General Count Peter Alexandrovich Tolstoy, he met the famous General Alexander Osterman-Tolstoy, of whom he made a striking relief bust in wax. This portrait depicts the General as markedly stiff and haughty (an appearance he provided to those who did not know him well), and Feodor described him at the time as "pompously patrician, and utterly cruel to his serfs": two charges which on the evidence are quite false.[7]

General Osterman-Tolstoy

An understandable feeling of resentment may also have been a contributing factor in his adoption for a period of mildly radical political attitudes, though the true sources of these views must be sought in the generous impulses of an altruistic young artist living at a time when a Byronic longing for public and personal liberty passed like an electric current through the intellectual community. Feodor's friends were for the most part high-spirited young noblemen, burning to fight with giants and tilt at windmills, many of whom were to be implicated in the Decembrist uprising of 1825. As he himself wrote, "these were not the types to which the greater part of our young aristocracy belongs, brought up only for balls and drawing-room prattle, but were people who loved their Fatherland and continually applied themselves to Science with the aim of being of some use to it." He joined masonic lodges and discussion groups, who spoke of a renovated Russia, with a Tsar truly representative of the people, abolition of serfdom, and legal protection for all. Popular enlightenment was seen as an essential key to the emancipated community, and Tolstoy urged emphatically that "our supreme aim consists in the swiftest possible spread of literacy among the ordinary people". He played a leading role in the move to found and multiply schools based on the English Lancaster system, which sought to overcome the shortage of teachers by arranging for senior pupils to assist in instructing their juniors. Three such schools were founded in the capital but, as Alexander I succumbed increasingly to reactionary influences in the latter part of his reign, the schools were frowned upon as sources of free-thinking and sedition and eventually closed.

However, though Tolstoy and his friends privately discussed such radical schemes as the replacement of the monarchy by a republic, he did not follow that uncompromising group which moved towards open revolt against the Government. "My undeviating readiness," he wrote, "was to be of use to all requesting or in need of help. Not having any understanding of politics or its implications, I acted from beginning to end in one way: I helped whom I could, and gave honest advice to those who requested it." In 1821 he left the principal reforming society which he had previously supported, and had no knowledge of the conspiracy culminating in the armed uprising of 1825. Learning of fighting in the Senate Square, he set off to observe events, but returned home without becoming involved. Despite this, his previous dabbling in political activity brought him under suspicion, as the new Emperor Nicholas I stamped out all vestiges of revolution. At the beginning of 1826 he was arrested and interrogated. Denying any knowledge or approval of the uprising, he nevertheless responded firmly and honourably to his questioners.

When a member of the Commission of Enquiry, Prince A. N. Galitzine, suggested that Tolstoy must know the names of members of other branches of the political society to which he had belonged, he replied sarcastically that, "Your Excellency himself has belonged to several societies of mystics, and still less than me do you know their composition." And when asked concerning a close friend who had participated, he replied still more forthrightly that "the enlightened intelligence, honest and sensitive heart, and noble soul of Colonel Feodor Nikolaevich Glinka always drew me to him, and I enjoyed a friendship with him which I still cherish." A manly response of this sort in fact appealed to the Tsar's soldierly instincts, and he was discharged without any reflexion on his character.

In fact, though he made no effort to ingratiate himself with the government of the new Emperor, he strongly disapproved of the December uprising. "My God," he wrote, "how many young men of excellent inclinations, education, and open-hearted love of their country, were compelled to sacrifice their lives for it . . . zealously working for the advancement of their country, honest champions of truth and defenders of the oppressed . . . in one unhappy, rash, profitless conspiracy and open rebellion, they ruined themselves for ever and deprived their country of their fruitful labours." He himself continued openly to advocate widespread educational and legal reforms, and the removal of the crushing burden of serfdom from the peasantry.

It is clear that Feodor Tolstoy, as he himself declared, was not primarily concerned with politics. His prime interest was in the striking of medals. Russian medals at the time were for the most part crudely designed in echoes of styles long passed out of fashion in Western Europe. As Tolstoy himself put it, "All those medals in the taste of Louis XIV's time were compounded of ill-conceived allegories representing mythological gods and suchlike caricatures, garbed in the sort of fantastical clothing used in the theatre of that time; wild beasts and birds, of species impossible to identify. . . . And all this was expressed without taste, quite incongruously to nature, and without any understanding of art or perspective. . . . This ridiculously pitiful position of our medallist's art in the Mint, quite unregulated and demanding totally new artistic forms, must be altered."

In Tolstoy's view no dilettante approach could possibly succeed. His first insistence was that the medallist must be capable of conducting the entire process, from the first design sketch to the final casting. The true medallist was not a technician, but as much an artist as in any other field; as such he must possess both the creative inspiration to conceive his design, and the professional skill to bring it to fruition. In addition he must possess a wide knowledge of history, architecture, natural history, and other sciences, since it was essential to good art that it should be based on authenticity and consistency. Above all, a medal's design should convey with instant clarity the personality, theme or event for which it had been designed. No better source of all these virtues, Tolstoy held, was to be found than in the masterpieces of the Greek and Roman world, with their unerring instinct for line and perspective, and wonderful clarity of concept. Tolstoy himself had already (in 1809) demonstrated in practical form the tenor of his theory, with a magnificent medal struck for the province of Volhynia, in recognition of the achievements of the Polish educationalist Tadeusz Czacki. Other designs, equally superbly executed, appeared in succeeding years.

Four years after his appointment at the Mint, Feodor Tolstoy set before himself a task which in its fulfilment was undoubtedly to become his *magnum opus.* "I am a Russian," he wrote in 1814, as the country rejoiced over the defeat of Napoleon, "and I am proud of the name. And being desirous to participate in my compatriots' glory . . . I am venturing on an undertaking which would daunt the greatest artist. But the unprecedented glory of our times . . . can so inspire a mediocre talent that he will enter the gates of the future. Filled with feelings, I shall venture to portray through medals the remarkable events of the years 1812, 1813, 1814 and pass on to posterity in those weak shades of feeling of which I am capable; being desirous to tell them how in our time everyone felt as I do, and all were happy to bear the name of Russian."

The first medal, which he thereupon designed, moulded and cast, displayed a bust of the Tsar Alexander I, represented as the Slavonic divine hero Rodomysl. Feodor Tolstoy presented this to the Academy, together with designs for a further nineteen medals. "If the Academy could find the means of rendering me assistance," he wrote in his accompanying letter, "I would then set about engraving nineteen medals of similar design." He was reduced to making this request, as he absolutely lacked funds to accomplish his project independently. "It is an enormous undertaking; besides my own arduous and prolonged labours, modelling all the drawings in wax and carving their moulds requires expenses of an extent which I, existing on a lone salary, cannot meet. I fear, what would be terrible for me, that if I don't receive the allowance from the Government I am about to request, then I will be obliged to abandon what for me would be such a deeply interesting artistic enterprise."

But the Academy was indeed greatly impressed. A special committee was set up to examine Tolstoy's petition; their enthusiasm was swiftly aroused by the grandeur of the project, coupled as it was with the artist's previously demonstrated abilities. He was granted twenty thousand roubles to enable him to complete his task. The sum appears lavish, until one contemplates its magnitude. Tolstoy aimed at nothing less than perfection, and his meticulous attitude to his project expanded it enormously at every stage. Even before he began preliminary sketches he was concerned to conduct extensive literary researches on the events he commemorated, seeking out also eye-witnesses of the campaigns. He talked with Marshal Kutuzov and with veterans of all ranks, absorbing their memories and impressions until his conceptions flowed together in a creative whole.

From the beginning he eschewed any idea of conventional representations of victorious generals or contemporary arms and uniforms. Equally he turned his

Kulm medal   *Czacki medal*

back on allegorical or symbolic obscurity. His inspiration lay in his beloved Greek and Roman past, which he saw not as a legendary aesthetic conception but as a real world, where the virtues of patriotism, heroism and civic duty were exalted. Classicism had been developed from French and German models in Russia in the middle decades of the eighteenth century, deriving fresh impetus from Western Europe after excavations at Herculaneum and Pompeii had brought the old world vividly to life once more. What both Europeans and Russians admired in the ancient world was, in the phrase of the great German scholar Winckelmann, "a noble simplicity and a calm grandeur" appropriate to the romantic art and civic sense of the Enlightenment. Feodor Tolstoy's adoration of the Greek world echoed Herder's rapturous encomium: "Greece will remain the place where mankind experienced its fairest youth and bridal beauty . . . noble youth with fair anointed limbs, favourite of all the Graces, beloved of all the Muses, victor in Olympia and all the other games, spirit and body together in one single flower in bloom. . . . Greece, type and exemplar of all beauty, grace, and simplicity! Youthful blossoming of the human race – Oh would that it could have lasted forever!"[8]

Tolstoy felt that his neo-classical approach raised the events he was commemorating to a higher, aethereal plane. The graceful, energetic figures that so boldly stood for the turbulent events of recent history generally personify whole classes of the heroic Russian people, or high ideals of gallantry and chivalry. It is all on a Homeric scale: to the French he conceded a martial boldness, and to the Russians those characteristics on which they had begun to pride themselves: massive, patient strength, resilience, and a calm confidence in the justice of their cause and ultimate victory. In some of the medals the fighting is fast and furious, with swords snapping, axes raised aloft, and anguished figures reeling from deadly blows. In others all is purposeful haste, as when Napoleon apprehensively flees across a recumbent figure symbolizing the River Niemen, or when two Russian warriors rush forward over fallen bodies at Katsbach. At General Osterman-Tolstoy's crucial victory at Kulm in 1813, a Russian champion wrests the sword

163

from a falling Frenchman. At the struggle on the Beresina, a terrible calm momentarily descends as a stalwart Russian, his sword and shield slung on his back,
points grimly behind him to a field littered with tumbled corpses. Then the
movement gathers pace, and when the Russian armies finally enter France in
1814, we see at Brienne, Fère-Champenoise and Arcis-sur-Aube the enemy sinking
ever lower as the Russian conqueror strikes him fiercely down with lance and
mace. The medals are not only individually harmonious, but move as a series with
a varying flow and momentum reflecting the epic events they commemorate.

Raising the militia, 1812

The task was immense. Applying himself with all his exceptional energy and
concentration, Tolstoy struck the first medal in the series (that of Alexander I) in
1814. It was not until 1836 that he completed the final touches of the last, *Peace in
Europe*: he had been at work on his masterpiece for twenty-two years. As the
magnificent series began gradually to appear from the Mint, public acclaim and
honours descended on the grateful artist from every quarter. Russians naturally
waxed ecstatic, patriotic pride being allied to artistic appreciation, and in 1828
Tolstoy was nominated Vice-President of the Academy of Arts. Almost equal
enthusiasm arose abroad as it became apparent that Russia possessed artistic
genius largely unsuspected. Virtually all European academies bestowed honorary

membership on him. The British Government invited him to design a similar series commemorating British victories, an offer which he declined on the patriotic grounds that he was constitutionally incapable of doing full justice to a cause not his own. From Vienna the medallists of the Austrian Academy wrote to declare that "no country had created anything finer in recent centuries", and the Chancellor, Prince Metternich, wrote in similar terms. Still more valued praise came from the great Goethe, who in 1817 expressed deep admiration for Tolstoy's abilities, and a keen desire to meet him. It was during this time, too, that Tolstoy produced (1820–1840) the delightful illustrations to Bogdanovich's *Dushenka* already described.

A faithful friend, Nikolai Longinov, who had been the one person to stick by the family after the unfortunate episode of the poodle-thief, had taken opportunities of praising Tolstoy's work to the Empress Elizabeth, wife of Tsar Alexander I. The good-natured Empress expressed interest in meeting him, and the young artist was brought to court and presented to her. During their conversation the Empress mentioned that Longinov had praised the Count's skill with water-colours, and asked whether she might not see some specimens of his work. A little embarrassed, he explained that he was first and foremost a medallist, and that his painting was simply an amateur's hobby. But the Empress was insistent, and Tolstoy returned home, highly delighted with this warm reception.

The painting he selected for his sovereign's inspection was a favourite, and had an amusing anecdote attached to it. The picture depicted, with astonishing truth to life, some sprigs of red, white and black currants tumbled together at random. On one occasion Longinov and his wife had called when Feodor was out, and asked the artist's wife Annette if they could look at some paintings. She pulled out an album containing the picture of the currants, which amazed the Longinovs with its uncanny realism. Suddenly there was a cry: the Tolstoys' baby daughter, whom Annette was holding in her arms, was demanding to be fed some of the succulent fruit! Everyone laughed, when Mrs. Longinov cried out sharply, "Countess, what have you done? Look, Mashenka's tears have gone on the page!" But the "tears" were drops of dew painted by Tolstoy's unerring hand! Surviving examples of his skill show that the story need be no exaggeration.

The picture was presented by Longinov to the Empress, who was delighted beyond measure. A grateful message came back, followed not long after by the gift of a valuable diamond ring, which when sold enabled the Tolstoys to exchange their little house by the Smolensk cemetery for a larger house nearby on the north side of Vasilievsky Island, overlooking the wooded park and mansion of an old Count Stroganov. Its light and airy rooms, with sparse but tasteful furnishings in the Grecian style are recorded in a delightful watercolour Tolstoy executed not long after. But matters did not end there: so pleased was the Empress with her picture that she ordered a succession of copies, to present to her relatives abroad. For each one there arrived another diamond ring, and it became a familiar joke of Feodor's that he had fed an entire family on those currants. The Empress continued to be a generous benefactress to the Tolstoys, arranging for their sick daughter Lisa to be treated and educated at her expense.

Tolstoy's industry was extraordinary; and nothing seemed to disturb his concentration. "In the morning," his daughter Maria remembered, "my father generally arose about cock-crow and sat at a little window working on his medals. . . . Or he would disappear somewhere, probably attending his duties at the Mint. . . .

At four o'clock Papa would return home and immediately change into a pink linen Russian shirt. Grandfather and one or other of the uncles practically always came to dinner. The table was laid below an awning of the outhouse. Having dined speedily on whatever God provided, all poured out in a jovial crowd to the courtyard and, each doing what he could, began to enjoy the bright summer air. The ladies played hoop-la, while the boys drove sticks into the ground and often played at knucklebones." The Count would entertain the family with feats of juggling, and took them boating on the Chernaya Reka, or walking in Count Stroganov's park beyond.

Family Portrait, *1830*

Meanwhile a series of bas-reliefs illustrating the Odyssey received general acclaim, as did a powerful terracotta bust of the god Morpheus (1822). He designed reliefs depicting (in the Grecian style) scenes of rural labour for a ceremonial gold plate presented to Nicholas I at his coronation, and later modelled a set of doors with Christ seated in judgment with the four evangelists for the Cathedral of Christ the Saviour in Moscow. At the same time that he was working on these grandiose projects, he experimented more and more widely with the painting which he had over-modestly described to the Empress as his hobby. There were exquisitely delicate studies of flowers, fruit, insects, and birds, all as fresh and vivid to the eye as the famous currants which made his fortune. There were sketches of rural life, drawings of imaginary scenes from the Roman and Greek past, and brilliant individual tours-de-force, such as a *trompe d'oeuil* of a country scene apparently lying beneath a sheet of tissue paper – all as three-dimensional

Studies of fruit and flowers, by F. P. Tolstoy

as reality. Then there were larger landscapes, and evocative effects of dark night-clouds over expanses of water, the moon half glimpsed in the still obscurity. A girl sits at an open window (perhaps his own Annette), gently strumming her guitar, while outside boats silently glide down the moonlit Neva. Pushkin wrote of Feodor Tolstoy as the fitting illustrator of his masterpiece *Eugene Onegin*. "What if one were to employ F. Tolstoy's magical brush? No, too expensive," he sighed.

At the window on a moonlit night, *1822*

Yet another art Tolstoy made his own was that of the silhouette. Silhouettes as portraits had been popular for some time, but Tolstoy diverted himself with a series of vignette scenarios, principally lively and naturalistic scenes of campaign from the Napoleonic Wars. Though designed as usual with exquisite attention to detail, movement and realism, the artist regarded them merely as amusing *jeux d'esprit*. They portray armies on the march, Cossacks, artillery, Napoleon seated at a fire, fights, and so on; also entrancing scenes of peasant and rural life. These panoramas were particularly entertaining for children. When, as so often occurred, his home was filled with a cheerful crowd of friends, relations and visitors, he suffered no resentment at the distraction, but his indefatigable brain and hands continued working. One of his daughters recorded how he "was not put out by the presence of visitors, but continued drawing while he listened to conversations, readings and music." He also contributed to the entertainment by cutting out his silhouette scenes and stories from glossy black paper. This delightful genre was to Tolstoy simply an exercise of skill and means of amusement, but no serious art. As a result many examples were carelessly thrown away or lost: a tragedy which is evident from the striking naturalness and verve of surviving specimens.

As if all this were not enough, Feodor Tolstoy branched out into yet another field of creative inspiration. At an early age he had attended the ballet in St. Petersburg, and had experienced the greatest enthusiasm for an art that literally lives and breathes. His first creation was *The Golden Harp*, a ballet with an Ossianic theme. Tolstoy, who had earlier studied the whole art under the great *chef de ballet* Didelot, wrote the libretto, designed dramatically striking costumes *à l'écossaise* for the dancers, drew up suitably wildly picturesque scenery for the backdrops, and in a series of sketches indicated to the ballet-master poses for the principals indicative of their roles in the dance. The ballet, composed in 1838, promised to be a sensational feast of colourful spectacle. One is astonished by the ability with which Tolstoy succeeded in blending the flow of the dance, with his picturesquely barbaric costumes, and rocky hillsides and forest glades, before which his figures spin on the grass, and float in the mountain air. There is also a certain balletic style in Tolstoy's contemporary engravings for *Dushenka*, but there the atmosphere is still and contemplative; in *The Golden Harp* bare limbs and flowing draperies awake from the languorous Mediterranean sun to vigorous life in the clear air of Northern mountains and mists.

In 1842 Tolstoy created a second ballet, this time set in that Grecian clime, which was to him "when all the world was young". In fact neither ballet was ever performed, owing to some whim of the Tsar, who declined to permit performances in the imperial theatres. Perhaps the attractive nudity which adorns some scenes shocked imperial sensibilities, though it can hardly be supposed it was intended to be literally translated to the stage. Tolstoy was disheartened, though not daunted, by this unexpected frustration.

His absorption in every field of artistic creation enabled him to overcome a much more poignant reverse. In 1835 his wife Annette, his inspiration, helpmate and refuge during the years in which he rose from impoverished obscurity to recognition as one of Europe's foremost creative talents, died, leaving two daughters, Lisa and Maria. Three years later, at the age of fifty-five, he married again. The bride was Anastasia Ivanovna Ivanov, the twenty-two-year-old daughter of a poor army officer. She was also attractive and clever, and succeeded to the supportive role of poor Annette. She too bore him two daughters, Catherine and Olga, born in 1843 and 1859 respectively.

The birth of Olga, when her father was already seventy-six, suggests that Feodor Tolstoy had inherited the physical vigour enjoyed by most of his family. But in middle age his health had begun to deteriorate. He found himself worryingly short of breath, and his heart was giving trouble. His medical advisers recommended a trip abroad for treatment at a spa. Tolstoy had long been anxious to visit the great art galleries and architectural treasures of Italy, but owing to his straitened circumstances (he was still dependent on his salary, and had extensive family commitments), it seemed impossible. He reluctantly decided to appeal to the Tsar for assistance. Supported by the President of the Academy, Tolstoy petitioned for a grant of four thousand roubles to enable him to follow the doctors' recommendation. Nicholas I consented to the appeal, ungenerously however halving the sum requested. Despite the hardship this entailed, Tolstoy decided he had no choice and set off on his travels, accompanied by his wife, on 5 June 1845. He crossed Germany, visited France, and then settled in Italy. Throughout his travels he kept a diary, in which he recorded wide-ranging reflexions on the people and politics of the lands he visited. He also made continual record with pencil and brush of the scenery, quaint costumes and characters, and picturesque remains of all he saw. Whilst he revelled in all this living evidence of ancient civilization, he shared his compatriots' conviction that their homeland possessed qualities that were somehow deeper and truer than those of the frivolous and superficial Europeans. "We are still young," he reflected, "we don't yet have continuity of creation, precision or accuracy. But in spite of our youth, let us only acquire the direction, the means, and we will immediately overtake the Germans despite their centuries-long enjoyment of the fruits of civilization. And Europe will recognize what Russians can do. The cleverness, boldness, and all those innate qualities of the Russian people will far, far outstrip her." One may detect that peculiarly Russian characteristic: the frustrating sense of inferiority coupled with consciousness of vigorous talent. To a Russian, overwhelmed by the creative experience in all fields from political to artistic, it was maddening beyond measure to encounter placid German nobles "whose only conversation concerned cattle-breeding, farming, hunting and horses".

Staying in Rome and Naples, Feodor Tolstoy was at last physically able to immerse himself in the antique world of the Caesars which had been his greatest single source of inspiration. But he expressed a continual disgust at the degraded appearance of much of the poverty-stricken populace, which reflected a great deal his deeply-cherished instincts of humanity – and also perhaps a little of that patriotic self-consciousness which led Russian travellers in Europe, from Fonvizin onwards,[9] to draw unfavourable comparisons with the Motherland.

In Rome Tolstoy's impatience with bureaucratic philistinism performed a useful service for the colony of Russian artists, granted scholarships by the Academy to study and work abroad. The Russian Government had for reasons best known to itself selected as director and supervisor of the expatriate painters a German General named Kil, who coupled a sublime ignorance of all matters aesthetic with boorish manners and an unpleasing personality. Fortunately Tolstoy's prestige and influence at the Academy sufficed to secure the General's removal: an event which aroused the heartfelt gratitude of the young painters.

There was much to rejoice in. He was reunited with his old friend Gogol, and spent fruitful hours with Russian and Italian painters and scholars. The mingling of the old world with the new in teeming cities, where the colourfully-clad inhabitants still lived in tenements, crowding streets where Virgil walked, and worshipping in churches familiar to Dante and Boccaccio, struck the artist with delicious freshness. He strolled and sketched in the ruins of Pompeii, visited the galleries of Florence and Genoa, and mentally peopled the Coliseum with crowded scenes of Imperial glory and cruelty his imagination had conceived long years before his arrival.

The parsimony of the Government cast a shadow over this pleasant round. Tolstoy felt increasing nostalgia for St. Petersburg and his comfortable home, but his funds had run so low that he lacked the means of his daily subsistence, let alone the expenses of a journey home. His original funds were exhausted; after taking the waters at Franzensbad he had lain ill for six weeks. Driven to desperation, he petitioned Tsar Nicholas to grant him the further two thousand roubles required to take him back. He possessed no private property or income beyond his house on the Chernaya Reka, and with a wife and three children to support life was always difficult. The Emperor granted him a further thousand roubles, and in April 1846 he returned home with his wife to an unrelenting round of work, labouring on his design for the doors of the Cathedral of Christ the Saviour, and on drawings, paintings, designs for ballets, medals, sculptures, and illustrations.

Feodor was glad to be home. From Italy he had written to a friend to express his longing: "I find things so much better at home, not just because one is used to it, but carefully going into all aspects (setting aside climate and architecture – but that's another matter); comparing everywhere I've been, the good and bad with our good and bad; I say that according to my understanding and instinct we in Russia are several hundred times better off . . . I can't wait for the moment when I will know the joy of being back in my native land."

Not only his native land but those others which were rated so much lower showered accumulating honours on his greying head. He was awarded a gold medal at the Great Exhibition in London in 1851. In the same year he was made an honorary member of the Moscow Society of Arts, and in 1859 he was elected Vice President of the Academy of Arts for life. On Sunday evenings, when he was "at home", his house on Vasilievsky Island had long been the rendezvous of many of the greatest creative minds in Russia. In early years there were Pushkin, Zhukovsky, Gogol, Krylov, Belinsky, Bryullov and Glinka. As the decades passed their places were taken by Shevchenko, Maikov, Turgenev, and a promising young cousin, Leo Tolstoy. Many lesser-known artists and scholars were welcomed, and in particular young and struggling artists were given unstinting encouragement and advice. Tolstoy remembered too well his own years of struggle not to wish to help those entering on the same arduous road.

He was an inspiring guide, as all who knew him concurred to testify. It was not merely his generous and sympathetic character which gained him universal love and respect, but the unfailing freshness of his approach and the eternal youthfulness of his enthusiasm. He himself was always learning; not merely the multifarious skills at which he had at an early age become proficient, but virtually every other discipline which might further reveal to him the extent of the beauty and wonder of God's creation. He regularly attended lectures on physics, chemistry, zoology, statistics, political economy, history, archaeology, and even astronomy. There was no dilettantism in this, as his profuse notes and essays testify. Thoroughness was his watchword; it was not enough for him to paint exquisite watercolour landscapes – first he had to master the art of preparing paints.

Gradually, however, his cruel ill-health gained an increasing ascendancy. He suffered from a glaucoma in his left eye, and from terrible headaches. "I am sometimes ready to long for death," he confided in a bitter moment to his diary. In 1861 he travelled to Italy again, principally in search of medical treatment. But his personal suffering did not check his concern with his countrymen's wellbeing. He was overjoyed at the news of the Emancipation. "Longing for the emancipation of the serfs was the dream of his whole life," wrote a daughter; "he was unspeakably happy that he lived to see it happen, and his last work was a medal commemorating an event which for him was so important and dear to his heart."

Despite extensive treatment during his stay abroad, Tolstoy returned home in 1862 little the better. His health continued to deteriorate, until in latter years he was almost completely blind. What never declined were his unfailing goodness of heart, generosity and fascination with every aspect of man and his creation. He died on 13 April 1873 at the age of ninety. He, who had done so much to enrich the lives of his countrymen and all humanity, was able to leave his widow precisely a hundred roubles – insufficient to cover his funeral expenses.

7
Two Reactionaries

$\mathcal{D}$mitri Nikolaevich Tolstoy was born on 12 March 1806 on the family estate of Znamenskoe, in the province of Ryazan. The estate was inherited from his great-great-grandfather, Count Peter Andreevich Tolstoy, whose services to Peter the Great were described in Chapter Three of this book. His father, Count Nikolai Feodorovich, had enlarged the estate and built a splendid church there, designed by the celebrated Rastrelli.[1]

Dmitri was the youngest of five sisters and three brothers, and they lived in a happy-go-lucky turmoil characteristic of many noble mansions at that time. The house was filled with people coming and going, as well as with those who came but never went. These included the Polish dancing-master, engaged from Moscow for four months but who lingered on for forty years and died at Znamenskoe. There were also the customary tutor and governess, the German steward and Dutch housekeeper, wandering travellers and retired officers. The transient visitors would die and be replaced, themselves sleeping peacefully in the family church-yard. Then of course there was the customary stream of buffoons and idiots who found temporary asylum with the Tolstoys, followed by singers and even entire choirs. The regular servants comprised some eighty men and women, each with a particular duty and place at table.

The Count and Countess appeared perfect parents, and were adored by their children and army of attendants and visitors. Old Count Nikolai Feodorovich and Countess Natalia Andreevna would bustle out delightedly to greet the latest stream of guests, and with their elder children were popular visitors at neighbour-ing homes. When Dmitri came, years later, to write his memoirs in the library at Znamenskoe, he recalled his conviction that no one else had so large and happy a home or played quite as he and his brothers and sisters did.

Once a year, generally in the summer, came the great family expedition to Zadonsk. Count Nikolai made this pilgrimage to visit his uncle's tomb and that of the holy Bishop Tikhon. The organization of this annual outing was a very lengthy business, and the journey itself never took less than a week – though Zadonsk was not more than seventy miles away. When everyone was at last assembled a long train of vehicles slowly began to debouch onto the highroad. First came a carriage containing Mama, Dmitri and his smallest sister. This was followed by another containing the four elder sisters and their governess. Next came Papa's barouche, with the Tolstoy arms on the side, followed by that of Dmitri's two elder brothers

Previous page: Dmitri Andreevich Tolstoy   Autumn, *by F. P. Tolstoy*

174

with their tutor. Behind them straggled an endless stream of droshkies, wagons and carts bearing the servants. At the rear, providing the final impression of a regiment on the march, came the Znamenskoe baggage-waggons piled up with the household's beds and bedding, tents and kitchen utensils.

The progress was made at a snail's pace. When the weather was warm and the scenery inviting, the Count would signal for the train to stop. A lavish meal was spread out on the greensward, after which he would sip tea in the shade. The day drew on – why not dine as well? – and it ended with the tents going up and all sleeping under a spangled violet sky. Next day there was no pressing haste, and generally the column got under way after lunch. For the children these journeys were a never-failing kaleidoscopic paradise.

When they eventually arrived at Zadonsk they stayed in the monastery. Before unpacking all trooped into the church to attend a memorial service for Bishop Tikhon. Little Dmitri gazed, afraid and excited, at the sarcophagus surmounted by its golden image of Tikhon. Lamps and candles gleamed in the darkness, and the melancholy funereal chant, punctuated by the shrieks and sobs of deranged women in the congregation, had a terrifying effect upon him, until he longed for the moment they would escape into the daylight. But once outside, the Tolstoy household and the monks were the best of friends; presents were exchanged, and Dmitri was treated with cherries. His parents were extremely devout, and the annual fasts and ceremonies of the Church were observed rigorously.

When Napoleon invaded Russia in 1812 it made only a dimly remembered impact on the little boy, who was still only six. He recalled endless serious discussions amongst his elders, the only one of which that made any impact was a tale of a gallant General Raevsky, who set off for war accompanied by his two young sons. Dmitri dreamed several times that Raevsky had with his own hand slain the monster Bonaparte. He was however an eye witness of two of the eddying currents of war. Across the park in one direction streamed wild Bashkir and Kirghiz light horse, whilst in the other marched a column of French prisoners-of-war. His father bestowed equal hospitality on friend and foe: the French officers dined at his table, and their men in the courtyard below.

One officer, a Captain Pagan, was billeted on them. He became a family friend, and continued to correspond long after his release and return to France. What was remarkable was that this generous treatment in no way angered the peasants

Al fresco meal, *by F. P. Tolstoy*

who flocked to gaze on the prisoners. Some were even heard to remark sensibly that "they didn't want to come here; Bonaparte sent them." This spoke a great deal for the essential good nature of the Russian peasant, who had suffered considerably as a result of the war.

Sadly, time flew on and the children began growing up. Dmitri's father, who adored them all, became increasingly unhappy as the time came for the eldest to leave for his military service. However Alexander, who was the family favourite, could not wait to join his regiment in Moscow and was in ecstasies when his new uniform arrived. But when in 1818 the moment arrived even he was overcome with sorrow, and the whole household wept bitterly. It was the first moment of sadness Dmitri had experienced.

Old Count Nikolai never recovered from the loss. His cheerful happy nature left him and he became melancholy and withdrawn. He was soon obliged to walk with a stick or with the support of a servant's arm. Thinking of his son at church, his hands would tremble and his old eyes fill with tears. As he grew more enfeebled and solitary, so the family's condition deteriorated. Friends moved away, lost touch or died, and the Tolstoys at Znamenskoe faded from their central position in the locality. It was as a result of this that the old Count was subjected to a horrible indignity.

A certain Vasily Anokhin, a government clerk in the neighbourhood, had appeared as a lowly but kindly-treated guest at Znamenskoe. An ambitious fellow, he afterwards managed to get himself enrolled onto the ranks of the serving nobility. This required certificates from local men of standing, which Count Tolstoy was the first to sign. But Anokhin was an ambitious, embittered man, one of those to whom a kindness is a patronizing favour to be resented. One pleasant, sunny morning he burst into the house with some policemen, announcing arrogantly that he had come to take away recruits for the army from the household. Armed sentries were stationed at the entrance, whilst Anokhin and his men rudely ransacked the house and manhandled men of suitable age downstairs. As he saw his shrieking servants hauled off, the Count was so insulted and horrified at his own impotence that he almost suffered a stroke. His wife fainted, and the frightened children were in tears.

Eventually it was over, and Anokhin carried off in triumph a number of men shackled together. They included the Count's valet, butler and favourite cook – dear friends, with whom he used to play cards. Fifty years later, when Dmitri

Taking a recruit

came to write his account of this outrage, he found he could not do so without once again experiencing the same sense of pain. Eventually strings were pulled in Ryazan and the abducted servants returned, but not before they had suffered the usual treatment of having the front halves of their heads shaven bald. Little Dmitri watched their arrival from the porch.

This incident illustrates as well as any other the capricious and cruel nature of the old autocracy. What in theory exalted the despotic power of the Tsar, in practice enabled mean-minded men like Anokhin to act on occasion as petty tyrants over the highest in the land. It was this essential lawlessness of the autocracy that drove many high-spirited young men of the time into the ranks of the Decembrists and other reforming or revolutionary organizations.

Meanwhile the children's education proceeded in typically eccentric fashion. *All* subjects in their little domestic school were taught by the Polish dancing-master, Vikenty. Vikenty taught them the little French he knew (with a strong Polish accent), geography, universal history and arithmetic: all out of what primers he could find in the house. That there existed other branches of knowledge he never suspected. At the age of thirteen Dmitri's education had progressed so far that he could read French without understanding a single word, possessed a fragmentary knowledge of Greek and classical history, and knew (up to a point) the first four sections of the arithmetic course. On the other hand he knew all the liturgy and catechism, and was thoroughly familiar with the Bible and other sacred writings. As he remarked later, there was a little lack of balance in this system; yet he grew up to become one of the finest scholars of his age.

However, a great change was looming in the lives of the peaceful inhabitants of Znamenskoe. After thirty years of bucolic contentment, the Count found himself obliged to visit Moscow. The most ecstatic excitement reigned in the household when the news became known. Moscow! What magic lay in the very word! Dmitri's brain buzzed with a turmoil of magical images. He pictured the great city with some difficulty, presuming that it must be a much larger version of the village of Znamenskoe, surrounded by even lusher corn-fields. He was particularly fascinated by the concept of bridges, never having seen one. That they were built of stone was the most remarkable factor, and Dmitri pictured sparks flying from the shoes of horses passing over, like those of the knights in his childhood ballads.

In Moscow the family was to stay at the home of a cousin who at that time was occupying a post at Revel on the Baltic. The house was near the Presnensky Gate and in order to reach it, it was fortunately necessary to traverse all Moscow. To young Dmitri, peeping from the carriage window, it was a panorama of unalloyed excitement. Magnificent *stone* houses and churches crowded every street, stone lions at the doors and golden cupolas glinting on high, and crowds of carriages and people startled his excited imagination at every turn. Especially appealing was the succession of colourful shop signs which Dmitri took to be a sort of public art display. So crowded and splendid was the noisy vision that it seemed to the child like something projected from a magic lantern. How strange, for example, to see all the traffic moving on wheels through the snow, instead of on sledges as at home!

Soon after their arrival Dmitri was taken by a servant on his first walk through the city. At close quarters it all seemed more wonderful still, for now he could gaze into shop-windows piled high with glittering treasures of every sort. At Pedotti's, the famous confectioners, they stopped to gaze at ascending pyramids

177

of vases and jars of multi-coloured sweets. The temptation was too much and, extracting a small coin from his companion, he entered the treasure-house. A magical bell tinkled from above and they were inside. There all was even more stunningly wonderful: the great room appeared like one of those enchanted chambers his nurse had described in fairytales, and the magnificent figure who came forward to greet him even more like their magical proprietors. "What would you like?" enquired this godlike being: a question more easily asked than answered. The choice was limitless, but what could one buy with a five-kopek piece? After long deliberation he fastened on a cake made in the shape of a hen's egg, and promptly ate it in the shop with indescribable delight.

Gradually the family settled in to the new life. There were visits from numerous relations, who to the Tolstoys appeared awesomely sophisticated in their manners, whilst they in turn must have seemed incurably homespun. Numerous dinner invitations arrived, causing some distress to the Tolstoy girls who had little idea what to wear. The elder girls, charming and beautiful, were soon attending balls at the Nobles' Assembly Rooms, where the cream of Russian society congregated. It was difficult at first to obtain tickets to this exclusive circle, but all was soon arranged by an influential uncle, Count Feodor Andreevich Tolstoy, a General and Senator who possessed one of the finest libraries in Russia, which the great historian Karamzin had used as his principal source.

Despite their willing induction into society, the Tolstoys lived at home just as they had done at Znamenskoe. Hordes of servants filled the house, one of whom

Feodor Andreevich Tolstoy

provides an example of the extraordinary continuity of Russian life in the early nineteenth century. This was the *skazochnik*, or storyteller. When Count Nikolai retired to bed and his valet had drawn the curtains, the *skazochnik* in a loud clear voice told stories until his master was asleep. A similar functionary had doubtless told the same stories to his ancestor Indris nearly five centuries earlier.[2]

But, alas, the old gentleman was nearing his end. Despite constant attendance by Dr. Pfeller, one of Moscow's most distinguished physicians, and a course of the fashionable electrical treatment, he grew weaker all the time. A French specialist, Dr. Cantou, was called in, to the outrage of Pfeller, who denounced him as an ignorant horse doctor. But even Cantou's treatment was of no avail, and at the end of May 1820 the Count suffered an apoplectic fit. The closely-knit household was in despair, the Countess scarcely conscious and the daughters weeping continually. A priest was summoned, who found Count Nikolai already unconscious and seemingly unable to receive the Last Sacrament. Only the tears of Dmitri's beautiful sister Anna could persuade the kindly priest for once to condone the irregularity and administer the rites. Dmitri rushed into the room, to find his beloved father seated still and pale in his armchair. He threw himself down, kissing the cold hand and covering it with tears until he was borne away.

Dmitri went to stay with some cousins nearby. They treated him with every sympathy, and he was particularly touched by the solicitude of their six-year-old son, who tried to give him all his toys. But it was no good; all this kindness merely served to remind him with greater poignancy of what he had lost. Perhaps at that very moment his father's soul was departing from this world! In fact the old man recovered consciousness for a few days, and bestowed a blessing on his son. Then, on 2 June, he died and his body was taken home for burial. When the cortège neared Znamenskoe the weeping peasants accompanied it to the church. There he was buried beside his father and grandfather, Count Feodor Ivanovich (the grandson of Peter Tolstoy, Peter the Great's Ambassador in Constantinople), who had originally built the church.

After this tragedy the family could no longer bear to continue life in the same Moscow home, so a house was rented where life passed idly enough in the daily round with neighbouring relatives. Dmitri took up drawing lessons, and soon became convinced he would one day become a great artist. He became close friends with a cousin, Maria Dokhturov, who was gifted and intelligent, and who introduced him to German philosophy which at that time reigned supreme in Russia. To improve his sadly neglected education, Dmitri took up quarters in a French *pension*. But despite the efforts of the Polish dancing-master, his French remained so bad he had to be removed after a few weeks, and subsequent efforts at tuition proved unavailing.

One day his mother announced that they would spend the summer in the country. Now Dmitri was happy at last, and could spend his days roaming freely in the gardens and woods around. And it was now, oddly enough, that his real education began. His father had left a very fine library of books on all subjects, in which Dmitri browsed by the hour. As he admitted, this method of self-teaching might have resulted in a harmful dissipation of his intellectual resources, but fortunately an innate feeling for scholarship led him in the right direction. It was for this that both he and the library had been waiting, and long happy hours spent in the company of dead or distant writers and scholars were to bear rich fruit.

Then, when the sun beamed down on the lush lawns of Znamenskoe, he would tear himself away from his books and set out for the open fields. Hawking was his passion. "I bought a falcon," he recalled, "and for a whole night trained him on my wrist. I did not actually hunt with him once. To me it was pathetic to see the defenceless quail when the bird of prey pounced on it; what interested me was to release the wild falcon, which from a savage bird had become an obedient instrument of my will. Occasionally, when I released him to swoop aloft, he would joyfully hover in the air, describing flowing circles in the great void above. Now he soared higher and higher . . . but I only had to whistle and he, at the familiar sound, was back on my wrist and preening his feathers with his blood-thirsty beak."

But these blissful days were drawing to a close. Dmitri was sixteen, and had to prepare for his state service. For young men of the best families the military was the only choice, the civil service being despised as a near disgrace. Since Peter the Great instituted his Table of Ranks in 1722, nobles were firstly obliged and, after Peter III issued a fresh Charter in 1762, later expected to enter the state service. In Nicholas I's reign, in particular, any attempt to evade this service was regarded with the utmost suspicion: such a man must surely harbour thoughts disloyal to Government. However, as the Table of Ranks had permeated the whole outlook of society and offered the only regular path to high office and lucrative rewards, most people accepted it as a fact of life.[3] Dmitri was entered for the Guards, and as a result obliged to study earnestly for his entry examination to the cadet school.

In the winter of 1822 he returned to Moscow and took up quarters with a cousin who lay under something of a cloud for having married a mere Titular Counsellor. They had a flat in a wooden house in Great Presnensky Street, and Dmitri slept in a screened-off bed in the hall. Despite this he was treated as one of the family and became very fond of his odd hosts. The husband was a freemason, cryptic allusions to which mystery interlarded his speech, whilst another cousin lodging with them, an attractive young widow, was not unusual in speaking good French and exceedingly poor Russian. She soon married a masonic friend.

Meanwhile Dmitri, perpetually short of funds, ran out of money to pay for his tutoring. He was saved by the intervention of his kind landlord, who arranged for two masonic friends, Stepan Maslov and Ivan Kalaidovich to provide lessons at a nominal charge. "For my part," wrote Dmitri much later, when he had become a distinguished public figure, "I nurtured for [Maslov] all my life the deepest gratitude and filial devotion. Today, when he is 79 and I 66, after meeting him I feel like a timid schoolboy before his master." Maslov arranged for his young friend's introduction to the magic circle of the "aces" of Russian aristocratic society: Prince Dmitri Galitzine, Prince Sergei Gagarin, and his famous cousin General Peter Tolstoy.

All this while Dmitri Tolstoy had been brought up in a climate of opinion which was in his experience unquestioningly loyal to the Tsar, the Orthodox Church and the Motherland. That uncomplicated world received an irreversible shock when, during holidays at Znamenskoe in 1825, the family read in the newspapers of the death of the Emperor Alexander I. There had been no previous indication that the Tsar had even been ill, let alone dying, and for a while the report was simply disbelieved. Then, when the truth became known, incredulity gave way to anguished sorrow. The noble-hearted Tsar, who had led Russia to victory over Napoleon, restored the liberties of Europe, and established the Holy Alliance was no more! At Znamenskoe the mourning was heartfelt and sincere, until it was abruptly interrupted by even more startling news. In swift succession the Grand Duke Constantine had refused the appalling burden of the throne, his brother Nicholas had instead been declared Tsar . . . and a rebellion against him had broken out and barely been suppressed in St. Petersburg! "Rebellion" was what everyone locally termed it, since the word and concept "revolution" were as yet unknown.

Few people in the province looked on the Decembrist uprising with anything but revulsion. The landowning class saw it as a treacherous attack on the central edifice of Russian society, while the peasantry either shared this view or presumed (from the conspirators' background) that it was all a plot of discontented nobles. Only in the towns did the disaffected liberal intelligentsia bitterly regret the failure of the coup. When Dmitri returned to Moscow he found a very different climate of opinion from that prevalent in rural Ryazan. Many of the greatest families had youthful relatives at that moment in the Peter-Paul prison awaiting trial and condemnation. Whilst the older generation agonized over their children's impending fate, among the young romantic sympathy for the gallant young idealists now destined for Siberia or the scaffold reached enthusiastic proportions. Young Dmitri, two of whose friends turned out to have been implicated in the attempted coup, did not escape the contagion. His young and attractive cousin, Maria Dokhturov, an avid reader of Byron, Lamartine and Pushkin, gathered around her a devoted band of young people dedicated to the idea of bringing harmony to the discordant old world. Dmitri joined their ranks.

His recollection in later years was that the majority of society condemned the rebels. But the severe (by nineteenth-century standards) punishments imposed on gallant young men whose principal fault had been blind enthusiasm for liberty and justice aroused widespread distress and sympathy. In the privacy of drawing-rooms opinions divided sharply, and the Tolstoys were ranged on both sides of the issue. Prominent among the dignitaries presiding over the Supreme Court of Justice was the Tsar's favourite Count Peter Alexandrovich Tolstoy, fifty-five-year-old general and former Ambassador to Napoleon. Amongst those he helped to try and condemn was his young relative Vladimir Tolstoy, Ensign in a regiment of foot, who "knew of the plan to kill the Tsar; belonged to a secret society with knowledge of its aims, but without participating; was 18 when he joined the society in 1824" and was sentenced to two years' penal servitude.[4]

Dmitri was saved from the consequences of committing himself overtly to the revolutionary cause by the powerful intellect of his friend Maslov, but privately he was deeply influenced by the passionate dreams of Maria Dokhturov. "This dual influence," he remembered, "divided me in my mind: on the one hand, I not only did not sympathize with the Government but looked privately on the Tsar as a tyrant who created so many victims out of personal vindictiveness; and on the other recognized in him the personification of the state, whom it was my personal duty to serve as supreme overlord of the Russian people. I worked diligently at my studies, but not for anything in the world would I have accepted court service." When the Tsar came to Moscow for his coronation in the ancient capital, the whole family from Znamenskoe rented a room overlooking the route of the procession. Dmitri, however, stayed at home, resolved not to participate in the "despot's" arrival.

Fortunately for Dmitri's immediate prospects his elders remained ignorant of the revolutionary fervour. Maslov found him a place in the Commission of

General Count Peter Alexandrovich Tolstoy. By George Dawe

Requests, which at that time was undergoing a radical reform. His task was the uninspiring one of summarizing petitions for the consideration of the Commission. The subsequent procedure was typically Russian. No petition was turned down outright, nor on the other hand was any final decision arrived at. It was explained to the petitioners that the matter was being attended to, whilst the petition itself was moved on to another department. No one in the department, from the Minister down to Dmitri Tolstoy, had any knowledge whatever of laws, procedure, or even the powers of their own department.

As an example, which may stand for the methods of the Russian bureaucracy of Nicholas I's day, a petition arrived on Dmitri's desk from the widow of General Zimmerman, a landowner of Tambov, concerning her late husband's property. The letter was a simple assertion of her claim, without any legal ratification or other correct procedure. After considering Dmitri's summary the Committee, whose policy was never to turn anything down outright, explained that it was necessary to process the petition "in the proper manner". But what was "the proper manner"? The Commission had not the faintest idea. It was up to the lawyers in Tambov to puzzle their heads over the problem, who put the matter to the District Court. The District Court, which had previously rejected the widow's petition, received the impression that the Commission of Requests wished it granted and accordingly did so. Justice appears to have been done, though more by luck than design.

Another petition, from a Kalmuck chieftain, began with words that remained in Dmitri's head: "One of the Government's biggest mistakes lies in its rushing to arrange its subjects' happiness – without understanding the people."

Not long after, the Tsar returned to St. Petersburg, and soon after that a shower of indiscriminate awards and medals descended on the clerks of the Commission. Dmitri to his surprise found himself promoted to the lowest rung (*chin*) of the civil service ladder after a few weeks' desultory service. Despite his recent revolutionary tendencies he was overwhelmed with joy at the promotion, as was his proud mother. He now enjoyed an increasing circle of acquaintances among young men of similar rank and class and soon engaged in a delightful social round. His best friend, encountered by chance in the theatre, was a dashing and bright young man named Gregory Volkov, who introduced Dmitri to all the pleasures of the sophisticated and cultured elite: fine wines, liveried servants, the soaring exchange of ideas and the penning of verses.

All this, however, was but the prelude to a still more glittering existence. He was promoted to the Chancellery of State-Secretary Longinov in St. Petersburg. At last he was destined for the great capital, where any ambition could be realized. The journey itself seemed quite an adventure. In 1826 there was as yet no made-up highway between the capitals, and as a result Dmitri travelled post with a friend. He fretted fearfully over the loss of a packet given him by Longinov's father-in-law, but all ended well. In St. Petersburg he obtained lodgings with a German, and next morning sought out the Ministry. This was in the lower part of Longinov's private house, where Dmitri found the whole family at breakfast. He was at once received as one of them, and they teased him over the loss of the important parcel. It had contained some favourite jam, which he was accused of having devoured on the way. The only cloud in a bright sky was the Longinovs' preference for speaking French, which Dmitri still had difficulty in even understanding.

After breakfast he was introduced to his new duties. Longinov next suggested Dmitri occupy a small flat within the house. He accepted with glee, bought some pleasant furniture, and found himself for the first time in the exhilarating position of having his own home. He had an open invitation to dine when he liked with his kindly hosts, was paid 200 roubles a year in salary and received another 2,000 from home, made new friends, and had attained the peaks of youthful pleasure and excitement.

As the years slipped by, Dmitri Tolstoy's strong intellect gained him steady promotion and a succession of interesting posts. In 1831, after the suppression of the Polish revolt, he served under Count Stroganov and helped in the reimposition of Russian rule. Later he was attached to the Governor-General of the Baltic States at a time of considerable confusion and stress. The peasants were agitating for emancipation, their German noble landowners sought to consolidate their unique position within the Empire, while the Government made tentative efforts to extend Russification to the area (an Orthodox bishopric was founded at Riga in 1836). Dmitri found all this stimulating, "furnishing an abundance of memories, the more so in that my time of service at Riga was unusual and the tasks entrusted to me were unprecedented".

Tolstoy was rewarded for his industry and loyalty by being appointed Serving State Councillor, and later Governor of Ryazan province, which enabled him to spend part of every year on his beloved Znamenskoe estate. He entertained the gallant Welsh Colonel William Williams, who during the Crimean War long defended the Turkish fortress of Kars against its Russian attackers. Finally taken prisoner, Colonel Williams was travelling to Petersburg as an honoured guest of the Tsar. The Governor was fascinated by Williams's stirring tales (they conversed in French) of daring deeds in India and the Caucasus, where he had had dealings with the famous mountain chieftain Shamil. The wild Shamil had kidnapped two Georgian princesses, upon which he received a stern note from the Welshman, pointing out that he had committed an act unworthy of a gentleman.

In 1856 Tolstoy was transferred to the Governorship of Kaluga, and subsequently to Voronezh. Each year he spent much time refreshing his spirit and reviving memories at Znamenskoe. He was amused to note, however, that were he to take literally the official round laid down by statute for his duties he would have precisely three hours in every twenty-four to eat, sleep, and receive petitioners, and none for exercise. Count Tolstoy was a loyal servant of government and devoted subject of the Tsar, but the confusion and contradictions of the bureaucratic mesh infuriated him. He held old-fashioned views on most issues, but was widely loved by his subordinates for his integrity and good nature. He was, above all, a deeply cultured man with wide literary and historical interests. He had known Pushkin, and was by the poet's side as he lay dying after the fatal duel in 1837.[5]

In 1861 Tolstoy's old chief at Riga, P.A. Valuev, was appointed Minister of the Interior. An able and intelligent statesman, he was a conservative who despised the old, mindless autocracy of Nicholas I, but who wished to strengthen existing institutions in a way that would revitalize Russian government. He fully recognized the need to contain and harness the growing reform movement, and wrote shrewdly that "World history testifies to the fact that in the development of states there are times when the suppression of ideas that are undermining social order cannot be accomplished by the use of government power alone precisely because of the limited number of unconditionally subordinate weapons at the government's disposal. What is needed is the co-operation of that part of society that is imbued with or may be imbued with opposing ideas."

To assist him in his task, Valuev appointed men to office whose reliability he had proved in earlier cooperation. They included Dmitri Nikolaevich Tolstoy, who in August 1861 became Director of the Department of Executive Police. He has been described by a recent authority as a "fine example of traditional officialdom and its ministerial power ethos."[6] It may seem strange that so humane and high-minded a man should have been chosen for this particular Department, but at that time the Police held much wider responsibilities than those of simply maintaining order. Tolstoy's relative, Pavel Golenishchev-Kutuzov-Tolstoy (grandson of the famous Marshal Kutuzov) wrote later of the dedication and idealism he and many of the highest nobility felt when they entered a service devoted to protecting Russia from disruptive influences at a time when so many vital operations of reform were in motion. When many branches of government remained non-existent or at most in embryo, it lay to the police to ensure that society was nurtured and protected on its delicate course.[7] Needless to say, this high ideal remained far above the attainments of the service, but for men like Dmitri Tolstoy that was a spur to renewed efforts.

An idea of what police work in nineteenth-century Russia involved can be gained from the succession of problems placed before the new Director: Ukrainian nationalist agitation, peasants and landowners, regulation of the affairs of the Kirghiz Horde, reorganization of the Church, and (not least) of the Police itself. Above all there was the colossal tremor that shook the Empire with the promulgation on 19 February 1861 of the statutes abolishing the institution of serfdom. Tolstoy's views were strongly conservative; as he put it, "The masses only respect strength." He wished for a just, ordered society, autocratic but not subject to the arbitrary whims characterizing Nicholas I's reign. He found in Alexander II a ruler who was sufficiently enlightened to make such a vision feasible. But everywhere he saw his measures obstructed by incompetent or obstructive officials, and eventually even Valuev appeared distanced from him. On 17 April 1863 he resigned his post on the pretext of ill-health, and retired from public life. He was granted lands in Samara province by the Government, but was denied the post of Senator which he had requested. He departed, grieved that his more than thirty years' service to Tsar and Fatherland had not been more generously recognized.[8]

During the remaining twenty years of his life, Tolstoy devoted himself to writing and scholarly research. He was elected President of the Society of Russian Antiquities from 1876 to 1879, and published a number of books and articles on historical and archaeological subjects. Happily his retirement was not solitary. As a provincial governor he had, as an old bachelor, provided the customary balls and receptions. Later, however, he married a gardener's daughter, Efrosinya, by whom he had a son Sergei. In 1872 he completed a biographical memoir, from which much of the foregoing is drawn. "My life," he began, "had nothing remarkable about it, save only that I spent it more fruitlessly than many others. Many of my souvenirs are unfortunate ones and should not from self-respect be included in these notes. But on the one hand there was my friends' insistence, and on the other a total absence of any occupation impelled me to embark on this labour; especially with the idea that these lines will be perused, if not with profit, I hope by God's grace with the love of my son, whom I love more than anything else on earth. . . ."

Dmitri Nikolaevich Tolstoy died on 14 March 1884. His grandson was killed in the Great War, and the family of Tolstoy-Znamensky (he was authorized to adopt the extra surname in 1878 through love of the estate) appears to be extinct. The old manor-house, if not destroyed, was presumably "socialized" at the Revolution and must now be inhabited by a high Party or KGB official. Nothing is known of the career of Tolstoy's son Sergei whom he so loved, but another relative who was in many ways a son to him fulfilled every promise Dmitri Nikolaevich could have hoped for.

The Count had a first cousin, Andrei Stepanovich Tolstoy, who was thirteen years older than himself. This Count Andrei had inherited the ancient Tolstoy estate of Shelbovo in the province of Suzdal, which had been held by the family since the time of Vasily Ivanovich Tolstoy, Voevod of Suzdal from 1621 to 1625.

In 1830 Andrei Stepanovich was shot dead, so it was said, by his host in the midst of a dinner-party, where he (Tolstoy) had drunkenly boasted of being on too intimate terms with his hostess.[9] He left two sons aged seven and six, and the kindly Count Tolstoy-Znamensky offered his protection to the orphans in view of the fact that their mother had remarried and they were homeless. The younger son was tragically drowned at the age of nineteen, but the elder, also called Dmitri, lived on to enjoy a career as distinguished as it was controversial. Ultimately the two men were united by marriage as well as cousinship, for Count Tolstoy-Znamensky's son Sergei was to marry his ward's niece Maria.

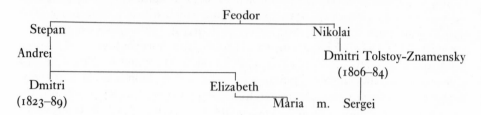

Dmitri Nikolaevich enjoyed wealth and position great enough to send his young cousin at the age of thirteen to the elite Imperial Lyceum at Tsarskoe Selo. (The non-Russian reader is begged to excuse the presence of two Dmitris within the same chapter; henceforward we will be exclusively concerned with the career of young Dmitri Andreevich.) The Lyceum, without question Russia's most prestigious and exclusive place of education, had been founded in 1810 with the declared aim of educating "youth especially intended for the important sectors of state service". Throughout its century of existence it was to prove superlatively successful in this respect, its graduates occupying the highest offices of state in disproportionate numbers. Despite this, its main claim to fame when young Tolstoy arrived there in 1836 was that it had been the place of education of the immortal Pushkin.

The course was rigorous, as befitted its purpose not only of developing the students' intellectual powers but of producing loyal and pious servants of state and Tsar. The Lyceum was exclusive, and carefully designed to be so. It occupied splendid premises in a wing of the imperial palace at Tsarskoe Selo, where students could also make use of the magnificent park. The Emperor Nicholas took great personal interest in the school, and his tall, soldierly figure was familiar to all the boys. There were just over a hundred, divided into four classes, and instruction was on an intimately personal level scarcely paralleled elsewhere in Russia or Europe. Entrants were almost all of noble birth and the fees exceptionally high.

In order to ensure total dedication of pupils to their future careers as the Tsar's first servants, the boys became entirely absorbed into the institution during their six-year course. Leave and visitors were severely restricted, and only in the summer holidays did boys have any real chance to be amongst their families again. A strict daily programme supervised the students' movements from their rising at 6 a.m. to retirement at 10 p.m. In school hours and in public places they were obliged to wear a military-style uniform. Reading-matter was strictly censored, and the work-load and examination requirements so arduous as theoretically at least to leave scarcely a moment for idleness or mischief.

None of this was remarkable by the standards of the time, and is in many respects comparable to the perfectly tolerable regime of the English public school I attended thirty-five years ago. There were also numerous compensations, which go far to explain why most graduates sustained lifelong feelings of affection and loyalty to their old *alma mater*. Subjects taught were broad in scope, chiefly comprising law, languages, literature, history and political economy. There were occasional subsequent complaints that the curriculum was too liberal and not specialized enough. Extra-curricular activities were lessons in art, fencing, dancing, music and gymnastics. Food and medical care were excellent, and most students agreed they had much to be grateful for. Discipline was rigid, but punishments rarely inhumane. In this respect the Lyceum may be favourably contrasted with contemporary English public schools, as also in the absence of bullying.

Young Dmitri Andreevich Tolstoy found this atmosphere of industry and loyalty entirely satisfying. His capacity for hard work was extraordinary, and as he possessed a first-class brain he was not daunted by the demanding programme. With his father dead and his mother remarried he could not feel the draw of home that must have affected many of his comrades. Indeed, the sense of being a virtual orphan appears to have instilled in him a determination to be self-sufficient and make his own way in the world. His one tie of affection was to his kindly cousin, Dmitri Nikolaevich.

A story which circulated later illustrates this marked, even extreme, independence of character. In his last year at the Lyceum he upbraided a fellow-student for immoral behaviour. As the boy left school immediately afterwards, Tolstoy was sent to Coventry by the other boys, who presumed he was responsible. To the one boy who generously offered to remain friends with him, he allegedly remarked bluntly that he "did not need anyone, but could make do without any contact with his companions".

Pupils at the Lyceum, despite every pedagogical resource, could not be successfully quarantined against the doctrines of disaffection that were gaining moment with each decade of the early nineteenth century. The rigid censorship of Nicholas I was evaded with virtual impunity: "There was not a single foreign forbidden book which might not appear at the Lyceum in the hands of fourteen- or fifteen-year-old boys," wrote a former student. Tolstoy's contemporaries included Petrashevsky, an advanced socialist theorist, and the gifted satyrist Saltykov-Shchedrin. Though thoroughly hostile to all seditious ideologies, Tolstoy was fully aware of his opponents' way of thinking, and was never afraid to encounter them personally in intellectual argument.

Tolstoy graduated with distinction on 31 January 1843, receiving a gold medal for the way in which he had exemplified the ideals for which the Lyceum had been founded. In general the Lyceum was highly successful in producing graduates not only of high intellectual capacity, but who were also loyal servants of government. Tolstoy emerged possessed of these qualities in marked degree, and also with a profound conviction of the efficacy of the regime to which he had been subjected.[10]

With these impeccable qualifications, and the influence of his highly-placed patron and cousin, D. N. Tolstoy-Znamensky, Dmitri Andreevich was assured of a promising career. For four years he served in the Chancellery supervising girls' schools and charitable institutions, and then transferred in 1847 to the Department of Spiritual Affairs in the Ministry of the Interior. One of his major duties there was the compilation of an important report on the non-Orthodox religions of Russia, and this research was also put to good use in a book subsequently published in 1863 and 1864 under the title *Roman Catholicism in Russia*, a work scholarly but far from impartial to a religion which Tolstoy saw as an insidious instrument intent on undermining Russia's most essential national institution. Well before that, however, he had published in 1848, at the youthful age of twenty-five, a detailed history of Russian financial institutions in Catherine the Great's time. His capacity for industry was so remarkable that at thirty he was appointed Director of the Department of Spiritual Affairs.

It might seem that from all this evidence of astonishing dedication to his career that Dmitri Tolstoy was from the beginning the heartless bureaucrat *par excellence*, and it comes as a relief to learn that he found time also for the sort of foibles to which most young men are subject. He formed one of a group of lively and talented young men who gathered at the home of the rich and hospitable young Count Alexei Bobrinsky in Mikhailovsky Square. It happened within a year or so of Tolstoy's graduation that a rich landowner named Yazykov arrived at that time in St. Petersburg with his family. He had two beautiful daughters, who were the involuntary cause of much anguish and quarrelling among the youth of the capital. Dmitri Tolstoy found in one of them a draw stronger far than that of Catherine II's budgetary system. It was the time of Lent, when the girls were obliged to attend church regularly. Crowds of young officers and nobles swiftly became very devout, appearing in the same church to conduct their devotions. Tolstoy was there too, and he persuaded a friend who happened to be a gifted artist to use the opportunity of providing him with a lifelike sketch of his *inamorata*. The two young men placed themselves in a convenient corner of the church, and the artist duly made a pleasing likeness on which Tolstoy could gaze in privacy. To conceal this operation from the congregation, the sketching-pad was ensconced in the artist's hat. Unfortunately the whole affair had been observed by the burning eyes of a young prince, also distraught with love for the lady. Consumed with jealousy, this rival flew to the girls' mother, providing her with a disinterested warning of the scandal to which Tolstoy's flagrant conduct would give rise.

The next time Dmitri appeared at the girls' home he found himself declined entry. It was not long before the truth got abroad, and the furious young Count arranged for Alexei Bobrinsky to take round a challenge to a duel. This the prince resolutely declined, on the not very creditable grounds that he knew neither Count Tolstoy nor Count Bobrinsky. But now he found himself the object of increasing criticism by his friends, who adjudged his refusal as unworthy of an officer. Goaded at last to action, but unable to fight with Tolstoy whose challenge he had refused, he provoked Bobrinsky to a quarrel. The whole complicated affair was quietened down only with the greatest difficulty. Count Dmitri Nikolaevich intervened to prevent any prospect of marriage between his nephew and Miss Yazykov, who later married a Dutch diplomat.[11]

Not for some years did Tolstoy marry. On 8 November 1853 he was wed to Sophia, the plain and simple, but good-hearted, daughter of General Dmitri Bibikov. Bibikov had become Minister of the Interior in the previous year, and was second to none in his admiration for the autocracy. As a recent historian points out, he "had blind faith in state power and believed all forms of social organization to be inherently evil". As Governor-General of Kiev he had been noted for enthusiastic implementation of his master's obscurantist policies, boast-

General Dmitri Bibikov

ing in a speech at the end of his term that he had done nothing to build bridges between state and society, and that in any case he was not interested in popularity.[12]

Thus every converging influence bearing on the formation of Dmitri Tolstoy's views was in greater or lesser degree conservative. His uncle, Dmitri Nikolaevich, was kindly, charming, honourable, and also enthusiastically loyal to the person and powers of his Emperor. The Lyceum was specifically designed to bring up young men to serve that ideal, and now his wife was the daughter of one of the most devout bureaucrats of the age. It would have been surprising if Dmitri Andreevich had not turned out a thoroughgoing reactionary. This he undoubtedly was: as Professor Seton-Watson points out, "Tolstoy has become known in Russian historical literature as one of the most bigoted and most influential reactionaries of the nineteenth century. He was uniformly hated by educated Russians of liberal or radical outlook. The rather conservative Chicherin wrote in his memoirs: 'One can name but few people who did more harm to Russia.'"[13] There is truth in all of this . . . yet nothing in Russia is ever quite as it appears.

From 1853 to 1860 Tolstoy was appointed Head of the Chancellery of the Naval Ministry. The first part of this period saw the disastrous setback to Russia and the autocratic policy of Nicholas I of the Crimean War. The Emperor himself died in the midst of hostilities, and after the Treaty of Paris had in 1856 imposed humiliating terms on Russia, voices rose on every side demanding reform. Russia's defeat was not the cause of this upsurge but the pretext. The whole justification for Nicholas's virtual militarization of all Russian life was that it made the nation irresistibly powerful, and here she was, beaten on her own soil by the army of "Napoleon the little", just forty years after her armies had entered Paris on the heels of Napoleon the Great. Something was wrong, and to most people (including the new Tsar Alexander II) that was the stifling oppression of the previous reign. Not only was it patently morally wrong, but hopelessly incompetent. What gave the British and French their advantage was their free political system, which developed that intelligence and independence which, among other things, wins wars.

The greatest issue at this time was of course the Emancipation of the Serfs. As in most other communities, serfdom (and slavery) had probably existed in some form since the beginnings of Russian society. But up to the end of the fifteenth century, the majority of Russian peasants appear to have been free tenants. In 1497 their right to shift was regulated by law, and subsequently they became gradually bound to the land. It was the law code (*Ulozhenie*) of Tsar Alexei Mihailovich in 1649 that finally enserfed the Russian peasantry.[14] The sweeping reforms of his son Peter the Great, which in so many striking ways brought Russia into line with Europe, bound the serfs even more rigidly to the soil with the decree of 1722, which in turn was designed to increase the taxable resources of the nobles required to pay for Russia's enlarged military power and prestige. In 1785 Catherine the Great's Charter to the Nobility still further increased, if not by intent then by implication, landowners' control over their serfs.[15] (It is an odd fact that the social history of the Russian labouring class developed virtually in reverse order to that of the rest of Europe, passing from the free peasantry of the Kievan period through serfdom to the imposition of slavery (under the GULag system) in the present century.)

The institution which it was now proposed to abolish must be seen, therefore, not as a decaying relic of an age passed away, but as in many ways a relatively new estate, whose significance permeated virtually every aspect of Russian life. Although by the nineteenth century the effects of European enlightenment had so extensively penetrated Russian opinion that the majority of educated people had come to regard it as an anomalous evil to be abolished if Russia were to become a full member of the comity of civilized nations. Nevertheless the nobility were extremely vociferous in demanding accompanying political and administrative reforms which would in effect recompense them for the loss of privilege which deprivation of serf dues would necessitate, by giving them compensating political power.[16]

All this apparent disorder and challenge to the *status quo* horrified Dmitri Tolstoy at the Naval Ministry. The same dangerous proposals menaced the autocracy and offered to deprive the nobility of its economic base. In the beginning of 1860 he sent the Emperor an intemperate and sarcastic memorandum, bitterly lamenting the coming measure, which he foresaw would inevitably ruin the landholding class. Alexander II was angered by this criticism, which he condemned as ignorant or malicious in intent. Tolstoy was so distressed by the way things were going that on 19 September he resigned from the liberal-minded Naval Ministry. For a year he worked for the Central School Board, fulfilling his lasting interest in education.

On 19 February 1861 serfdom was abolished throughout Russia. To Dmitri Tolstoy, the predictable confusion that followed was proof of the harmfulness of the whole measure. Many peasants had only the haziest idea of what was intended. On Leo Tolstoy's estate at Yasnaya Polyana the peasants refused on one occasion to cut the hay, and the crop was only saved by the author and his family taking up scythes and rakes.[17] Dmitri Tolstoy, unlike his celebrated cousin, did not regard such incidents as inevitable teething troubles. To his sympathetic uncle, Dmitri

Nikolaevich Tolstoy, he wrote indignantly on 30 April 1861 (six weeks after the Emancipation; peasants were obliged, however, to fulfil their former commitments for another two years): "Out of four of our villages, three are performing the obligatory labour more or less satisfactorily, but the fourth (Fursovo . . .) refused pointblank to do any work, so that today I was obliged to telegraph a request to Muraviev [Minister of State Properties, and another opponent of Emancipation] to send a company of soldiers there. There is some hope that we shall be left without income and Russia without bread. All neighbouring and very big estates around Lesishch are finding work refused. How can we not thank the Editorial Commission! . . . In Petersburg they are now adopting a rule of recognizing it as disorder [only] when the peasants break out into open rebellion; but if they only don't work or don't pay quit-rent that isn't taken into account, and they find that such a place is perfectly peaceful. So it is that things are only troubled in Kazan and Penza, where the peasants drove away the soldiers, but in other places all is just as it should be."[18]

To men like the two Tolstoy cousins, whose estates were organized on benevolently patriarchal lines, remote from feverish discussions in Petersburg and Moscow, the Emancipation appeared an entirely pernicious move which destroyed the peace of the countryside and relationships that had stood the test of time. It was all too much, and the disgusted Dmitri Andreevich resigned his post in the Education Ministry that December on the day the liberal A. V. Golovnin was appointed Minister of his Department.

During the next two years, when the reforms continued, Tolstoy lived in semi-retirement, acting as trustee for the two famous girls' schools, the Alexander and Catherine Institutes, and engaging in scholarly research. As befitted his solitary and self-sufficient character, the latter was an enduring love of his life. At his country estate in Ryazan he had a special tower built to house a library of forty thousand books. There were works in every major European language and, stemming from his early interest in the reign of Catherine the Great, he built up a valuable collection of manuscripts of that period.

His interests ranged wide, and included the publication of his ancestor Peter Tolstoy's diaries in Italy in 1697–99. The major work at this time was, however, his history of Catholicism in Russia, written in French under the title *Le Catholicisme romain en Russie*.

Tolstoy was clearly deeply influenced by the anti-Russian uprising in Poland and Lithuania, which broke out on 22 January 1863 and was not suppressed until the following year. It had been preceded by an attempt by Tolstoy's old chief at the Naval Ministry, the Grand Duke Constantine, to introduce large-scale reforms. Though land reforms followed the extinction of the rebellion, to Tolstoy here was irrefutable proof, if proof were needed, that weakness and concessions only invited further assaults on Russian territorial integrity and the authority of the Tsar. Tolstoy's pessimistic views did not attract any great following, and he remained in the political wilderness, obliged to watch helplessly as the old Russia that he valued so much was dismantled about him. It might have seemed that his day was done, when the sluggish flow of Russian history was once again diverted by a sudden jolt.[19]

On 4 April 1866 the Tsar Alexander was strolling in the Summer Gardens at St. Petersburg, when a youth stepped out of the crowd of respectful onlookers, drew a double-barrelled pistol from his coat and fired at the Tsar. A peasant managed to jerk his arm, and the bullet missed. As the would-be assassin tried to flee he was seized by the police. Under interrogation the prisoner was revealed to be a certain Dmitri Karakozov. Twenty-five years old, he was of unattractive appearance, with "a pale and tired face, hair flowing onto his shoulders . . . noticeable for the carelessness of his clothes." He was that familiar revolutionary figure, the failed student, expelled from both Kazan and Moscow Universities. Imbued with a vaguely defined call to liberate the masses by some striking deed, he decided that the murder of the Emperor would be the most dramatic. Though there was at that time little revolutionary sentiment in the country, which was if anything inclining to the right after the great reforms, Karakozov was found to be linked to a conspiratorial socialist group enjoying the melodramatic title of "Hell". He was hanged on 3 September, and a couple of dozen of the gang exiled to Siberia.[20]

Much more significant than the punishment of those involved in the attempt on the Tsar was the effect on public and official opinion. There arose immediately a widespread feeling that the path of reform might be being pursued too fast, and a firm hand on the brakes was called for. New ministers with uncompromising views on agitation were appointed, and these included Dmitri Tolstoy. Within ten days of Karakozov's attempt, on 14 April 1866, the liberal-minded Golovnin was dismissed as Minister of Education and Tolstoy was installed in his place. His hour had come at last, at the age of forty-three. His qualifications for the post were pre-eminent. He enjoyed a reputation as a scholar, and had already worked in the field of educational administration since his graduation in 1843. But it was his stern views on the dangers of compromise with the forces of opposition to the autocracy that now appealed as strongly as they had previously repelled. What he also possessed, as his many enemies conceded, was an iron will that would not baulk at any measure necessary to protect Russian society and its institutions.

The Ministry of Education was now regarded as being in the front line of the war to be waged against the secret advocates of revolution. Not only had Karakozov and many of his fellow-conspirators been students, but in the universities at large there had been rising agitation. In 1861-62 mass demonstrations had occurred at St. Petersburg University and the Technological Institute, with 300 students arrested, 659 suspended, and the University closed for two years. During the decade before 1866 a remarkable breeze of excitement had wafted through Russia's universities. In 1861 a number of Moscow professors signed a report which noted that "Russian society had instilled in the student a high conception of his own worth, a conception which can hardly be found in any other country. . . . At the present time every Russian person profoundly senses the need for education, as the only escape from our oppressive social ills. . . . In the eyes of many, the student represents the future hope of Russia".[21] It was, moreover, through the universities that dangerous ideas were imported into Russia from the West; in the words of Professor Riasanovsky, they "constituted the main conduit of Western knowledge and thought into Russia".[22] Here was the inflammable material which appeared ready to respond to any spark thrown down by a malevolent or mischievous hand. It was Dmitri Tolstoy's assigned task to damp down the smouldering threat.

Sweeping changes would clearly follow the induction of the new Minister, and his appearance was greeted with justified apprehension in the academic world. It was not just his declared reactionary views that left professors and students alike under no misunderstanding that things must change from the relatively easy-going regime of Golovnin, but also Tolstoy's legendary industry and pertinacity, and his uncompromising expectation that others should measure up to the same inflexible standard.

No sooner had the new Minister familiarized himself with problems which from their sheer scale and the critical phase through which they were approaching must surely have been greater than those faced by any Minister of Education in the world, than he announced his intention of making a tour of inspection down the Volga. Between 4 August and 23 September he travelled from his home in Ryazan province to Moscow, the whole length of the Volga to Astrakhan on the Caspian Sea, back again through Saratov, Samara and Simbirsk to Kazan, and so via Nizhni-Novgorod, Kostroma and Yaroslavl to St. Petersburg: a journey of some four thousand miles. Nor was this a mere display of ministerial authority, such as Russians have been accustomed to for centuries, as accounts of Tolstoy's arrival at Kazan exemplify. The former Tartar city, captured by Ivan the Terrible in 1552, had been accorded a Gymnasium by the Empress Elizabeth in 1758, and this had been transformed into a University in 1804. Russia's easternmost outpost of enlightenment, it swiftly built up a first-rate academic reputation.

The University's Curator, Peter Shestakov, always remembered the fear which he and his colleagues felt as they awaited Tolstoy's first arrival at the railway station on 3 September. "This Count Tolstoy is going to replace the Kazan Curator chosen by Golovnin, with whom the new Minister is at daggers drawn," went round a cheerful rumour. His appearance was indeed daunting, but not quite as had been expected. His first words after descending from the train were "What are you afraid of?"

With his pale, thin face, brisk movements, and lively manner of speech, he appeared younger than his forty-three years. In no time at all his hosts were vastly impressed with his powers of concentration, enthusiastic interest in everything to do with the University, and capacity to absorb information.

"The Count inspected subsidiary educational institutions very carefully, listening attentively to each director's account of his institution's resources, and what was required to improve those institutions. . . . Count D.A. Tolstoy stayed at Kazan a whole week; apart from university lectures, he attended lectures at the Theological College, and was at the boys' and girls' Gymnasia. At home every evening he received several professors arranged in turns, and over glasses of tea got to know them."

Universities and schools swiftly learned from first-hand experience that the new Minister's legendary capacity for hard work had been if anything understated. Moving tirelessly from one person and one subject to another (he was known to allow precisely two minutes for an interview), he impressed on all his capacity to grasp an idea in its totality the moment it was put to him, and to retain complete clarity of mind and perspective in a seeming turmoil of appointments. As for his scholarly researches, which continued throughout his ministerial career, they appeared merely a relaxation from work. Amidst such superhuman activity he inevitably made mistakes, "but what struck all with particular pleasure and attracted them irresistibly to him was – his straight-forwardness, cheerfulness and candour, which had an infectious, charming effect."

This was the Curator's view, and that of many senior colleagues. However, lower down the line a more daunting impression was conveyed. To students, junior lecturers, and others he appeared a terrifying figure. A priest who encountered him on his journey fled in terror on merely learning his identity. (Tolstoy had been appointed Procurator of the Holy Synod, responsible for Church affairs, in the previous year. That was, however, one duty which through indifference he neglected.)[23] Former students in later years recalled the frantic weeks of meticulous preparation anticipating the visit. In obedience to a circular from the Ministry, all lecturers presented to the Minister were obliged to shave their beards, which were apparently regarded as the mark of a free-thinker. A former pupil at a gymnasium recalled the Minister's chilling appearance. Dressed in ministerial uniform, with a star on his breast and the symbolic gold key of a Court Chamberlain (which he had been since 1858) at his back, this "tall, spare, dry figure . . . slowly looked around with an icy, dry gaze at the pupils who were standing to attention and without a word of greeting, without a smile, invited us to sit and found himself a place at one of the foremost desks next to a shrinking pupil; behind him his entourage arranged themselves similarly.

"'Continue the lesson!' ordered the Count, and the pupil Sergeev brightly, clearly and intelligently began parsing grammar on the blackboard; several times the Minister interrupted him, putting his questions in a sort of dry, constrained voice; afterwards he asked other pupils to do a dictation and inspected particularly closely the Bashkir Kutlemetov's exercise book. He spent forty minutes in the classroom and then, giving a nod, slowly and sedately left the room. Vladimirov [the teacher], quite pale, trembled for 40 minutes over his fate (he had a large family and was dreadfully poor), sank down from exhaustion at the nearest desk, and was speechless with agitation.

"There was complete silence in the classroom, and all that could be heard was the buzzing of a fly and the teacher's deep breathing. So the lesson ended. Teachers and pupils alike were left with a heavy, oppressive impression for a very long time: for their whole lives. There were neither reprimands nor scoldings, but the icy gaze of the Minister conveyed something cold and sinister."

This account provides an unpleasant impression of Tolstoy's approach. He is a complex figure, about whom contemporaries held violently differing opinions. It is possible, in view of his unnaturally reserved and self-sufficient character, that mistrust of others' feelings towards him caused him to appear withdrawn and impersonal. But in the instance just described, it seems likely that the impression he gave was intentionally severe. This was his first visit to Kazan, whose University had experienced serious unrest, and whose rollcall had included the Tsar's would-be assassin, Karakozov. The Minister may well have wished to indicate that a new era of obedience and discipline had arrived.

This seems the more likely in that ample evidence exists that he could shew a very different face when occasion demanded. Another former pupil, this time from the Gymnasium at remote Orenburg, out in the Siberian steppe, describes a rare visit from the Minister. The school was scrubbed and burnished from top to bottom as usual. The boys were issued with new uniforms and had their hair close cropped (perhaps long hair was another tell-tale mark of agnosticism). The teachers appeared in class in full-dress uniform, and wore cocked hats and swords. For days and days they studied the identical lesson, until they could repeat it like *Our Father*.

"In those days there was still no train to Orenburg, and so the exact day of the Minister's arrival could not be known. So it was that for more than a week we sat in this state of anguished expectation; finally, one day Mihail Matveevich Tarakan [a master], scarcely able to breathe and flushing scarlet, heaving his whiskers about in the most frightful way, flew into our class and, standing on one leg, raised a finger on high and whispered: 'He's arrived! He'll soon be here!' "

The next lesson was Russian language, and the master, Danilov, hastily told the boys to open up the lesson they had been preparing all week.

"Almost at once we heard footsteps, and the Minister walked into the classroom. He wore a plain frock-coat with a star. Coming up to the boys, he simply said: 'Good day, children. Sit down.' Then he shook hands with Danilov, who was covered in confusion; he asked what we were studying, and added: 'Please continue your lesson. I am not here.' He went round the whole class, and came up to my desk. I stood up. He smiled, put his hand on my shoulder and said quietly, 'Sit down, sit down,' and sat down himself with me on my seat. Danilov called up K. . . . and began to question him and explain something. Count Tolstoy listened attentively to him, at the same time quietly asking me how many pupils there were in the class, were there many Kirghiz, how they learned, and all sorts of other things. I was not a coward, and in any case then understood nothing of ranks and grades, and so replied frankly."

Things proceeded in this genial way, but Danilov could hardly teach for anxiety to overhear the Minister's murmured conversation with the boy. Finally the great man departed, saying "Well, goodbye, children! Study, and love your Gymnasium!"

The boy suffered somewhat for the attention paid to him, as Danilov reported the conversation to his superiors, who in an agony of apprehension interrogated the pupil at length as to what precisely the Minister had said. And when, three months later, some changes in the staff were ordered by the Minister, suspicion fell on him as having been the instigator.[24]

The principal aim of the new Minister of Education has been well epitomized by Professor Allen Sinel. The key problem facing Tolstoy, he writes, was "how to reconcile his country's need for a viable school system with the inherent dangers for autocracy of such a system. Nowhere would this dilemma be more acute that at the university, for its student body provided the technical elite the government sought and at the same time had from the late 1850s contributed greatly to Russia's instability by actively demonstrating for its rights and by joining the revolutionary movement in large numbers." It was a later Russian prime minister, Count Witte, who pithily set out the paradox: "Education foments social revolution, but popular ignorance loses wars." A problem which today bedevils the Soviet regime as much as it did its imperial predecessor. In 1866 both stings in the scorpion's tail had made themselves forcibly apparent, in the shape of the débacle of the Crimean War, and the student agitation which followed soon after. One result of the apparently insoluble anomaly was a continual swing to extreme remedies by a frustrated government; "the position of Minister of Education was one of the most insecure posts in the Russian bureaucracy. During the period 1802–1917 no fewer than twenty-seven individuals occupied that position."[25]

Tsar Alexander II, however, was remarkably stalwart in support of ministers in whom he placed his confidence, and Tolstoy remained Minister of Education for fourteen years, from 1866 to 1880.

His approach to the main problem, that of student unrest, was unimaginative but surprisingly effective in achieving his purpose. Again quoting Professor

Sinel, for Tolstoy "the solution was simple, in conception if not in execution. Improve higher education by more teachers, better schools, extra funds for research; combat student unrest by stricter controls over faculty and more careful supervision and selection of students." There was thus a negative and a positive side to his approach. The trusted weapon of authoritarian governments, censorship, was one which Tolstoy greatly favoured. Text-books in particular were carefully vetted by a Central Committee of the Ministry, and discretionary powers previously devolved on university authorities over the selection of schoolbooks were largely withdrawn to the Ministry. Libraries, too, were sifted for any material the Ministry regarded as seditious. But Tolstoy's acceptance of the need for censorship was not wholly obscurantist. A scholar himself, he had no wish to stultify young Russia, and took care to staff the censorship board with reputable and, in some cases, famous scholars, whose rôle was intended to be positive. Books were graded according to their estimated value, and between 1866 and 1877 more than 55 per cent of those considered were passed as permitted reading. Of those rejected, a large number were simply considered sub-standard irrespective of possible political content.

Pedagogues as well as books required monitoring and purging. In order to remove what he regarded as excessive autonomy within the universities, he replaced all but one of their curators (the chief administrators) with his own nominees, who in most cases had an administrative rather than educational background. He also dismissed the dedicated but over-permissive Nikolai Pirogov from his post supervising students training at foreign universities – a dismissal not very graciously or generously implemented.[26] Perpetually concerned that universities geographically remote from his control would allow things to slide back to their former dangerous condition, he increased the numbers and powers of district inspectors who, if they fulfilled the letter of their instructions, should have spied on and regulated virtually every move of staff and pupils on and off duty. In practice, however, the number of inspectors was so small in relation to the gigantic size, adverse climatic conditions and poor communications of Russia that the surveillance remained quite inadequate. Above all, Tolstoy was determined to gather authority to the centre, and to ensure that everything of moment, even down to schools curricula, was settled according to his direct decision. Again, this deliberately repressive measure possessed its positive side. Provincial administrators could be idle and procrastinatory, and the Minister intended to see that these slipshod ways came to an end.

The single purpose of all the increased control was of course the suppression of student dissidence. There can be little doubt that Government was correct in seeing the student body as one pre-eminently receptive to extreme ideas. The attractions of revolutionary new ideas, uncompromising measures, panaceas for the solution of the human condition and the like possess a natural attraction for half-formed minds, bursting with all the vigour of incipient manhood, though lacking any yardstick of experience. In Russia the danger posed was much greater than in other countries, for a number of reasons. Sandwiched between an intransigent and unthinking bureaucracy on the one hand, and the superstitious, illiterate millions on the other, it was natural for students to regard themselves as a Platonic or Nietzschean elite. The danger was susceptible to statistics; in the 1870s, 36 per cent of revolutionary activists proved to be students.

But brash idealism was far from being the only cause of university dissent.

Many students were pitifully poor, living in drab lodgings on city outskirts, and subsisting on grim fare supplied by the student canteen. It was all too often a struggle to exist, and these conditions were in part caused or exacerbated by regulations designed to nip agitation in the bud. All student associations were strictly banned, thereby preventing young men from collaborating to raise funds for cheap books and food. Other regulations, designed to prevent an irresponsible attitude to life, simply insulted students' self-respect. Rigid rules controlled their behaviour in and out of class, smoking, clothing, and recreation; and these rules were enforced by a correspondingly strict set of punishments.

Though many of these regulations had been inherited by Tolstoy from previous Ministries, he enforced them more rigidly and added to their number. He was convinced that it was possible to legislate against the twin evils at work on impressionable minds: harmful outside influences, and student idleness. Censorship and police and inspectorate control combatted the former, while restrictions on entry and greater compulsion to study gave students little time for anti-social activity.

Tolstoy was on the whole remarkably successful in his declared aim of taking the universities out of the revolutionary movement. Only after 1876 did renewed agitation begin, when the autocracy began to be faced by a new crisis abroad. Russia's successful if bloody war against Turkey in 1877–78 was deprived of its fruits at the Congress of Berlin, while in 1879 there was another assassination attempt on the Tsar. New repressive measures were temporarily introduced, which further alienated the student body. All in all, Tolstoy's commitment to improving university standards was real, and stemmed in large part from his own love of learning. He was, after all, the author of three solidly scholarly books and eleven learned articles and monographs. His sincere belief in the lasting capacity of discipline and enforced commitment to hard work to remedy adolescent discontent was clearly misguided, but must in part at least have stemmed from his own astonishing proclivity for unceasing industry at the Lyceum and afterwards. It should not be forgotten that many of the controls which appear so unacceptable today were also enforced in universities throughout Europe at that time; also that "it was 'backward' Russia . . . that enrolled more students in higher educational institutions than any other country in the world except the United States."[27] Finally, resources in finances and manpower available to central government in nineteenth-century Russia were so limited as to make anything approaching effective implementation of its decrees impossible. And the frustration arising from this permanent obstacle was a continual incitement to increasingly repressive but dead-letter legislation. It was all a far cry from the ideologically motivated police states of the twentieth century.

Dmitri Tolstoy's work was not confined to the universities. Indeed, it was secondary education which attracted his main attention, since it was there that the possibility lay of real influence for good. The secondary school, writes Professor Sinel, represented for Tolstoy the most crucial phase of the formal learning process. "Not only did it determine who would go on to university and hence indirectly into the higher levels of state service, but it provided the best opportunity for properly moulding this future elite."[28]

What he required was that the universities draw on the products of an elite schooling system, which would recruit from stable elements of society and provide them with the right mental training. Tolstoy decided that the latter lay primarily in the field of classical studies. Many conservatives and reactionaries objected that the history and literature of ancient Greece and Rome provided more striking examples of rebellion, tyrannicide and free-thinking than any other available subject. A yet more valid objection lay in its largely impractical value to an increasingly technological and scientific world.

Tolstoy's view was however decisive. Firstly, he accepted the view, almost universal in contemporary Europe, that the classics afforded a unique mental training, particularly suitable for future administrators and public servants. The logical and orderly structure of Greek and Latin grammar, and the stately world-outlook of the major figures of the ancient Mediterranean world brought about in those who studied them a balanced and reasonable attitude to life. The natural sciences, on the other hand, were in a highly experimental stage. Young men, suddenly faced with the half-digested and apparently revolutionary implications of recent research, became over-receptive to startling new theories of every sort. Most nineteenth-century socialist theories, from Fourier to Marx, depended on a more or less convincing "scientific" basis. It was not possible to challenge such views directly, since in doing so it would be necessary to place tempting but deceptive ideas before those who might otherwise not encounter them. Far better to provide young people with sound, analytical methods of thought and a broadly cultural background against which the wild claims of enthusiasts could be calmly examined. Such, for example, appeared to be the situation in England, that envied model of stability, where classics predominated in public schools and universities, and ideologists scarcely raised their insidious heads.

There was another, more practical consideration. Tolstoy's plan called for the universities to recruit as exclusively as possible from the elite Gymnasia, into which the right type of entrant could be introduced from the beginning. Not only was the Gymnasium considerably more expensive than the parallel "Real-Schools" (*Realschule*) introduced by Tolstoy to replace the old Real-Gymnasia, but the rigorous curriculum dominated by classical studies would tend to put off or weed out idle children and those from a less socially responsible background. All in all, Tolstoy hoped to draw bright intelligent children from that gentry class which ought to be supplying Russia with dedicated, efficient officials; and, after forming their characters and tastes at the Gymnasium, supply them with first-rate higher education at universities cleansed of vapid would-be intellectuals. It was an incredibly ambitious aim, one which few people could have thought likely to succeed, but Dmitri Tolstoy was the last person to be daunted by the mere magnitude of a task.

Of course this elite rôle accorded the Gymnasium necessarily involved a down-grading of the Real-Schools. No longer would they provide a route to the charmed bourne of the university. Moreover, if only a classical education served to avert radical sentiments, would not the Real-Schools become hotbeds of sedition in their turn? Tolstoy's answer was to direct the curriculum of the Real Schools towards the sort of practical subjects their alumni would require for their future careers.

The proposed stratification of schooling could only come into effect if the Ministry possessed the power to dictate subjects and timetables, and that in turn required careful legislation. There was strong opposition from both left and right, and it was not until 1871 that the measures were laid before a special conference to review them. Argument was fierce on both sides and in the end, despite all Tolstoy's eloquence, the majority decided against him. It was felt that the programme heralded a return to a general policy of reaction similar to that which had already done Russia enough harm. But the Russian see-saw, never still for long in the last century of Romanov rule, was inexorably tilting towards the conservative side.

The revolutionary movement at home and abroad had once more assumed threatening proportions. Following the Prussian victory over France in 1870, the Emperor Napoleon III had been deposed and a Republic instated. In Paris the revolutionary Communards had risen and taken control of the city, and were only suppressed after committing appalling atrocities and destruction. At home after a lull of more than a decade wide-ranging conspiracies seemed to have reappeared. At the end of 1869 Sergei Nechaev entered Russia from Switzerland, founded a small revolutionary clique entitled The People's Reckoning, and drew widespread attention to his activities by arranging the brutal murder of one of his co-conspirators before fleeing back across the frontier. (The crime and its instigator were memorably brought to life in Dostoevsky's novel *The Possessed*.) The revolutionary movement in which he was prominent was extensive and dangerous, advocating the Tsar's murder and the replacement of his rule by a reign of terror and totalitarian dictatorship remarkably similar to that eventually established in 1917. Nechaev in turn had received the blessing and patronage of a far more celebrated revolutionary: Mihail Bakunin, then an émigré in Geneva.

It is undeniable that opinions and activities hostile to government in nineteenth-century Russia were frequently the direct result of illiberal policies pursued by that government. As the late Tibor Szamuely argued in his brilliant book *The Russian Mind*, terrorism was in large part the reverse side of the coin to autocracy, its child and its enemy. But whatever the historical sources of terror, Alexander II and his advisers had to reckon with the fact that they were dealing as often as not with people recognizable in any society as suffering from personality defects causing social alienation expressing itself through the "revolutionary act". Nechaev, for example, "was a thin, undersized nervous creature, with burning little eyes and brusque gestures, continually gnawing at and around his nails, so that his fingers were covered with sores."[29] It seems unlikely that such a man would have laid aside his dagger had Russia become a parliamentary democracy. Nor did the relatively small number of active conspirators debar them as a potent threat to society. 1917 was to shew what a handful of dedicated Nechaevs could achieve in a time of crisis.

The danger was clear, and on 18 June 1871 the Tsar used his prerogative to uphold Tolstoy's minority view outvoted by the State Council. The scheme became law a month later. Henceforth the Gymnasium course concentrated on Latin, Greek and mathematics. 41 per cent of weekly teaching was devoted to the classics, concentrating principally on linguistics. Disproportionate as this may appear, the percentage of time spent on classics fell behind that in use at Prussian and Saxon schools, where it was as high as 47–48 per cent.

Tolstoy did what he could to improve the quality of education at the Gymnasia. Entry qualifications were raised, and he added a year to the course. Within severe limits imposed by the impoverished state of the Imperial treasury, he improved salary incentives to attract superior staff. On the negative side, restrictions were increased on the pupils' activities, and controls on those of the staff. It is scarcely necessary to state that this form of teaching by rote and rule was indescribably dull, and aroused much hostility and resentment. Both subject-matter and approach, however, were not strikingly different from those obtaining in, say, contemporary Britain, and Tolstoy believed firmly that mental training, like its physical counterpart, could achieve little without great effort and some pain. In one major aspect, too, he could claim striking success. Examination finals produced a satisfyingly high rate of passes, as high in the dreaded Latin and Greek as in more congenial subjects.

In accordance with his belief in "streaming" pupils – those from the Gymnasium into government service, the professions and the university, and those from the Real-School into business and industry – Tolstoy arranged a much more practically inclined course for the second rank of schools. Backward Russia was beginning to industrialize at a surprising rate, and increasing numbers of men with good technical qualifications were required. The first four classes studied religion, Russian, mathematics, geography, history, penmanship, mechanical drawing, and two foreign languages. The last two had courses in natural science, physics, chemistry, and mechanics. The commercial course substituted for the last two bookkeeping and clerical tasks. Since Real-School students were not intended for university, the course of study was intended to be as complete and practical as possible.

Between them the Gymnasia and Real-Schools catered for the needs of a few thousand of Russia's most gifted sons. But what of the untutored millions, the Dark People, most of whom a bare ten years previously had been serfs? In 1864 there had been a mere 1,846 elementary schools under Ministerial control throughout all Russia. A much greater number were organized by the clergy, but standards there on the whole were primitive. Initially Tolstoy hoped that the Church and local councils (*Zemstvos*) might increase the quality and quantity of schooling, but when this failed he began in 1869 to extend Ministry control over elementary education. Demanding sweeping improvements in standards, he employed a relatively large and active inspectorate with increased powers of control. He established teachers' seminaries and model schools, and within the scope permitted by the limited financial resources available applied pressure to increase the number of schools under Ministerial control and the quality of those run by local authorities. The model schools were regarded as a particular success: after squeezing additional funds from government, the Ministry increased their number from 166 in 1873 to 1,009 six years later.

All this, with Tolstoy's determined opposition to reactionary proposals by ministers to reinstate elementary education under clerical control, "demonstrates again the Minister's sincere desire to promote and improve Russia's primary schools. He established a fairly rational system of elementary education with teacher training institutions and government inspectors. Unlike some conservatives, Tolstoi acknowledged his country's great need for a literate population and worked conscientiously to fill this need."[30]

Perhaps Tolstoy's most striking success during his fourteen years' period as Minister of Education lay in his improvement of the quality, status and number of teachers. Swiftly overcoming his initial hostility to existing (and woefully inadequate) pedagogical seminaries, he set to work to make Russia "equal all other international powers in learning as well as politics". As with the schools for which the teachers were intended, elaborate measures were adopted by the Ministry to ensure that seminaries fell under central control, and the inmates' daily round

Dmitri Andreevich Tolstoy

was suitably circumscribed to avoid the revolutionary infection. That said, his achievement remains remarkable. Continually extorting funds from the hard-pressed Minister of Finance, he founded fifty-nine teachers' colleges during his fourteen years of office, and transformed the number, quality and motivation of teachers qualifying at government institutes.[31]

Tolstoy's overall purpose was overtly political, and in this he was surprisingly successful. No students from philological institutes took part in the radical movements of the 1870s and, as he pointed out with pride, only three seminarists appeared among the thousands of people under suspicion of revolutionary activity at that time. But he resisted purely reactionary measures such as attempts to define legally the social class intakes of differing institutions, or the reimposition of a clerical monopoly in primary teaching. "We make only one distinction among pupils – a distinction on the basis of merit. . . . Our gymnasia must produce aristocrats, but what kind? Aristocrats of the mind, aristocrats of knowledge, aristocrats of labour. May God grant that we gain more such aristocrats." So he declared in a speech at Kherson: words that received loud applause from listening Jewish leaders. Tolstoy had encouraged increased Jewish involvement in the state school system, a policy that was to be reversed by illiberal successors. A devoted lover of learning himself, Tolstoy was patriotically resolved that "in the world of learning, just as in the world of politics, Russia's international relations will be based only on complete equality."[32]

Dmitri Tolstoy was bitterly hated by most liberal and some conservative opponents of his policies as Minister of Education, whose writings and memoirs bear eloquent testimony to his defects as they saw them. B.N. Chicherin described him as "a bureaucrat to the core hating . . . every appearance of freedom . . . deceitful, greedy, evil, vindictive, insidious, ready to do anything to achieve his personal aims which usually pleased tsars but which aroused loathing in all respectable people". A speciality of Russian liberals was the blackguarding of the personal characters of those whose political policies they disliked, but so far few or none of the more vitriolic charges have been substantiated. To Soviet scholars, whose researches have greatly added to our factual knowledge of his work, he was the reactionary *par excellence*, second only to Alexander III's bigoted adviser Pobedonostsev, Tolstoy's successor as Procurator of the Holy Synod in 1886. None of this would have troubled Dmitri Tolstoy, who was little concerned with others' opinions. "I do not want popularity, I despise the seeking for popularity," he declared publicly in 1867, at the beginning of his term of office.[33]

Only in recent years have scholars like Nicholas Hans, Patrick Alston and Allen Sinel placed his achievement in a juster context. Of course he was a reactionary. He believed in the autocracy as the only suitable form of government for Russia. He believed that, if Russian history had anything to say, reforms were invariably forced upon a people, as often as not reluctant to accept them, from the top. A firm, paternal hand was essential to direct the destinies of a country as large, ignorant, volatile, and perhaps cruel as was Russia. It was precisely in accord with these views that Tolstoy believed the Tsar and his ministers had a God-given duty to improve the lot of those placed in obedience under the Autocrat. Hand in hand with his stern determination to eradicate radical doctrines went the resolution that Russia should be able to hold up her head intellectually among the nations of Europe. No Slavophile, chauvinist, or black clerical, he recognized the achievement of European civilization, and saw no reason why Russia should not benefit from its gifts.

At the highest level he followed his own scholarly inclinations by assisting laboratories, libraries, observatories and the Academy of Sciences. He set up three new higher education institutions, reinvigorated seven other faulty ones, and laid the basis for a future university in Siberia. He put pressure on the Finance Ministry, as a result of which the proportion of the national budget spent on education was nearly doubled within a decade. In 1865 there had been six students in secondary education for every ten thousand inhabitants; by 1880 the proportion was more than sixteen, despite a great increase in the population.

The inherent weakness of the whole system, paradoxically, lay in the nature of the autocracy itself, which was no more consistent in its policies that the parliamentary regimes of Western Europe. Alexander II was more loyal than most Tsars to deserving ministers, but crises inevitably brought about changes. In 1878 and 1879 riots and disorders broke out afresh among peasants, workmen and students. A new wave of assassinations occurred, culminating in a dynamite attempt on the Tsar's life in the Winter Palace itself on 5 February 1880. The explosion destroyed a room in which the Tsar was due to meet the Prince of Bulgaria. The Tsar escaped assassination for the third time, but it was decided that sweeping changes must be made. The security forces had been unable to protect the sovereign even in his own palace, and it was clear that mere repression would not do. General Loris-Melikov, chief of the Supreme Executive Commission, was appointed Minister of the Interior in August 1880. A war hero (he had captured Kars from the Turks in 1878), he advocated policies of combined firmness and

General Loris-Melikov

reform. Dmitri Tolstoy was singled out as a Minister whose reactionary policies had helped to bring about the existing turbulent state of affairs. He was paradoxically accused of provoking radical outbursts by his harsh policies, and simultaneously of breeding revolutionaries in his new seminaries. Tolstoy had to go, and on 22 April 1880 he fell from office.

Loris-Melikov's "Dictatorship of the Heart" (as his administration was known) attacked the crisis on two flanks. Firstly, liberal public opinion would be placated or won over by the removal of overtly authoritarian institutions and measures, which hitherto had provoked offence without securing public order. Secondly, a vigorous offensive campaign would be conducted against declared revolutionaries, keeping strictly within the framework of law. The underlying aim was to provide Russia with stability through legality, doing away with the traditional system whereby rival ministries lashed out blindly in different directions, obstructing each other and antagonizing society with every blow.

Loris-Melikov took a first cautious, preparatory step in the direction of representative government. He proposed that elected local representatives should play a limited advisory rôle in the preparation of legislation. On the morning of 1 March 1881 Alexander II approved the proposal, ordering the Council of Ministers to meet three days later to arrange its enactment into law.[34] That afternoon he was assassinated by agents of the "People's Will" organization, who blew up several of the Tsar's mounted escort and a number of bystanders with an improvised grenade. When the Tsar descended from his bomb-proof carriage to comfort the wounded, he too was mortally wounded by a second explosion.

After a few weeks' indecision, the new Emperor Alexander III was persuaded to reject the path of constitutional reform. On 29 April he issued a manifesto

The murder of Tsar Alexander II

declaring his intention to rule with full autocratic powers. Loris-Melikov resigned the next day, to be replaced as Minister of the Interior by the reactionary Count N.P. Ignatiev.

Ignatiev swiftly proved quite unequal to the task assigned him. Neither violently oppressive policies nor the proposed revival of the *Zemsky Sobor*, an archaic representative assembly, had any success in suppressing the activities of the radicals – actually quite few in number, though the authorities saw them as a massive international conspiratorial organization. So ineffective were the efforts of the police that the Tsar himself retreated from his capital to the isolated palace of Gachina, "a complete prisoner".[36]

Now the public began to take a hand in the game, notably in persecution of the Jews, held in some way to have been responsible for the murder of Alexander II. It must be made clear, however, that the assertion by a recent historian that Alexander III himself "launched a vicious wave of pogroms against the Jews in southern Russia"[36] is completely unhistorical fantasy. That the riots were not prevented was due, as might be expected, to administrative incompetence: in the north-west they were firmly put down, and Professor Bruce Lincoln's claim that none of the riots were suppressed is simply false. Failure to prevent them in the Ukraine and Poland was an important cause of Ignatiev's downfall.[37]

A further source of disorder in Ignatiev's time was "The Holy Host", a group of imaginative noblemen organized as a secret society, devoted to "the protection of His Majesty the Emperor and eradication of sedition". The Host's activities were more romantic than effective. Attempts were made to infiltrate the universities by granting scholarships to Ruthenian agents ("very cunning people"). Three apocryphal journals were lauched, one moderate in tone but the other two preaching revolutionary doctrines so horribly bloodthirsty as to put off the average decent radical for life. Elaborate plans to eliminate revolutionary leaders living abroad came to naught when the potential victims were alerted by no less a person than the former Minister of the Interior, Count Loris-Melikov. The last straw came when agents of the Holy Host triumphantly arrested a number of plain-clothes policemen whose activities they misunderstood.

The Tsar himself became impatient, and his wrath fell upon the Minister of the Interior, Count Ignatiev. Ignatiev, like the Tsar himself, had originally bestowed his blessing on the Holy Host. Now he was blamed for its continual interference with police work and the two-edged effects of its counterfeit liberal propaganda. Alexander III began to cast about for a new Minister of the Interior.

Dmitri Andreevich Tolstoy had already attracted the Emperor's favour with a very capable study of Russia's relations with the Vatican. Now, prompted by his reactionary adviser Constantine Pobedonostsev, the Tsar's choice fell on Tolstoy. The circumstances were related by his cousin, Mihail Vladimirovich Tolstoy, a seventy-year-old ecclesiastical scholar. He was playing cards with Dmitri's wife at their house in Mokhovaya Street when there was a ring at the door. The Count, who was in his study, came out to find a messenger bearing a letter and packet from the Tsar. Inside was a message explaining that "Sorting out my father's things, I came across his favourite seal, which I am sending you in his memory." Tolstoy was delighted with this mark of favour, and telephoned the Minister of the Palace.

"When may I have the happiness to express my gratitude to His Majesty for his kind attention?" he asked. In reply he was invited to dinner the next night. Clearly something was in the offing, and Countess Sophia invited cousin Mihail to be present when the Count returned. At nine o'clock next evening Tolstoy came back from the Imperial palace at Peterhof in an exultant state, explaining that he had just been appointed Minister of the Interior. When the Emperor announced this to him, Tolstoy had replied: "Your Majesty, I am already old and have developed views which I am incapable of changing. Now is it your wish, Sire, to have a Minister whose views can be changed?"

"Of what views are you talking?" enquired the Tsar.

"Well, for example, I believe that our history is centred around the nobility, and over the past 25 years everything has been done to undermine that class."

"Yes, I agree with you."

"In that case I am delighted to have the honour of renewing my services," replied the Count.[38]

This was on 30 May 1882, when Tolstoy was fifty-nine. After the bitterness of his dismissal as Minister of Education he had imagined himself to be at an age when his star must set. Now he found himself as the nearest thing to a Prime Minister that Russia possessed, with the full confidence of his Emperor. His colleagues were virtually all men of similar outlook. From now on Russia's policies were to be dictated by the triumvirate of Dmitri Tolstoy and the Tsar's two reactionary advisers, Procurator of the Holy Synod C. P. Pobedonostsev and the publicist M.N. Katkov. The alliance was even cemented by marriage, as Tolstoy's son and heir Gleb Dmitrievich was married to Katkov's daughter Olga. All three men were similar not only in their entrenched political opinions, but also in their undoubted intellectual talents. Katkov was editor of the excellent literary journal *Russki Vestnik* which, amongst other work, had published the writings of Leo Tolstoy.

Tolstoy's first task as Minister was to clear up the mess bequeathed to him by his predecessor Ignatiev.

Count Dmitri Andreevich Tolstoy

Of the Holy Host, he remarked to Alexander III that "a colony for young thugs is the right place for Count Bobby (P.P.) Shuvalov and Co". The Tsar agreed at the outset of Tolstoy's appointment that the Holy Host should be suppressed, but in view of its distinguished membership there was some delay before this could be accomplished. Not much time passed, however, before the Host predictably provided a pretext for its suppression. A grandiose circular was composed by its Executive Committee, inviting members of the public to join the "secret" brotherhood. Regrettably a copy fell into the hands of some young wags, who appended to the document the anagram name of a high police officer, much disliked by the public. Sealed with a magnificent wax seal, the circular began its round in the usual improbable circles. The outraged police official whose name had been attached saw to it that the Minister was informed, and the Emperor at last agreed to a total suppression. This came in the form of a letter from Count Tolstoy, congratulating the society upon the brilliance of its successes, but pointing out that for that reason its continuance had become unnecessary. It was all too much for poor Bobby Shuvalov, who had a nervous breakdown.[39]

Violence against Russia's Jews was dealt with much more sharply. Tolstoy, in company with many Russians, disliked the "Hebrew leprosy", but he disliked lawlessness much more. "My entire programme," he declared, "can be summed up in one word: 'Order'." The pogroms were brought to an abrupt halt, and on 25 June 1882, less than a month after he assumed office, Tolstoy issued a circular threatening dire penalties on officials who did anything to persuade Jews to emigrate. About 20,000 had fled in 1881 and 1882, of whom about 3,000 returned with his assistance. Nevertheless restrictive laws inhibiting Jewish settlement, occupation, and so forth remained in force, and voluntary emigration continued throughout the decade. All Tolstoy could do was rescind some of the laws restricting Jews, and ameliorate the effects of others.[40]

Tolstoy believed that autocracy was the form of government best suited to the genius of the Russian people. He believed equally strongly that the autocracy should be efficiently and fairly administered. He was particularly anxious to fine down the bureaucracy, making it at once a more streamlined vehicle for putting into effect the wishes of government, and more receptive to the needs of those whom it controlled. Within the limits of this concept, Tolstoy undoubtedly brought valuable talents into play. He possessed an iron will, tireless capacity for hard work, contempt for popularity, and great administrative ability. He could also display great charm, especially to those subordinates who satisfied his exacting expectations. What he wished to see was the same sort of progress over which he had presided as Minister of Education extended now to all other aspects of Russian life. He believed in stern repression of anything likely to disturb public tranquillity during this critical time, and by the same token tended to refrain from actions likely to be unnecessarily provocative to any sizeable section of the populace.

Though not responsible for foreign policy, Tolstoy exerted his considerable influence with the Tsar to bring about the generally placatory and unprovocative nature of Russian external policy characteristic of the reign of Alexander III. Many Russians today look back with approval on a policy which, by and large, ensured Russia's continuing status as a great power, without continually seeking to extend her frontiers or strike hostile attitudes towards her neighbours. In 1886–1887, for example, an unsuccessful Russian attempt to intervene in the affairs of Bulgaria caused tension between Germany and Russia at a time when

German-French relations were also poor. Many Russians saw here a chance to fish in troubled waters. Tolstoy was so worried by this that he wrote to the Emperor on 28 December 1886, apologizing for interfering in what was not directly his concern, but emphasizing that external affairs inevitably influenced internal ones, and *vice versa*. After a brief but exceedingly perceptive résumé of the European scene (he noted in passing that Germany's long-term aim must be to absorb German-speaking Austria), he concluded with a strong appeal: "For these reasons, it seems to me . . . that Russia should preserve her freedom of action, not linking herself disadvantageously in separate treaties."[41]

Fortunately Foreign Minister Giers held similarly moderate views, and the result was the Reinsurance Treaty with Germany, which committed Russia to very little. Ultimately, of course, Russia came to link her fortunes to those of France, but that is a story outside the province of Dmitri Tolstoy's career.[42]

Dmitri Tolstoy's administration of Russia's internal affairs during his seven years of office was largely successful in terms of his own policy aims and, despite the shrill claims of his many opponents, beneficial to his country.[43]

A minority group which had suffered much more cruelly at the hands of the state than the Jews was the sect of Old Believers, who rejected changes in the Church introduced in the seventeenth century. Measures to improve their standing had been included among the reforms of the previous reign. As in his dealings with the Jews, Tolstoy was lenient in his treatment of individual cases of infringement of the laws, and allowed them further concessions, the greatest of which was the granting permission for a Congress of Old Believers to be held in the holy city of Moscow itself in 1883. In general Old Believers were allowed freedom of worship provided it was unobtrusive and there was no attempt to make conversions among the Orthodox population at large. This accorded with the Minister's belief that nothing should be allowed to divide or weaken the Russian Orthodox faith, which, with the autocracy, was one of the twin pillars of Holy Russia.

Less amiable was the Minister's policy towards the Catholic Church in Poland. His views on Catholicism were bigoted, as his early polemical study *Romanism in Russia* reveals. Catholicism was regarded as the bonding of Polish nationhood, which the Government was determined to eradicate. Russian Poland, bordering vulnerably on Russia's powerful neighbours to the west, was regarded as the Empire's dangerpoint, and a harsh policy of Russification was unleashed on the population. The aim, which thanks to Polish toughness proved illusory, was to eradicate their language altogether. The extreme harshness of this policy was bitterly resented by the Poles. Still recovering from the suppression of the 1863 uprising, they were obliged to suffer this insulting and tyrannical assault on their nationhood. Ultimately, of course, it only resulted in greatly increased patriotic fervour in Poland. In the Baltic States, where Tolstoy feared the Germanizing influence of the Baltic barons, he undertook similar measures to enforce Russian speaking and undermine the barons' dominance of the region.

All this is very unpalatable, and the intolerant policy eventually inflicted much political damage and a great deal more moral harm on Russia herself. All that can be said, less in extenuation than to set the matter in perspective, is that Russia was adopting policies pursued by virtually every other power in Europe. Germany was equally oppressive in her treatment of her Poles, and even in comfortable Britain the Ministry of Education sought from 1847 to eradicate the Welsh language (Welsh-speaking was equated with evidence of immorality!), and so civilised an

Englishman as Matthew Arnold could look upon its demise as "an event which is socially and politically so desirable for them".[44] Only in Austrian Galicia were the Poles relatively well treated under the benevolent rule of the Hapsburgs.

Unjustifiable as the policy of Russification was, it is clear that Dmitri Tolstoy's concern was as ever solely with the preservation of security, and not with any purely chauvinistic attempt to instil one culture as superior to another. He made no attempt to apply the policy to Finland, or to infringe the autonomy she had possessed since annexation from Sweden in 1809. There was no danger of Swedish intervention in Finland, which he was therefore glad to leave in peace. Similarly, Tolstoy pursued a cautious approach towards the Moslems of Central Asia. There, where on the frontiers Russian columns were still annexing territory, a largely conciliatory attempt to integrate the native peoples took place. Russification was a long-term aim deferred in all major issues to a more appropriate time. At the same time native revolts in 1882 were suppressed with the same severity the British accorded the heirs of the Mahdi in Sudan. All in all, Tolstoy's policy towards the minority peoples and creeds in the Russian Empire was cautious and essentially pragmatic. The attack was strong where he feared a challenge to order and relaxed when that seemed secure.

Polish and Central Asian nationalism were not a direct threat to the integrity of the Empire, though they might well become so in the event of a crisis. The really dangerous adversary, as Tolstoy saw it, was the revolutionary movement within Russia itself. The Russian population at large remained relatively quiet throughout Tolstoy's ministry. Police administration had been reformed by Loris-Melikov, a procedure which Tolstoy continued. The Minister's formidable reputation was probably sufficient to cow most potential unrest, whilst he reminded the police force (which was tiny for a country the size of Russia) that they could always call upon the Army for support. The bugbear of Government was no longer the appearance of another Stenka Razin or Pugachev, but the spectre of assassination. The succession of attempts on the life of Alexander II, culminating in the death of the Tsar in 1881, provided eloquent proof of the resolution and resource of the People's Will party. Soon after that its agents succeeded in murdering a deputy minister of the interior and a military procurator of a court martial in Kiev. Despite this, successful arrests had drastically reduced active membership of the movement, but this the Government had no means of knowing.

Dmitri Tolstoy carried the campaign over onto the attack, attempting to infiltrate the People's Will with spies and informers. This necessarily involved skirmishing on dangerous ground, and the Ministry of the Interior not infrequently found itself the victim of a double agent, who switched sides or worked for both at once. Sergei Degaev, a man of limitless personal ambition, agreed to betray the People's Will, and pulled off the satisfying coup of arranging the arrest in 1883 of its intrepid leader, Vera Figner. But Degaev's rôle came under suspicion from the exiled remnants of the leadership, who under threat persuaded him to arrange the murder of a particularly obnoxious police officer. Degaev escaped, ending his days as a university professor in South Dakota.

Despite this débacle, the People's Will did not survive long. Degaev had purveyed the normal stock-in-trade of the informer, submitting grossly exaggerated accounts of the strength of the organization, and with his departure these alarmist reports also subsided. The movement's back was broken. In 1884 its newspaper suspended publication, as it could no longer be successfully circulated in Russia. Finally the

People's Will wound itself up in a manner both pathetic and ludicrous. Tikhomirov, exiled leader of the organization since the arrest of Figner, suddenly saw the light and wrote a grovelling apology to Alexander III for all his misdeeds, begging to be allowed to return to the Fatherland. He was forgiven, and later received a golden inkpot from Nicholas II as some sort of reward.

Apart from an isolated project to murder the Tsar in 1887, for which Lenin's brother was among five organizers sentenced to death, Russia remained outwardly quiet for the rest of the decade. A fascinating insight into Tolstoy's thinking is provided in the memoirs of Bernhard von Bülow, afterwards German Foreign Minister, who in 1885 travelled to join his country's Embassy at St. Petersburg. From Warsaw he rode in the same train compartment as Count Tolstoy. The journey took some thirty hours, during which the all-powerful Minister of the Interior spoke freely and animatedly to the intelligent young diplomat. He spoke first of his disappointment at the hostility his programme weighted towards classical studies had aroused in Russia, hoping that in Germany at least, home of the humanities, his efforts might be appreciated.

He then moved on to his current problems, particularly his attitudes towards the revolutionary movement and demands for constitutional reform. "He told me, not without humour, that a week before he had visited in prison a leading Nihilist intellectual, Miss Vera Figner, a general's daughter. This lady had aroused widespread interest as a brave and active agent of the Nihilists' Executive Committee. He had spent about two hours chatting with her.

"'You know how we Russians love to talk.'

"As he was bidding her goodbye, he said to her: 'I regret, Vera Petrovna, that I must now leave you. If I could spend another two hours with you, I would convert you to loyalty to Government.'

"She riposted neatly: 'And I too regret your going, Dmitri Alexandrovich [sic]. If you had been able to allow me two more hours, I should have won you over to *my* ideals.'

"The Minister pursued this stimulating account as we travelled, providing a penetrating exposition of the state of Russian affairs. He did not believe that the autocracy in Russia would survive in the long run. But the West European parliamentary system was still more unsuitable for Russia. The Russian people would be no more able to cope with that than a great clumsy peasant with a dainty toy. Count Tolstoy said to me, and I have recalled it many times since the outbreak of the Russian Revolution: 'Every attempt to introduce a West European parliamentary government in Russia will collapse. If the Tsarist system, which for all its shortcomings and weakness (I admit) has held Russia together for the century, were to break down, you would get pure, plain Communism in its place – the Communism of Mr. Karl Marx in London, who has just died and whose theories I have studied with the closest interest.'"

Tolstoy went on to explain that the only hope for Russia in her precarious position was the development of the *Zemstvo* system of local councils, and the continuation of a lengthy period of internal tranquillity during which Russia's infant industries could develop. When Bülow pointed out that this programme made no concessions towards the sort of personal freedom, security before the law, and religious toleration accepted as prerequisites in Western Europe, Tolstoy responded emphatically, "Certainly; oh, certainly! But first of all we have to destroy Nihilism. We're on the way to that."[45]

If, as seems probable, von Bülow's recollection of this conversation was accurate, Dmitri Tolstoy was remarkably prescient as to the course the revolutionary movement would adopt. For in 1885 there can have been very few people in Russia who foresaw Marxism developing as the prevalent revolutionary doctrine. Insofar as any subversive movements were surviving Tolstoy's stringent repression, it was the Populists and Anarchists who engrossed all perceptible enthusiasm. Populism, if one may summarize a complex set of beliefs, was a sort of romantic socialism, tinged with Marxism but unrestricted by Marx's prophetic historical exegesis. Anarchism, in the person of Mihail Bakunin, looked cheerfully forward to a Pugachev-style uprising, with rivers of blood, blowings up of churches and palaces, etc. Tolstoy did not mention which of Marx's works he had studied, but he certainly could have read *Das Kapital* in the original German or in the uncensored Russian translation of 1872.

But Marxism only really entered Russia through the works of Georgi Plekhanov, a converted Populist who settled in Geneva. In 1883 he formed a Marxist Party which had five enthusiastic members, and wrote two books, *Socialism and the Political Struggle* (1883) and *Our Differences* (1885), explaining and popularizing Marx's teaching. It was these which first made it apparent to Russian radicals that Populism and Marxism possessed important distinctions, and it was only about the time of Tolstoy's conversation with von Bülow that a little Marxist discussion group established itself in St. Petersburg. [46]

It was clearly not the existing strength of Marxism among the radicals that convinced Tolstoy that, were Russia to undergo a revolution, it would be a Marxist regime that succeeded it. His shrewd, cynical mind grasped at once the effect a doctrine like Marx's must have upon susceptible Russians. Marx himself thought it unlikely that revolution would come to Russia in the near future, but that was because he believed his own theory, which held that the country had first to pass through a capitalist stage. Tolstoy appears to have appreciated what Marx surprisingly never did: that Marxism itself formed a discrete political-historical entity. It was not the intricate, hair-splitting ratiocination that would appeal. To Russians, their vast country in a state of internal flux and moral incertitude, what would attract were, firstly, the convincing "scientific" chiliastic prophecy of a total destruction of the present decaying, evil old world, and its replacement by a regenerated New Jerusalem; and, secondly, "the intellectual satisfaction of a system that leaves practically nothing to contingency, making it possible to believe in the iron regularity of history and 'in principle' to foresee all future events."[47]

Most people at this time probably perceived the Russian state apparatus as formidably, even excessively, strong. Tolstoy, as he confessed to von Bülow, sensed its essential weakness. It operated largely in an intellectual and moral vacuum. Everywhere there was an unconscious yearning, which Marxism fitted to a T. A Scotsman travelling in Russia in the early 1870s encountered the spirit in an early guise. Mr. Mackenzie Wallace is writing about the peasants he encountered in Northern Russia: "A large proportion of them can read and write, and occasionally one meets among them men who have a keen desire for knowledge. Several times I encountered peasants in this region who had a small collection of books, and twice I found in such collections, much to my astonishment, a Russian translation of Buckle's *History of Civilization*!

"How, it may be asked, did a work of this sort find its way to such a place? If the reader will pardon a short digression, I shall explain the fact. At the commencement of the present reign there was a curious intellectual movement – of which I shall have more to say hereafter – among the Russian educated classes. The movement assumed various forms, of which two of the most prominent were a desire for encyclopaedic knowledge, and an attempt to reduce all knowledge to a scientific form. For men in this state of mind, Buckle's great work had naturally a powerful fascination. It seemed at first sight to reduce the multifarious, conflicting facts of human history to a few simple principles, and to evolve order out of chaos. Its success, therefore, was great. In the course of a few years no less than four independent translations – so at least I have been informed by a good authority – were published and sold."[48]

It was on this extremely fertile ground that Marx's far more comprehensive vade-mecum was to disseminate itself in due course. Unlike Marx, Dmitri Tolstoy understood the Russian predicament, and saw clearly how great an appeal his ideas, suitably popularized by Plekhanov or others, must have in Russia. His own policy was to hold the ring and buy time whilst with maximum haste Russia built up a solid industrial base, together with schools, hospitals and other institutions, until the spread of educational enlightenment ensured a sufficiently wide-based rational approach to life on the part of the population. Judging from the tone of his conversation with von Bülow, however, his assessment of the capacities of rationality were not optimistic. During his time as Minister of the Interior he was largely successful in the aims he set himself. The revolutionary peril was banished, Russian industry did indeed enter a boom period, the *Zemstvos* gained in strength despite continuing restrictions. Whether this combination of firmness and (generally) fair-mindedness could, if continued by successive ministers of the interior, have saved the dynasty is impossible to tell. It is to be regretted that he was not as enterprizing as Loris-Melikov in his attitude to fruitful reforms.

The greatest problem facing the autocracy in the 1880s was that of peasant discontent. At the time it appeared as if the Emancipation of 1861 had created as much peasant dissatisfaction as it had dispelled. This was probably inevitable, even had a Solon presided over the legislation; the transference of property was after all by far the greatest accomplished in the history of the world by a ruling class in a non-revolutionary situation. There was no Solon in nineteenth-century Russia; merely a disparity of interests and a general intention to stabilize the countryside. That this did not occur was all too predictable, and accounts for the hostility of otherwise enlightened men like Dmitri Nikolaevich Tolstoy to the whole reform. As it was, there was increasing anger among widespread sections of the peasantry, who often enough found themselves worse off than in their days of serfdom. It was generally objected that land allotted to the peasants when the post-Emancipation apportionments were eventually settled were unsatisfactory, being in frequent cases smaller than those tilled in the days of serfdom. Then again, as the landowners could not have their property expropriated, the peasants frequently found themselves saddled with debts and obligations which they simply did not have the resources to meet. A bad situation was disastrously exacerbated by extraneous factors, principally the financial crisis brought on by Russia's war with Turkey in 1877–78 and a world-wide depression in grain prices in the years following 1873. (Even in England, in retrospect so secure and prosperous and lacking most of Russia's peculiar problems, landlords had reason at this time to fear "a violent movement . . . the assaults of an insidious Socialism" amongst the rural poor.)[49]

With the enormous impetus to Russia's industrial development heralded by Alexander III's reign, large numbers of recently-emancipated serfs left the land to work in factories in towns and cities. As they maintained close links with their home villages, discontent and agitation developed widespread links, and town and country responded to the same pressures. On 7 January 1885 a serious strike broke out among 8,000 workers at Morozov in the province of Vladimir. Troops intervened, and at the end of a week the strike was broken by the arrest of nearly six hundred of the men. They were tried and acquitted, but a tremor ran through the Empire. Henceforward a feeling of unanimity developed between peasants and workers in their struggle. The movement was not as yet overtly hostile to the Tsar and his Government, but it could not be long before agitators and seditious literature began to reap from so fertile a soil. For Dmitri Tolstoy the danger was not revolution, but a continuing breakdown of order, ranging from illegal felling of landowners' timber to assault, arson and murder. Time and again the Minister was called upon to despatch troops and gendarmes, a state of affairs far from the law-abiding *Rechtstaat* Tolstoy was striving to build up.[50]

The Minister's belief was that the fault lay chiefly with Russia's paralysingly inefficient bureaucracy. The justification of the autocracy was to provide motion and purpose in an Empire too vast and diverse to be governed by any other method. Excessive consultation, deliberation or participation in government by the population at large must result in the whole cumbersome machinery breaking down. But for the autocrat to fulfil his rôle as the decisive centre of this complex community, he must possess not only the power but the capacity to cut across vested interests and the sheer dead weight of the country's vast size and backward outlook. Dmitri Tolstoy saw clearly that the intentions of the Government, expressed through his Ministry, were more often than not frustrated as they percolated downwards through the ever-muddying waters of the provincial bureaucracy, so effectively satirized by Gogol in an earlier reign. Equally, the genuine complaints of the peasantry were filtered off by the same clogging process and prevented from reaching the Emperor and his advisers.

Tolstoy's proposed method of obviating these gigantic problems was hotly debated and fiercely opposed in Government circles in the 1880s. He advocated the creation of a new category of local official, known as "land commander" (*zemsky nachalnik*), allocated sweeping powers, executive and judicial, who could act as a direct link between populace and administration. He would be able to make instant judgments, cut corners, and break through existing bottle-necks caused by the local *Zemstvo* or bureaucracy. These men were preferably to be selected from respected men of the local nobility. Given the premise of Tolstoy's belief in the necessity of autocratic rule, it might have seemed a brave new way out. In fact it was swallowed up all too predictably in that prevailing morass of Russian public life: the lack of suitable personnel. As one of the land commanders himself pointed out, "their powers were so broad that a good man would make very good use of them – but by the same token a bad man could do a great deal of harm. Unfortunately the choice of candidates for this post was in many cases far from satisfactory, as a result of which they not infrequently did more harm than good."[51] In essence, all that had arrived was yet another arm of the bureaucracy, one mistrusted by colleagues and feared by the peasantry.

But even as this unfortunate measure was receiving the Emperor's final approval, the brain that had prepared and urged it was removed abruptly from the scene. For some time Dmitri Tolstoy had been a sick man, though his single-minded devotion to duty had for long prevented him from mitigating his strenuous daily round. In 1885 he suffered a heart attack. Alexander III loaned him the imperial estate at Livadia in the Crimea in which to recuperate. He recovered, but was set back by a stroke in 1887. Early in 1888 he was back at work, but much debilitated in health. Devoting the remaining months of his life to supervising the legislation regarding the land commanders, he died quite suddenly from a heart attack on 25 April 1889. He was sixty-six.[52] The British Ambassador, Sir Robert Morier, described his death as leaving "a great gap" in the administration,[53] and Alexander III despatched a telegram to Countess Sophia Dmitrievna: "With what dreadful grief have I learned of the passing of dear Dmitri Andreevich; for you this is a tragic loss, but for me it is perhaps even worse, particularly at this moment: such a devoted, noble and stalwart man and colleague will be hard to replace. God preserve you in your deep sorrow!"[54]

Dmitri Andreevich was buried on the family estate of Zavidovka near Tula, where he used to spend part of each summer.[55] Countess Sophia Dmitrievna lived on to witness the 1905 Revolution, and died in 1907.

There can be no doubt of the fitness of the Emperor's epitaph. Dmitri Tolstoy possessed many sterling qualities. He was loyal, high-principled, honest, highly intelligent, and so industrious that it may fairly be stated that he literally worked himself to death in his country's service. His integrity appears beyond doubt, but what is unlikely ever to receive agreement is whether his achievement was beneficial or harmful to his country. Both before and after the Revolution the overwhelming majority opinion has come down heavily against his policies, and he shares with Pobedonostsev the reputation of being the most benighted reactionary of the nineteenth century. More recent scholarship, particularly that of Professors Sinel and Taylor, provided a healthy corrective to this extreme view, and his administrative achievements as Minister of Education and Minister of the Interior have at last received their due.

His political achievement must remain largely a matter of unverifiable opinion. It was a tragedy that Alexander III lacked the vision to allow Loris-Melikov his head, and few rejoiced at that fine stateman's fall more than Dmitri Tolstoy. But, given the fatal Russian condition, it would be a bold man who would confidently assert where and how the old Russia could have reformed itself. Tolstoy believed that what the country needed above all else for years to come were stability and order, and these to a large extent he provided in the 1880s. Believing that at that time the alternative to the autocracy could only be rapine and dictatorship, he set his face firmly in favour of the *status quo*. Things after all, he may have felt, could be much worse. There was much in Romanov Russia that was wholly admirable, and observers at home and abroad were impressed with her progress. Many men of his generation preserved not wholly illusory memories of a stable patriarchal existence in the countryside of their youth, such as that on his uncle's estate at Znamenskoe described in the early part of this chapter, and saw few benefits in hastening the demise of that society. Ultimately, he sensed, it might well be doomed, but what lay beyond that doom he fancied he knew. He had, after all, read Karl Marx and listened to Vera Figner.

8
Quentin Durward in a Frock Coat

f Alexei Constantinovich Tolstoy, a recent critic has written: "Among the poets of his generation, A. K. Tolstoy was the most versatile, original, and ultimately the most interesting." He was poet, playwright and historical novelist, and of all the Tolstoys chronicled in this history was, perhaps, the most winning and delightful character. He was the *beau idéal* of a Russian nobleman of the nineteenth century, and forms a pleasing contrast to other wild if brilliant relatives. Romantic and civilized, he was beloved by all he encountered.

Alexei's grandfather, Major-General Count Peter Andreevich Tolstoy, was remembered as a straightforward soldier of such extreme integrity that he left his thirteen children in a state of great poverty. His third son Constantine was born in 1780, and fought gallantly in the wars against Sweden and France until he was invalided out of the service at twenty-six with a damaged left arm. He remained somewhat soldierly in his bearing, bluff, clumsy, with blue eyes and a large nose, fond of drink and jollity. His first wife died soon after their wedding, and on 13 November 1816 in St. Petersburg he married the beautiful young Anna Perovskaya. She was the illegitimate daughter of Count Alexei Razumovsky, whose uncle had been the secret husband of the Empress Elizabeth and Hetman of the Ukraine.

Constantine Petrovich Tolstoy

Sadly, the marriage was a disaster. On 24 August 1817 Anna gave birth to a son, christened Alexei, and only six weeks later she left her husband, never to return. It seems that, whatever the Count's feelings, the young girl had allowed herself to be swept into a marriage which had meant little to her from the beginning. Constantine's brother Feodor, the artist, observed that "My brother Constantine ought never to have married Anna Alexeevna. She is too intelligent for him. It was hard to hope for compatibility." It was hinted too that Count Constantine's military penchant for strong liquor had played a part in alienating the strong-minded young bride.

Without any apparent bad blood between the families, Anna and her baby left Constantine Tolstoy for good and took up residence with her brother Alexei Perovsky, who became young Alexei's "father" in place of the real one he had

Previous page: Alexei Constantinovich Tolstoy

never known. This sudden flight of the young mother and baby led to persistent rumours that Alexei was the product of an incestuous union between brother and sister, and that the marriage had been hastily arranged to conceal the fact. Such a story is certainly not borne out by the dates of the wedding and christening.

The baby Alexei's new home was at Krasny Rog in the province of Chernigov, where both the Tolstoys and Perovskys originated. Krasny Rog was a magnificent European mansion deposited in the midst of wildly beautiful Russian countryside, making a perfect setting of romance for the impressionable boy as he grew up. Set on a hill, with a landscaped park around, the house was the creation of the famous Italian architect Rastrelli. It was a feast of luxury and beauty, possessing a magnificent library filled with rare books and valuable manuscripts. Alexei Perovsky, the owner of this paradise, an estate extending to 25,000 hectares (61,775 acres), was a man of great learning and artistic feeling. He had served with distinction in the army against Napoleon, but took an early opportunity of resigning his public duties and returning permanently to his beloved Krasny Rog. A learned botanist, he filled the park with rare and beautiful plants. Little Alexei played on the lawns and walks, but what most influenced his precociously romantic nature was the great forest beyond, whose sombre depths could be glimpsed across the gently meandering river Rog. Below primeval trees roamed goats, deer, foxes, wolves and boars, wild denizens of a land of imagination and adventure.

As he grew up under the benevolent care and inspiration of his gifted uncle, Alexei discovered treasures in the great library which, borne off to the freedom of the woods, led his impressionable mind to soar to ecstatic flights of creative imagination. Later he recalled finding at the age of six an old anthology of Russian poetry. He soon knew it by heart and mastered the rhythms. He used to confess that its dirty red cover "is imprinted on my memory and sets my heart beating when I see it". From an old nurse he heard Russian fairytales of the hut that walked on chicken's legs, of the hideous hag Baba-yaga, and of the Grey Wolf and the Firebird. His uncle, who was in everything but reality his father, relished an enthusiasm he himself had never lost, and set the child wild with excitement over stories of knights and troubadours, vampires, and midnight castles inhabited only by hooting owls.

A year before his death Tolstoy recalled that "my childhood was supremely happy and remains with me as a glittering memory". At Krasny Rog a cross word or an unkind deed was a rarity. The peasants looked with affection on their benevolent master, Alexei's mother and uncle adored and encouraged him, and the little boy grew up with nothing but laughing memories and a warm conviction that God and love were one. Turtle-doves patrolled the luscious lawns in loving pairs, and as Alexei somersaulted beside them he was building up a memory-world to which he would return to the end of his life in the joyful certainty of recovering the golden age. Around this little paradise the forest and plain stretched to an illimitable horizon, and a harsher world was too remote for conception.

When Alexei was nine his uncle was recalled to duty in St. Petersburg, and his mother and he accompanied him to the capital. There Alexei became a playmate of the eight-year-old Heir to the Throne, the future Tsar Alexander II. With other little friends, the boys romped all day with an energy that startled all around. Alexei Tolstoy was remarkable for his strength, tossing the others upon his shoulders and galloping about neighing like a horse. One day a tall, powerful figure appeared amongst them. It was the formidable Tsar Nicholas I, come to see the Tsarevich at play. At once little Alexei offered to wrestle with him. The Tsar smiled: "With me? But you forget that I am stronger than you, and much bigger." "I don't mind!" cried Alexei, "I'm not afraid to take on anyone: I'm jolly strong, I know!" "All right then," laughed the Emperor, "come on then. But as I am so much bigger I shall only fight with one hand." Alexei flew at him, but struggle as he might he could not shake the powerful Tsar. Eventually Nicholas swept up the panting warrior, kissed him and complimented him.

In 1827 young Tolstoy travelled with his "parents" to Germany, where he made the acquaintance of the great Goethe "who instinctively impressed me with enormous respect, thanks to what I had heard people say about him. What I recall from this visit are the majestic features of Goethe, and also that I sat on his knees," he recalled later. Alexei Perovsky himself was venturing into literary fields, and wrote stirring Gothick fantasies in imitation of the *Tales of Hoffmann*. For his nephew he specially composed a story entitled *The Black Hen*. It was a magic hen which came one night to Alexei's bed, led him away to indescribable adventures, and presented him with a charm that enabled him to remember all his lessons without really working. This was a charm the boy possessed in reality, but the story ends with an impeccable moral, and Alexei never forgot that industry is as vital as imagination to a writer.

In 1831 the family travelled to Venice, where Alexei kept a diary of all the wonderful sights he saw, just as his ancestor Peter Tolstoy had done there in 1698. He was infatuated with the glories of Italian art, many specimens of which were despatched home as his uncle cheerfully disbursed vast sums on works by Titian, Tintoretto and Michelangelo. He was also fascinated by the gloomy dungeons of the Inquisition, the cell whence Casanova escaped, and the Palace of the Doges. His writing, perception and taste were exceptional for a thirteen-year-old boy, and presaged his future tastes and interests. "These dilapidated houses, the deathly quiet of the streets, and particularly the black gondolas give Venice a melancholy air," he noted on 23 March 1831.

They travelled on to Rome, where they met the sculptor Thorwaldsen and watched the Russian painter Bryullov at work on his gigantic canvas *The Last Day of Pompeii*. At Pompeii itself the future historical novelist was upset to find most of the artefacts removed to a museum; he wished to dwell on them *in situ* and bring the past flooding back to life. Alexei returned to Russia with his heart brimming over with love for the warmth, scents, noise and beauty of sunny Italy. His soul had been seized by this rapturous experience, and the notion of beauty's perfection now absorbed his whole being.

But Russia in the early nineteenth century was not Europe, and the inexorable demand of the Russian Imperial bureaucracy advanced their shadow upon him as they did upon everyone, no matter how distinguished his birth. On 9 March 1834 Tolstoy was sent to study at the Foreign Ministry Archives. He derived some pleasure from acquaintance with the manuscript material of Russia's terrible past, but when he qualified nearly two years later the thought of government service aroused only repugnance. His uncle's anxiety to see him advance creditably up the ladder of *chin* promotion for the first time set him and Alexei apart.

But a melancholy blow was to remove the impediment his uncle's ambition had placed before him. Alexei Perovsky became seriously ill, and his nephew obtained leave from the Archives to take him to recuperate in Nice. The sickness had taken its grip, and they had only reached Warsaw when, on 9 July 1836, Perovsky died in young Tolstoy's arms. Tolstoy was griefstricken. His Uncle Alexei had provided him with a grounding enviable for any young man, but for one possessed of such founts of poetry and romance as Alexei Tolstoy it had been a boon beyond price. He returned to St. Petersburg to console his mother; she fell ill from the shock.

On 13 January 1837 he received a fresh government appointment attaching him to the Russian mission at the Diet of the German Empire being held at Frankfort-on-Main. There he met the writers Gogol and Zhukovsky, and amused himself with the glittering company there assembled.

Tolstoy was now on the threshold of his public literary career. Every advantage seemed to lie before him. He was rich (his uncle had bequeathed him Krasny Rog and his fortune), handsome, charming and brilliantly talented. His appearance we know from a marvellous likeness painted by Bryullov in Moscow in 1836. Tolstoy is represented in his huntsman's clothes, with dog and gun in the forest, but the expression on his face powerfully suggests his rapt love for the untamed country-side.[1] A friend recorded at the time that he had never "seen in a man such a clear

Alexei Constantinovich Tolstoy. By Bryullov

and candid soul, such a responsive and tender heart, such a consistently high moral ideal as in Tolstoy". His nature appeared clouded by no regrets, doubts or troubles, and his infectious laugh and convivial ways won him friends wherever he went. At times he would delight them with enthusiastic demonstrations of his colossal strength, driving nails into walls with his open palm, twisting thick silver forks into knots, and straightening out horseshoes.

His duties at Frankfort were not onerous, and in October 1838 he travelled to Italy with the heir to the throne, the Grand Duke Alexander, and wintered there with his mother. At Como he fell in love with the pretty daughter of the major-domo of a neighbouring villa. In a room with closed shutters, where the warm sun could insinuate itself only through the cracks, Alexei Tolstoy poured out his love to the blushing Peppina. The romance ended with his departure from Italy, but pretty Peppina lingered affectionately in his memory and reappeared in his writings. Love for him was not suffering or obsession, but a rapt state of intoxicated elation and absorption in a world where nothing jarring or ugly intruded.

He fell in love too with his friend Prince Meshchersky's young sister, who had just returned from delighting the English with her charms at Queen Victoria's coronation. But Alexei's widowed mother prevented the match; as Meshchersky correctly surmised, through a jealous desire to keep her son by her.

> "I believe in love,
>   In the union of souls;
>   All my thoughts, my life, my blood,
>   The pulsing of each artery,
>   I would give joyfully to her
>   Whose dear face
>   Fills me to my tomb,"

wrote Alexei in his adolescence. His possessive mother was to ensure that it was a love that perforce remained checked in her lifetime. That he was not heartbroken suggests he was too much absorbed in a general state of love to require abandonment to the particular.

Back in St. Petersburg Alexei resumed his carefree life. He had inherited a love of practical jokes not only from the Tolstoys (his celebrated cousins Feodor Ivanovich and Leo shared his taste), but also from his uncle Alexei Perovsky, who once initiated an impressionable friend into a wholly imaginary masonic order. With two young cousins, Alexei and Vladimir, he was the bane of the capital's respectable inhabitants. From their sledge would project a long pole over the pavement, causing passers-by unexpectedly to spring in rows high in the air. At the theatre one of them would "accidentally" tread on the toe of some lofty dignitary, and then plague the life out of him with persistent apologies, continuing for days and weeks after. On another occasion they released the horses from an ambassador's carriage, which galloped off delightedly down the streets. When a famous German actor portrayed *Hamlet* on the stage in his own language, Tolstoy and his cousins ensconced themselves in a box with a gigantic dictionary. "Sein, oder nicht sein," declaimed the tragedian in sonorous tones. "Just a moment!" cried out young Tolstoy, as he hunted for the word "sein" in his dictionary. However, they finally went too far when one night they summoned St. Petersburg's most famous architects to the Winter Palace, explaining that the St. Isaac Cathedral had suddenly collapsed. The stern Tsar Nicholas I was not amused.

Despite his popularity with the city's *jeunesse dorée*, particularly the ladies, Alexei continued to succumb to the lures of the open countryside and of literature. He was still developing his talents in leisurely fashion, and devoted himself principally to a series of weird and fantastic tales calculated to provide sleepless nights for all the imaginative young girls of St. Petersburg. *The Vampire* was the most ghastly, and is certainly not to be read in a darkened study above moonlit canals. Horrors and fantasies follow in sinister dreamlike succession.

> Under the castle the Danube runs and roars
> And darkest clouds roll over . . .
> The deed is done, the old man's throat is torn,
> And Ambrose feasts with his gang.
> The moon is bathed in the bloody waters –
> And the false wife feasts with Ambrose.

Tolstoy was not deterred by some critical reviews, one of which unkindly suggested that the whole thing could only be explained by the author's addiction to opium. In fact his love for ideas fantastic and sinister may be attributed to the weird old Russian fables he had absorbed from his nurse, developed by an untrammelled imagination floating free in the dark forest of Krasny Rog. This in turn was encouraged by his uncle's tastes and the public's enthusiasm for Gothick horrors.

But there was never anything morbid about Alexei Tolstoy. A melancholy bout of nostalgia might creep over him, but not for long. It was also at this time that he developed a veritable passion for the hunt. "Alongside my longing for Italy soon began to develop a strange contrast, which at first glance could appear contradictory: this was a passion for the hunt. In my twenty-second year it gained such a hold on me, and I abandoned myself to it with such zeal, that all my spare time was devoted to the chase. At that time I was attached to the palace of the Emperor Nicholas and followed that glittering life which was not without enjoyment for me, but I often slipped away from it in order to lose myself for a whole week in the woods, sometimes with friends but generally alone. Among regular huntsmen I soon acquired a reputation as a hunter of the bear and elk." Out on the wild Cossack steppes of Orenburg Alexei discovered a new exaltation. He loved the open plains, so vast that the Cossack choruses "were lost in the limitless void without being repeated by a single echo". Then, from time to time, he would slip back to the lush scenes of his childhood in the Ukraine, where he derived exquisite pleasure from sadly recalling the lost years.

All the time more poems and tales poured from his fluent pen, reflective, bizarre, wild, nostalgic or humorous. *Artemy Semeonovich Bervenkovsky* was the

Hunting scene, by F. P. Tolstoy

tale of an eccentric landowner who took up mechanical inventions. Amongst his achievements was a turnspit operated by three mechanics to roast one chicken; a carriage whose axles simultaneously operated a coffee-grinder and a barrel-organ (which played only patriotic tunes); a basin disguised as a three-cornered hat and a razor-case indistinguishable from a violin; and a movable roof which unfortunately let in the rain. This nonsense annoyed the distinguished critic Belinsky, but delighted Alexei's friends.

In everything but his Herculean strength and vitality Tolstoy resembled his spiritual mentor Walter Scott; in his equable and affectionate nature, deep love of the historical past, devotion to the countryside, absorption with the wild and fantastic, and in his gifts as lyric poet and historical novelist. On one occasion, when in love, he could find no satisfactory inspiration for verses he required. He then recalled the melancholy song of a Kirghiz camel-driver he had encountered in the wastes of Orenburg. Tolstoy made arrangements for this man to be fetched from the other end of Russia and sent him to sing to the lady, explaining that all his skill could not rival this song, the product of so many souls over so many centuries. Certainly this tale reflects the aristocratic opulence of Tolstoy's life, but there is also a sincerity of feeling for the immanent grandeur of the earth's wonders and the richness of her past.

During the 1840s Alexei Tolstoy continued to receive promotion at court. He had not sought these duties, but they were not onerous and his social and literary life continued to flourish. He played no direct part in the increasingly violent controversies developing between Slavophiles and Westernizers, and those of differing literary schools. He detested anything that savoured of ill-will or fanaticism, but was inevitably influenced by the new school of historical realism precipitated by the writings of Pushkin and Lermontov. A fascination with the reality and recreation of the past was fast banishing to their native mists the vampires, witches and phantoms of Hoffmann and his devotees. Like Scott, Tolstoy always retained a juvenile love for those grim emanations, but was far too sensible to allow their pallid forms and bloodstained talons to spirit him away.

In company with the galaxy of genius that glittered over Russia in the reign of Nicholas I, Pushkin, Nekrassov, Turgenev, Gogol and Zhukovsky, Alexei Tolstoy was always a favoured guest at lavish entertainments provided by the millionaire Prince Demidov, Prince Viazemsky and other great society hosts. He dined too with the amateur chemist Prince Odoevsky, who with his own hands prepared sauces so revolting as to cause one guest to feel ill at the memory forty years later. At home Tolstoy's possessive mother watched over his official and social life, and (it is said) never went to bed before his return home.

During a leisurely official mission to Kaluga in 1850 his friendship and literary collaboration with the eccentric Gogol developed closer bonds. Despite marked differences in personality, Tolstoy always sustained a great love and admiration for the great satirist, playwright and novelist. Politically, too, they shared a devotion to the monarchy. When Gogol died in 1852, an absurd whim of the censorship banished Turgenev from the capital for publishing too eulogistic an obituary of his fellow-writer. Alexei Tolstoy was horrified at this act of mean-minded despotism, and exerted himself with unwonted energy to have the sentence rescinded. Despite his relations with the Tsar Nicholas and his heir, it was not until nearly two years had passed that his efforts were successful. His credit with the Imperial family had been dangerously stretched, but his reward lay in the ecstacy with which he read Turgenev's *Huntsman's Notebook*, that wonderful work which he aptly likened to a Beethoven sonata.*

It seems inevitable that with a nature like his he would succumb to a *grande passion*, and it is only surprising that it was not until he reached the relatively late age of thirty-four that the inevitable happened. At one of those masked balls which for some time he had come to regard as the epitome of vapid tedium, he came face to face with a young girl whose lively eyes and mellifluous voice drew him irresistibly to her, despite the fact he could see little of her behind the mask beyond a mass of lustrous blond hair and a lithe, active figure. But when he advanced towards her she laughed and drew away. It was not for a year that he was to meet her again, but she had already made an impression not to be effaced. "This time you won't escape me!" he cried, and she showed no inclination to do so. The fair unknown proved to be Sophie Andreevna Bakhmetev, who in 1846 had married a Guards officer who shared none of her enthusiastic passions. They soon separated, and Sophie retired to her family estate, her favourite occupation being to gallop across the fields astride a Cossack saddle, a musket slung over her back.

Her beauty, charm, love of the countryside and enthusiasm for literature appeared to make her indeed the destined partner of Alexei Tolstoy.

"I found this piece in your diary," he wrote in 1851; "'to achieve truth it is necessary once in your life to cast out all former ideas, and start your whole mental approach afresh.' How joyfully would I work for such a renewal, with you by my side! I am like a coach-house or a huge chamber full of all sorts of things, some very useful and a few very precious, but which are heaped up one upon another; I want to sort it all out with you. . . ." A series of limpid verses, some exultant, some melancholy, pressed the same theme. Sophie invited him to her home at Smalkov, where he found real happiness in an atmosphere which was at once charming and informal, casual and intimate. He intensely disliked the formal

---

* *A propos*, it is interesting to note that, close as were Alexei Tolstoy's relations with Gogol, it was another Tolstoy who became Gogol's nearest associate, who provided a home for him, and in whose house he ultimately died. Count Alexander Petrovich Tolstoy, born in 1801, was the son of Alexander I's Ambassador to Napoleon after the Treaty of Tilsit. He had a distinguished career in the army and diplomatic service, had been Governor of Tver and Military Governor of Odessa, but retired in 1840 to study religious questions. A man of enormous learning, he was a determined defender of the ideas of Orthodoxy and Autocracy. He met Gogol on a trip abroad and, finding their literary, political and religious beliefs coincided, became his closest friend. Thenceforward his homes in Russia and abroad were thrown open to the writer. Alexander Tolstoy was a nobleman of great wealth and lavish whims: his dentist, for example, was in London. Gogol frequently accompanied him abroad, and in Rome met at his house the great sculptor, medallist and painter Feodor Petrovich Tolstoy (uncle of Alexei Constantinovich), who however left a very sarcastic account of the meeting. (Not all the family approved of the writer, and when Gogol's great work, *The Government Inspector*, appeared, the duellist Feodor Ivanovich Tolstoy ("the American") was heard to growl out that Gogol was an enemy of Russia who should be packed off in chains to Siberia.) In Moscow Count Alexander Tolstoy lived in a magnificent mansion at 314, Nikitsky Avenue (today 7, Suvorov Street). There Gogol was provided with his own suite of rooms (decorated entirely in green), waited on by the Count's servants and, in short, wanted for nothing. It was there that Gogol burned his manuscript of the second part of *Dead Souls* in a distressing episode famous in literary history, and it was there that he died in 1852.[2]

round of court and society existence, and only his close friendship with the Grand Duke Alexander and his respect for the Tsar Nicholas kept him from breaking the golden chains binding him to the capital.

"When I think of you," he confesses in another letter, "I see a cottage half hidden by trees, I see the countryside, I hear your piano and that voice which sets me trembling since the first time I heard it. And everything which clashes with that quiet, good life – all the rattle of the world, ambition, vanity, etc., all the hypocrisy necessary to sustain such an artificial existence so harmful to conscious-ness – all that appears to me from afar like an ugly miasma, and I seem to hear your voice go straight to my heart: 'I give all that up for ever for love of you!' And then an overwhelming happiness enters into me, and your words set up a vibrant response in my heart with their affirmation that henceforth nothing can do you harm; and I immediately see that all that imagined happiness, that cottage, that good, calm life – it is all within us. *It is your heart which sings with happiness and mine that listens*, and as all that is inside us, it can never be snatched away and we can be alone and happy in the midst of turmoil."

But the turmoil, without and within, was not so easily banished. On 4 May 1851 Alexei was appointed Master of Ceremonies at Court. Sophie fell very ill, so ill he thought at one point she might die, and contemplated a very desperate measure; but she recovered. He made a brief trip to Paris, writing to her continu-ally to revel in his love for her and the melancholy which seized him when they were apart. Most dangerous of all was his mother's unmistakable hostility to their relationship. Possessive as ever, she tried unsuccessfully to persuade her son that Sophie's past must be held against her.

Tolstoy's verse continued lyrical, sighing, nostalgic, until a gathering storm aroused his enthusiasm for more stirring rhythms. During a prolonged visit to his beloved Ukraine he felt the draw of the countryside more strongly than ever.

> Do you know the land where is lushness and plenty,
> Where rivers are purer than silver,
> Where feathered grass waves beneath the steppe-wind
> Where farms lie embowered in orchards of cherries;
> The trees in the gardens lean over the earth,
> Their weighty fruit hanging right down to the ground?

An inimitable picture is painted of the heavy, sleeping countryside, a distant bell, larks rising as the sun burns over the plains,

> Remember that night in the sleeping Ukraine,
> When out of the pond rose a smoky white vapour,
> The world was apparelled in shadowy gloom,
> And the Bear gleamed down on the breadth of the steppe. . . .

But the mood is changing. After references to remote warrior-heroes, Tolstoy burst out

> Do you know the land where once the Great Peter
> Boisterously caroused on the wide open plain,
> Bugles and battle-cries martially mingling,
> And Sweden's proud King decamped in disorder,
> Where our forefathers gathered in glory for battle?
> It's there, over there, that my soul longs to be!

Russia's invasion of the Balkans, which aroused the hostility of Britain, France and Austria had brought about this upsurge of patriotic fervour. Alexei Tolstoy believed passionately in Russia's mission to liberate her fellow-Christians and Slavs suffering Turkish oppression. And then he became filled with indignation against the British and French, who intervened on behalf of the infidel oppressor and despatched their armies to his aid.

Russia's poets were united in raising a levy of patriotic verses, good, bad, and generally indifferent. This was not enough for the frank and direct nature of Alexei Tolstoy, who detested humbug. In the spring of 1854, when sailing on the Volga with Sophie, he resolved on action. He was a large, immensely powerful man, a superb horseman and shot, and the thought of riding into battle against the enemies of his beloved country greatly appealed to his chivalric spirit. The Allies did not land their forces in the Crimea until September, and the first actions of the war were at sea. In April a British fleet under Admiral Napier appeared in the Baltic bombarding Hangö in Russian Finland and threatening the great naval base at Kronstadt. Tolstoy joined the crowds on the coast, gazing through his telescope at that distant line of sails, on one of which the ferocious Napier was planning his crimes.

Alexei decided to buy a small steamboat, which he would crew with a hundred well-armed sailors, disguise as a pleasure-steamer, and launch a series of hit-and-run raids against the enemy. With a friend, Count Bobrinsky, he bought quantities of arms from the Imperial factory at Tula and set about drilling and training peasants on his estate. But ultimately the Russian malaise prevailed again; the peasants proved undrillable, and a hundred obstacles obtruded themselves. Alexei Tolstoy, burning with frustration, had to content himself with riding furiously up and down the Baltic coast with his valet, and chafing over war bulletins from the Caucasus and Crimea. Reports of the soldiers' suffering greatly affected him, and he volunteered to enlist in a regiment of sharp-shooters. It was at this moment (18 February 1855) that the Tsar Nicholas died. The country in general breathed again after its long night of autocratic regimentation. Tolstoy had found the oppression as galling as anyone, though he strongly respected the Tsar's honesty of purpose and upright character. As Master of Ceremonies, Alexei Tolstoy was responsible for the Imperial obsequies, which occupied him fully for some weeks.

As soon as he was free of this responsibility he approached the new Tsar Alexander II, who had been a close friend since childhood, and received permission to join the regiment of his choice. He was commissioned as a major in a detachment officered entirely by noble volunteers. For a while they led an idle and merry life in cantonments in remote Novgorod, Alexei composing patriotic verses and drinking songs for the mess, in which his sunny nature earned instant popularity. But he was chafing inwardly: he had joined to serve his country in the field, and he desperately missed his darling Sophie. "When I was fifteen," he wrote to her, "I wrote the poem *I believe in pure love*. . . . I only talked then of loving enduring to the grave, and I did not realize that it goes much further than that. . . ."

Eventually the regiment was despatched to Odessa, where dysentery and typhus were destroying more troops than were dying on battlefields outside Sevastopol. Alexei had to nurse his friend Bobrinsky, who nearly died of the fever, and then he himself was attacked. The anxious Emperor telegraphed daily as his friend came very close to death. One day as Alexei lay sweating and trembling in his bed, he woke to find Sophie Bakhmetev bending over him. She had flown to his side when she learned the news, and continued with him when he eventually recovered and convalesced with his comrades. As the débâcle of the campaign manifested itself, fierce arguments, at one point narrowly averted from continuation on the duelling ground, broke out among the friends. Alexei's proud and passionate spirit longed for a war *à outrance*, and rejected utterly the prospect of a dishonourable peace. Others saw this as futile quixotry, seeing in the defeat clear condemnation of Russia's helpless backwardness in face of Europe, and of the thirty years' benighted policy of Nicholas I.

Alexei's powerful constitution soon effected a complete recovery and, once more bursting with animal high spirits after his long confinement, he drove by the sea, drinking in the salt air with a sublime feeling of exhilaration. Armed with pistols and dagger, he explored some quarries where brigands were supposed to resort, and then with Sophie set off for an inspiring tour of the untamed grandeur of the Crimea. Alexei drank in the brilliant atmosphere of craggy defiles, distant sea views, deserted Tartar villages and legends of a picturesque past. As usual, he gratefully poured out his feelings in verses permeated with enthusiastic adoration of the natural world. His writing has been criticized, then and since, for its lack of social commitment, of psychology or metaphysical dissection. His devotion to lyrical exaltation of beauty and sentiment have been compared to his contemporary Tennyson. But the closest analogy is perhaps with the poetry of Walter Scott, also a superb master of the lyrical mood and lover of the countryside and its attendant historical and legendary associations.

Alexei Tolstoy intensely disliked artistic artifice and urban sophistication. So-called "natural" writing, with its attendant aspects of sordidness or obscenity, repelled him. When the famous French actress Rachel portrayed her rôle of Adrienne Lecouvreur with over-vivid representation of suffering acquired (so initiates delightedly reported) in actual visits to hospitals, Tolstoy withdrew in disgust. Repulsion and ugliness were not the business of art. To the end of his days he retained a child-like enthusiasm and imagination, which the passing years failed to overlay with cynicism or world-weariness. On his return from the Crimea he spent with an uncle a night in a reputedly haunted house by the Dnieper. Pistols at the ready, they waited in vain for the werewolf's return!

Here Alexei and Sophie parted, for he had resolved to return home to Krasny Rog and seek his mother's approval for his marriage to Sophie, when she should become divorced. But that was predictably withheld, and the Countess Anna Alexeevna exerted all the skills of a possessive mother to prevent the union. Alexei was heartbroken, roaming his childhood haunts in the grounds in an extremity of despair. He idolized his mother and could make no move without destroying a relationship essential to his happiness. He left for Moscow with the residual hope that time might somehow settle matters.

In the old capital the Emperor Alexander II was preparing for his coronation. Anxious to retain his old friend by his side, he pressed Alexei to accept the post of aide-de-camp. Though deeply torn by rival attractions, he accepted with misgivings and received his appointment on the day of the coronation, 26 August 1856. Once again public duties must interfere with poetic inspirations. On the other hand it soon dawned on him that he could put his close friendship with the Tsar to good use on behalf of the Russian people entering on the Great Reforms. This virtuous resolve produced its own reward. The charming and sensitive thirty-two-year-old Empress Maria Alexandrovna, listening one evening at the Palace of Gachina to Tolstoy reciting his verses, became his enthusiastic admirer and friend. It did not require Alexei's romantic devotion to the monarchy to reciprocate this feeling, for she was besides being an Empress a warm-hearted, sincere personality. He became quite infatuated with his beautiful sovereign, which in a less spontaneous and enthusiastic personality must have aroused the jealousy of his lady-love. Henceforward, at her request, he read all his new compositions to the Tsaritsa, who asked him to dedicate his first volume of verses to her. His responsive enthusiasm did not offend Sophie, who knew him too well, but did provoke sarcasm from some.

Tolstoy's return to Court, however, brought him just the sort of attention he was anxious to avoid. Without any consultation with him, the Emperor appointed Tolstoy head of a committee to look into the affairs of the Old Believers. He wrote to Sophie, expressing his extreme distress at submitting to this burden. He was a writer, not a functionary; besides, he had little knowledge or liking of day-to-day affairs and found his birth and tastes inevitably distanced him from the rest of the community. "Whatever they do, they won't find any way of linking me to the masses." But the Emperor had chosen him precisely because he needed someone of humane and independent character to supervise this delicate business. He undertook his duties conscientiously enough, but in all matters political he was confessedly out of his depth. The task obliged him to postpone completing a long contemplated ambition: an historical novel set in the sixteenth century. Instead he continued with his poetry, which at least could be written between interruptions. In 1857 *The Contemporary* published next to some verses of his the story *Youth* by his cousin Leo Tolstoy. The two were never very close, but they dined together, and Alexei wrote enthusiastically to Sophie about the younger Tolstoy's talent, prophesying a great literary future. Alexei shared Leo's gift for enthralling small children. When Sophie, for reasons of health, left in the spring of 1857 for a foreign tour, Alexei called often to see her young nephew and nieces. Four-year-old Andrei especially delighted him with his enthusiasm for tales of exploring among animals, and his eager questioning. "How many monkeys are there in the world? Ten million, or less?" Tolstoy told the boy that as a special treat two American frogs would appear to him in a dream that night, one grey and one yellow. Appear they did, but Andrei indignantly informed his "uncle" next morning that they had only been green and white, and accused him of deception! The Count consoled him by asserting that tonight he would dream of a whole palm-forest of his favourite monkeys, one playing a violin on each tree. . . .

This was the family life for which he longed, but which his equally deep love for his mother denied him. Then came news which shattered the dilemma, but left Alexei quite struck down. On 1 June 1857 the Countess Anna Alexeevna died suddenly. Sophie was not there to console him, and he was desolated. "I am not yet what I should be to say I love you, but I can't wait to tell you," he wrote; "all is over, my mother sleeps in her tomb, everyone has gone and I am alone with her!" For some time he was plunged in a despair, alleviated only by attendance at religious services and occasional glimpses of the possibility of communicating with his mother in that more beautiful world where she now dwelt.

Gradually the underlying optimism and good sense of his character reconciled him to the loss, without ever allowing him to forget. 1858 and the years which followed were a time of unparalleled excitement in Russian public life, and Tolstoy was willy-nilly caught up in the attendant intellectual upheavals which shook the placid Russian land. Reform was in the air; the liberation of serfs in Vilna, Grodno and Kovno ordered by the Emperor at the end of 1857 was the preface to a general emancipation which should free not only millions of serfs, but also the whole Russian people, for whom serfdom was, symbolically wholly and in reality partially, the expression of their ancient bondage.

Alexei Tolstoy was as patriotic, religious and imbued with love for the Russian past as any Slavophile, but he disliked their exaltation of the traditional Russian commune (*mir*) as Russia's unique way forward; one which left government to the autocracy, allowing Russians the freedom to develop socially and morally without the trammelling fetters of private property and legal proprieties. To Tolstoy this was a form of communism, linked though it might be to tradition and the soil, which was a denial of the individual, "the only fruitful principle of civilization". It smacked of "egalitarianism, that silly discovery of [17]93 which has never existed, in no matter what republic". The projected unity of the classes which was purported to result from the projected soil-bound community he saw as at worst a levelling down, at best a hollow sham. He himself maintained a close *rapport* with his own peasants, one stemming however from patrician benevolence, not radical conviction.

Imported Western doctrines of materialism, utilitarianism and the like he found equally repellent, with their implicit overtones of "*sans-culottisme*" and reductionism. As for the reactionaries, he perceived their policies as not essentially different from those of their arch-opponents the radicals. In essence, all three extremes wished in the name of all-embracing theories to reduce mankind to a featureless mob, a sort of shapeless sea-beast blundering through an unmarked murky landscape. As a poet he loved the variety of natural beauty and the richness of individual character. As a public man he detested extremes, vulgar, strident and divisive; and admired the temporizing philosophy of the seventeenth-century Lord Halifax, as portrayed by Macaulay.

> In neither camp a soldier, only a passing guest,
> For truth I am ready to draw my good sword,
> But to struggle with both was my strange fate
> Always, and none could draw me to obedience.
> We could never enter into a full alliance,
> Without commitment; under whatsoever flag I travel,
> Weary of the entrenched views of my friends,
> I will defend the honour of the enemy flag.

As Tolstoy's verse implies, Russia had no place for neutrals at this time. Tolstoy was widely criticized for his lack of commitment to political views, which those who were anxious to enrol him under their banner termed selfish irresponsibility. In fact he did have a view, but not one with a sufficiently clear-cut, all-embracing message to appeal at a time when arguments were being exchanged like javelins. His outlook was essentially aristocratic. He believed in hierarchy, variety and mobility; in honour, mutual respect, and the decencies of life. Whilst he saw the rival ideologies as wishing to crush the human condition into their particular Procrustean mould, he saw the world as an unbelievably rich creation to be studied, experienced and admired. As much at home in the courts and vineyards of Germany and Italy, he could not share the Slavophiles' contempt for "decadent" Europe; still less could he relish the Westernizing radicals' reduction of society to a Serbonian bog, its pulpy, uniform surface diverted only by the fetid exhalations of demagoguery.

He could only retreat from the indecent struggle, defending his timidity in verses characteristically looking back to other times of trouble.

> As a villager threatened
> By war's cruel strokes
> Bears his wealth to the thicket,
> Flees the fire and the sword,
>
> In the gloom and the silence
> Digging deep in the ground,
> He inscribes on the pine-bark
> Runes of protection.
>
> So in these harshest of days
> When devilry rules
> In rhymes secret and close,
> Poet, hide your true thought.

Tolstoy set out his predicament, thinly disguised, in the long poem *John Damascenus*, published in 1859. Freely adapted from an eighth-century hagiography, it tells how the saintly John decides to quit the court of the Caliph, in which he is a pampered favourite. He wishes to abjure the vanities of this life and devote himself to praise of God and worship of His creation. The Caliph offers him half his kingdom to stay, but relents when he sees John's determination. The saint enters a monastery at Jerusalem and, to exorcise vanity and worldliness, is compelled by a stern elder to substitute a vow of silence for the one gift he desires to celebrate: his gift for poetry and the creative exaltation of the Divine mystery. He agrees, then later succumbs to a monk's pitiful plea for him to compose a song to commemorate a dead brother. In the midst of the recitation of his magnificent prayer, the elder enters, sternly reproving him for his backsliding and pride. The poet is chastened at first, but ultimately vindicated as the Virgin appears in a dream, requiring John to use his God-given talent to celebrate His works and confound the sceptical. The poem ends with John's consequent glorification of the ideal world and its reflexion on earth below. Alexei Tolstoy's chafing at his court service, and his view of the poet's purpose are clear.

In June 1860 he travelled to England, where he attended séances conducted by the celebrated medium Daniel Dunglas Home, whom he had already known in Russia. With his Platonic convictions of the reality of an ideal world of which mundane existence was a pale shadow, he found in the manifestations of spiritualism a convincing parallel with his own conception of the poet's rôle as mantic source and interpreter. It was inevitable that he developed an irresistible penchant for table-tapping, flying furniture, detached voices and music, animal magnetism and all the other persuasive apparatus of illusion, extremely fashionable at the time.

Returning home via France and Germany, Alexei Tolstoy arrived just in time to witness the emancipation of the serfs. He at once travelled to his home at

Krasny Rog and, with Sophie at his side at the head of the steps, read out the proclamation to the assembled peasants. There was some confusion, eventually resolved, when the peasants decided this was a false manifesto, concocted to deprive them of significant rights. Undisturbed by this little contretemps, he lingered on in his favourite retreat, writing happily among his six thousand books and all the comforting disarray of a Russian rural household. This prolonged spell away from court convinced him that at last he must make his final break with official life. It had been hard, for they were links of friendship rather than authority which bound him, but "chains are always chains, even when made of flowers". A lengthy appeal to the Emperor resulted in his release from all official duties, announced on 28 September 1861. Alexei Tolstoy was liberated in the same year as the peasants.

Alexei Constantinovich Tolstoy

He celebrated his freedom by completing the work by which he is perhaps best known, the historical novel *Prince Serebryany*. He had begun it as early as the late 1840s, but repeatedly laid aside his pen. The subject-matter was the reign of Ivan the Terrible, a topic which has in some respects remained a litmus test of Russian political attitudes. The story is that of the young and gallant Prince Nikita Romanovich Serebryany, who returns to Russia in 1565 after five years' service abroad in Lithuania. This device enabled Tolstoy to present through an innocent contemporary's eyes the revolution which had taken place in Ivan's character and rule. Much of the plot is derivative or conventional in historical romance. Prince Serebryany loves a pallid beauty married in his absence to the dignified boyar Morozov; there are kidnappings, magical enchantments, fights, dreams, black-hearted villains and noble robbers. All this draws rather belatedly on Walter Scott and his not unsuccessful Russian imitator Zagoskin, author of *Yury Miloslavsky* (1829). The historical and naturalistic detail is however coloured in with a richness worthy of Scott at his best, as a result of extensive research and feeling for the Russian countryside.

The most convincing character in the novel is Tsar Ivan himself. Highly intelligent and, when he chooses, gracious and charming, he has nevertheless degenerated into a terrifying tyrant, in whose court no one is safe. By means of his *oprichniki*, a band of base-born hirelings ready to commit any atrocity without compunction, the Tsar arbitrarily deals out torture and execution on anyone arousing his resentment. Tolstoy admirably evokes the appalling atmosphere of fear permeating Ivan's feast at the *Alexandrova sloboda*, where Serebyany first encounters the Tsar in his new guise. Crime after crime ensues, Ivan recovering each time from frequent bouts of desperate remorse, culminating in a monstrous mass public execution based on an historical event of 1570. Rejecting all interpretations of historical necessity or changing moral outlook, Tolstoy conveys starkly to the reader his unmitigated horror that such things could ever have been in Russia. The principal defence offered by some writers, that Ivan was obliged to create and unleash the *oprichnina* in order to chasten the ambitions of the great boyars, is seen by Tolstoy as Ivan's worst crime. Alone at nightfall, Ivan "prayed for calm in Holy Russia, prayed to the Lord to enable him to overcome treachery and disobedience, and to crown with blessing his great endeavour to level the strong with the weak, so that there should not be in all Russia one man higher than another; that all should be on an equality, and that he should stand alone above all, like an oak in an open field!

"The Tsar prayed, prostrating himself on the ground. The stars gazed down on him through the window, fading in the obscurity, as much as to say: 'Oh, you Tsar Ivan Vasilievich! You began your work in an unchancy hour, you began it without consulting us: two stalks of grain do not grow equally, tall crags cannot be levelled to small hills, there will never be lack of boyars on the earth!'"

It was this moral, or an interpretation of it, which aroused ridicule in hostile quarters. It was suggested that Tolstoy viewed Ivan's actions purely from the point of view of his own class and ancestors. (In *Yury Miloslavsky* Ivan IV is upbraided for his brutal treatment of the Miloslavskys of his time.) Critics scoffed at what they took to be Tolstoy's belief that society in 1570 comprised the Tsar, the *oprichniki*, the boyars, and some picturesque bandits. That the remaining 90 per cent of the population did nothing to show disapproval of Ivan's treatment of the boyars was doubtless due to the fact that they were only too pleased to see belated punishment visited on their tyrannical masters. Such was the viewpoint of Dostoevsky's journal *Vremya*, and most other periodicals.

The near-unanimity of the intellectual journals' hostility suggests there is some truth in the criticism, and if the quotation given above were to be taken at face value there is certainly something ludicrous in the suggestion that the Muscovite nobility formed an integral part of the natural order. Aspects of the novel might appear to confirm this view. The toiling masses are (as in all historical literature of the period) almost entirely omitted from the picture. The boyar characters, such as Serebryany himself and his old patron Morozov, bear as much similarity to the sixteenth-century serving nobility as do Tennyson's Knights of the Table Round to those of Malory. Serebryany's chivalrous, independent nature might have been at home in the Spain of Philip II or the France of Henri II, but is quite out of place in Ivan IV's Muscovy. That he might pen a sonnet to his mistress's eyebrow, or play a lute beneath her balcony, seems quite conceivable. That he should order the flogging of serfs, belch and vomit at table, or squabble over points of *mestnich-estvo*, is not.

Nevertheless, the criticism appears unfair, despite its seeming plausibility. The hero's vapidity and lack of social historicity are doubtless due in part to the tradition established by Scott and adopted by Zagoskin (though not by Dumas), as well as an attested desire to create as hero a type of quixotic "holy fool". Artistically such a character afforded the opportunity of recording all the mon-strosities of Ivan's reign in stark contrast to civilized standards of behaviour, though clearly at a severe cost to historical realism and artistic effect. This objection can be raised in the case of virtually all Scott's novels, though few would deny Scott's literary genius.

The more serious objection, that Tolstoy's viewpoint was absurdly narrow in viewing events exclusively from the viewpoint of his own class, seems unjustified. He possessed a deep knowledge of history, and must have been well aware of the generally harsh character and rough behaviour of the sixteenth-century boyar class. What he appears to imply, though, is that Ivan's ferocious attack on the class which alone possessed social consciousness and the rudiments of civilized behaviour, and which alone possessed powers capable of checking the despotic power of the Tsar or developing institutions capable of forming a permanent check on that power, was ultimately an attack on liberty itself. If the boyars possessed no legal protection, then what chance had the people? A scene at the beginning of the book illustrates the concept. Serebryany and his servant enter a village near Moscow whose inhabitants are cheerfully preparing a wedding-feast. The villagers press the travellers to join them, but soon afterwards they are brutally attacked by a band of horsemen. Serebryany takes the assailants to be robbers, and assists in beating them off. In fact they are the Tsar's *oprichniki*, who prey on high and low alike, and the Prince narrowly escapes execution when the leader of the *oprichniki* presents a complaint to the Tsar. Tolstoy's clear impli-cation is that they were indeed robbers, and that Ivan's abuse of his autocratic powers meant that in effect there *was* no law, society being in a state where there was no government in any true sense – only arbitrary oppression by (the Tsar's) bandits. When Tolstoy makes the stars warn Ivan that there will always be boyars, he is simply implying that there will always be the strong and the weak, and the destruction of legally constituted privilege must inevitably substitute the rule of lawless leaders infinitely more cruel and ruthless.

In theory Alexander II possessed the same powers as Ivan IV, and if he so wished could exercise his autocratic power in a similarly despotic manner. What inhibited him was not law but the refined outlook of the nineteenth century, which in turn helped form the honourable character of the Tsar himself. In *Prince Serebryany* Tolstoy appears to be warning his readers against two converging extremes threatening Russia in his day: the Slavophiles' advocacy of the tra-ditional equality of the peasant commune, presided over by a benevolent autocrat, and the Westernizing radicals' belief in a socialist levelling down. In Tolstoy's dedication to the Empress he seems to hint of the danger of a recurrence of ancient tyranny, and reminds his public of how much they have to be thankful for in the existing state of affairs: "Your Majesty's name, which you have allowed me to place at the head of this romance of the time of Ivan the Terrible, is the best guarantee that an unbridgable gulf separates the dark circumstances of our past from the enlightened outlook of the present day."

Tolstoy would no doubt have wryly concurred with a hostile critic, who described Ivan IV as a "democratic sovereign and bold revolutionary". Within seventy years Russia would once again know such a ruler, with effects even more horrifying than those experienced under Ivan's bloody rule. Eisenstein's film, under Stalin's direction, presented precisely that picture of Ivan extolled by Tolstoy's critics. Tolstoy's portrait of the Tsar could equally be held to provide a grimly prophetic vision of the future. Chapter 8 in particular, with its vivid picture of Ivan the Terrible's feast, needs only the names changed to become a Kremlin gathering in 1940. The suspicious brooding tyrant, his terrified boyar guests, the baleful *oprichniki*, even the weak and drunken Tsarevich – all have their parallels.

Alexei Tolstoy continually experienced attacks by reviewers, who resented his refusal to enter into debate over the specific political and social issues of the day. If he deserted his cherished belief in art for art's sake, it was to paint a broader picture than was acceptable to his socially committed contemporaries. Fortunately the reading public did not share these intellectual misgivings. *Prince Serebryany* continued to appeal to a wide readership, appreciative of its lavish pageantry and dramatic incident. *Prince Serebryany's* brilliant evocation of an exotic past gave it an international appeal, and it was translated into Polish, English, French, German and Italian. It continues to enjoy broad popularity in Russia today.

Alexei Constantinovich Tolstoy

In his brief autobiography, Alexei Tolstoy cheerfully accepted that it was especially the middle classes that enjoyed the work, and appeared little put out by the critics' largely hostile reception. It was in any case a time of celebration. At long last Sophie's divorce from her forgotten husband had been finalized, and on 15 April 1863 she married her lover at the Greek church in Leipzig. His happiness should have been complete, but for a serious relapse in his health. Despite his exceptionally strong and vigorous constitution, he suffered at this time from increasing attacks of what appears to have been asthma. He was obliged to travel abroad extensively in search of healthier climates, missing Sophie greatly but enjoying as much as ever the picturesque beauties of old Europe. As always, he took his misfortunes with good humour, writing to Sophie of his encounter with three russet-coloured snails in a path near Schlangenbad: lucky snail, who breathes through a hole in his side!

His cheerfulness is extraordinary when the tribulations of his life during these years are fully appreciated. No previous biographer was aware that Tolstoy's wife Sophie was for several years, if not the whole of their married life, a very sick woman. I am indebted to a descendant of Count Alexei Bobrinsky for providing me with copies of her ancestor's correspondence with Alexei Tolstoy, his closest friend, revealing this hitherto unknown aspect.[3]

On 21 November 1863 Tolstoy wrote from Geneva to his friend: "Here is the reason why I haven't written to you until now from where we are staying. I have missed you this winter more than I can say. Your influence on my wife is always good and healthy. You would have helped me to draw her out of a mood so sad that she sometimes seems to be in despair."

Sophia Andreevna Tolstoy

Five years later, on 18 May 1868, he alluded again to what was clearly a psychological disorder.

"It is a great consolation to me to know that she has a real affection for you. Two days ago it was the anniversary of her brother George's death. She showed me much affection and told me that she recalled all I had been to her. In such moments I feel really happy. But she really does have a mental illness. The idea of spending a winter at Krasny Rog appears quite impossible to her."

Her suffering grew worse. On 30 September 1871 Tolstoy writes from Krasny Rog, "You know, I believe, that my poor wife has lost the ability to read and write. Her eyes, far from getting better, give me the impression of getting worse. This has been going on since February, and you who know how much reading was *her life* (she could be at it for 24 hours) will be able to imagine her misery since 'the night it came upon her', as she puts it. Something of relatively small importance has happened in connexion with it. Her horse fell under her and she dislocated her left hand, which for some time now she has had strapped up. She must have voluntarily sacrificed her two hands and arms to save her eyes. In Vienna we will consult A.H., who is said to be the best oculist in existence."

But so gallant was the public face Tolstoy put upon his domestic trouble, that no one but Bobrinsky had any inkling of what was passing behind the scenes.[3]

He was as popular as ever in the *beau monde* of European cities, where the King of Prussia eagerly awaited his high spirits, good humour and fascinating conversation, and the Empress Maria Alexandrovna, watering at Schwalbach, listened breathlessly to a reading of Tolstoy's new drama, *The Death of Ivan*, "turning red and then pale as she listened". Still more intoxicating praise for *Prince Serebryany* came from Goncharov (the author of *Oblomov*), whom he encountered at Carlsbad in 1864, and who declared the novel a masterpiece which would only receive its full meed after the author's death.

In those far-off days many Russians mingled in a civilized European society that was supranational, without any invidious levelling of individual national *traits*. It was here that Tolstoy encountered the aristocratic ideal he so valued, that odd but valuable late flowering of mediaeval chivalry imposed on Europe by the genius of Walter Scott. What Russia needed, he seems to have felt, was not the sordid squabbling over political and social issues that categorized his partially emancipated countrymen, but a true aristocratic order, confident in the example of its ancestry, and providing an example of culture, polish and benevolence which would penetrate all society. At the court of Weimar, surrounded by grand-ducal portraits and other picturesque evidences of long-standing aristocratic power and independence, Tolstoy felt his heart beat "more freely" in this European mediaeval environment, to which he felt certain he "had formerly belonged". His ancestors had lived in Russia for five centuries, but before that (as the story of Indris's arrival indicates) their predecessors had also been among the nobility of the Holy Roman Empire. Though his Russian patriotism was not dimmed during the Polish insurrection of 1863 (when his cousin Leo prepared to ride off to the wars), when the "hangman" Muraviev began his subsequent brutal suppression, his sympathies were with the Poles, who possess "elements of European culture and civilization which are superior to our own".

A practical instance of how far the rude Muscovite nature still flourished beneath the façade of nineteenth-century Russian *politesse* occurred at this time. The famous radical writer Chernyshevsky, whose materialistic views were anathema to Tolstoy, had been sentenced to fourteen years' forced labour. This offended Alexei's profound belief in liberty of thought, and he took advantage of his proximity to his friend the Emperor during a hunt in the province of Novgorod, to enter a plea for the exiled writer. Alexander II interrupted sternly with the words, "I beg you, Tolstoy, *never* speak to me of Chernyshevsky!"

Still, at beautiful Krasny Rog he felt as contented as ever, and when he departed on his perennial travels that charmed estate was always in his mind. From abroad he would write to his little nephew Andrei, planning trips on the river, fishing, shooting and expeditions by night. They would build a hut together in the forest, drink tea, play chess, and watch for the wolves. "Isn't it true, Andreika, that there's nothing better in the whole wide world than to live in the countryside, and especially in the forest?" In 1865–66 Alexei and Sophie spent some months in England, first in the Isle of Wight and then in London. There he came to know the writers Wilkie Collins and Dickens, one of whose public readings Leo Tolstoy had attended two years previously. What an enviable life it seems, when Europe was at the summit of its glory and greatness! After England came Italy once again.

"We returned by the road from Ostia and saw afar off mountains which are not precisely mountains, clouds, music, flowery scents. And we heard the larks singing and donkeys braying. And we came into the streets, which smelt horrible, and were let into a church by a picturesque monk . . . we strolled in the Coliseum . . . and we went in galleries where Sophie copied the pictures. . . . Then we went out at night into the Piazza del Popolo and heard water splashing from the marble lions and saw the moon come out from behind Mount Pincio. . . . It was so warm, and the scent of the orange-trees wafted out, . . . and the print-shops were lit up, and we bought a transparency of St. Peter's. . . . My heart felt so light when I saw you so tranquil! And then I loved the whole world the more. . . ."

In Rome the Tolstoys became close friends of the composer Franz Liszt and his mistress, Princess Helena Sayn-Wittgenstein, who gave the Russian writer sound advice: return home, seek Russian sources of inspiration, and do not dissipate your great talents. "Don't allow posterity to regret that you were rich and happy . . . pleasure passes, but a book remains." Sound advice, but it is hard to tell how applicable it was to the author's perennially boyish enthusiasm and undiluted love of the changing images of life. To Tolstoy Rome possessed attractions as great almost as those of Krasny Rog.

Meanwhile Tolstoy's play *The Death of Ivan* had finally emerged from the censor's grubby handling to a mixed reception from the critics, to which the dramatist was by now accustomed. The next step was to place the drama on the stage. With strong court backing, the producers were enabled to stage the production with a splendour that can rarely have been equalled. Aided by the distinguished historians Zabelin and Kostomarov, the artist Vyacheslav Schwartz, and the designers Chichkov and Bocharov, Tolstoy's piece proved a stunning *coup de théatre*. The astonishing splendour of costumes and scenery provided an overwhelming effect of the heavy, jewelled, embroidered costume of old Muscovy, and the darkened, flickering, incense-laden atmosphere of the Kremlin's cavernous chambers. The première was held on 12 January 1867 at the Maryinsky Theatre, in the presence of the Emperor, the court, the diplomatic corps, the *beau monde*, and the intellectual elite of St. Petersburg. Their enthusiasm was overwhelming, and night after night the stage was deluged with flowers and applause. Despite this the critics remained divided. As the former censor Nikitenko sardonically commented in his diary, "Oh, it's well done! But why doesn't he belong to some literary circle? And he's an aristocrat into the bargain, at least in name and court position. But that he's a man of great talent and that he has written a very fine piece, what is that to the grave-diggers and charlatans who instruct the young generation?" That there was some truth in this is borne out by the sarcasms of one critic who, with the surprising freedom of expression tolerated in Imperial Russia, made barbed reflexions on the "gentlemen and high dignitaries" attending the first night. Tolstoy, however, after some changes of cast and staging, was delighted. An access of depression brought on by his fiftieth birthday swiftly passed.

The sequel to *The Death of Ivan the Terrible, Tsar Feodor*, appeared to suffer by contrast with its predecessor. This was in part because of the ineffective character of the formidable Ivan's successor whom Tolstoy had in part intended as another sympathetic "holy fool". Even in this capacity the character was compared unfavourably with Shakespeare's similar Henry VI. But once again the chief attack was not directed on aesthetic grounds at all. It was held in the increasingly conservative government circles of the time (1868) that the whole piece, with its portrayal of the actions of a feeble-minded Tsar seemingly justifying a rebellious attitude on the part of his subjects, was of an anti-monarchical and radical nature. Tolstoy, a confirmed monarchist, was particularly angry with this blundering attack; but the censorship intervened to prevent its dramatic representation. The author protested vigorously: was Shakespeare a republican because he wrote *Macbeth* and *Richard III*? (He clearly ignored Queen Elizabeth's suppression of *Richard II* in 1601, whose implications she found dangerous.)

However great his disappointments, Alexei Tolstoy could always restore his spirits among the lawns, forests and lakes of Krasny Rog. Nothing deterred by the fate of *Tsar Feodor*, he began work on the last part of his dramatic trilogy, *Tsar Boris*. His researches led him to increased revulsion against the barbaric strain running through Russian history, which he put down to the effect of the Tartar conquests. The Mongols had destroyed the civilization and liberties of the old Kievan state, turning Russia from her true heritage as a member of the commonwealth of Christian European nations towards Oriental paths of despotism and serfdom. Developing this theme, he wrote a number of charming ballads exalting the robust individualism of pre-Tartar Kiev, stressing by authentic historical passages her close links, dynastic, religious and mercantile, with Germany, France, England and Scandinavia. In *The Knight Potok* he created a Rip van Winkle who fell asleep in the reign of Vladimir of Kiev, bold and free, to awake five hundred years later in the oppressive atmosphere of seventeenth-century Moscow, where the Tsar, like a Tartar khan, moves slowly through silenced streets with accompanying executioners. Despite the deep feelings underlying these themes, Tolstoy wrote with a deftly humorous touch, moving easily and effectively from the satirical and the Gothick to the heroic and prophetic. Those critics who accused the poet of dilettantism might have detected the consistent theme running through all Tolstoy's work, had it not been one which was objectionable to Slavophiles and radicals alike. That it offended the advocates of autocracy was understandable, and may argue a certain shrewdness on their part.

Tolstoy's love in his writings for rich, lavish descriptions of the idiosyncratic and picturesque was the expression of his deepest central convictions. It was the variegated tapestry of European life that made her unique in her cultured existence, where the contribution of Bavaria or Tuscany to the human heritage was as great as that of whole civilizations elsewhere. Tolstoy was predictably horrified at the implications of the Russification policy instituted by Government after the Polish uprising in 1863.

After a public denunciation of repressive measures in a speech at Odessa in 1869, the poet retreated into verse, but this time there was no disguising sarcasms directed against the principal advocates of uniformity. After listing various national groups whose very existence appeared to terrify the Government publicist Katkov and his supporters, Tolstoy goes on to suggest that:

> For fear of frightening Katkov,
> I'll whisper when I say
> That we've also lots of Polish –
> But that's just by the way.
>
> And quantities besides that –
> No limit to our store.
> What a pity that among them
> We've no negroes to the fore!
>
> Only then could Prince Cherkaskoy,
> Whom zeal makes so upright
> Smear upon their lawless faces
> Some dye – to make them white;
>
> With equal love for duty
> Up friend Samarin comes
> With a bucket and some chalk
> To whiten all their bums.

But it was rarely that Alexei Tolstoy struck out as sharply as this. His poetry expressed what he loved; what he hated was painful to him. "All the Napoleons of the world," as he put it (it was 1870), "are not worth Krasny Rog with its forests and bears." Among primeval oaks and swaying birch-trees he composed resounding ballads in the style of mediaeval *byliny* poetry of that happier time, when the spirit of chivalry reigned over all Christian Europe from the Guadalquivir to the Dnieper.

Times were becoming less happy for Tolstoy. In Germany the old unchanging world of the courts of Weimar and Nymphenburg was being replaced by the blood and iron of that of Berlin, while he felt his beloved Rome threatened by the destruction of the temporal rule of the Papacy. The old Europe, so painfully reconstructed after Napoleon's devastation, was being broken up. In Russia herself the two extremes that Tolstoy loathed – autocracy and radicalism – were gaining ground with every year.

> I fear progressive people,
> I am frightened of the dear nihilists

he wrote presciently, and similarly good-naturedly castigated the communists, who:

> are also quite literal-minded –
> not very fond of what's subtle;
> I suppose, not being very handsome,
> With beauty they wish to do battle.

The extremes were taking up position and becoming more threatening. His cousin

Dmitri Andreevich Tolstoy's measure to make the Classics the basis of Russian higher education gained the support of Alexei Constantinovich, the devotee of Europe's classical heritage:

And I think my namesake is justified
In giving Classics the place of pride;
For Latin and Greek plough the furrow straight
Where seeds of Science may germinate.

The measure was good, but Alexei expressed reservations over the application . . . "all rests on the extent." These increasing fusillades against nihilism and communism aroused accusations of his having gone over to the reactionary camp, even from his wife Sophie. But he stoutly maintained the times had changed, not he. "Do I write to please one party? I praise what I find good and condemn what I believe bad, without asking whether I am dealing with conservatives or progressives."

There can be little doubt, however, that he was conservative at heart. He believed in a society that was hierarchical, harmonious, diverse and organic in its growth. He detested uniformity and profoundly mistrusted blueprints for the perfect society. The two apparent extremes, autocracy and nihilism, he saw as children of the same parent. Life should be a rich and varied pageant, a colourful tapestry, its characters and setting as distinctive yet harmonious as a flower-garden. Tolstoy shared the preoccupation of his age in projecting this vision onto an idealized Middle Ages, with its proud, chivalrous barons, grandiloquent prelates, ascetic monks, stalwart yeomen, and cynical jesters. The glitter of armour, the flaring colours of baldric and cloak, the gorgeous devices of heraldry, the blare of trumpets and trampling of hooves . . . all this was contrasted in Tolstoy's eye with the frock-coat of the functionary and the radical's red shirt. To the end of his days he never ceased to revel in what was weird or exotic: vampires, spectres, the forest witch Baba-yaga. In this sense he had never deserted his childhood; whether that is a bad thing is for critics to decide.

It was a world whose sun was setting fast, and dark clouds continued to gather. In May 1872 Alexei's nephew Andrei, whom he loved as a son, died tragically at the age of nineteen. Tolstoy was abroad at the time, suffering increasingly from agonizing headaches. On his return home to Krasny Rog in 1873 neuralgic pains grew sensibly worse, attacking his eyes, teeth, shoulders and back. Despite appalling pain, he set down to write what is recognized as his masterpiece of satirical verse, *The Dream of Popov*. Popov is one of those soulless, mechanical bureaucrats, the butt of Russian writers from Gogol to Chekhov. He sets off to congratulate a Minister on his namesday, wearing his full uniform. But in the antechamber he realizes to his horror he has forgotten to put on his trousers. It is too late; he almost sinks through the floor in terror, until he recalls the Minister's strong liberal views. Such a man might even see in the trouserless condition a certain spirit of freedom, of emancipation! The Minister is indeed a strong liberal, and his speeches are interlarded with references to "freedom", "the people", "emancipation", and so forth. But when he sees Popov his fury knows no bounds. What are you trying to do? Have you read too many of Scott's novels, and become a Highlander? Or do you think you are a Roman patriot? Or are you trying to symbolise the Russian budget?

Beside himself, the Minister decides Popov's move must be part of a scheme to overthrow the Government, and delivers him up to the dreaded Third Section (political police). There an officer interrogates him, first with gentle enquiries, finally with terrifying threats. Popov gives way, and signs a long confession implicating numerous other "conspirators". At this point Popov wakes, sees his trousers hanging on a chair, and realizes it was all a dream. Tolstoy concludes by putting forward strong arguments against the veracity of the whole story. It really is absurd: how could there exist in Russia such a man as Popov, or such an overbearing official as his Minister? And could there really exist such an institution as that to which Popov was sent? It is all quite impossible: people simply do not forget to put on their trousers. Tolstoy dismisses these questions with the reminder that he is not Popov, and cannot be held responsible for his dream.

It is hard to believe when one reads this poem, with its lightness of humour and elegance of language, that Alexei Tolstoy was a very sick man. In a letter accompanying the manuscript (12 October 1873) he wrote: "These last two months . . . have been real torture, to the extent that not even for an hour or a quarter of an hour have I been free of the most fearful neuralgia in my head. . . ." He travelled abroad once again in vain hope of appeasing the malady, receiving brief consolation when on 13 December 1873, in company with his cousin Leo Tolstoy, he was elected a member of the St. Petersburg Academy. The asthma and neuralgia grew ever more crushingly painful, but Alexei's boyish cheerfulness and high spirits never left him. Visiting his Empress at San Remo in January 1875, he read her *The Dream of Popov*, which reduced her to tears of laughter. He withheld, however, his latest *jeu d'esprit*, *The Rebellion in the Vatican*, which treats in not very serious style of an uprising of the Pope's choir of *castrati*, who demand that their master undergo the same operation imposed on them.

He returned to Krasny Rog in the late summer for the last time. He was very enfeebled, and was obliged to take frequent injections of morphine to relieve the constant pain. Presentiments of death appeared, without troubling his serenity. Seeing a fine grouse fly over the garden, he exclaimed "That is my bird, it has come for me!" Another, an apparition in white, appeared before him. On 29 September 1875 he died peacefully in his sleep, and was laid to rest in a vault at the ancient wooden church of Krasny Rog, near the grave of his nephew Andrei. Sophie was reunited with them seventeen years later. It was a peaceful spot near the river Rog, where blackbirds sang in a meadow growing right up to the tombs, within earshot of children playing in the village. During the Revolution of 1905 the "dear nihilists" attempted to desecrate the sepulture; what their successors did after 1917 is not known. It is to be hoped that his spirit still, as he firmly believed it would, haunts the warm meadow in sunlit hours and roams the tossing forest at the magic midnight hour.

> The crescented moon rises from over dark woods,
> Where pale mists in ravines start to roam,
> The hag Baba-yaga rides by on her mortar,
> In the Dnieper the sprites toss the foam;
> Across the Dnieper a forest goblin is heard,
> By the edge of the stables a brownie has stirred,
> And a witch waves a wild scarf from a chimney-top –
> But Potok goes dancing on . . .[4]

9
The Pursuit of Innocence

One of the first places of pilgrimage for any visit to Russia is the fine country home and estate of Count Leo Tolstoy at Yasnaya Polyana ("Bright Glade") in the province of Tula, south of Moscow. Despite successive occupations by the Bolsheviks and the Germans (who converted the house into a sanatorium during the occupation in 1942),[1] the house is carefully maintained as closely as possible to the condition it was in during the great author's lifetime. To all Russians it is a place of great sanctity because of its lifelong association with one of the greatest creative spirits of all mankind. Few other places bear such evocative memories: here Tolstoy's passionate struggles with himself and the world beat themselves out in the long, white two-storeyed building set among lush rolling fields, lakes and birch-forests. Here Tolstoy experienced that innocent, happy childhood whose memory was to dominate his life. Here he returned from the wars, a dashing, ambitious soldier and would-be author. Here he wrote *War and Peace* and *Anna Karenina*, novels through which he grasped hold of the whole world; and here at the age of fifty he underwent the crisis of conscience that was to send him out on his crusade against the darkness of man's condition.

Not a little of the attraction of Yasnaya Polyana, at least for its Russian visitors, lies in the solitary physical evocation in the Soviet state of the old manorial way of life, preserved through the chance of Tolstoy's being not only a great writer but also the inheritor of an aristocratic demesne. Every room, so far as is possible, is maintained with the writer's possessions dotted around, as in life, and the estate too is farmed and tended, rather more efficiently than it was by its wayward and enthusiastic owner. Implicit admiration and envy for the old order is encountered frequently in the Soviet Union, and nowhere more so than at Yasnaya Polyana.

Count Ilya Andreevich Tolstoy

Members of my family are frequently asked whether we have visited "our family estate", to which it is necessary to explain that, not only do we belong to a different branch of the family, but that Yasnaya Polyana was not a Tolstoy inheritance. Other houses, such as my greatgrandfather's home at Murzikha near Kazan, had been in the family for two centuries or more, but Yasnaya Polyana

Previous page: Leo Tolstoy, by I. N. Kramskoy, 1873

was acquired by Leo's father through marriage. Leo's grandfather, Count Ilya Andreevich Tolstoy, was third in descent from Peter Andreevich, Peter the Great's celebrated Ambassador to Constantinople. Count Ilya was Governor of Kazan, but when he died in 1820 his financial affairs were so embarrassed that two years later his son Nikolai was obliged to marry the heiress of Prince Nikolai Volkonsky, hereditary proprietor of Yasnaya Polyana. In this way the estate passed into the hands of the Tolstoys.

Prince Nikolai Volkonsky

Count Nikolai Tolstoy had served, like so many others of his name, in the Napoleonic wars. He was captured by the French and liberated in 1814 when the Allies entered Paris. After his marriage to Princess Maria Volkonsky he settled down to administer his newly-acquired estate. He was not a liberal, but as Alexander I's increasingly reactionary policies were continued and accentuated by the martinet Tsar Nicholas I, he deliberately avoided all contact with government service.

The Count's wife Maria was plain, but known to all for her gentleness and Christian truth and honesty. Married at the then late age of thirty-two, she died

243

eight years later, having supplied her husband with four sons and a daughter. The fourth son, following the Russian system whereby titles are inherited by all the children, was Count Lev Nikolaevich Tolstoy, better known outside Russia as Leo Tolstoy.*

Nikolai Ilich Tolstoy

Leo was born on 28 August 1828 (Old Style). His mother died on 7 March 1830. This loss had a profound effect on his whole life. "I do not remember my mother," he wrote later. "I was a year and a half old when she died. By some strange chance no portrait of her has been preserved, so that as a real physical being I cannot picture her to myself. I am in a way glad of this, for in my conception of her there is only her spiritual figure, and all that I know about her is beautiful; and I think this has come about not merely because all who spoke to me of my mother tried to say only what was good, but because there actually was much good in her."

From a very early age little Leo evinced an astonishingly heightened consciousness, which particularly displayed itself in an intense warmth of feeling for that mother he had never known. He noted that she "appeared to me a creature so elevated, pure and spiritual, that often in the middle period of my life, during my struggles with overwhelming temptations, I prayed to her soul begging her to aid me; and such prayer helped me much." Time and again in later life he was to feel a deep upsurge of longing for maternal love and its reciprocation. It remained a powerful mainspring of his motivation, and near the close of his life poured forth as heartfelt as ever.

* In view of this, and the fact that he always used this form when signing letters in English, Leo is the name I propose to use here.

"All day a feeling of gloomy dread. Toward evening this state of wretchedness was transformed into a feeling of deep tenderness, into a desire to be caressed, comforted. Like a child, I long to press myself against some loving, sympathizing being, to shed tears of love and affection, and to feel myself being consoled. But where is the being with whom I can find such a refuge? In my mind I go through all those I love - not one is what I need. To whom am I to turn my affection then? Should I become a child again and hide my head against my mother as I picture her? Yes, you, mama, you whose name I never spoke, because I was still too young to talk. . . . Yes, you, the highest ideal of pure love I have ever succeeded in imagining, of human, warm, maternal love. That is what my weary soul cries out for. You, mama, you: comfort me, console me!"

There was no feeling of bitterness, such as frequently occurs in similar cases, and indeed Leo's was an exceptionally warm and loving nature. His earliest childhood memories were fonder and more acutely recalled than most. His first recollection was that of the frightening constriction of the swathing-bands with which Russian children were bound in their cots. He was alarmed and cried out. Grown-ups rushed to comfort him, but "I feel the injustice and cruelty – not of people, for they pity me, but – of fate, and I pity myself . . . this was the first and strongest impression of my life. And what remains on my memory is not my cries nor my suffering, but the complexity and contradictoriness of the impressions. I desire freedom, it would harm no one, but I who need strength am weak, while they are strong."

Until the age of five or six Leo spent virtually his whole existence in the familiar confines of the children's quarters upstairs. "All that I remember happened in bed, or in our rooms. Neither grass, nor leaves, nor sky, nor sun existed for me. It cannot be said that no one ever gave me flowers and leaves to play with, that I never saw any grass, that they never shaded me from the sun; but up to the time when I was five or six years old, I have no recollection of what we call nature. Probably, to see it, one has to be separate from it, and I was nature. . . . This is all I remember up to the age of five. Neither my nurses, aunts, brothers, sister, nor my father, nor the rooms, nor my toys, do I remember."

At about the age of five he left the infants' quarters and moved downstairs to join his elder brothers. It was a step which, innocuous as it appeared to all around, had a profound effect on the little boy.

"When I was moved downstairs to Feodor Ivanovich [the German tutor] and the boys, I experienced for the first time and therefore more strongly than ever since, the feeling which is called the sense of duty, the consciousness of the cross every man is called upon to bear. It was hard to leave what I was accustomed to from the beginning of things, and I was sad, poetically sad, not so much at parting from people – sister, nurse, and aunt – as at parting with my crib, the curtain and the pillow; and I feared the new life into which I was entering. I tried to see the jolly side of this new life awaiting me; I tried to believe the caressing words with which Feodor Ivanovich lured me to him. I tried not to see the contempt with which the boys received me, the youngest boy. I tried to think it was a shame for a big boy to live with girls, and that there was nothing good in the life upstairs with nurse; but my heart was terribly sad, I knew I was irreparably losing my innocence and happiness; and only a feeling of personal dignity and the consciousness of doing my duty upheld me . . . I experienced quiet grief at the irreparableness of my loss; I was unable to believe that it would really happen . . . it was sad, terribly sad, but had to be; and for the first time I felt that life is not a game but a serious matter."

Oddly enough, this feeling was to be shared by Leo's own son and namesake. When in 1872 he was faced with the same critical moment, he hesitated at the top of the stairs. "I don't really want to go down," he was heard to say. "I shall start being bad down there."

This consciousness of the early loss of innocence is a regular concomitant of growing up, but what was different in Tolstoy's case was the extremity of the feeling.

Already he possessed a disconcerting awareness of himself as an individual and of his emotions as identifiable properties. In his novel *Childhood* (1852), which is factually largely autobiographical and in sentiment almost entirely so, he describes a small boy's reaction to the death of his mother. "Before and after the funeral I wept continually and was miserable, but I am ashamed to recall my misery because it was always tinged with a certain feeling of egoism; now a desire to show that I was more grief-stricken than anyone else, now concern about the impression I was making on others, now an idle curiosity which made me observe Mimi's bonnet or the faces of those around me. I despised myself for not experiencing sorrow to the exclusion of all else, and I tried to conceal all other feelings; because of this my grief was insincere and unnatural. Moreover, I experienced a certain pleasure in knowing that I was unhappy and I tried to stimulate my sense of unhappiness, and this egoistic feeling did more than anything else to stifle my real grief."

Professor Christian has aptly compared this passage with a similar one in the early part of *David Copperfield*.[2]

Tolstoy's account cannot be referring directly to the death of his mother, which he could not remember, but undoubtedly reflects a bitter awareness of the precocity with which his powers of self-analysis had developed. The loss of innocence is a curse with which all mankind has been burdened since Adam tasted the forbidden fruit in Eden, whether in the collective transition from primitive to more advanced societies, or in each individual's passage from infancy to adolescent self-awareness. The beginning of Tolstoy's problem was that he valued the innocence more deeply than most.

"Happy, happy, irrecoverable time of childhood!" Tolstoy exclaims at the beginning of Chapter XV of *Childhood*, a book specifically written to make it recoverable. "How can one not love and cherish its memory? Its memory refreshes, uplifts my spirit and supplies me with the source of best delights." Leo's brothers Nikolai, Dmitri and Sergei shared his feeling. Together they organized their celebrated private fraternity of Ant-Brothers, "which consisted in sitting under chairs, sheltering ourselves with boxes, screening ourselves with handkerchiefs, and cuddling against one another while thus crouching in the dark." This was their shared secret, but there was another that Nikolai (five years older than Leo) did not reveal. The chief secret of the Ant-Brotherhood was "the way for all men to cease suffering any misfortune, to leave off quarrelling and being angry, and become continuously happy; this secret he said he had written on a green stick, buried by the road at the edge of a certain ravine, at which spot," Tolstoy continued in his recollections, "(since my body must be buried somewhere) I have asked to be buried in memory of Nikolenka."

Tolstoy was perfectly aware of the significance of the symbolism, as he was of everything else, and wrote more than sixty years after the event that "The ideal of ant-brothers lovingly clinging to one another, though not under two arm-chairs curtained by handkerchiefs, but of all mankind under the wide dome of heaven, has remained the same for me. As I then believed that there existed a little green stick whereon was written the message which could destroy all evil in men and give them universal welfare, so I now believe that such truth exists and will be revealed to men, and will give them all its promises."

To most people it is regrettable but axiomatic that the lost age of innocence cannot be recovered, but this Tolstoy would never allow. Acceptance of such a pessimistic view opened up a void too horrible to contemplate. After all, the intensity of childhood emotions is such that it is the subsequent rationalizing, sceptical existence which appears unreal in contrast.

Tolstoy's mother's place in the household was taken by his "aunt" (actually a distant cousin) Tatiana, who was more than a mother to the children and whom he adored. In 1852, when on military service in the Caucasus, he wrote to her half-humorously, telling of a fond dream he had.

"It's a beautiful dream but it's still not all that I allow myself to dream of. I am married – my wife is a sweet, good, affectionate person; she loves you in the same way as I do. We have children who call you 'grandmama'; you live in the big house, upstairs – the same room that grandmama used to live in; the whole house is as it was in papa's time, and we begin the same life again. . . . If they made me Emperor of Russia, if they gave me Peru, in a word if a fairy came with her wand to ask me what I desired; my hand on my heart, I would reply that my only desire is for this to become a reality."

But into the childhood itself stern reality was all too swift to intrude itself. When Leo was eight his father died suddenly, and a few months after that his grandmother also passed away. His father's death at the time seemed unreal; he died in Tula, and Leo did not attend the funeral. But he saw his grandmother in her coffin, a sight which filled him with dread. At the same time another part of him was flattered when he overheard an old woman refer to him and the other children as "complete orphans; their father only lately dead, and now the grandmother gone too". The frightening implications of death came to play an increasingly large part in his thoughts; as did unsettling discoveries that there existed other families to whom his existence meant nothing, and that he was actually rather a plain little boy. All these emotions and experiences, which most people come gradually to terms with throughout their lives, crowded in on him at an age when he seemed barely to have stepped from a chrysalis of love, warmth and goodness. The contrast was too great to be borne, and he felt certain there must be a way of reascending to those cosy rooms he once knew upstairs.

Yasnaya Polyana was calculated to fortify the feeling that the pristine age was reattainable. The house and park had been greatly expanded and embellished by Prince Nikolai Volkonsky in Catherine the Great's reign, but otherwise life there in 1840 was scarcely different from what it had been in 1740. The estate was peopled, master and man, with men and women whose parents and grandparents had lived there time out of mind. The usual mediaeval procession of monks, nuns, beggars and holy fools arrived and departed; the Count rode out to hunt wolves under the broad, unchanging sky; people were born, married and died in the arms of a Church that eschewed delusive novelties. In Leo Tolstoy's lifetime the greatest change was the Emancipation of the Serfs in 1861, but that was a change wholly

Yasnaya Polyana

praiseworthy, and one which left human relationships little altered. The type-writer, the telegraph and the bicycle arrived, but life in its essentials continued its archaic course.

Behind Leo Tolstoy's conscious despair lay a conviction that the Golden Age could be restored if one strove hard enough for it. In the contemporary England of Thomas Hardy, by contrast, the countryside changed beyond recognition in a lifetime. Railways and steam-ploughs, the threshing-machine and the chaff-cutter, cheap newspapers and agricultural unions, had virtually broken the back of traditional, slow, superstitious, rural England. Hardy, whose writings also reveal obsessive hankering for youthful intensity of emotion, could in contrast to Tolstoy only descend deeper and deeper into hopeless pessimism.

Life at Yasnaya Polyana, a nest of gentlefolk embowered among forests, lakes and meadows, with its continual renewal, spring following winter, births succeeding deaths, provided tangible experience of man's potentiality for static content and the intrinsic simplicity of the human experience. It was his microcosm of the world, one which affected him with conscious intensity. "Without my Yasnaya Polyana," he wrote, "I can with difficulty imagine Russia and my relationship to her. Without Yasnaya Polyana I would perhaps understand the general principles needed for my fatherland more clearly, but I could not love her with such fond partiality." It was in fact a little world, with its own government and economy, and it was hard to believe that it was not a model for that greater world beyond.

Without all this, Tolstoy's desperate desire to discover a pattern and purpose in the human condition might well have expressed itself in the form of an all-embracing ideology, such as his older contemporary Karl Marx was gradually formulating at the same time in a significantly different *milieu*. It became, indeed, Tolstoy's all-consuming aim to discover that "little green stick", with its key to social harmony. At the age of twenty-six he was to record in his diary an ambition to found "a new religion corresponding to the present state of mankind . . . a

Leo Tolstoy, aged 21

practical religion, not promising future bliss, but giving bliss on earth". Fortunately a quarter of a century passed before he began his attempt to put this remarkable scheme into practice, during which interval his restless energy had poured the desire for world-transformation into other channels.

The early loss of his parents – particularly his mother – appears to have inflicted from a very early age an intense sensation of cosmic vulnerability. It is not surprising that he later singled out the Old Testament story of Joseph for the "enormous" impression it made on him at a tender age. The theme of the boy abandoned by his family who, after exciting adventures, reappears as a glittering figure empowered to bestow enormous benefits upon them and everyone else, is

249

one supremely calculated to appeal to a boy in his position. That it suggests in addition a high degree of egoism need not surprise us. The other stories which made a similarly "enormous" impression upon him were the old Russian *byliny*; traditional folk-tales with their recurring themes of neglected younger sons achieving unexpectedly brilliant successes, valiant heroes riding out alone to do battle with evil beings, etc.

Along with these tales of unheard-of achievement gained in the teeth of daunting odds, the young Tolstoy experienced a feeling that happiness was ephemeral and could only be won through suffering. He would punish himself painfully in the hope of fulfilment. At the same time the prospect of corporal punishment, inflicted on himself or others, filled him with horror. Once his French tutor, St. Thomas, "first locked me into a room, and secondly threatened to flog me. I thereupon experienced a dreadful feeling of anger, indignation and disgust, not only towards St. Thomas himself, but towards the violence with which I was threatened." When he learned that an estate serf was to be flogged, he recorded that "I cannot describe the dreadful feeling which these words . . . produced on me." This aversion remained as strong throughout his life. In 1857 he witnessed an execution in Paris, an experience which filled him with such disgust that it was one of the prime causes of his rejection of the legitimacy of state power: "no theory of the reasonableness of our present progress can justify this deed . . . and therefore the arbiter of what is good and evil is not what people say and do . . . but is my heart and I."

This arose from Tolstoy's absolute capacity to identify himself with other people, so that what happened to them he at once felt happening to himself. In his novels suffering is described from this acutely personal and vivid point of view, the whole experience being hateful and injurious to the authors and victims of suffering alike. "Downstairs" death could and did snatch away inexplicably those on whom his previously secure childhood world had depended. Indeed, scarcely a single bastion of the seemingly impregnable stronghold of the nursery seemed defensible. He discovered himself to be unpleasantly ugly ("all I then had and all I would ever possess in the future, I would have given for a handsome face"), and even learned at the age of eleven from another boy that God Himself was "a mere invention. . . . We all . . . accepted the news as something very interesting and fully possible."

He became in consequence of these disturbing revelations a confirmed solipsist. "But no philosophic current swayed me so much as scepticism, which at one time brought me to the verge of insanity. I imagined that except myself no one and nothing existed in the world, that objects are not objects but apparitions, appearing only when I pay attention to them and disappearing as soon as I cease to think of them. In a word, I coincided with Schelling in the conviction that what exists is not objects, but only my relation to them. There were moments in which under the influence of this fixed idea, I reached such a stage of absurdity that I glanced quickly round hoping to catch Nothingness by surprise, there where I was not.

"The philosophical discoveries I made greatly flattered my vanity: I often imagined myself a great man, discovering new truths for the benefit of humanity, and I looked on other mortals with a proud consciousness of my own dignity; yet, strange to say, when I came in contact with these mortals I grew timid before each of them." As he was to note shrewdly many years later, "madness is egoism carried to its ultimate conclusion."

Many of these fears, as Tolstoy discovered during his voracious adolescent reading, had been shared by Rousseau, and indeed formed part of the emotional currency of early nineteenth-century romanticism.[3] "I have read the whole of Rousseau," Tolstoy once remarked, "all his twenty volumes, including his *Dictionary of Music*. I was more than enthusiastic about him, I worshipped him. At the age of fifteen I wore a medallion portrait of him next to my body instead of the Orthodox cross. Many of his pages are so akin to me that it seems to me that I must have written them myself."

Rousseau helped Tolstoy to crystallize and sharpen his own perceptions on a broad scale from an early age. Essentially both men were in revolt against the artificial constrictions of society, which had perverted and corrupted an older, harmonious order. *Then* men had simple, uncomplicated needs, and were able to develop their characters and tastes to the full without impinging detrimentally on those of their neighbours. *Now* the elaborate machinery of civilized society so effectively concealed the springs of human feeling, that men could be persuaded to commit and suffer the most abominable acts: unthinkable in naked isolation, legitimate when cloaked by the authority of the state. So men robbed, murdered and tortured each other without compunction, now that those crimes were disguised as taxation, judicial execution and war. What was Napoleon's invasion of Russia, but the legitimization of thousands of individual acts of murder, arson and pillage? Unacceptable if committed singly, "heroic" when inflicted *en masse*.

Scene from War and Peace (L. Pasternak, 1893)

Clear evidence, accessible to every man, lay in the experience of childhood. Children are not flawless; they lie, quarrel and steal. But these are trifling aberrations, lacking system or malice. In significant respects they are actually superior to adults, superior in imagination, spontaneity and depth of emotion, and in absence of hypocrisy, ambition and artifice. Tolstoy and Rousseau recognized, as they grew up, that they too were acquiring the false traits they despised. But even in the adult world there were people whom the "benefits" of civilization had barely touched, and who still lived in a state of relative innocence. The peasants of Yasnaya Polyana in large part retained the ethos of childhood. Close to nature, unsophisticated in their needs and desires, religious in a nobly untrammelled sense, consuming no more than they produced, they provided tangible evidence that the "natural" state of man formed indeed the daily existence of the overwhelming majority of Russia's eighty million inhabitants.

Sergei, Nikolai, Dmitri and Leo Tolstoy, 1854

In 1852 and 1853 Tolstoy served in the army of Prince Bariatinsky, which was engaged in subduing the mountain tribes of the Caucasus. He was stationed in the Cossack village of Starogladovsk, where he saw much both of the Cossacks and the Circassian tribesmen whom they were fighting. He became predictably enamoured of the carefree, rollicking existence of the Cossacks, set in some of the most spectacular scenery imaginable. He loved the frankness of their relations with each other, seemingly uncomplicated by any unnecessarily restrictive moral code. To ride, to hunt, to fight, to feast in comradely equality, was all they knew. The women in particular, as candid as they were beautiful, enjoyed very free relationships with the men, unclouded by false moral inhibitions. He fell deeply in love with one, Mariana, who rejected him because he lacked in some degree the essential Cossack capacity to "steal cattle, get drunk on Tchikir wine, sing songs, kill people, and when tipsy climb in at her window for a night, without thinking who he was or why he existed". The last qualification probably applied to Leo Tolstoy less than any man alive.

He had just completed and published his wonderfully evocative and perceptive autobiographical tale *Childhood*, and now he gathered materials in order to bring his mountain adventures to literary life. In March 1853 the magazine *Sovremennik* published his tale *The Raid*, but his major work on the subject was not completed until ten years later, when the much more important novel *The Cossacks* appeared. *The Cossacks* reveals the central problem of Tolstoy's life at this time. How could he reconcile his own all too typically aristocratic and European tastes with the admirably spontaneous and unsophisticated Cossacks, who led a "natural" existence beneath the pure snowy grandeur of the mountains?

Tolstoy's hero Olenin is an enthusiastic, contradictory young nobleman, who sets off for the Caucasus in an ecstasy of romantic anticipation. "All his dreams of the future were woven with visions of such heroes as Amalatbek, of Circassian maids, mountain gorges, tremendous torrents, and perils." He dreamed in particular of finding a lovely Circassian maid, artless and free, "with long braids of hair and deep, submissive eyes", whom he would educate in her mountain hut during the long winter evenings. Back in St. Petersburg his new wife would astonish society with her natural dignity. Characteristically, however, the dream is interrupted by Olenin himself, who mutters cheerfully, "Oh, what rubbish!" But the Caucasus proves to be not very far from his idealized vision. The mountains are more sublime than imagination could picture, the Cossacks reckless and uninhibited as in Gogol's *Taras Bulba*, and there is even a black-eyed beauty, Mariana, with whom Olenin falls in love.

But though Olenin throws himself wholeheartedly into the life of the Cossacks and is in turn liked by them, he finds ultimately that he cannot win Mariana from a handsome young Cossack rival, nor can he be a true Cossack himself. Try as he may he cannot escape from self-doubt and the awareness that his capacity to see the Cossacks from the outside prohibits his blending into their existence. It is the curse of the thinking man, a curse that he tries in vain to shake off. A fellow officer posted to the same village integrates himself quite happily, takes a Cossack mistress and moves with perfect ease among the villagers. He, however, is a genial, uncomplex soul, who simply seeks entertainment before moving on. Olenin is baffled by the Cossacks' easy morality, knows his motives are not theirs, and cannot accept death as a passing fact of life.

"God made everything for man's enjoyment," explains his old Cossack mentor, "Uncle" Eroshka, "There's no sin in anything." And he quotes laughingly a veteran's saying, "You will die . . . and the grass will grow over you, and that's all there is of you." The dashing Lukashka shoots a Chechen through the head, looking upon the muscular corpse with some admiration but no compunction. To Olenin, death means the horribly bloody, mangled mess of the Chechen's comrades shot down on the hillside. "Horror seized his eyes." He cannot marry Mariana, and is bidden an openhearted farewell by Uncle Eroshka.

"'Goodbye, father, goodbye! I shan't forget you,' shouted Eroshka. Olenin looked round. Uncle Eroshka was talking with Mariana, evidently about his own affairs, and neither the old man nor the girl gave him a parting glance."

It was Tolstoy's farewell to the noble savage. The Caucasian episode was in many respects an idyll, but an idyll in which a thinking man could only participate as an outsider. For if there was one propensity in Tolstoy as strong as his quest for innocence it was his obsessive love of truth. A stark sense of reality, of the pointlessness of deception which cannot deceive, and an acute love of the rich variety of creation made it impossible for him to side-step entirely into a world of illusion.

Immediately after his Caucasian adventure Tolstoy found himself plunged into the experience of real war. Russia, in the course of her ancient enmity with Turkey, had invaded the Turkish provinces of Moldavia and Wallachia (later Roumania). The Russian army crossed the Danube and laid siege to the great Turkish fortress of Silistria. In May 1854 Tolstoy joined Prince Gorchakov's besieging army and saw the fighting. The spectacle, which he witnessed from the heights of the Russian position, "was truly beautiful, especially at night".

"The view from that spot was not only magnificent, but of the greatest interest to us all. Not to mention the Danube, its islands and its banks, some occupied by us, others by the Turks, you could see the town, the fortress and the little forts of Silistria as though on the palm of your hand. You could hear the cannon-fire and rifle shots which continued day and night, and with a field-glass you could make out the Turkish soldiers. It's true it's a funny sort of pleasure to see people killing each other, and yet every morning and evening I would get up and spend hours at a time watching, and I wasn't the only one."

This was war as it appeared in popular lithographs: a gigantic brown landscape, spectacular cloud formations, zigzag trenches, puffs of smoke from the fortress, tiny coloured lines of advancing infantry, and only a picturesquely reclining soldier in the foreground to provide an acceptable image of suffering. Tolstoy greatly admired the commander, Prince Gorchakov, eccentric in appearance but absolutely fearless and adored by his men. "He's a great man, i.e. a capable and *honourable* man, as I understand the word. . . ." Unfortunately, just as the Prince was about to give the order for the assault that must certainly have brought about the Turks' downfall, orders inexplicably arrived from above to abandon the siege and recross the Danube. Though Gorchakov accepted the disappointment with equanimity, "I can say without fear of error that this news was received by all – soldiers, officers and generals – as a real misfortune. . . ."

What Gorchakov knew, and Leo Tolstoy and his comrades did not, was that there were compelling strategic reasons for the retreat. Alarmed by the incursion of Russian military might into the Balkans, Austria had concluded an alliance with Turkey and assembled an army on the frontier that outflanked Gorchakov's force. Field-Marshal Paskevich, the overall Russian commander, saw no alternative to a withdrawal of Russian forces. It will be seen how this débâcle probably influenced Tolstoy's philosophy of history.

Despite this Russian reverse of policy, Britain and France, Turkey's allies in the war, despatched an expeditionary force to the Crimea, and it was at Sevastopol that Tolstoy saw fighting as a combatant himself. The effect was overwhelming. He waxed ecstatic over the heroism of the Russian defenders, officers and men, and described in his letters and published writings scenes of stoical bravery and actions of daring gallantry. Though enthusiastically patriotic, he admired also the manly appearance and fighting qualities of the British, and his pen dwelt affectionately on the valour and cheerfulness of men suffering terrifying experiences.

But what swiftly struck him much more forcibly was the stark, pointless savagery of what was happening. Here, after all, were thousands of ordinary people, whose plain humanity was seen in all its individuality by Tolstoy's clear eye, assembled for the sole purpose of inflicting terrible pain and death on each other. None of them had any personal involvement in the quarrel, or had any reason to dislike each other; in fact the enemy was generally regarded with ungrudging respect. Yet "hundreds of newly bloodstained bodies of people who, two hours before, had been full of various lofty or trivial hopes and desires lay with stiff limbs in the dewy vale of flowers which separated the bastion from the trenches and on the smooth floor of the mortuary chapel in Sevastopol; hundreds of people with curses and prayers on their parched lips crawled, writhed and groaned, some between the corpses in the vale of flowers, others on stretchers, on beds, or on the bloodstained floor of the ambulance station; and still, as on previous days, the dawn broke over Sapun hill, the twinkling stars grew pale, the white mists spread from the dark roaring sea, the rosy dawn lit up the east, the long purple clouds spread across the pale blue horizon; and still, as on previous days, the sun rose in power and glory, promising joy, love and happiness to all the awakening world."

How to reconcile the beneficent world God has bestowed on man, and man's blind cruelty to himself within that world, was what Tolstoy had to discover. God in His benevolence started the world afresh every morning and every springtime; why could not man too start afresh? A premise to this conviction was the belief that man's nature is essentially good and that, were his eyes but opened to the fantastic abuses imposed by the accreted sophistication of civilization, he could be led to return to that good. That men are essentially evil, or that they may be made so with as equal facility as they may be improved, he recognized as a possibility but emphatically rejected. The alternatives were Hegelian acceptance and apathy, or Nietzschean despair and defiance.

Despite his contempt for it, war fascinated Tolstoy. "War has always interested me," he wrote; "not war in the sense of manoeuvres devised by great generals – my imagination refused to follow such immense movements, I did not understand them – but the reality of war, the actual killing. I was more interested to know in what way and under the influence of what feeling one soldier kills another than to know how the armies were arranged at Austerlitz and Borodino." In reality his view was not so constricted as this passage implies. As a supreme artist, he was fully alert to the excitement and dramatic quality of warfare, and of admirable qualities it brought out in the participants. He *was* interested, too, in questions of strategy, leadership, morale and other attendant factors, as any reader of *War and Peace* will know.

What appears to have attracted him to the study of war was its concentration of evil, the manner in which it brings to a head all the poison immanent but less easily detectable in civil life. There overt cases of physical cruelty are normally rare, and the real oppression constricts humanity in a thousand subtly disguised deprivations and distortions. In war, on the contrary, the brutality is practised on so large and open a scale and generally on so trivial a pretext, that the lie is apparent to all.

Tolstoy's purpose was that of the boy in *The Emperor's New Clothes*, to strip away all that was fraudulent and superfluous, in order to restore the true entity beneath. It was not a destructive aim, though frequently it appeared as such; but the constructive one of the restoration of purity and innocence such as he had known in childhood at Yasnaya Polyana, and of which he still saw abundant traces in the world about him. It is not surprising that his relationship with the opposite sex was strongly tempered by this complex outlook. Women are elemental creatures, retaining many of the qualities of childhood whose passing Tolstoy lamented in himself. Yet the strength of the sexual impulse provides them with an overpowering capacity to turn men's lives upside down; by the same action conferring on one man the most sublime happiness, and on another unbearable torture.

Paradoxically, it was the same quality of affection, innocence and beauty, which in childhood meant so much to Tolstoy, that transformed itself into a dangerous potential for extremes of jealousy, selfish desire of possession, and psychological imprisonment in situations as painful as any inflicted on the robustly harsh world of the battlefield.

Tolstoy's sexual drive was extremely strong, and in his old age he confessed that of all his bad habits it was the hardest to overcome. As a young man he enjoyed the favours of peasant girls on the family estate, of gypsies and prostitutes. He felt with varying degrees of passion that this was quite wrong, and like anyone else dreamed of love for a pure-minded young girl who would be a helpmate in his life's task. In the abstract, his view of women was low. He resolved "to regard the society of women as a necessary unpleasantness of social life, and to keep away from them as much as possible. From whom indeed do we get sensuality, effeminacy, frivolity in everything, and many other vices, if not from women?" He frequently expressed the familiar idea that women are children of passion, incapable of rational thought, and a fatal incumbrance to any man with an honest mission in life. He justified prostitution on the grounds that its absence would cause men to seduce each other's wives and daughters, so destroying family life.

Of course Tolstoy is the last person whose opinions should be taken out of context, nor do they necessarily reflect fully his real motivation. He enjoyed a perfectly rational and intellectual relationship with several women, including his "aunt" Tatiana Ergolsky and a real aunt, Countess Alexandra Tolstoy. But he had difficulty in falling whole-heartedly in love, though he ardently wished to do so, and when finally at thirty-four he resolved to marry Sonia Behrs he found as usual the intellectual Leo Tolstoy was busily and destructively analysing the emotional Leo Tolstoy. "I am afraid of myself," he wrote in his diary on 23 August 1862; "what if this be only a *desire* for love and not real love?" And, five days later: "Ugly mug! Do not think of marriage; your calling is of another kind." But a month later he was married, and his wife proved to be a highly intelligent helpmate. She bore Leo thirteen children, managed his household, conducted correspondence, typed and corrected his books, arranged for the publication of many of them; and, in short, devoted her life to him and his work – her expressed aim. In discussion with him of literary or social matters her views were always interesting and not infrequently more sensible than those of the erratic genius she had married.

There is not space here to discuss their stormy relationship in full, and many books have been devoted to the subject. She had a great deal to put up with from the first moment of marriage, when her husband chose to purge himself of some guilt complex by compelling her to read his diary records in all their salacious detail. He appears to have made little attempt to understand her, signing away his literary rights, installing as his literary aide the unpleasant charlatan Chertkov, and leaving a will which seemed to have been quite deliberately cruel. Sonia even had cause to complain about his personal habits. "I can never get used to the dirt, the smell," a desperate entry in her diary records.

It was Tolstoy's sexual code that was most hard to suffer. His views appear

*Sophia Andreevna Tolstoy
(née Behrs), 1863*

eccentric enough, though it may be that there is an explanation. The aphorism *post coitum omnia animalia tristia sunt* seems to have applied more closely to him than most. The act itself he regarded as disgusting.

"A man who doesn't feel what elephants feel, that copulation generally is an act humiliating both to oneself and one's partner, and therefore repulsive, an act in which a man pays involuntary tribute to his animal nature and which is only redeemed by the fact that it fulfils the purpose for which the need for this repulsive and humiliating act, irresistible at certain times, is implanted in his nature – such a man, despite his ability to argue, is on the level of an animal, and it is impossible to explain and prove this to him."

Though Tolstoy always suffered deep remorse after his visits to his wife's bed, he was quite unable to restrain himself from regular repetition. Even when writing the *Kreutzer Sonata* in 1889, a book whose principal theme is the advocacy of celibacy, he could not keep away from Sonia. In December of the following year, fearing she was pregnant, she confided to her diary her fear that Moscow society would scoff that the baby was "the true P.S. of the *Kreutzer Sonata*". Of a vegetarian menu Tolstoy was advocating, she noted sardonically: "I expect the person who wrote the menu practises vegetarianism as much as the author of the *Kreutzer Sonata* practises chastity."

What was the explanation for this exaggerated remorse? Certainly Tolstoy experienced post-coital revulsion more than most. He warned his son Andrei, who was contemplating marriage to a peasant girl in 1895, that he would have "a hated, repulsive wife round your neck (*as always happens as a result of purely sensual intimacy*)" (my italics). In addition he perhaps felt humiliation and self-betrayal at having conducted the most intimate of acts with a woman whose views in the daytime he had repudiated as utterly false. To gain temporary but irresistible pleasure, a man places himself voluntarily in bondage to a woman. The implication is that the sexual act cannot be regarded as an independent phenomenon, but is inextricably bound up with the whole complex of human relations. It was far too important to be otherwise.

Leo Tolstoy with his granddaughter, Tania

Moreover, the sheer overriding force of the impulse implied a vanity in supposing the human will capable of overcoming its component evil. No one would know what power it had over him, yet how false was any impression of him lacking that knowledge. In 1906 he wrote bitterly in his diary.

"All are writing my biography, and in my whole biography there will be nothing about my connection with the 7th Commandment (Thou shalt not kill). Nor will there be all the terrible filth of masturbation and worse, from my 13th and 14th year to the 15th, 16th (I do not remember when I began my debauchery in the brothels). And so up to my union with the peasant girl Axinia – she is alive. Then marriage, in which once more, though I never betrayed my wife, there was lust in my relations with her – nasty and criminal lust. There will be none of this and all the more important, since at least of all the vices this is one of which I am the most conscious, the vice which more than all others compels recovery."

But probably the guiding force behind Tolstoy's increasing hatred of the sexual act was straightforward jealousy, carried typically to extremity. When their first son, Sergei, was born in June 1863, Sonia was placed in torment by her husband's extraordinary behaviour. Without previous warning, he insisted that she should suckle the baby, despite the fact that her poor health made this highly dangerous. When a doctor warned him about this, Leo accused him furiously of having conducted his examination in an indecent manner. Bestowing the baby on a wet-nurse was morally dangerous as depriving Sonia of the "only means which might have kept her from coquetry". Tolstoy displayed violent jealousy of the baby, and was convinced that a former teacher at his school who talked to his wife politely was lusting after her. It was all quite absurd, but obsessively important to Leo Tolstoy. In a diary entry for 1900, the grotesque extent to which his jealousy could be carried is revealed when he recorded his conviction that it was several degrees *worse* for a man to be betrayed by his wife than for him to frequent brothels, engage in promiscuous sexual activities, or "to have intercourse with a young girl and abandon her".

Natasha's first ball
(L. Pasternak, 1893)

What agitated Tolstoy so much was an instinctive feeling that the sexual act represented a fatal loss of innocence when first experienced by a young girl. Her open-hearted childhood world had fled for ever, and all that remained was for further sexual relations to be subordinated to purposes of procreation and confined within marriage. To live up to his self-imposed rigid ideal was an impossible task for a man whose sexual drive was little impaired at the age of eighty, but he did not allow himself to be daunted.

Tolstoy's seemingly unreasonable sexual code was a reflexion of his unceasing search for a theodicy, a satisfactory moral explanation for existence, epitomized by his brother Nikolenka's "little green stick". His penetrating, restlessly destructive mind turned from one of humanity's illusions to another, until there seemed nothing left intact. All the accepted outward observances of religion were mere flummery designed to conceal the truth (Christ may even never have existed, he conceded at one time); marriage was a torture-chamber; government in Russia was simply a deadening impediment to the people's self-fulfilment, while in Western Europe "the original *spontaneous* sentiment of man . . . is not to be found, and it disappears just as civilization, that is to say the interested, rational egoistic association of men, spreads." Virtually every generally accepted institution and ideal was a poisonous illusion, designed to corrupt man's natural purity.

There was no avoiding the conclusion that life was a heartless joke, and death the "supreme moment of life". "How can man fail to see this?" he wrote in 1879. "And how go on living? That is what is surprising! One can only live when one is intoxicated with life; as soon as one is sober it is impossible not to see that it is all a mere fraud and a stupid fraud! That is precisely what it is: there is nothing either amusing or witty about it; it is simply cruel and stupid." He took the logical step on occasion of contemplating suicide by shooting himself when out hunting or hanging himself from a beam in his study.

Then there was the fear of death itself. Of course his restless, curious, probing mind could not halt at this point. There *must* be a logical answer, one that could survive his most destructive criticisms. After all, there had been a time when he had known the harmony of the Ant-Brotherhood; and there were even moments, such as a moonlight night or spring in the forest, when the world regained its placid equilibrium.

Leo Tolstoy walking.

Tolstoy sought the answer in history. Men were naturally disposed to good, as Rousseau, his own childhood and an underlying necessity to believe had taught him. What then was the source of all that evil which reigned in the world, and which most people misguidedly accepted as inevitable? How could thousands of sane householders leave their wives and children to follow a vain *poseur* like Napoleon, in order to stab and kill until thousands of other wives and children were left widows and orphans? How could the pure and simple teaching of Christ have become a priest-dominated instrument of persecution and superstition?

Into *War and Peace* he interpolated long excursions arguing his theory of history. Briefly, he held that the "swarm-life" of man – the great movements that occupied the principal attention of historians – was the effect of deep impersonal forces ebbing and flowing with independent force. All the pretexts provided at the time or since for Napoleon's invasion of Russia are demonstrable absurdities; hence the real motive was one unconsciously present in the whole French army and nation. The participants were compelled to do what they did by this under-swell of historical necessity, and allowed the man who ran out at the front of the swarm to declare himself its instigator.

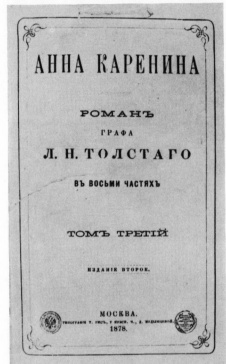 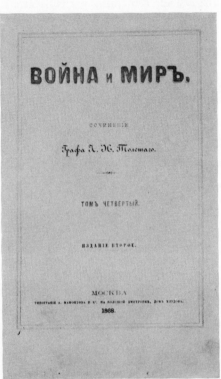

First editions of War and Peace and Anna Karenina

But despite these destructive waves, "natural" events not altogether susceptible to explanation, the life of mankind continued the only cycle that really matters, and which should be history's real concern: birth, marriage, the family, the daily round necessary to sustain life, and death. Though they no more influenced the movement of history than Napoleon, by understanding or better still *living* it, they embodied its true purpose.

On a purely factual level this theory, which is similar in its central respect to the contemporary one of Karl Marx, was simply a healthy reaction to the super-ficialities of historians like Mihailovsky-Danilievsky, who saw history in terms of Emperors' conferences and generals' movements of armies. But, as has often been pointed out, Tolstoy's theory of history is less an attempt at scientific investigation than a moral protest. It is in fact a polemical attack on Napoleon and the belief in "great men" which the French Emperor above all others epitomized.

Tolstoy intensely disliked Napoleon. As a Russian patriot, he hated the man who had, without the slightest justification, invaded and laid waste his country. He was correspondingly proud of the subsequent Russian victory. (When describing the war of 1812 to children at his school in Yasnaya Polyana, he set the whole class wild with patriotic fervour!) He instinctively viewed with aristocratic disdain the posturing of the *arriviste* usurper, and in any case mistrusted French superficiality.

Unaware of his true motive, he set about the destruction of Napoleon. Now, it was useless to stress the real reason he detested him: the terrible destruction and misery brought about by his selfish ambition. After all, many Russians (including Pierre Bezukhov in his novel) were fully prepared to admire Napoleon as super-man, while remaining perfectly aware of the harm his career had caused. What was necessary was to remove the real source of Napoleon's spurious "greatness": the power of his personality single-handed to alter the pattern of history. To prove that the French Emperor was as much the puppet of the Great Cause of history as the least of his grenadiers, Tolstoy was obliged to take considerable liberties with the evidence.

He detested him so much that he had to deny him the one quality that everyone conceded him: his astonishing abilities as a commander. This caused him to present Napoleon in an unconvincing light, which is detrimental to the novel. Even the most unpleasant Russian characters, such as Kouragin and Dolokhov, bear redeeming and, what is more important, human characteristics. Napoleon as Tolstoy sees him has none; he is a pure compound of blindness and vanity. This is not the Napoleon of history, nor is it conceivable within the context of the novel that such a man could have risen to the position he occupied. The portrayal has been unfavourably contrasted with that of Lenin by Solzhenitsyn. Lenin had fewer redeeming personal qualities than Napoleon and did far more harm to Russia. Solzhenitsyn undoubtedly accepts this, yet his Lenin remains a credible piece of breathing humanity.

Leo Tolstoy, by Ilya Repin (1891)

262

Tolstoy's Russian patriotism is also revealed in his portrayal of the Russian commander Kutuzov (whose daughter, incidentally, married a Tolstoy, founding the now extinct line of Kutuzov-Tolstoy). Clearly Tolstoy could not in the same work have Napoleon prevented by immutable historical laws from playing any part whatsoever in the outcome of the war, without also applying those laws to Kutuzov. So Tolstoy explains that Kutuzov, with a sort of earthy instinct, "understood" the course of events and used that understanding to advantage. Whilst the "impetus" lay with the French he knew it was futile to oppose them. When that "impetus" ran out in Moscow and the French retreated, he followed upon the heels of that retreat. Once again the historical record was tampered with and Kutuzov's character moulded to suit the interpretation. One may compare this approach with Marx and Lenin's claim that Communists are entitled to leadership of the proletariat, not because of their superior abilities but because of their superior understanding of the laws of history.[4]

It is unlikely that Tolstoy would have been unduly disturbed by criticism on these lines. Always searching for further insights of the truth, his beliefs were never static. He wrote his books with a moral purpose, and what really mattered in this instance was to convince people that Caesarian figures like Napoleon must be stripped of all the false glamour accorded them by foolish people. Then, having shewn him to be no more than other mortals, it is clear that his mass crimes must be judged by exactly the same criteria as the sordid offences committed by private citizens. There must be a morality in history or, once again, what is the purpose of existence?

Tolstoy was inclined to judge literary works by what he took to be the moral intentions of their authors, sometimes with eccentric results. Understandably, he greatly admired Dickens, and English novels in general. But he also bestowed extravagant praise on *Uncle Tom's Cabin*, whilst giving vent to withering contempt for works by Shakespeare and Goethe!

Fortunately for the world, Tolstoy's profoundly moral outlook was not only expressed in didactic form. It is his fiction that has so powerfully absorbed men's minds and there, unlike that of his admired English and American counterparts, any overt moral purpose is confined to explicit didactic excursuses, or obliquely expressed in attitudes and arguments developed by the protagonists. In his novels are many passages and themes that he would doubtless have condemned in other writers. It was of course the truth with which he was preoccupied, in its broadest sense. His characters must, once created, live and breathe an independent existence. He occasionally claimed to find himself surprised by his characters' unexpected behaviour. Art is the transmission of feeling: "Art is a human activity consisting in this, that one man consciously by means of certain external signs, hands on to others feelings he has lived through, and that others are infected by these feelings and also experience them."*

Tolstoy's ambitious aim was to take the totality of human experience and transmute it in this way. It was a vision extraordinarily multifarious which he sought to convey as a spiritual unity; a dramatic unity, and not an ideological one. There are hints of the imposition of a Tolstoyan justice, as in the occasional fortuitous coincidence or reward of virtue in *War and Peace*, or the possible implication of the repeating dangers of broken marriage apparent in *Anna Karenina*. But

* *What is Art?* (1898).

these are to be contrasted with other episodes, and Tolstoy certainly held no simplistic aim. The reduction of Napoleon is important; much more so is the portrayal of what *is* vital in humanity, the brimming life of "ordinary" people in its rich variety.

In 1918 Alfred Adler delivered a brilliant lecture on Dostoevsky, much of which is equally apposite to Tolstoy. After a resumé of the writer's disturbed upbringing, he described how Dostoevsky "walked step by step, gathering together all experiences, embracing all humanity in one broad embrace, for the sake of obtaining knowledge, of touching life in all its phases, to seek truth, to seek *the new teaching*.

"Anyone who holds within his breast such contrasts, who is compelled to bridge such contrasts, must indeed drink deeply if he desires to gain any repose. For he will be spared no trouble, none of the sufferings of life; he will not be able to pass even the most insignificant bit of life without trying to see how it fits into his formula. His whole nature impels him onward toward an *integrated* interpretation of life so that in his eternal oscillations when in this state of restlessness he may find security and rest.

"To gain repose he would have to be able to arrive at *truth*. But the road to truth is beset with thorns, demands great exertions, great perseverance, a tremendous training of mind and soul."

Like Dostoevsky, Tolstoy practised "his penetrative vision in order to attain to knowledge of the inter-connections of life and then to call a halt and unite in one synthesis all the antitheses that threatened to shake him to his foundations and confound him. Amidst the uncertainties of his psychic contradictions the goal of his striving was the discovery of some valid truth. He himself was alternately rebel and obedient slave, was drawn to abysses from which he shrank back frightened."

Finally, Adler perceptively identified the crisis towards which such a quest is leading.

"But we must remember first and foremost, that the orbit of artistic creation passes outside the battle of life. We may consequently assume that every artist will show a turning-off, a halt, a retreat, as soon as the normal expectations of society confront him. The artist who out of nothing, or let us say, out of an anxious attitude toward the facts of life, creates a world and who, instead of an answer in terms of practical life, gives us a puzzling artistic creation, such a man is averted from life and its demands. 'Well, but I am a mystic and dreamer!'"[5]

There is also the fear of death haunting the writer, impelling him to distil and recreate his experience, discovering a central purpose valid enough to neutralize the darkening menace. Tolstoy once wrote that "If I do not know how to act in any situation, I imagine: what should I do if I were going to die to-morrow?"[6]

Leo Tolstoy's own crisis came in 1879, after five years of great perturbation of soul. That year he wrote his *Confession*. "Five years ago something very strange began to happen to me. At first I experienced moments of perplexity and arrest of life, as though I did not know how to live or what to do; and I felt lost and became dejected. But this passed, and I went on living as before. Then these moments of perplexity began to recur more and more often, and always in the same form. They were always expressed by the questions: what is it for? What does it lead to?"

All the preoccupations and achievements of his life, including his literary work,

Leo Tolstoy in 1876

suddenly assumed a ghastly air of pointlessness. "I felt that what I had been standing on had broken down, and that I had nothing left under my feet." Death loomed near, and he was tempted to suicide. He became seized with the idea that his life hitherto had been a cruel joke: for thirty or forty years he was conceded the delusion that he was maturing and achieving great things; then came the moment for which all this was preparatory – the discovery that *nothing* lay ahead, "nothing . . . but stench and worms". Everything he had done would be forgotten, he and all he loved would be dead . . . the whole thing was a meaningless farce. It was no good doing as most people did; recognizing the problem as too vast for solution, and therefore to be dismissed. It was the only problem that mattered, and could not be dismissed.

Up to now his art had brought him satisfaction, but it could do so no longer. "As long as I was not living my own life, but was borne on the waves of some other life – as long as I believed that life had a meaning, though one I could not express – the reflexion of life in poetry and art of all kinds, afforded me pleasure: it was pleasant to look at life in the mirror of art. But when I began to seek the meaning of life, and felt the necessity of living on my own account, that mirror became for me unnecessary, superfluous, ridiculous, or painful. I could no longer soothe myself with what I saw in the mirror, for what I saw was that my position was stupid and desperate. It was all very well to enjoy the sight when in the depth of my soul I believed that my life had a meaning. Then the play of lights – comic, tragic, touching, beautiful and terrible – in life amused me. But when I knew life

265

to be meaningless and terrible, the play in the mirror could no longer amuse me."

Tolstoy was spiritually shattered by the culminating conviction that life was without meaning and all his achievements worthless. There was no evading the conclusion. There were many people too stupid to appreciate the fatuity of life ("mostly women, or very young or very dull people"!), and more still who simply did not have the imagination to care, living only for the unreflecting moment. But Tolstoy "could not imitate these people: I had not their dullness of imagination, and I could not artificially produce it in myself." As a result only two courses remained open for him: the "strong" way, which was suicide; and the "weak" way, which was to cling to life in the futile expectation that something might yet appear to provide it with meaning.

Tolstoy's endlessly exploring mind could not stick at this point. It was, after all, his reason which placed him in this dilemma, but reason was merely a product of life – and the product cannot deny its own creator! There was something essentially wrong in all this hair-splitting and circular argument. What dawned on Tolstoy was that Hamlet's rhetorical question existed as an issue only for that tiny, pampered, frivolous and introspective sector of mankind to which he himself belonged. He had acted as if that were the whole world; but *out there* were the millions whose work sustained the earth and who in turn were sustained by a superstitious but vital faith. It was there in the real world, among "the real labouring people" for whom he felt "a strange physical affection", that he must seek the truth, and not in the artificial superficialities of his own idle, liberal-minded class. "While we think it terrible that we have to suffer and die, these folk live and suffer, and approach death with tranquillity, and in most cases gladly." This was because they lived in unreflecting communion with God, and eked out a simple, productive existence without striving for the superfluities that inevitably corrupt body and soul.

In his search for God, Tolstoy had come to reject his own Orthodox faith and that of all established religions. Their exclusiveness made them a force for division, not brotherhood; much of their theology and ritual obscured man's close personal relationship with God, and was in any case impossible to accept; they accepted war and judicial killings; and, finally, their lives, which took as inevitable injustice, poverty, sickness and death – the world's real evils – were a stark denial of their teachings.

His road was now clear. The impulsion to suicide was simply the last, logical conclusion of his previous existence, and was as false as the rest of it. After five years of struggle he had found the solution. "I then understood the answer to the question, 'What is life?' when I said that life is 'evil', was quite correct. The only mistake was, that my answer referred to *my* life, but not to life in general. My life, a life of indulgence and desires, was meaningless and evil . . . and I understood the truth, which I afterwards found in the Gospels, that men love darkness rather than the light because their deeds are evil; and that to see things as they are, one must think and speak of the life of humanity, and not of the minority who are parasites on life.

"And indeed, the bird lives so that it must fly, collect food and build its nest; and when I see the bird doing that, I joy in its joy. The goat, hare and wolf live so that they must feed themselves, and propagate and feed their families, and when they do so, I feel firmly assured that they are happy and that their life is a reasonable one. And what does man do? He should earn a living as the beasts do, but with this difference – that he would perish if he did it alone; he has to procure it not for himself but for all. When he does *that*, I have a firm assurance that he is happy and that his life is reasonable."

All this represented a literal revolution in Tolstoy's outlook, as even his symbolism indicates. His acceptance of God's existence resulted from a realization that "I could not have come into the world without any cause or reason or meaning; I could not be such a fledgling fallen from its nest as I felt myself to be. Or, granting that I be such, lying on my back in the high grass, even then I cry because I know that a mother has borne me within her, has hatched me, warmed me, fed me and loved me. Where is she – that mother? If she has deserted me, who is it that has done so? I cannot hide from myself that someone bore me, loving me. Who was that someone? Again, 'God'? . . . And strange to say, the strength of life which returned to me was not new, but quite old – the same that had borne me along in my earliest days. I have returned to what belonged to my earliest childhood and youth."

Leo Tolstoy ploughing, by Repin (1887)

The results of this baring of his soul are well known; how Tolstoy took up in all seriousness many aspects of the material life of the peasantry, ploughing, reaping, cobbling, etc.; how he dressed in dirty peasant clothing, eschewing all social vanities; his educational experiments in the school he founded at Yasnaya Polyana; his vegetarianism; his desperate efforts to rid himself of the guilty inheritance of wealth. He carried the analysis expounded in his *Confession* to its extreme conclusion. The wealth of the few was enjoyed at the expense of the well-being of the many, and was protected from the latter by state-instituted violence. The government itself was a mere conspiratorial means for the dragooning of the people, and its staple pretexts for existence palpable frauds designed to deceive the masses and preserve itself. Thus the government maintained huge armed forces to protect its citizens from foreign invaders – yet all wars were instigated by governments and not peoples, who derived no benefit and much loss from them. Private property was protected by an armed police – yet the modest property of humble men was only threatened by rich men and government officials. And so on. There was no legitimate justification for government, whose real prescription was the original conquest of the people staged by the existing government's predecessors in the recent or remote past, and every reason for the abolition of an institution whose true rôle was no more than that of the robber levying blackmail on his neighbour-hood.

Tolstoy's political programme was different from the anarchism of Bakunin and others only in that he absolutely eschewed the use of violence to attain these ends, and in his more humane attitude towards the human components of government, whom he recognized as fellow human beings, pitying them at the same time as condemning the evil they practised.

Tolstoy in fact condemned all existing political movements as tending towards refinements of the identical evil. He was particularly hostile to the propositions of 'scientific" Socialism, remarking prophetically that it was "to be instituted by a fresh organization of violence, and will have to be maintained by the same means", and that a Socialist government "must, moreover, inevitably introduce laws of compulsory labour – i.e. they must re-establish slavery in its primitive form". To obviate the absolute inevitability of violence breeding further violence, Tolstoy advocated non-cooperation with the government, with its citizens refusing office and declining to assist state-directed violence, particularly in the army and police.*

Because of his brilliantly persuasive arguments and patent honesty, and still more because of his towering spiritual stature as the author of *War and Peace*, Tolstoy's flow of writings on political, economic and moral problems enjoyed enormous influence throughout Russia and the world. He was also looked upon with the greatest disfavour by the government of the day – not least by its Minister of the Interior, Count Dmitri Andreevich Tolstoy, a cousin whom he referred to ironically as "brother Dmitri Andreevich".[7] He could and did publish freely abroad, but within Russia Leo Tolstoy's polemical writings were frequently censored, and his staff and printers harassed. Despite these repressive measures, the Government shrank from touching the great author himself. It was said that Tsar Nicholas II had dismissed a suggestion of exile with the words "I do not wish to add a martyr's halo to his glory."[8]

This immunity must surely have helped to confirm Tolstoy's belief in the efficacy of non-violence as a means of opposing the state's unjust demands. He had challenged the Government to imprison him, being perfectly prepared to undergo the sentence, but also confident that the authorities were unlikely to go so far. Much of this confidence stemmed from his social eminence, and in a history of the Tolstoy family it is impossible to neglect the influence which his ancestry had on his outlook and conduct.

In 1901 Tolstoy felt that his son Andrei was leading a worthless life, and in a bitter letter asked him to "imagine clearly what you would be and what rôle you would play if it weren't for your money and your name – the very thing that isn't your own, but just happens to belong to you". At the same time Tolstoy was extremely conscious of the merits of ancient blood and a famous name, and

*Solzhenitsyn has advocated a similar method of resistance to the Soviet Government. His hostility, however, is to one specifically evil government, whereas Tolstoy was opposed to all.

continued throughout his life to display obviously aristocratic prejudices. He had been brought up on a great estate, everything and everybody on it being the hereditary property of his ancestors. As a young man, among the many facets of his various personality was a strong predilection for the outward marks of gentility. A fellow-student at Kazan University in 1846 remembered that he "kept clear of the Count, who from our first meeting repelled me by his assumption of coldness, his bristly hair and the piercing expression of his half-closed eyes. I had never met a young man with such a strange and, to me, incomprehensible air of importance and self-satisfaction. . . . At first I seldom met the Count, who in spite of his awkwardness and bashfulness had joined the small group of so-called 'aristocrats'. He hardly replied to my greetings, as if wishing to intimate that even here we were far from being equals, since he drove up with a fast trotter and I came on foot." He became quite a dandy, sporting a grey beaver collar to his overcoat, swinging a fashionable cane, and wearing a glossy hat set at a casual angle on his curly, dark-brown hair. He expressed a preference for the company of "*gens comme il faut*", and once ridiculed a gentleman driving without gloves.

When the family estates were divided among the brothers, Leo received his beloved Yasnaya Polyana. As a result he continued to live surrounded by the rich material evidence of his heritage. The patrician features of past Tolstoys and Volkonskys gazed down at him from every wall, and as a keen student of history he could not fail to be continually reminded of the distinguished part men whose

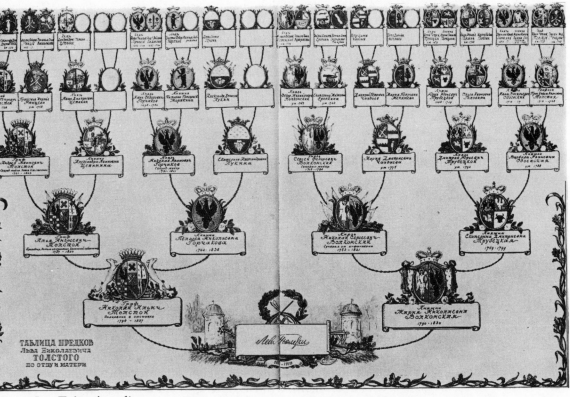

Leo Tolstoy's pedigree

blood he bore in his veins had played in his country's story. His eldest son, Sergei, later compiled a pedigree to illustrate his father's thirty-two quarterings. The names of Leo's immediate ancestors read like a roll-call of half Russia's history: Volkonskys, Troubetskoys, Gorchakovs, Galitzines, Odoevskys and Obolenskys.[9]

Tolstoy was particularly interested in the brothers Ivan and Peter Tolstoy, who had played such a distinguished part in the reign of Peter the Great. In 1870–3, in the course of preparations for a major novel set in the reign of that Tsar, he undertook extensive researches into the deeds of his ancestors. The uprising of the Streltsi in 1682 became a focus of Tolstoy's researches, being crammed with dramatic interest, and concerning as it did the most striking incidents in the lives of his Tolstoy and Miloslavsky ancestors. The notes provide tantalizing glimpses of the author's plans for presenting the characters in dramatic form. Peter Tolstoy he envisaged as "broad, clever, brilliant . . . speaks perfect Italian", while the cunning Ivan Mihailovich Miloslavsky he pictured with "a black beard growing below his middle". Possibly stemming from this interest, in 1873 he read to his son Zagoskin's historical novel *Yuri Miloslavsky*, set in the year 1612. Sadly, Tolstoy's pen never brought his ancestors to life, as ultimately he found the Petrine era too hopelessly cruel for his taste.[10] He particularly objected to his ancestor Peter Tolstoy's part in the abduction and judicial murder of the Tsarevich Alexei.

Tolstoy was perfectly conscious of his aristocratic prejudice, referring to it with disarming candour. His brother-in-law remembered that Leo "in my presence confessed to being both proud and vain. He was a rampant aristocrat, and though he always loved the country folk, he loved the aristocracy still more. To the middle class he was antipathetic. When, after his failures in early life, he became widely famous as a writer, he used to admit that it gave him great pleasure and intense happiness. In his own words, he was pleased to feel that he was both a writer and a nobleman." It is significant that, when travelling by rail, he always went first-class or third – never second!

Tolstoy was quite aware that such an attitude could offend thin-skinned persons, particularly among the intelligentsia, but made it plain that their opinions mattered little to him. In a passage written for *War and Peace*, but omitted from the published version, he set down his viewpoint in words which have startled some with only a partial knowledge of the Count's complex character.

"Up to now I have been writing only about princes, counts, ministers, senators and their children, and I am afraid that there will be no other people in my story later on either.

"Perhaps this is not a good thing and the public may not like it; perhaps a story of peasants, merchants and theological students would be more interesting and instructive for them; but for all my desire to have as many readers as possible, I cannot satisfy this taste for many reasons. In the first place because the historical monuments of the time I am writing about have survived only in the correspondence and memoirs of people of the highest circle – literate people; the interesting and clever stories which I have managed to hear, I also heard only from people of that circle. In the second place because the lives of merchants, coachmen, theological students, convicts and peasants seem to me boring and monotonous, and all the actions of these people seem to me to stem, for the most part, from one and the same motive: envy of the more fortunate orders, self-interest and the material passions. If all the actions of these people do not in fact stem from these motives,

Leo Tolstoy riding Délire

their actions are so obscured by them that it is difficult to understand them and therefore to describe them.

"In the third place because the lives of these people (the lower orders) bear less of the imprint of the time.

"In the fourth place because the lives of these people are ugly.

"In the fifth place because I cannot understand what a policeman thinks as he stands by his box, or what a shopkeeper thinks and feels as he invites people to buy braces and ties, or what a theological student thinks when he is being taken to be flogged for the hundredth time, etc. I cannot understand this any more than I can understand what a cow thinks when it is being milked or what a horse thinks when it is carrying a barrel.

"Finally, in the sixth place (and this I know is the best reason) because I myself belong to the highest order of society and like it.

"I am not a bourgeois, as Pushkin boldly said, and I say boldly that I am an aristocrat by birth, by habits and by position. I am an aristocrat because I am not only not ashamed, but positively glad to remember my ancestors – fathers, grand-fathers and great-grandfathers. I am an aristocrat because I was brought up from childhood in love and respect for the highest order of society and in love for the refined as expressed not only in Homer, Bach and Raphael but also in all the small things of life. I am an aristocrat because I was sufficiently fortunate that neither I, nor my father, nor my grandfather knew want or the struggle between conscience and want, nor had any necessity ever to envy anyone or sue for favours, nor knew the need to be educated for money or a position in society and so on – ordeals to which people in want are subjected. I see that this was a great fortune and I thank

God for it, but if this fortune does not belong to everybody, I do not see any reason to renounce it or not to take advantage of it.

"I am an aristocrat because I cannot believe in the high intellect, the refined taste or the absolute honesty of a man who picks his nose and whose soul converses with God."[11]

This was the Count Tolstoy who could beat an impertinent peasant with his own hands. It was also he who, in writing a letter of advice to Alexander III, told the Tsar that "I am not going to write in the tone in which people usually write letters to emperors – with flourishes of false and servile eloquence which only obscure both feeling and thought. I shall write simply, as man to man." And when similarly addressing his successor Nicholas II, he began simply, "Dear Brother, I consider this form of address to be the most appropriate because I address you in this letter not so much as a tsar but as a man – a brother. . . ." Much of this stemmed from Tolstoy's doctrine of Christian brotherhood, but one can detect also the conviction that a Tolstoy was fully the equal of a Romanov. Likewise, Tolstoy vigorously opposed injustice wherever he encountered it, but when it was an injustice imposed on himself there was a strong note of personal indignation in his response. In 1862 his home was raided by a party of police looking for revolutionary literature. Fortunately Tolstoy was not there at the time ("If I had been, I should probably be on trial for murder by now"), but when the news reached him his anger knew no bounds. The officers had threatened to return, to which Tolstoy reminded his aunt that "I have loaded pistols in my room, and am waiting to see how this matter will end." He asked her to consult the Tsar's close friend, his cousin Alexei Constantinovich Tolstoy (the poet), and wrote soon after to the Tsar himself, demanding that "Your Majesty's name be free of any possible reproach of injustice, and that those who are guilty of the misuse of this name be, if not punished, at least exposed." The Tsar swiftly send a message of apology.

As Marc Raeff has shewn in his book *The Origins of the Russian Intelligentsia*, the peculiar situation of the Russian aristocracy after Peter the Great's reforms placed them in a position quite different from that of other European nobilities. As a class they possessed little power, which was centred in the hands of the autocratic emperor. But at home in the country their personal power was almost limitless. Control over their serfs was actually increased, as a reward for loyalty and as a means of controlling the countryside. When the fathers disappeared for years on end to fulfil their obligatory military or civil service to the state, the sons remained at home in the care of the womenfolk. Their companions were the children of local serfs, for whom they felt all the overflow of affection natural to deprived children; yet at the same time they exercised absolute authority over their young friends.

As noble youths grew to manhood they in turn departed for their state service. Removed from their homes, they suffered increased feelings of isolation from the people, a sensation tragically exacerbated by the spread of European culture among the educated classes. Guilt, deprivation and isolation made the nobleman, once reinstalled on his estate, potential prey to a number of conflicting emotions and attitudes. The artificial nature of government administration could induce him to hold an exaggerated, sentimental love of the "natural" peasantry on his estate. At the same time he was alienated from them in culture, and even language and dress. There was a strong impetus for the aristocrat at home to do what he had been powerless to do during his hidebound years of state service: implement far-reaching schemes of innovation and reform. As his legal powers were scarcely circumscribed at all he tended to regard his estates much as Western intellectuals have regarded Russia herself in the eighteenth, nineteenth and twentieth centuries: as a *tabula rasa*, ideal material for any utopian scheme of improvement. What this attitude did not make for was any concept of reality, of caution, of the value of settled institutions, or the encouragement of individual initiative among the startled serfs.

The Russian nobleman was not accustomed to accepting limitations to his ideas, which soared untrammelled across the open Russian steppe. On his estates, which were often vast beyond the conception of a European magnate, his was the only will that existed. As for government, that appeared in the main as an arbitrary, obstructive institution, remote but threatening, whose actions tended to be characterized by blundering incompetence and insensitivity. After the collapse in 1825 of the Decembrist revolt, conducted by idealistic young nobles whose fate had excited great sympathy among their peers, and the consequent repressive government of Nicholas I, the aristocracy as a class became still more isolated from central authority. Some threw themselves into schemes of improvement on their estates, while increasing numbers flung their bursting energies into the free world of ideas, into the arts (particularly literature) and into abstract – frequently utopian – political theorizing.

Leo Tolstoy's personal experience of government gave him cause to believe that it was at best a pointless nuisance, at worst a bullying incompetent. A year of local government service in 1861–62 disgusted him with politics, and his military service so convinced him of the incompetence of the general staff that he ultimately came to believe that to be a general it was necessary to be deprived of valuable human faculties, and that in any case war was a science which could not be mastered. (His own indifference towards any aspect except gallantry under fire was such that he missed receiving the coveted St. George's Cross: firstly, because he had mislaid some essential documents; and secondly because he forgot to go on duty when absorbed in a game of chess!) Thereafter government activities assumed a role that could only appear stupidly obstructive. His books were censored, often for motives too obscure for comprehension. Early on in his literary career he complained that "*Childhood* was spoilt, and *The Raid* simply ruined by the Censor. All that was good in it has been struck out or mutilated."

Small wonder that Tolstoy felt only "malice and disgust, almost hatred, for that dear government which searches my house for lithographic and typographic machines . . .", as he wrote in 1862. In fact Tolstoy's fame, and the general acceptance of the essentials of European enlightenment throughout educated Russian society, made the government extremely hesitant to oppose his activities too openly or consistently, and this uneasiness paradoxically served to confirm his view that society, given sufficient pressure, could be radically altered by moral pressure. Government and the artificial society of the two capitals were, he became increasingly convinced, false, superficial entities imposed on a countryside with which they had little contact and no beneficial effect. Needless to say this was true so far as it went. The autocracy *was* an artificial conception, imposed on an unwilling or indifferent population; and the Russian educated classes had become alienated from the general population.

Where Tolstoy went wrong was in supposing that this unique situation, arising from particular historical circumstances (the Tartar conquests, the size of Russia, her lack of natural frontiers, etc.) supplied a model from which the human experience could be judged. The fierce intensity of his destructive analysis led him to cut intellectually through everything that was false, insincere and unnecessarily complex. Thus Anna Karenina's tragedy arose less from the sin of adultery than from the fate of straightforward, elemental passions trapped in an over-sophisticated society. Reaction against this complexity led Tolstoy to some characteristically extreme conclusions, such as a belief in the harmful effects of telegraphs and railways ("the railway is to travelling what the brothel is to love – just as convenient, but just as inhumanly mechanical and deadly monotonous"). Pessimistically he became convinced that political and social reforms represented a mere patching of the worn-out garment, a view which led him into expressions of view foreign to his true nature, such as an initial refusal to participate in famine relief work in 1891, or declining support for a a sensible move to improve women's educational opportunities in 1895.

However interesting as a partial explanation, it would be facile to dismiss Tolstoy's convictions as simply the unconscious outcrop of his environment as a nineteenth-century Russian landowner. Few people were more trenchantly critical of these views than his English disciple and biographer, Aylmer Maude: "A knowledge of the social surroundings in which Tolstoy grew up makes it easier to understand the doctrines he subsequently taught. It was partly because he grew up in a detached and irresponsible position that the state of his own mind and soul were to him so much more important than the immediate effect of his conduct on others, and the same cause led him to remain in ignorance of lessons every intelligent man of business among us learns of necessity."

But it was Maude too who stressed the intellectual advantages with which this life equipped the great writer. "His independent position made easier the formation of that state of mind free from intellectual prejudice which enabled him later on to examine the claims of the Church, of the Bible, of the economists, of governments, and the most firmly established manners and customs of society, untrammelled by the fear of shocking or hurting other people. . . . He thus came to see things in a way we do not see them, while he remained blind to some things with which we are quite familiar. That is one reason why he is so extraordinarily interesting."

The most harrowing personal aspect of this discrepancy, between what every fibre of his being told him was the right course and the grim realities of life, was the rift it caused between himself and his wife. There was one vice he eschewed and that was hypocrisy. If he could not put into practice himself what he so ardently believed, then of what value was that belief? Sonia bore unstinted admiration for her husband's talents as a novelist, but felt that his provocative attitude towards the authorities could only bring trouble on the family with small benefit to anyone else, and that his pamphleteering was a cruel waste of his creative ability. There also seemed to be a great deal of hypocrisy in his attitudes towards sex and money. She was not the only one of his admirers to hold these views. In 1883 the dying Turgenev wrote a last unavailing plea: "Kind and dear Lev Nikolaevich . . . I am writing to you especially to say how glad I have been to be your contemporary, and to express my last sincere request. My friend, return to literary activity! That gift came to you from whence comes all the rest. Ah, how happy I should be if I could think my request would have an effect on you! I am played out. . . . My friend – great writer of the Russian land – listen to my request!"[12] Chekhov, who also greatly loved Tolstoy but was much sharper in his judgment, expressed his view privately in 1894: "Logic and a sense of justice tell me that there is more neighbourly love in electricity and steam than there is in chastity and abstention from eating meat."

Even Turgenev's most moving of appeals could achieve nothing. At the end of 1885 Tolstoy wrote a long, agitated letter to his wife in which he set out his position very clearly. After lamenting the differences that had arisen between them, he went on: "I came to the conclusion nearly 10 years ago that my only salvation, and that of any man in this life, is to live not for oneself but for others, and that the life of our class is entirely arranged for the sake of living for oneself and is entirely based on pride, cruelty, violence and evil, and that therefore a man in our circles who wants to live a good life, to live with a clear conscience, to live joyfully, has no need to look for any difficult and remote feats to accomplish, but needs to act this very minute, to work hour by hour and day by day in order to change this life and to go from bad to good; this alone constitutes the happiness and virtue of people of our circle, but you and the whole family are not moving towards changing this life, but, as the family grows and the selfishness of its members increases, towards aggravating its bad sides. That is the cause of the pain. How can it be cured? Should I renounce my faith? You know that's impossible. If I said by word of mouth that I renounce it, nobody, even you, would believe it, any more than if I said that 2×2 is not 4. But what should I do? Profess this faith in words and books, and do something different in actual fact? Again, even you can't advise me to do that. Should I forget? Impossible. But what should I do? The point is that the subject which occupies me and to which, perhaps, I have been called, is the business of moral teaching. And the business of moral teaching differs from all others in that it can't be changed, it can't remain mere words, it can't be binding for one person and not binding for another. If conscience and reason demand a thing, and it is clear to me what conscience and reason demand, I can't fail to do what conscience and reason demand and be at ease – I can't look at people, bound to me by ties of love and knowing what reason and conscience demand and not doing it, without suffering. . . . You think that I am one thing and my writing is another thing. But my writing is the whole of me."

There was no middle way. There were writers who advocated pious platitudes from the comfort of their studies, but Tolstoy could not join them. The French writer Renan, whose insincerity Tolstoy suspected, he described as "a eunuch with his moral testicles cut off", and Bernard Shaw was aptly labelled "clever-foolish". He was not, as many thought, obsessive; he could cheerfully laugh at himself and satirize his own views. But he had spent a lifetime in search of the truth, and could not now abandon it to gain domestic peace.

The agony of mind increased with every year. In the nineteenth century the central debate had on the whole been conducted by civilized men who, with all their faults of venality and inertia, at least discussed the issues in an atmosphere of civility and mutual respect. But with the coming of the twentieth century it was apparent that something dark and terrible was stirring in the abyss. The chances of a peaceful, Tolstoyan revolution were scarcely propitious. And what, after all, was there to show for all the work and agony? If governments and political parties were changing for the worse, what were the fruits of his work among the people? There were all over the world men and women who corresponded with the great man and led, or believed they led, more rewarding lives in consequence. But most of the well-meaning attempts at Tolstoyan colonies had foundered in squabbling incompetence, and his doctrines inevitably attracted cranks and neurotics who sought contact with the great writer from motives of vanity, and whose doctrines might appear to justify the situation of people incapable of achievement in their personal lives.

Not unnaturally, the old Count on occasion could become irritated with people of this stamp. "There is neither a Tolstoyan sect nor a Tolstoyan teaching," he rebuked one enthusiast. "There is only one unique teaching, that of truth – that universal and eternal teaching so perfectly expressed, for myself no less than for others, in the Gospels." And when he sensed an unhealthy fanaticism among those who, so to speak, "out-Tolstoyed Tolstoy", he did not hesitate to contradict his own teaching. To a man who urged, just as he had done, universal labour on the land, he replied smartly that it "would be slavery". And another, who outdid Tolstoy's own fulminations against printed literature, he accused of being uncandid and insincere.[13]

Unfortunately Tolstoy himself became greatly dependent on one of these disciples, Vladimir Chertkov. Though intelligent and a sincere follower of Tolstoy's ideas, Chertkov was a devious, vain man, whose ambition was to "manage" Tolstoy. He was largely successful in this, and did much to exacerbate Tolstoy's differences with his wife. He has been suspected with some reason of being an embezzler and thief of Tolstoy's income and manuscripts, and the author was unpleasantly aware at times into what hands he had consigned himself.

The only truly satisfying success in his new life had been his relationship with the schoolchildren of Yasnaya Polyana. He was perpetually entranced by the freshness, imagination and what he saw as the intuitive brilliance of their unspoiled minds, and they in turn adored the great man and were entranced by Tolstoy's stories, tricks and jokes. "He easily won their confidence, and seemed

to have found the key to their hearts," noted his brother-in-law. "I remember his children sometimes running up to him, and telling him they had a great secret; and when they persisted in refusing to divulge it, he would quietly whisper in their ears what it was. 'Ah, what a papa ours is! How did he find it out?' they would cry in astonishment."

With such inspiring guidance it is not surprising that the children worked both industriously and with immense pleasure, producing far better results than others subjected to the insensitive and unimaginative discipline universal at the time throughout Russia and Europe. Was it really necessary for man to grow out of that spontaneous existence, where an idea, a reflexion, an emotion would expand in an instant to fill an entire consciousness? Surely it could not be God's intention that all this should wither away at the age of twelve? If the grim straitjacket imposed by governments were withdrawn from the grown man, would not the result be analogous to his own freeing of the children's minds?

Leo Tolstoy,
by Repin (1909)

Yet it had not worked. Despite the superhuman effect of his own personality, which could win over a man like Chekhov against his will, Tolstoy could see that the world had not changed. Outside the circle of his personal influence, his "movement" comprised many admirable people, but also crowds of oddities and misfits. Worst of all was the situation in his own family. His wife was thoroughly hostile to his way of life, and most of his children rejected it. His whole world was upside-down: he taught universal love – and make his wife wretched; he preached the virtues of poverty – and lived in enforced luxury; he hoped for unity with the Almighty – and spent his time in domestic squabbles; he despised personal vanity – and was surrounded by autograph-hunters and photographers;[14] he denounced the sexual act, even in marriage, as "nasty and criminal lust" – and yet at eighty felt as strongly as ever the "bad feeling"! Once before, on the evening of 17 June 1884, he had suddenly left home on the Tula road. Unable to bear any longer the discordant demands of home and conscience, he contemplated fleeing . . . perhaps to France. But feelings of pity and duty towards his wife had drawn him back.[15]

This time, however, there would be no turning back. He was eighty-two years old, and the fear of death he had experienced since childhood, and which he expressed so vividly in *The Death of Ivan Ilych*, now stalked him remorselessly. In the night hours of the morning of 28 October 1910 he fled secretly from Yasnaya Polyana, leaving behind a note to Sonia.

Leo and Sonia, in his study

"My departure will upset you. I regret it, but understand me and please believe that I could not have done otherwise. My position at home was becoming – has already become – intolerable. Without mentioning anything else, I cannot continue living in the luxury which has surrounded me up to now, and I am doing what most old men of my age generally do: they give up the world to spend their last moments in solitude and silence. Please understand this, I beg you, and don't try to find me, even if you discover where I am. Your arrival will only exacerbate your position and mine, and won't alter anything in my position. I thank you for the forty-eight years of honest life you spent with me and beg you to forgive all the wrongs I've done you, in the same way that I forgive those you may have done me."

It was characteristic that, though these were the true reasons for his departure, the final provocation that drove him to his desperate act was a "Countly" irritation at his wife's intrusion into the privacy of his study. (She was searching for the new will, which, as she correctly surmised, he had recently executed, assigning his literary rights away from her and his children to the unspeakable Chertkov.) He overheard her from his bedroom. "My aversion and indignation grew," he wrote angrily; "I choked and counted my pulse – 97. I could lie there no longer, and suddenly took the final decision to go away." Leo Tolstoy had no more been able entirely to free himself of that notorious Tolstoy family pride (already known to Gogol in 1846)[16] than of his other weaknesses.

In his hurried and rather undignified flight, Tolstoy called at the convent of Shamardino, where his eighty-year-old sister Maria had long been immured as a nun. She was the only remaining survivor of those Elysian childhood days, to which he returned so often in his thoughts. He decided to finish his days there, but on receiving disturbing messages from Sonia and his children, changed his mind and took the train with a vague plan of settling in the sunny Caucasus, where as a young man full of energy, hopes and ideas he had served with the free-riding Cossacks. He was accompanied by his doctor, Dushan Makovitsky, and his youngest daughter Alexandra, who had joined him at the monastery. By a curious chance she had been born early on the morning of 18 June 1884, a few hours after her father's previous flight from home. Now Tolstoy felt closest to her, and was persuaded that she alone of the family understood what troubled him.

But, as the train rumbled slowly towards the South, it became clear that the sick old man was in no condition to travel seven hundred miles in winter. At a little station called Astapovo the party disembarked, and a temporary home for the weakening fugitive was established in the stationmaster's house. Tolstoy was dying, pausing from a journey pursued with relentless conviction but with uncertain destination. He lay feverish, his temperature rising, his heart beating irregularly, wracked by stabbing pains in his head and an unassuageable thirst. From a neighbouring room came the clear voices of the stationmaster's three little children, laughing and singing, a sound which filled him with pleasure.

But it was not long before their insouciant prattle was replaced by the subdued hubbub of visitors hastening from all directions to this obscure spot. The devoted Chertkov, publicity agent and stage manager, arrived at the head of an ever-increasing host of "Tolstoyans", all eager to be linked in person with the approaching event on which the eyes of the world were now fixed. Countess Tolstoy, having missed a train at Tula station, hired her own and arrived with the young Tolstoys, Tatiana (46), Ilya (44), Andrei (33), and Mihail (31). But at the insistence of Chertkov and Alexandra, Sonia was not admitted to see her husband. They feared that in his weakening state the resultant agitation could prove fatal.

Sonia, now quite distraught, paced the railway platform, desperately asking from time to time whether she might not be permitted to see the husband with whom she had lived for forty-eight years. His protectors were adamant: the world's greatest writer must not be disturbed. Meanwhile, a Pathé cine-camera team arrived to immortalize the great moment. They eagerly filmed the station sign, the line, the platform and the stationmaster's house. They could not shoot the great man himself, but did secure delightful scenes of his wife's agitation and distress. Rarely indeed has a humiliation been so public. She went to the window of the house (cine-cameras whirring) to see if she could catch a glimpse of Leo: a considerate hand within drew the curtain across in her face. Eventually she could bear it no longer, and went round to the entrance. She was faced by her twenty-six-year-old daughter Alexandra, who forbade her to enter. The weeping Sonia then pleaded to be allowed to come inside the doorway, so that the clustering mob of reporters and spectators might at least imagine that she had not been turned away by the husband for whom she had sacrificed her whole existence. Alexandra generously permitted this for a few moments, and then returned to the crowded room, where Chertkov and the other elite Tolstoyans peered and whispered in the dark.

For nearly a week the drama persisted. Tolstoy lay, intermittently conscious, in the little house, while Sonia stayed with her sons in her railway carriage, parked in a siding. The ever-increasing horde of reporters fought for space in the neighbourhood, whilst the authorities ordered squadrons of mounted police to prepare for some unspecified emergency. The dying man was troubled by memories. When his wife's secretary approached him, he called out energetically "Masha, Masha!" He thought it was his daughter Maria, who had died four years before. "Many things have fallen upon Sonia," he reflected aloud; but did not reply when his daughter Tania asked if he would like to see her. "I ask you to remember this," he said firmly, raising himself on his bed; "there are plenty of people in this world besides Lev Nikolaevich, and you're only concerned with him." And again: "And the peasants? How do peasants die?" All present strained eagerly forward, committing every word to memory. "Search . . . keep searching." His strength was utterly spent. "I am going somewhere, so that no one can stop me. Leave me alone!" The crowd waited respectfully. Only the occasional distant shouts of the stationmaster's children threw a jarring note on the historic deathbed scene.

Shortly before the end he called for his eldest son Sergei, who had by now also arrived. Sergei came forward and knelt by the bed. A single candle burning by its side cast a light on the patient's pale features.

"The truth," murmured Leo Tolstoy faintly; "I love it so much . . . they all. . . ."[17]

The final sentence remained uncompleted. They were his last words, and just after six o'clock on the morning of 7 November he was dead. Dr. Makovitsky bent over and closed his eyes: a scene Alexandra Tolstoy described to me in May 1979 with deep emotion, as she in turn lay dying.

Leo Tolstoy was buried in a glade at Yasnaya Polyana, at the spot his brother Nikolai had pointed out in their childhood as the resting-place of the little green stick, the talisman of eternal charity, harmony and content. It had been a long, hard, bitter road, but he was there at last.

Glade of the Green Stick, by I. P. Pokhitonov (1905)

10
The Aristocrat at Stalin's Court

*I*n order to ensure the presence of the celebrated writer Count Alexei Tolstoy among her house-guests that summer, the well-known society hostess Valentina Khodasevich took the precaution of sending him an invitation months before, in the winter. The Count was, after all, a great catch. He was the country's most famous novelist and playwright and a nobleman of high rank, and also the richest man below her ruler in all Russia. In country houses and city mansions he was always in demand: charming, affable, talented and generous, his presence ensured the success of any house-party, reception or dinner. Frequently he spent part of the summer at Sorrento in sunny Italy, but this year the troubled political situation in Western Europe was likely to raise difficulties in the path of foreign travel. Perhaps this time Madame Khodasevich would trap the lion!

"My husband and I," she recalled, "invited Alexei Nikolaevich and his wife to come to us in the summer at the village of Dubovo on lake Seliger, where we had a delightful, fair-sized house. That summer we had already several friends staying, and many others lived in the neighbourhood by the lake. Many too were friends of Tolstoy. It was always merry and noisy at our place, so there was nothing to keep Alexei Nikolaevich away – rather the contrary. For the use of guests we kept a couple of yachts and several canoes. The house was situated right on the edge of the lake. . . . Generally we crossed in our canoes to the opposite shore, where there was a marvellously sandy beach.

"At the beginning of August we received an express telegram: 'We've arrived – come to meet us – Tolstoy.' The painter V.S. Basov, who also lived with us at Dubovo, set off early in the morning by steamer to Ostashkov and by eleven o'clock they had all returned by the boat and were at Dubovo.

"We wanted to provide these favoured guests with a worthy reception. On the lake side of the house we had a huge open terrace with a broad flight of steps in the centre. The flooring of the terrace, its steps and balustrades were supported by eight thick pieces of timber, carved in the shape of tall pedestals. We decided to paint them in honour of the solemn arrival of our visitors. On the two lower pillars perched my two tame hawks, already half grown; on the upper two, two ballerinas were to stand *en arabesque* (one of them was the tireless Tatiana Vecheslova, a match for Tolstoy), and on the remaining pillars stood in huge clay pastry bowls an improbably large quantity of bouquets of wild flowers.

"Tolstoy's sleep having been disturbed on the train, he had slept on the steamer and was now quite astonished, recovering himself in a trice. All his luggage was swiftly unpacked, and Alexei Nikolaevich hastened to revel in all the merriment with which Lake Seliger and its picturesque surroundings abounded."

Unfortunately spirits became dampened by the onset of persistent rain, until the Count elegantly paraphrased Cardinal de Polignac's *bon mot* to Louis XIV at Marly, by declaring that for them the rain need not exist. "He convinced us, and we decided to accept, that there was no rain. In any case it did not prevent us from making long trips in our yachts and canoes, from swimming all day long, catching fish, wandering in the woods in search of mushrooms, and calling on acquaintances living on the other bays. In the evenings, occasionally soaked through and shivering after the day's outing, we dried out in front of our huge fireplace. Alexei Nikolaevich seated himself on a large stuffed Pacific tortoise, used as a stool

Previous page: A. N. Tolstoy at the St Petersburg Technological Institute

before the hearth. The rest of us gathered round, lying on the carpet or reclining in the ottoman, and began the most enchanting conversations. Next morning we set out once more to discover new beaches and islands in the setting of Lake Seliger. Thus in the beautiful countryside around a fortnight of uninterrupted idleness slipped by unnoticed, and urgent business was demanding Alexei Niko-laevich's return to Moscow. He had already fallen in love with Seliger (that happened to virtually everyone who came there) so much, that he decided to spend the whole of next summer with us writing the third part of his novel on Peter the Great."[1]

By now most readers may justifiably imagine that we are back in the palmy days of Tsar Alexander III, when peace reigned from the Baltic to the Pacific, the spirit of revolution had been stilled, and the Russian nobility led a life of unimagin-able luxury and pleasure, migrating each summer from gilded palaces in Petersburg and Moscow to great country estates sleeping in the shimmering haze of summer. Splendour and comfort combined to make life one long course of contentment, at least for those privileged enough to enjoy it.

Those unfamiliar with Russian history may be surprised to learn that Count Tolstoy's Elysian holiday was not spent in the summer of 1890 . . . but that of 1940. Twenty-three years earlier Revolution had swept away Russia's aristocracy in torrents of blood, and in their place had proudly risen up the world's first socialist state. In 1918 Lenin stated that "the old bourgeois apparatus – the bureaucracy, the privileges of wealth, of bourgeois education, of social connexions, etc . . . all this disappears under the Soviet form of organization . . . The same thing applies to the best buildings, the palaces, the mansions and manor-houses."[2] This was the theory and Professor A.J.P. Taylor has written sympathetically of the practice, that "the greatest crime of the Soviet Union in Western eyes is to have no capitalists and no landlords".[3] However, the career of Count Alexei Nikolaevich Tolstoy may serve to illuminate some surprising realities of Soviet society.

He was born on 29 December 1882 (old style) at the town of Nikolaevsk, in the province of Samara. His most distinguished near relative was his grand-father's first cousin, Count Dmitri Andreevich Tolstoy, reactionary Minister of the Interior under Tsar Alexander III. This was not however a relationship that Alexei drew attention to in future years, preferring to speak of his connexion with more distant relatives, such as Peter Andreevich (Peter the Great's colleague) and the great Lev Nikolaevich (Leo). It was in the summer of the year of Alexei's birth that the author of *War and Peace* had reached the peak of his disillusion-ment with contemporary existence. "What will be the outcome," he wrote on 31 May, "I do not know, but I am convinced that matters are drawing to a head, and that life cannot continue in its present form."[4] Tolstoy was right, of course; but the career of the cousin, whose birth was taking place almost as he wrote, was to illustrate in a remarkable way the unanticipated paradox of revolutionary change.

The circumstances of Alexei Tolstoy's birth parallel in a striking respect those of another relative, Alexei Constantinovich, the great lyric poet, after whom he was named. His father had been a rake-hell cavalry officer, whose rowdy excesses proved too much even for his fellow hussars. He was obliged to leave his regiment and the two capital cities, and retired to an estate in Samara. There he met and married Alexandra Leontievna Turgenev, a lively girl of good family but slender means. She bore him two sons, Alexander and Mstislav, and a daughter Elizabeth.

But the wild blood of the Tolstoys did not allow him to settle down to an existence of domestic harmony. Within a year the retired hussar had been exiled to Kostroma for insulting the Governor of Samara. When strings were successfully pulled to arrange his return, he celebrated it by provoking a fellow-noble to a duel. This was more than his high-spirited wife could stand. She found life intolerable with the turbulent Count and inevitably fell in love with a staid, kindly young gentleman of suitably liberal and anti-aristocratic proclivities, named Alexei Apollonovich Bostrom.

In May 1882, already two months pregnant with her fourth child, Alexandra fled to the arms of her new lover. The scandal that followed was appalling. The Count loosed off his revolver at Bostrom and was exculpated by the courts, whilst the ecclesiastical court in granting a divorce ruled that the guilty wife should never be allowed to remarry. In order to be allowed to keep the expected baby, Alexandra was compelled to assert that it was Bostrom's child. Ostracized by society and even for some years by her own parents, she left with her lover for Nikolaevsk, where he held a modest post in local government.

It was there that the baby Alexei was born. He was officially registered as the son of Count Nikolai Alexandrovich Tolstoy, but until the age of thirteen he bore the name of Bostrom and believed him to be his father. Given these circumstances, it would not be surprising if the boy's paternity had been called in question. In fact it seems certain he was the son of his mother's husband. It is unlikely that she would have wished, or the registrar have agreed, to give him the surname "Tolstoy" if there were serious doubt of the matter. Similarly, the Tolstoy family would presumably have challenged his resumption of the name in 1895 had they not accepted the legitimacy of his conception. Finally, when his father died in France in 1900 he left a legacy of thirty thousand roubles to Alexei, which he would not have done had he believed the child he had never seen to be another man's bastard.

Despite this, there can be no doubt that the scandal and its aftermath exerted a profound influence on the young man. He had never known any of his family, by whom his mother had been totally rejected, and for the same reason he had never encountered the society his father would have regarded as his by right. The man whom he had accepted as his father was for reasons of circumstance and conviction a bitter opponent of the class to which young Alexei knew himself legitimately to belong. Bostrom maintained his mistress and adopted child on the inadequate income provided by a poor farm. He was a convinced materialist and atheist and (Tolstoy claimed later) avid reader of the works of Karl Marx. In later years Alexei's nature was divided between hatred for that proud class which had cast his mother and him forth into the wastes of Samara, and inordinate pride in the title and name that raised him in his own mind above social ostracism and sordid poverty.

The farm which formed his childhood home was a lonely single-storeyed wooden building, with no neighbours beyond the local villagers. But his mother and adoptive father were a cheerful and devoted couple, and Alexei's earliest years were filled with happiness. Later he lovingly recaptured his impressions of those sunlit days when his world was bounded by the garden and pond of Sosnovka, and the outside world comprised the village of Pavlovka. In 1921, suffering lonely exile, he brought his childhood back to life in the charming autobiographical novel *Nikita's Childhood*. Gleb Struve judged it "worthy to stand beside Leo

Tolstoy's *Childhood* and Aksakov's autobiography", and there must be few readers who would quarrel with that enthusiastic verdict.[5]

In it every corner of the Bostrom home is recreated in loving detail, and Alexei clearly shared with other writers an intense regret for the days of his childhood, when the worlds of reality and imagination were still inextricably merged. But alongside the excitement of the family Christmas tree and snowball fights with the village boys, Nikita finds himself unconsciously growing and changing. The arrival of a pretty little girl, Lilia, brings him to an awareness of powerful emotions of intense happiness, previously purely immanent in all around him. For it is a home filled with love, centred on the adored figure of Nikita's mother Alexandra. Only allusive and incomprehensible references to an unhappy passage in the lives of his great-grandparents, whose portraits hang in a neglected room, provide a hint that love can also bring pain and regret. The book was dedicated to Alexei's young son Nikita, whom he clearly hoped would enjoy as happy a childhood as he had done.

The Nikita of Alexei's memory is understandably a tough little fellow, fearless when faced by rough boys from the hostile end of the village, or an angry bull in the yard. In reality Alexei was not strong, and not markedly courageous. A later acquaintance recalled him at the age of eight, walking in the Strukovsky Gardens at Samara with his mother.

"Near us sat a mother with a fine little boy, not like the other children. The boy was dressed in a dark velvet suit, whose jacket had a large round collar and short trousers. On his feet he wore short socks and shoes tied with ribbons. We liked the boy, and christened him 'little Lord Fauntleroy'. He gave the impression of being rather lacklustre, with a dozy expression and fair ringlets on his head. We tried to talk to him, but he was shy and clung to his mother. His mother, a magnificent blonde, seemed to us a very strict and grand lady. She explained to us that the boy had grown up alone and was shy. We invited him to play hide-and-seek. He took the game very seriously and nearly cried when he was found."[6]

It is not difficult to reconcile this picture with Alexei's self-image portrayed in *The Childhood of Nikita*. A possibly spoiled and over-protected child, the adored focus of an isolated family group, he developed a vivid imaginary existence. Perhaps also one may detect that his devoted mother, resentful of the stigmas of poverty and social ostracism, was determined to shew that her son was as good as any of the offspring of the pompous gentry. It may be seen, too, how Alexei grew up highly self-conscious of the inheritance of the title and name he rightly bore, but which from the unusual circumstances of his upbringing must in reality have appeared a little phantasmagorical. At any rate the most marked characteristics of his adult nature were hatred of poverty, social pride, resentment of the class from which his unknown father sprang, and a brilliant imagination.[7]

As with so many Russian children at that time, little Alexei picked up his earliest education at home. There were lessons with his not over-strict tutor, his mother taught him to read and write, and his stepfather read aloud to them in the evenings from the writings of Tolstoy and Turgenev (to both of whom Alexei was related through his parents). His attention was perfunctory, and in his earliest years it was his imagination and dreams that absorbed his energy. His mother was an amateur writer and poetess of modest abilities but infectious enthusiasm. When he was ten, she urged Alexei to write stories. He did so, and both were delighted to find how easily prose flowed from his pen, despite his inattentiveness at formal instruction. His mother's encouragement bore swift fruit, and with every year his talent became more apparent. Tolstoy himself wrote later that, "looking back, I think that my creative inspiration profited by the loneliness of my childhood years. I grew up alone in contemplation and development among the great images of earth and sky. Summer lightning over the darkened garden; autumn clouds like milk; bare twigs, slithering in the wind over the pond's first ice; winter snowstorms piling snowdrifts up to cottage chimneys; springtime sounds of running water, the cawing of rooks alighting on last year's nests; the rotation of the seasons, birth and death, like sunrise and sunset or the cycle of the grain; animals and birds; red-cased beetles living in cracks in the ground; the scent of ripe apples and of bonfires in twilight dells; my friend Misha Koriashonok and his tales; winter evenings with a book by the lamp, dreaming (I fear I was a poor student) . . . what a succession of wonderful memories can I see and hear with heart-catching intensity. . . ." There was much in later life that was insincere about Alexei Tolstoy, but these words undoubtedly reflected deep emotions.

Proofs of the wickedness of the existing social order his parents found in a close study of the works of Marx and Plekhanov, which also confirmed them in their atheism. Church and society, which had rejected them, were in their turn rejected. More tangible evidence of the *ancien régime*'s iniquity came in the form of the dreadful famine of 1891–92, whose ravages locally made a deep impression on the young Alexei Tolstoy. Despite frantic – and not unsuccessful[8] – efforts by the government, and appeals by Leo Tolstoy, millions died and suffered terribly.

In 1896 the fourteen-year-old boy was sent to school, and in the following year he attended the high school in Samara. There he studied physics, chemistry, engineering and other more practical subjects than those he would have learned had he attended the aristocratic gymnasium. That he resented the unjust discrepancy is perhaps attested by his adoption about this time of his true surname. The farm at Sosnovka had to be sold, and the Bostroms bought a town-house in Samara. Their circumstances were even further reduced, and their ambivalent social position far more galling.

But to the growing boy there were considerable compensations. In the town's excellent public library he came across the dashing adventure stories of Maine Reed, Fenimore Cooper and Jules Verne. These made an indelible impression on his imagination, which always thirsted after what was dramatic, picturesque and vast in concept. All the petty constraints of his life vanished as he roamed with the Deerslayer in the forests of North America or traversed the oceans with Captain Nemo. Science fiction in particular appealed to his love of the fantastic, as did history with its evocation of brilliantly-coloured and widely-differing societies and individuals. After juvenile literature he discovered Victor Hugo, for whom his enthusiasm knew no bounds. "With angry sweeps of his broom," wrote the adult Tolstoy in significant phraseology, "he dispelled the dreary world of petit-bourgeois existence, and drew me into the unknown world of the Great Man." The reassumption of his name and title was clearly attuned to these glamorous discoveries.

In 1898 a touring company performed Lermontov's *Masquerade* in the Samara theatre, arousing too an undying enthusiasm for drama. An actor there introduced him to the name of Maxim Gorky, whose works he was eagerly to explore. Groups of disenchanted youths, among them Tolstoy, used to gather on summer days in the meadows by the Volga. There they raised their voices against the generally unsatisfactory state of the world, and on occasion listened to an orator "with a red beard and pince-nez", who began his speech with the word "Comrades!", talked of Karl Marx, and told of the coming era when class distinctions and feelings of alienation would be relegated to a dusty past. He did not, however, make a great impression on the young Tolstoy, who at the time was absorbed with ideas of a higher humanism, in which bonds of love – the all-embracing love of *Nikita's Childhood* – would override such petty considerations as class and wealth. It was about this time, too, that he fell deeply but distantly in love with an attractive peasant girl.

In May 1901 Alexei finished his studies at the high school. He was eighteen, and suffered from all the inadequacies of his age, accentuated by his peculiar circumstances. In his diary he recorded fears that he was "insignificant, a nobody, stupid, frivolous". He contemplated suicide: "faintheartedness in the struggle to overcome obstacles, apathy towards life arising from the single idea of my misfortune" daunted him; yet he resolved to battle on. His mother frequently tried to encourage him, but from her he now concealed his emotions. Writing alone seemed to console him. None of this made the young Tolstoy very different from his contemporaries; only two things distinguished him: the unusual circumstances of his birth and upbringing, and the dawning awareness of his brilliant abilities as a writer.

Thanks to the unexpected legacy received from his real father, who had died abroad in the previous year, Alexei was now able to take up further studies in St. Petersburg. Eager to join in the exciting throng of student life, he enrolled at a coaching establishment outside the city. Overcoming his former lethargy, he was soon studying for thirteen hours a day. By September he had applied himself sufficiently to obtain a place at the St. Petersburg Technological Institute. After the intensive work required to enter, he found life there delightfully free and easy. Attendance at lectures was not compulsory in any case, and increasing political unrest caused alternating student strikes and police closure to disrupt whatever work was in progress. To a boy from Alexei Tolstoy's sheltered upbringing it was all intoxicatingly exciting. Like most of his comrades, he was hostile to the government and spent much time in heated political discussions. On 12 February 1902 he took part in a protest march on the Nevsky Prospekt which was broken up by police and Cossacks, and he was enrolled in the Institute's Social Democratic Party. He was popular with the students, who elected him to their committees. But his enthusiasm for politics was perfunctory and eclectic, and when the Social Democratic Party split into Mensheviks and Bolsheviks he joined neither grouping. He was essentially a liberal humanist at this impressionable stage of his life. He intensely disliked the existing social system, but thought socialist promises of a coming society as terrestrial heaven too absurd for contemplation.

Besides, life was too rich to batten himself down in such narrow categories. At last he could indulge what was to prove a lifelong enthusiasm for the theatre. There were books, music, art and philosophy to share with his equally enthusiastic contemporaries. The great city was buzzing with intellectual and political ferment, and merely to be there was to be alive. His income was modest, but what of that? "My economy consisted in dining with my aunt and breakfasting at the Institute. Lunch, to my mind, was useless nonsense. I didn't lunch." Instead he would stroll all day in St. Petersburg's beautiful parks, accompanied more often than not by one of the lively and attractive girls for which the capital was famous.

It was here that a far more potent danger lay than in the sabres of the Cossacks.

It was virtually inevitable that a young man of Alexei's warm-hearted and romantic nature should fall passionately in love at the first opportunity. At the age of nineteen in June 1902, he rushed into a hopeless marriage. The girl was Julia Roshansky, daughter of a doctor in Samara, who was also pursuing higher education in St. Petersburg. The effect was once again to isolate the impressionable young man. "I married very early, and this distanced my comrades from me and for a while retarded my spiritual development." He became more intense and serious. Part of his engineering course consisted of practical work in factories, where he learned to respect the workers and despise the bourgeois factory-owners whose caste had already aroused his intense dislike at Samara. His attachment to the movement for radical social reform became greater, particularly after the tremendous revolutionary upheaval of 1905.

January 1906 was spent at his in-laws' home at Kazan, but the next month he travelled to Dresden to further his studies. There he met the attractive, black-eyed young sister of a fellow-student, Sophia Dymshits, who had escaped from a loveless marriage to become a student at Berne. Tolstoy was increasingly fascinated by her, and one day told her brother: "You know, Leo, if I were able to marry again one day, then my wife would be your sister." Aware that Tolstoy already had a wife and child, Leo hastily removed his sister to St. Petersburg. But Tolstoy too came home, and with his wife Julia paid a call at her family home. The calls continued, and eventually he came without his wife. Despite her parents' objections, Alexei continued his pursuit until he finally proposed marriage. By now Sophia was also hopelessly in love but, in view of the fact that they were both still officially married to other partners, she suggested that Alexei and Julia take a trip abroad to come to a final decision. Tolstoy agreed, and set off to Italy with his wife in the summer of 1907. The experiment predictably failed, and within a month he was back.

Despite Julia's intense distress, Alexei departed to set up home with Sophia. His baby son was already being cared for by Julia's family, and he seems to have deserted his little family with no regrets. His second "honeymoon" was spent in a cottage in the wilds of Karelia. For three months he wrote industriously in "The Cat House", as the lovers christened their retreat. His poetry and essays were now being published and receiving increasingly favourable reviews. His mistress was a stimulating companion, devoted to encouraging his literary endeavours. His old life was thrust behind him. He left the Institute without troubling to sit for the examination, and forgot the wife and child of his student days. There were no regrets there, but a bitter blow had been the death of his mother on 25 July 1906. "I never knew since," he wrote, "any woman as exalted, pure and excellent . . . from the day of her death I always felt her presence. And the more involved my affairs, the more intensively I experienced a spiritual existence and the more easily could I sense her nearness."

Another personal tragedy at this time seems to have affected him much less nearly. After returning to St. Petersburg from their love-nest, the couple took the well-trodden path to the Russian Mecca, Paris. Whilst there he heard from Julia that his three-year-old son had died of meningitis – the same dreadful scourge that had struck down his mother. Sophia claimed in a pious official memoir published in Moscow in 1973 that Alexei "took the child's death very much to heart". One may question this. The father, after all, made no attempt to visit his ailing son before his lonely end, nor did he return for the funeral (though he did make another, business, journey to Petersburg from Paris). As subsequent events were to shew, he could evince extraordinary callousness towards individual members of the human race, whatever his broadly liberal viewpoint towards the species at large.

In Paris the couple took up lodgings at 225 rue de Saint-Jacques. The other tenants were of every nationality and calling imaginable, including two African princes who were being educated at the expense of the French Government. Alexei was at pains to stress his Russian origin, appearing everywhere in a fur coat and hat. When spring arrived he took to even more resplendent garb, sporting a top hat and English frock-coat. He was beginning to relish the belated discovery that there were distinct advantages in being Count Alexei Tolstoy, now that he was among people who knew nothing of his humiliating upbringing. It was a happy time. Russian poets and painters crowded Paris, and long noisy sessions continued deep into the night at the restaurant *Closerie de Lilas*. There Tolstoy came to know the poet Constantine Balmont, the painter Elizabeth Kruglikova, and the writers Ilya Ehrenburg and Maximilian Voloshin. In August he wrote to his stepfather that his continued success in writing had earned him extraordinary acclaim among the Paris Russians. The only sour note was scarcely a fair one: "With such a name he ought to do better." Voloshin more shrewdly suggested that Alexei, with his real talent, could profit by it.

"You know, you are an extremely rare and interesting man," he ventured one day. "You certainly ought to be the one to carry on the old tradition of the literary 'nest of gentlefolk'." Tolstoy, he added, should achieve a suitable style and write a massive epic.

Alexei was delighted both with the praise and the advice. He could scarcely write from personal experience of the life of the great nobility, with whom he had no acquaintance; but he portrayed in a series of biting pieces the hog-like existence of the Samara smaller landowning class. He would be more than avenged for all the slights his mother and he had suffered. A note of aristocratic disdain was beginning to obtrude itself; who, after all, were these trans-Volga boors compared with the great House of Tolstoy?

That autumn the couple returned to Russia, and in the summer of 1910 they visited his stepfather Alexei Bostrom at the familiar home in Samara. Alexei received a rapturous welcome, with many neighbours calling to pay their respects to the rising author. The recognition after which he had hankered so long was at last coming his way. His poetry and fiction were becoming widely talked about. In October Gorky wrote: "Look to the new Tolstoy, Alexei – writing without question broad, strong and totally truthful respresentations of the psychological and economic collapse of our contemporary gentry. . . . It will be good and rewarding for you to acquaint yourselves with this new and powerful Russian literature."

It is no reflexion on Tolstoy's literary ability to note that his vivid portrayals were highly subjective. It was from his mother and her relations that he heard tales of the prototypes on whom he based his characters, and real or fancied slights which the irregularity of the Bostrom household aroused cannot but have influenced their attitude. Similarly the romanticized peasants whom Tolstoy contrasts favourably with the self-satisfied gentry must have been based partly on the reality of the boy Alexei's cordial relations with peasant boys at home, but also on their position as a class that could display only respect for the rather grand and correct Mrs. Bostrom. The tales' success was enormous. Sophia provided a glimpse of the enthusiasm with which he wrote them in their flat on the Nevsky Prospekt.

"Usually . . . Alexei Nikolaevich read them to me, avoiding the presence of visitors. But this time he was so thrilled with his stories and so proud of them, that he did not wait for the departure of our guest (a paintress) but came out of his study with the manuscript in his hands straight into the dining-room and, resting his elbows on the back of a chair, stood reading his story. We both responded enthusiastically."

Despite this success, Tolstoy underwent for some time a period of frustration and disillusionment with his writing. He seemed to have exhausted his *métier* and could not find a new road. Later he put this down to the "reactionary" influence of the Symbolist writers with whom he consorted. He was depressed by the appearance of critical reviews, whose effect was the more damaging in that they reflected his own dissatisfaction with the turn his writing was taking. In August 1911 he wrote his first play, but the celebrated Moscow director to whom he showed it tactfully explained that it was "interesting – but too difficult to stage. He also advised me not to have it published, and not to show it to anyone." Tolstoy was realistic enough to accept these cautions in due course. "It was a very nasty, improbable, complicated and boring play," he recalled. "In spite of that I liked it very much."

Another play, about a decadent nobleman, was better, though too much derivative from his "trans-Volga" series and Goncharov's *Oblomov*.

Of these doldrum days, Tolstoy wrote later that "I loved the life, my whole temperament being opposed to an abstract, idealistic outlook. I knew perfectly well that such an existence could not last much longer. I always worked hard, and now I worked even more pertinaciously. But the results were pathetic: I did not see the true life of the country and its people." There was a tense, anticipatory feeling in the air. The failure of the 1905 revolution had secured a return to autocratic rule in Russia, yet there was little feeling of stability abroad. An edgy sort of exhilaration amid the close atmosphere of pre-war Russia conveyed an impression of excitement round the corner. To an artist such excitement offered a challenge, and a way out.

Alexei and Sophia travelled again to Paris, where his second child and her first was born. She was christened Mariana at the Russian church. In the train on the way home to Russia they read a newspaper bearing the news of the assassination of the Prime Minister Stolypin, whose land reforms were fast providing Russia with a stable base lacking since the autocracy's inception. Tolstoy was overjoyed at the news, and to a friend present who angrily objected to this exaltation of murder he replied that one could only rejoice at the killing of a man who had himself been responsible for others' deaths.

By now Alexei Tolstoy was an established literary figure and from the autumn of 1912, when he and his family set up home in the house of Prince Shcherbatov in Moscow, he found himself moving at last in the mansions of the wealthy. Wealthy patrons and literary enthusiasts pressed him with invitations. Sophia remembered later how "they invited us to their *soirées* and salons, because Alexei Nikolaevich impressed them as an established writer of repute from the capital [St. Petersburg], and as a titled man of letters: a Count. They invited me as

Tolstoy's wife and as an artist, whose pictures in 1912 were beginning to appear in exhibitions in Petersburg and Moscow." Understandably, though, he never felt wholly at ease in this new world, and his writings continued to satirize obliquely that class whose homes he frequented. They were, after all, vulgar millionaires with whom his father's family would have scorned to associate. Madame Nosov, for example, "loved to flaunt the fact that her ancestors rose from simple peasants to millionaire merchants," and Sophia would complain, on returning to their flat from scenes of magnificent ostentation, that it was "not the exhilarating atmosphere of art that reigned there, but tasteless bourgeois luxury". What a contrast with their landlord, Prince Shcherbatov, whose house was furnished with refined good taste contrasting strongly with the snobbish vulgarity of upstart millionaires. The Tolstoys resolved to assert themselves.

A. N. Tolstoy, by Bakst, 1909

"Carefully observing the lavish receptions given by these patrons of the arts, we resolved to cut them down to size by arranging a masked ball in our very modest apartments. So many guests flocked to us that we had to take all the furniture out of our five rooms. One room was given over to a buffet. We did not provide a very wide range of dishes: Russian salad, cold veal, champagne and lemonade. Everyone was very amused that the wine and lemonade was standing in ice in the baby's bath! It was the greatest fun. At midnight the cast from the Maly Theatre arrived and put on a show. The place was crammed with every sort of people, from journalists to authors and from painters to art patrons." The latter were overcome with surprise at the brilliance of the evening and Madame Nosov in particular "was amazed at the success of our masquerade and could never understand how people who, judging by the standard of their entertainment must be impoverished Bohemians, could arrange such an effective entertainment".

A general style of grandeur crept into their lives. "My wife, Countess Tolstoy," Alexei would declaim sonorously – despite the fact that they do not appear to have been married. She dressed simply enough, "but Tolstoy appeared like some important noble from the provinces, in a top-hat and huge bearskin cape". In their flat he hung darkened portraits claimed as ancestors before impressionable visitors. To those more perceptive or aware of his upbringing he laughingly admitted buying them in a secondhand shop.

Despite these triumphs, the couple's home life was entering on a troubled period. On holiday in the Crimea in the spring of 1914, Alexei became greatly drawn to a young ballerina, Margarita Kandaurov. The break with Sophia was as abrupt as it had been with Julia. Out on a stroll, Alexei said significantly, "I feel that this winter you're going to leave me." Sophia did not reply, but took the hint and departed for another visit to Paris. The baby Mariana was deposited with an aunt. The outbreak of war in August caused Sophia to return to Russia, but though his seventeen-year-old ballerina soon left him, he and his mistress lived separate lives thereafter. Mariana, however, came to live with her father two years later.

By December Tolstoy had established himself with another mistress, Natalia Vasilievna Volkenstein, who was separated from her husband. They did not marry until after the February Revolution, as Natalia was unable to secure a divorce.[10] She came from a literary household and was herself a poetess of some merit, so the new household started a little more promisingly than its predecessors. In any case the advent of the Great War fully occupied his energies. He was gripped with the war fever that spread like flame across the country. "Brothers, to Berlin!" went up the cry, and no-one was more enthusiastic than Alexei Tolstoy. He became a war correspondent, writing highly patriotic articles for the journal *Russian News*, whilst continuing to work hard on literary productions. The war appeared as a logical outcome – perhaps even a little as a welcome relief – to the strange, listless, impatient and apprehensive decade which had preceded it. Already that summer in the Crimea Alexei had observed just before the outbreak, "the whole world and everyone in it is on the edge of catastrophe."

Russian News catered largely for the intelligentsia, who at this stage of the war were as fervently patriotic and bellicose as the most reactionary supporters of the government. Only Lenin and the Bolsheviks opposed it from the outset, though ultimately it was to prove the major vehicle of their success. With his usual energy, Tolstoy departed at once for the south-western front, where the Russian Army was already engaged with the Austrians. The experience proved extraordinarily vivid and valuable. "I was so tired after four days' uninterrupted galloping in wagons and traps on forest roads in the rain, receiving the unique impression of my life. . . . I reflected so vividly that I fulfilled a whole year of experience in that week, and this is only the beginning of the war."

Alexei already possessed a deep love of the picturesque and dramatic elements of history, as well as the ebb and tide of vast social and political movements sweeping with irresistible force once in a generation or more through the apparently static social condition. He who could understand that elemental flow became part of it and in a sense controlled it. Rattling alongside Plehve and Ruszky's glittering columns as they pushed deep into Galicia, Alexei Tolstoy was participating in events magnificent and gigantic enough to satisfy even his historically-obsessed imagination. His curiosity led him everywhere on horseback, by car and on foot: to staff headquarters, frontline positions, supply bases and hospitals. It was an intoxicating experience, and he felt none of the doubts of Russia's glorious purpose that were to gather as the dreadful struggle hardened and darkened.

. In February of the next year Tolstoy again visited the front, this time in the Caucasus where Russia's southern armies were battling against the Turks. For the moment, however, he seems to have gained the experience he needed, and spent the rest of the year in the two capitals and the Crimea with his wife, engaged in creative writing. Early in 1916, however, he travelled much further. At the request of the British Government, he visited England with a group of Russian writers. Landing at Newcastle, the party travelled by train to London, where they were lavishly entertained at banquets attended by ministers and members of the royal family. They visited King George V at Buckingham Palace and Lloyd George at 10 Downing Street; and, doubtless even more interesting to the young writer, called on the novelists Conan Doyle, Edmund Gosse and H.G. Wells. Britain's immense industrial power and the cohesion and discipline of her people greatly impressed him. Next they were whipped across the Channel to view the front, of which they had an extremely close experience. On 12 March, Tolstoy wrote home to Natalia, who had been prevented from accompanying him by an attack of influenza, that "we have come back from the outpost. We were less than sixty yards from the Germans and Nabokov and I were nearly killed. They threw grenades, two of which burst a few feet away, so that we were covered in mud and smoke. We spent about an hour in the trenches under fire."

All in all, Alexei Tolstoy was excited and flattered by his reception, though the English opinion of *him* was less enthusiastic: "a sleek, fat Bohemian with a great literary talent but a strong predilection for the creature comforts of life", was how the diplomat who invited him described him.[11]

On 18 March Tolstoy was back in Petrograd, as the capital had been patriotically rechristened. As the war ground on its bloody course Tolstoy detached himself again into creative and even escapist fiction, beginning a tale seemingly derived from H.G. Wells's *The First Men in the Moon* with a similar, though inferior, blend of scientific and sociological imagination. The motivation may have been once again Tolstoy's instinctive attraction to what was wild, exotic and grandiloquent, coupled with an experimental desire to establish the genre for which his talents qualified him. As many writers have experienced, he combined a burning conviction that he was capable of something sublime with a profound dissatisfaction for his current achievements. Critical acclaim did little to dispel his restless strivings.

But an event was now pending so enormous that its gale was to sweep him and millions of others with terrible force into a whirlwind of turmoil, agony, creation and destruction. In February 1917 the unfortunate Tsar Nicholas abdicated and the Provisional Government took his place. Natalia was in hospital, where she had given birth to a son Nikita a few days earlier.*

Alexei's attitude to the fall of the monarchy and the Revolution was one of

---

* Strictly speaking, Nikita was illegitimate, and neither he nor any of his descendants living in the USSR should be reckoned as Tolstoys. The couple were not married until 7 May 1917, but three weeks later they took care to have the baby christened.

unbounded enthusiasm and optimism: hopes probably shared by the vast majority of the population. His view from the beginning had been that out of all the suffering the nation would arise forged anew. He had believed that "our chaos of mental disarray and debility, of introspection and party struggle – all suddenly recedes, like the sea from its shores." Poor military organization and leadership merely confirmed that all that was needed for the liberation of beneficent Russian energies was the removal of the corrupt bureaucracy of the autocracy. Now that had happened, in "the most bloodless Revolution in history," and hope untrammelled seemed to reign, particularly for poets and thinkers.

He had recently been working for the Minsk *Zemstvo*, helping in the daunting task of providing services for the troops with hopelessly inadequate resources.[12] Now he was appointed Commissar for the Registration of Printing, with responsibility for direction of the new art forms the Revolution would bring in its train. Emigré writers returned to the homeland. On the Kuznetsky Bridge in Moscow literary figures gathered at the Trefoil Café, and there of an evening one could hear recitations of their latest works by Tolstoy and his wife, the poetess Marina Tsvetaeva, or the newly-returned Ilya Ehrenburg, whom Alexei had known in Paris. A writers' union was formed with Tolstoy on the committee, and an astonishing literary renaissance flowered for an all too brief period. Caught up in the centre of these great events, Tolstoy read widely in Russian history and began intensive research into that other period of revolutionary change, the reign of Peter the Great.

But disillusionment was tragically swift to arrive. The Provisional Government was determined to bring the war to a successful conclusion, and Alexei Tolstoy was among those who laid greatest stress on vindicating "national honour". But events on the front proved increasingly disastrous, and the Bolsheviks began to gain widespread support from their stance as the only party to advocate an instant cessation of hostilities, whatever the terms. Prime Minister Kerensky's belief that revolutionary enthusiasm would prove an effective substitute for military discipline was dispelled by the inexorable advance of the German armies. Then, as the summer wore on, and Bolshevik agitation increased, Kerensky lost his nerve. In August he ordered General Kornilov to advance on Petrograd to restore order. But as Kornilov began preparations, Kerensky panicked again and appealed to the Bolsheviks to protect him from Kornilov. The perplexed Kornilov was arrested and the Bolsheviks prepared themselves at last to seize power. In October they struck and, after brief fighting in the capitals, the Provisional Government ignominiously melted away. Initially not much more blood had been shed than in the February Revolution eight months earlier, but the struggle had only just begun.

Bolshevik propaganda was skilful and effective, above all in its promises to end the war and give the land to the peasants. War-weary soldiers and land-hungry peasants responded largely by taking the law into their own hands, but widespread sections of the population were equally determined not to suffer lawlessness and abject surrender to the enemy they had been fighting at such terrible cost for three years. Alexei Tolstoy was among the latter. Kerensky's faith in the uplifting if indeterminate virtues of liberty, equality and fraternity was strongly echoed by Tolstoy's own liberal humanist enthusiasm.

The first angry days of the Bolshevik coup in Moscow were spent by the Tolstoys in a temporarily blockaded flat. Two stray bullets had ricocheted off the dining-room windowsill, and improvised screens of carpets and cupboards swiftly barricaded every window. The children (Mariana and Nikita) slept in a window-less bathroom, whilst everyone else found refuges in corridors and corners out of the line of fire. The occupants of the house took it in turns to oversee the main entrance, where a samovar boiled night and day to provide mugs of tea for armed skirmishers darting in for a moment's respite. One of their visitors, a leather-jacketed blond youth, re-emerged into the street and shot down two officer-cadets before their eyes. On another occasion a combatant was killed and his body dragged to rest on their front steps. When in a few days it was possible again to move about the streets, groups of puzzled citizens could be seen gathered before placards posted up by the Bolshevik victors. Tolstoy was greatly struck by a snatch of conversation he overheard at one point. "Russia is finished!" groaned an elderly man. "It's finished for you, daddy," cheerily replied a voice from the crowd; "but for us it's only beginning!"

Tolstoy shared his fellow-intellectuals' fear and disquiet at what was happening. A Revolution was, after all, meant to be a cultural experience (Tolstoy had frequently emerged into the streets during the week of fighting to gain an artistic impression of the real thing).

"The truth is," he wrote on 4 December, "that we thought we were approaching a beautiful lady dressed in a *kokoshnik* and blue *sarafan*, sweet and good-natured." But face to face, "we recoiled in horror. . . . Who is this terrible, wild being, with her soiled clothes, up to the elbows in blood and wounds, and with distorted, tortured, mad face? I don't recognize you! Who are you?" The intellectuals' lament was beginning. Tolstoy contemplated emigration to Switzerland, but decided against it. Life continued, after all, and his work was still being published. A few very able men had actually accepted the new order. Mayakovsky was brimming over with enthusiasm for the Bolsheviks, and urged Alexei to join him. "Ah, Count! Accept my invitation to a proletarian bonfire, Your Excellency! Make yourself at home."

But the Count was not amused. Ehrenburg, who was close to him at the time, later gave a sardonic description of his indecision. "In 1917–1918 he was lost, unhappy, sometimes depressed; he could not understand what was happening. He sat in the writers' café 'Bom', attended the house committee, cursed everything and complained about everything – but above all, he was puzzled. . . . He observed the cowardice of the people, the small-mindedness, but did not himself know what to do. Someone shewed me the brass plaque on his door inscribed 'Count A.N. Tolstoy', and muttered ' "Count" to some, but "Citizen" to others!' But he laughed at that himself."

As the political climate darkened over that winter, privation bit hard at every-one, whatever his position. "No supper tonight," declaimed the servant, returning empty-handed from the market. "No provisions today," announced a notice outside a shop – "and none tomorrow," as a wit had inscribed beneath. Jam pancakes and black coffee could keep the family alive a little longer, but how much? At last they decided to leave Moscow and travel south to Odessa, with visions of sea-bathing and vineyards. In June 1918 the whole family, excluding Mariana who was left behind with her mother Sophia, set off by train to Kursk and then on to Odessa. In order to cement their hold on the country the Bolsheviks had made a disastrous peace at Brest-Litovsk in March 1918, whereby the richest and most populous parts of southern Russia were ceded to the Germans. Odessa was in their hands, and there Tolstoy was safe from the Bolsheviks, to whom he was now thoroughly hostile. ("I would not hesitate to put out the eyes of Lenin and Trotsky with a rusty bradawl, if they fell into my hands.") He earned a small wage working in a gambling-den.

But events moved chaotically fast in those hectic days of 1918. Germany was defeated by the Allies in November, and forced to evacuate Russian territory. Her garrison at Odessa was replaced by a French expeditionary force, despatched in the first place to help anti-Bolshevik White forces restore the front against Germany, and then to join directly in the fight against Soviet power. By the spring of 1919 the French in turn found themselves obliged to withdraw. As their fleet prepared to sail, thousands of terrified Russians crowded the quays in a desperate effort to escape the Red Terror, which was unleashed a few days later. The Tolstoys were among the lucky ones, and in June they found themselves in Paris.

The city was crowded with Russian refugees of every type and class. Princes and generals swept streets, waited in cafés and, if they were lucky, drove taxis. The Tolstoys were no exception amid the general misery. Staying at first with friends, and later in a flat in a house crowded with Russians, they were totally dependent on what work Natalia could find as a seamstress. Alexei was greatly depressed at this life of privation, which was not many degrees better than that which he had left Moscow to escape. He missed acutely the old life of ease and amusement. The Revolution had come at just the wrong moment. After years of struggle he had begun to achieve artistic recognition and material success, while here he was worse off than he had been in 1908 when he had only a hundred roubles in the world. Now, as then, he found his refuge "in the troubled waters of literature".[13]

Fresh from the extraordinary events he had witnessed during recent years, he plunged into work on an epic novel with the Revolution as its setting. Here was a theme even more earth-shaking than the Napoleonic wars his great relative had employed. The central intent of the book was to be the effect of this whirlwind on the intelligentsia, who had been uprooted and hurled about the face of the earth. They experienced the unfolding melodrama, but failed to comprehend it. This conception and much else in the novel were of course unashamedly autobiographical. Tolstoy sensed his good fortune in being presented with a theme such as no writer in the world before had known, but can have had no conception of the nature of the task lying ahead. More than twenty years were to pass before he completed it, by which time both he and the events in which his inspiration moved had changed and changed again. And in the very hour that his task was completed, a fresh cataclysm seized upon him and bore him and millions up in its swell.

The novel was the trilogy whose title (*Khozhdenie po Mukam*) is generally translated into English as *The Road to Calvary*, though a more correct interpretation would be *Pilgrimage through Torment*. Soon afterwards he broke off to write *Nikita's Childhood*, the touchingly evocative autobiographical novel described earlier. Clearly the most vivid and painful nostalgia gripped him, as it did his fellow-émigrés. Somehow his writing (sold to émigré publishing houses) and Natalia's sewing kept them going. Less reputable and more lucrative sources of income were funds begged from rich French families, whom he flattered to their faces and traduced behind their backs. Still worse was the sale (for 18,000 francs) to a speculator of his non-existent estate in Russia. Alexei took this hand-to-

mouth existence very badly, railing continually against the futility of their existence. The pathetic politics, quarrelling and introspection of the émigrés annoyed
him. He did not belong to all this. "Take Europe," he exclaimed one day to his
wife; "this cemetery. The whole time I smell the stench of decay. . . . To live
surrounded by corpses! I hate the people. We've got to get out of it." His wife
asked him where he wanted to go to. He did not reply, but the trend of his
thinking was clear. In Russia the likeness to a vast cemetery and the stench of
corpses was horribly literal. But it was in Russia that Alexei's roots lay and where
his inspiration had flowered.

The family shifted aimlessly from one home to another. The next year they
took a cottage in Brittany, where megalithic columns stood expressionlessly in
forest clearings overlooking the white-flecked Atlantic. But, lamented Alexei to
himself, "the artist's place isn't here, amid these Cyclopean stones and solitude,
whose stillness is only broken by the murmur of the breakers; but amid that
boiling turbulence, there, where out of tortured suffering a new world is being
born." The White armies had been crushed in a welter of bloodshed, except where
Baron Wrangel's army held out in the Crimea. On 25 April the Poles had invaded
Russia, and all that summer war burned across the Ukraine and Byelorussia. The
Soviet state (the name of Russia was soon abolished) was fighting for its existence.
Like all the émigrés, Tolstoy followed events in the East with avid interest,
though as yet no personal concern.

In 1921 the family was again by the sea, near Bordeaux. Alexei was more
irritable and restless than ever. Little Nikita already spoke with faults in his
Russian, saying *catastrophe* for *Katastropha*. His father, muttering angrily that
his son was no longer a Russian, left for Paris. A letter arrived a few days later.
Over her morning coffee, Natalia read his ultimatum.

"Life has drawn to the point of death. . . . I'm burning everything behind me; it
is necessary to be born again. My work demands swift decisions. Do you grasp the
imperative purpose of these words? We must go back. Get rid of the flat. We'll go
to Berlin and, if you like, further still."

That Tolstoy began at this time to feel an irresistible tug of the heart towards
the Motherland, the *rodina*, is what this account by his wife implies and what all
Soviet biographers have asserted since. It is, however, open to serious doubt. It
may well be that he was, like any good Russian, upset at the thought of his son's
growing away from the traditions of his ancestors, and that the quoted letter to his
wife is authentic. But the sentiments were certainly far from representing any
settled conviction. In his own letters written at the very time from Bordeaux he
himself employed unashamed Gallicisms such as *komfortabelny*, 'comfortable'
(instead of the more Russian *uyutny*). And when, a few months later, his family
moved as planned to Germany, he wrote enthusiastically of their improved standard
of living. In January 1922 he still had no intention of going to the USSR, declaring that "if I get something for the staging of my play, then I'll be secure for the
summer." In 1921 he had certainly been discontented with his poverty in France,
but did not seriously contemplate abandoning life as an émigré.[14]

In October 1921 the family migrated to Berlin, where Tolstoy became a col-
laborator on the journal *Nakanune* ("On the Eve"). *Nakanune* was the organ of a
group of dissatisfied émigré intellectuals who, in combination with Soviet writers,
urged that the only future for Russians lay within Russia herself, and as that today
meant Lenin's Russia there was no alternative to supporting the Bolsheviks'

efforts to restore the shattered country. Berlin was at that time a meeting-place for the different shades of Russian opinion. Amongst other gifted writers congregated there was Maxim Gorky, who had come in the opposite direction from Tolstoy, having left the Soviet Union recently sick and depressed by what he had experienced.

The two well-known writers collaborated for a while on *Nakanune*, but a split was inevitable. Gorky had broken with Lenin, angered by the increasing intolerance of the Soviets towards any form of intellectual dissent, fearful of the savagery perpetrated by peasants in the countryside, and revolted by the ever-increasing cruelty in general. Tolstoy on the other hand regarded Russia's tragedy as a sublime source of literary inspiration and, at least in the abstract, held no marked aversion to cruelty. Where Gorky expressed horror at the account of a victim who had been compelled to wind his own entrails onto a stake, Tolstoy saw only proof of the tragic grandeur of the Russian spirit.[15] At the Russian club attached to the Soviet diplomatic mission Tolstoy met his old friend Mayakovsky, whose continuing enthusiasm for the Bolsheviks greatly influenced him.

The decision was by now inevitable. In May Tolstoy visited Moscow, to receive a hero's welcome. He was received ecstatically by writers, actors and producers, and addressed a packed meeting on the subject of the contemptible nature of the White emigration and the degradation of art in the West. Public and press attention was overwhelming, in sharp contrast to the increasingly hostile attitude of the White Russians in Paris. Returning in a few weeks to Berlin to retrieve his family, he penned his farewell to emigration in *Nakanune*. "I am leaving with my family for the homeland, for ever. If there are people here abroad close to me, my words are addressed to them. Do I go to happiness? Oh, no: Russia is going through hard times. Once again she is enveloped with a wave of hatred . . . I am going home to a hard life."

There can be little doubt that his professed motives were real; both before and after his exile Tolstoy's writings reveal intense patriotism, together with what a Western writer termed "unquenchable, visceral love for his land, for its very sounds, smells, and landscapes which played the decisive role in bringing him to the decision to return to Soviet Russia".[16] But neither this, nor his professed belief that it was Lenin and the Bolsheviks alone who could extricate Russia from her terrible predicament, can satisfactorily explain his dramatic decision.

It is the words "I am going home to a hard life" that are impossible to accept in any sense of the words. If there was one thing that Alexei Tolstoy hated above all else, it was any sort of hardship or privation. Everyone who knew him, Whites and Reds, friends and wives, is unanimous in testifying to his lifelong dread of poverty and corresponding love of comfort, luxury and wealth. "He liked the good things of life with a love often encountered among members of the shabby-genteel families who suddenly come into money."[17] It was not only material comforts that he treasured: it was essential to his well-being that *everything* around him should radiate pleasure. If one city or country house proved unstimulating he shifted to another. When a wife no longer fulfilled his expectations by growing dull or old, he selected another; they remained on good terms, since if there was one thing he abhorred more than an unwanted wife it was a strident scene.

A friend, Kornei Chukovsky, who knew him well, tells how he "always craved for happiness, like a little child, he craved for laughter and celebrations; but gloomy, frowning people were spiritually alien to him. . . . In general he was psychologically incapable of listening to accounts of unlucky events, illnesses, misfortunes and infirmities." Chukovsky himself, a friend of thirty years' standing, experienced a striking instance of this aversion. During the Second World War he was walking one day with Tolstoy in the Tashkent Botanical Gardens, when he rashly began a conversation by saying flippantly: "Now, when we're both old men, clearly, very soon about to die. . . ."

Tolstoy fell silent, replied not a word, but scarcely had they returned home and gained the threshold than he announced to the household: "Never again will I walk anywhere with Chukovsky. He talked so vi-i-ilely on the way."[18]

How can it be explained, then, that Count Tolstoy was prepared to abandon the relative comforts and limitless freedom of life in Paris or Berlin for a country just emerging from the devastation of the Great War, the Revolution, the Civil War and the Polish war? Stricken with famine and disease, it was ruled by a self-proclaimed dictator whose aim was enforced egalitarianism and physical destruction of the wealthy and privileged. As Tolstoy himself admitted in his reply to an émigré's reproaches, Russians now "live, it is true, badly, hungrily, lousily. . . ." His patriotism is not in question, but how could such a sybarite without any evident qualms voluntarily have immersed himself in so horrifyingly harsh an environment?

In fact he never experienced the "hard life" of which he wrote, and it seems certain that he never expected to do so. Clearly he would not have contemplated return without the motives already noted: a profound patriotism and *nostalgie de la boue*. It was probably Mayakovsky who finally persuaded him to take the crucial step in Berlin, together with overtures from members of the Soviet diplomatic mission. (Some fifteen years ago I received a similarly flattering invitation from a high Soviet official.) They would certainly have assured him as to the social status he would enjoy in a society where the artist was for the first time freed from the degrading shackles of bourgeois patronage. On a more prosaic level it was clear that Mayakovsky and others like him enjoyed a comfortable standard of life, unaffected by the appalling tribulations suffered by ordinary Russians.

Hatred of the bourgeois found a ready echo in Tolstoy's heart. Real or fancied slights suffered during his youth at Samara, the supercilious ostentation of rich merchant patrons during his rising Moscow days, and what he took to be the smug indifference of the wealthy in Paris and Berlin had left him with a burning hatred for their whole class. At first he had also felt indignation against the old aristocracy, which in the person of his father's family had displayed such cruel neglect towards his mother and himself. But his father was dead, and Alexei had long discovered that his name and title brought him unshakable social recognition. His associates tended to be Bohemian artists who affected to disdain hereditary rank and privilege, but whose every response betrayed intense pleasure, romantic or snobbish, in the illustrious (as well as conveniently literary) antecedents of their easy-going friend. Amongst them Count Alexei Tolstoy was the nobleman *par excellence*, a rôle he clearly enjoyed. It was from an essentially aristocratic point of view that he despised the wealthy middle class and felt attraction towards the unspoiled and respectful peasantry.*

There was of course an element of risk in return. The distinguished historian

* The Italian film director Visconti is said to have become a Communist for similar motives.

Prince Dmitri Sviatopolk-Mirsky, for example, returned to the USSR in a fervour of enthusiasm in 1932. He had become a convinced Communist, and was eventually repaid for his loyalty with a one-way ticket to a GULAG camp.[19] But Tolstoy possessed the great advantage of *not* being a sincere Communist. He too had a profound knowledge of history, which enabled him to take a much more perceptive view of the situation. It had always been the great cataclysms of history that fascinated him. In 1934 he was to contemplate writing a novel on the fall of the Roman Empire.[20] Already, in 1918, he had translated the German Georg Büchner's *The Death of Danton*, a play whose overriding theme is the pointlessness of revolutions, which spill torrents of blood only to return full cycle to their starting-points. Above all, he had been fascinated since the age of sixteen by the career of Peter the Great, who had engineered a political and social revolution fully comparable to that of the Bolsheviks. In the same year as *The Death of Danton* Tolstoy published a twenty-five page novella entitled *Peter's Day*, describing in vivid terms the appearance and character of the great Tsar. In strong contrast to his later writing on the same subject, the overall picture is distasteful and depressing. Though touched at moments by a tragic grandeur, Peter is represented as a barbaric tyrant, all of whose efforts to turn Russia upside down are doomed to failure. The human condition is too heavily rooted to be altered by the efforts of individuals, however powerful and determined.[21]

In particular it was clear that every single revolution in history, however ruthlessly egalitarian its aims, had resulted in the appearance of a fresh ruling class as wealthy and privileged as its predecessor, and not infrequently obliged to be a great deal more ruthless in its determination to preserve hard-won gains. One is reminded of the reply of the former private soldier, Napoleon's General Junot in 1803, when "asked what steps he would take if there should happen an insurrection of the people: He clinched his fists and with a terrible scowl replied '*il n'en resteroit pas un*'."[22]

It cannot have escaped Tolstoy's notice either that on parallel occasions in the past clever and unprincipled members of the dispossessed ruling group (such as Talleyrand) had found it possible to make the transition to a comparable place in the new oligarchy. After all, the most striking example in Russian history of such a successful transference was one in which Alexei Tolstoy had a strong personal interest. It was his ancestor Peter Tolstoy who, as a partisan of his uncle Ivan Miloslavsky, had been the principal instigator of the murders of Tsar Peter the Great's uncle and other relatives in 1682. Yet when Peter triumphed, Peter Tolstoy played his cards so skilfully as to become one of the new Tsar's principal advisers. Yet another "Napoleonic" parallel lay in the career of Mihail Tukhachevsky, who shared with the Tolstoys a descent from the fourteenth-century Indris. The former Tsarist officer Tukhachevsky's ruthless ambition and dashing military capacity had raised him at the age of twenty-seven to the position of Commander-in-Chief of all Soviet forces on the Polish front in 1920.

Everything suggests that Alexei Tolstoy's historical and personal assessment of the Revolution of 1917 led him to the conviction that it would inevitably follow the pattern of previous revolutions in throwing up a ruling class of its own. As has been seen, he took the sensible precaution in the summer of 1923 of checking on conditions in the USSR before returning to Berlin to collect his family and take the irrevocable step. He was right in supposing that members of the Soviet elite from the moment of seizure of power would enjoy a grandiose life-style of ever-increasing luxury;[23] but it is the subsequent career of Count Alexei Tolstoy himself which illustrates the point most effectively.

On 1 August 1923 the Tolstoy family returned to Soviet Russia and set up home. Not surprisingly, it took Alexei some time to come to terms with the realities of Soviet intellectual existence. The first gush of revolutionary exhilaration was still in full flow, and dozens of new art-forms were being trumpeted by eager advocates. They ranged from the undeniably great (Mayakovsky and Blok) to inane, eccentric and even insane groups of "artists" who believed that any form of unreflecting self-expression constituted a revolutionary art-form. Tolstoy, of course, was traditional in his approach, holding strongly by purity of diction, richness and accuracy of description, and dramatic unity of plot. All these concepts were in varying degrees anathema to rival authors banding themselves together in the schools of Proletkult and Forge, VAPP or RAPP, Constructivists, Expressionists, Futurists, Neorealists, Simple Realists, Imaginists, Romantics, Serapions and the like.

The most important and hostile of these was RAPP: "the Russian Association of Proletarian Writers", which at this time bore semi-official status under the Party. RAPP was not only opposed to all forms of "bourgeois" art ("In the name of our tomorrow – burn Raphael, destroy the museums, trample down the flowers of art!") but even objected to artists who did not possess pure proletarian ancestry. Alexei Tolstoy, who was as far as possible from possessing this qualification, was an especial target for vilification. Even before his final return, he was claimed to be "scrubbing the white horse of his *Complete Works* in anticipation of a triumphant entry into Moscow."[24]

For nearly a decade Tolstoy frantically struggled to find a literary rôle that would simultaneously be an expression of the best of which he was capable, and at the same time satisfy the revolutionary vigilance of RAPP and other Party watchdogs. This was not easy. Before his return he had never really discovered his true *métier*, his only completely rewarding work being the unrepeatable *Nikita's Childhood*. There were points of contact, of course. His satirical, but not altogether unaffectionate, portrayals of decadent pre-Revolutionary society could pass muster with Lenin's followers, as could his more strident exposés of the futile existence of squabbling émigré intellectuals. But though his sympathies lay entirely with the Communist victors, his type of picaresque narrative, rich in historical detail and vivid characterization, was not what appealed to the enthusiasts of RAPP.

What they wanted from history were neat parallels presaging the ultimate Communist triumph, together with exaltation of heroic figures identified as unwitting precursors of Marxist fulfilment as apotheosized in Lenin and Trotsky's victory in 1917. The biographies of savage Cossack bandits like Stenka Razin and Pugachev, against whom Tolstoys had fought in the seventeenth and eighteenth centuries, were altered beyond historical recognition in order to represent them as popular saviours, dimly conscious of their self-sacrificing rôle in Marx's pattern of predestination. The record for this sort of prescience was probably held by the slave-hero of A. Glebov's play *Zagmuk* (1926), set in Ancient Babylonia. In a lyrical passage he foresees the coming of the October Revolution, only twenty-seven centuries away.

"I see an end to this night. What does it matter if I perish myself? . . . I know that another man – a great and fortunate one – will pick up my torch and disperse the darkness with it!"

Even this politicized rewriting of history was insufficient to satisfy the more advanced writers' revolutionary consciousness. Some Futurists held that language itself must be freed from the shackles of its bourgeois-dominated past. Vasily Kamensky's play *Stenka Razin* (1919) contained exciting specimens of this breakthrough in communication. Enter a group of peasants in a thunderstorm:

"1st: Ogo-go. Ogo-go. Grrr . . .
2nd: Zhzhzhy . . . zhzhu . . . zhzhu . . .
3rd: Chur, chur, chur, chur, . . .
4th: Khkho-kho-kho. Bzzz . . .
5th: Byz-byz-byz-byz . . ."

And so on.[25]

Against this Tolstoy could only continue to plough his own furrow, lose no opportunity of flattering the ailing Lenin with abject asseverations of loyalty and obedience, and argue at times in spirited fashion in defence of his literary motivation. "We don't need fractionary literary groups. We want talent," he stressed in dignified protest; advocating instead "monumental realism" and literary recreation of the rich speech of the Russian masses. But he knew well the dangers which menaced him in such a society. Several factors probably served to protect him during the early years of his return. Lenin himself, whose attitude to literature was largely utilitarian, came to consider the various proletarian cults as divisive and harmful.[26] Then there was the return of Maxim Gorky to the Soviet Union in 1929. Though he and Tolstoy had agreed to disagree in Berlin in 1923, Gorky had at last taken the same path. He was in any case an admirer of Tolstoy's work, and in view of his enormous international prestige was prized and cosseted by Stalin. This made him a very powerful protector. Finally, there is the simple fact that Tolstoy's writing afforded the public a great deal of pleasure. Proletcult and other *outré* forms of literary expression could on occasion be highly dramatic and included some striking achievements. But to the half-starved Russian public, living in conditions of inconceivable discomfort and drabness, all these wild or earnest endeavours appeared more or less depressing. What they wanted were excitement, colour and romance in their reading, and magnificent costumes, splendid sets and dramatic dénouements in their play-going. All these Tolstoy provided in abundance. In March 1925 his play *The Empress's Plot* was performed in Moscow, and swiftly achieved a *succès d'estime*. It was in fact a rather vulgar, melodramatic, but not wholly inaccurate, representation of court life under Nicholas II, culminating in the sort of set-piece at which Tolstoy excelled: the murder of Rasputin. The play was politically acceptable in that it necessarily portrayed the Romanovs in a poor light, but what the audience loved was the excitement, the glittering court uniforms, ball gowns, gilt furniture, rich hangings, and so forth.

The Empress's Plot was violently attacked by Tolstoy's opponents in *Izvestia* and other organs, but Tolstoy continued unrepentant. A year later crowds flocked to see his *Azev*, the story of a real-life agent-provocateur who worked simultaneously for the Tsarist police and the revolutionaries. Once again plots and counter-plots abounded, and the evil Azev appeared as black as ink.

Tolstoy's proletarian detractors again objected, adding to their previous strictures the fact that Azev's villainy appeared quite unmotivated. The author struck back with a pamphlet vindicating his reintroduction of the classic villain. His viewpoint was unashamedly patrician, though tricked out with a specious appeal to socialist realism. In the good old days of drama, he explained, villains' hearts had been as black as pitch, or as their sweeping cloaks and broad-brimmed hats. It was the wretched bourgeois who demanded the introduction of domestic dramas, where vulgar dentists, lawyers and their neurotic wives drank tea and snivelled their way through some sordid marital misunderstanding. No room there for sneering, blackavised bravoes, who swindled, lied and murdered their way through every scene.

Tolstoy knew his public, who supported him with enthusiasm. This included the Soviet leadership, which saw no harm in such an enjoyable release of popular frustration, and indeed shared the public's naïve pleasure. Tolstoy's defence of villainy caught on with the playwrights, and in the same year I. Platon brought out what must surely be the classic of its kind. *Arakcheevshchina* portrayed typically everyday scenes on a Tsarist estate. A summary provides the flavour of the play, which was presumably not for the fainthearted:

"Life on the Arakcheev estate in the play consists of almost continuous debauchery on the part of the owners as well as monks from the nearby monastery and of indescribably painful suffering on the part of the serfs. In preparation for a visit from Tsar Alexander, the General orders the prettiest girls brought in from surrounding villages; for one month they are scrubbed and polished so that the Tsar can choose bedmates from among them. In another scene, Arakcheev's mistress, furious over a missing glass of liqueur, tortures some of the serfs to the point where several commit suicide to escape their misery. The breaking point finally comes when the serfs rise up and murder the mistress. In a fit of revenge, the General has all of them tortured – some before the audience. Platon's naturalism goes so far as to display in one scene the bloody severed finger of Arakcheev's mistress."

Such was show business in 1926.[27]

But despite his successes Alexei knew that his critics were dangerous men, who made ample play of his aristocratic and White émigré background. He took to setting his novels in outer space, and gave them fantastic plots that stood (as he hoped) outside ideology. Already in Berlin he had published *Aelita*, which concerned an expedition to Mars, the love of its leader for the beautiful Martian girl Aelita, and the attempt of a Soviet agitator to lead the Martian proletariat to revolution. *Engineer Garin's Hyperboloid* is the story of a megalomaniac capitalist's scheme to rule the world, and *Seven Days in Which the World Was Robbed* explains how a group of dishonest American capitalists sought to gain world power by blowing up the moon. The standard of writing is on the whole inferior to that of similar adventure stories in the contemporary English *Boy's Own Paper*, and reflects what so many of his friends found his most endearing characteristic: his ebullient childishness.

None of this, however, can have been very satisfying to the ambitious author. Tolstoy does not give the impression of having been very critical towards his own work, most of which he appears to have regarded as being of a very high standard. But there can be no doubt that it is by his two *chefs d'oeuvres* that he would wish to be remembered: the epic novels *Pilgrimage through Torment* and *Peter I*. During the troubled twenties and early thirties he devoted much time to researching and writing these massive works. For the first he travelled widely in Russia, interrogating countless survivors from Voroshilov downwards. And for his fictionalized biography of Peter the Great he not only saturated himself in literature of and about the period, but surrounded himself with Petrine impedimenta precious and trivial. His collection must eventually have been extremely precious, containing as it did portraits and holograph letters of the great Tsar. But the small chance artefacts of everyday life fascinated him equally. The sickle held by the wondering peasant who from the door of his hut watched Peter's ships glide down the Don from Voronezh was to Alexei as important an evocation of the past as the telescope used by Peter at the siege of Narva. Like many good historical novelists, he was an historian manqué.

Both works absorbed the major part of his working life. The earliest section of *Pilgrimage through Torment* had already been published in Paris during his period of exile in 1920–21. Instalments of the second part of the trilogy appeared in the Soviet literary journal *Novy Mir* from 1927, under the title *1918*, and the final section (*Gloomy Morning*) from 1940. The whole work did not appear in volume form until 1943.[28] It is a work of very uneven character. The opening passage, with its unforgettable picture of doom-laden St. Petersburg in 1914, at once introduces the reader to the best of Alexei Tolstoy: marvellous attention to apt detail, evocatively rhythmic language, and an ability to bring a vast canvas to turbulent life – reflecting perhaps his earlier ambition to be a painter. The novel sprawls, but it is a sprawl in keeping with the vastness of the historical events and geographical space it explores. Drawn as much of it is from the life, the vivid narrative sweeps the reader from dusty roads in the German-occupied Ukraine to forgotten Cossack *stanitsas* in the Kuban; from the oily shattering stench of Petrograd factories to the puff and distant thunder of Kornilov's guns bombarding Ekaterinodar.

Other aspects of Tolstoy's writing, however, prevent his epic from matching the achievements of *The Quiet Don* or *Doctor Zhivago*. Whether because of a consciousness of his dangerously non-Party background or through a juvenile tendency to envisage issues in black-and-white, Tolstoy was incapable of portraying the opposition in the Civil War as anything but the stage villains he had placed so successfully on the stage. Clearly aware that dramatic truth requires that all characters behave with conviction and consistency of character, Tolstoy allows his fictional Whites full expression of their views. But scarcely a line passes without clumsy indications to the reader of the falsity, hypocrisy or self-deception of these doomed figures. The most they are allowed is a degree of tragic heroism in thus hopelessly setting themselves in opposition to the iron laws of history. No such restraints appear, however, where the major historical characters are concerned. All the opponents of the Revolution, Tsarist and White, are represented as vicious, degenerate and insincere. Kornilov is a suicidal fanatic, Denikin a weak poseur, Shkuro a cornered rat, and so on. Once again we are in the world of mad scientists seeking to take over the world.

Pilgrimage through Torment achieved resounding success in the USSR. It was not just that it was a rattling good yarn, containing genuine literary merit. Probably more than any other work, it set the Revolution in a historical context which on a huge and intricate scale proved its inevitability and strong roots in events and people of the past. The Revolution was not a *deus ex machina*, as some of the Futurists liked to think. The frenetic Soviet interest in history was, as Professor Spencer Roberts has pointed out, "in a way ... a quest for legitimacy", a situation analogous to one in which a *nouveau riche* spends his leisure time frantically searching the family tree for respectable ancestors. It was the quest for "the genealogy of the Revolution".[29]

Alexei Tolstoy's reputation has never waned within the Soviet Union, and he continues to be the subject of innumerable biographical and literary studies. This is not surprising. What is on the face of it extraordinary is his physical survival during Stalin's purges. Why did he continue high in favour, seemingly never in danger, at a time when so many of his fellow-writers disappeared? His noble and émigré background, together with his earlier anti-Soviet writings, cried out after all for his identification as a Trotskyite wrecker or White Guardist saboteur.

Two factors served to preserve him. The first was that innate historical awareness that enabled him to gauge the likely direction of the Revolution. From the moment Stalin's ambitions became clear Tolstoy was second to none in adulating the new dictator:

"I want to howl, roar, shriek, bawl with rapture at the thought that we are living in the days of the most glorious, one and only, incomparable Stalin! Our breath, our blood, our life – here take it, O great Stalin." Simultaneously, he extolled the dictator's "modesty". A good courtier, Tolstoy knew which side his bread was buttered. As a good courtier, equally, he was merely expressing what was his master's due; real conviction did not come into it. To a fellow-writer he confided cynically in 1930, "You know, my friend, you and I are awful fools. All we have to do to win acclaim is read the stenographic report of the latest Party Congress and faithfully follow its political line."[30]

But grovelling alone was not enough – had it been there would have been no purges. Other writers could ladle on the same syrup in even greater quantities, but that did not save them. What Stalin appreciated about Alexei Tolstoy was that his well-received novels and plays provided the Revolution with lasting historical antecedents, and more than any other created the myth that the Communist triumph in 1917 was the logical outcome of centuries of historical parturition. In particular he skilfully inferred that Stalin's inspired leadership had likewise been presaged in ages gone by.

Alexei's fascination with the figure of Peter the Great dated from before the Revolution. In 1928–29, after his return, he came back to the subject with a play entitled *On the Rack*. In twelve scenes, ranging from 1698 to Peter's death in 1725, a picture is provided, similar to that in *Peter's Day*, written in 1918. The squalor of his personal life, his epilepsy and the brutal pointlessness of his career were again highlighted. But inevitably the fuller perspective of the play took more note of Peter's mighty achievements, such as the building of St. Petersburg and the victory of Poltava. Fearful of being accused of conniving at a presentation too sympathetic to a Romanov, the Moscow theatre director invited Stalin himself to the dress rehearsal.

When the great man left early the worst was feared. Many people, after all, had marked the inevitable parallel between sufferings experienced by the masses under Peter's dragooning with the use of forced labour occurring in their own time during the implementation of the first five-year plan. The agitated director, Bersenev, ran out to try to placate the testy Leader before he could enter his car. Meanwhile critic after critic mounted the stage to voice their indignation at the disgraceful piece of monarchist propaganda to which they had just been subjected.

305

A. N. Tolstoy, Constantine Fedin and H. G. Wells in Leningrad, 1934

After the eleventh speaker had voiced this view, Bersenev reappeared. Reminding the audience of the dialectical aphorism that "from a clash of opinions, truth is born", he congratulated the eleven speakers on their unanimity. However, he felt that others might think differently . . . in fact someone had already expressed a contrary view. Comrade Stalin had thought the play "wonderful" in every respect, save that of not portraying the Tsar heroically enough. There was a stunned silence, followed by a crescendo of cheers. "Long life Comrade Stalin!" All subsequent critics and reviewers shared Stalin's favourable impression.

In 1934 Tolstoy produced a revised version, in which much of Peter's cruelty and coarseness was omitted, and the positive gains of his career given more prominence. But by now the critics were confident of the required attitude, and again attacked the playwright for having "distorted history". He took the hint properly in the third version. A totally new Peter trod the boards; a calmly beneficent ruler, devoted only to the reconstruction of his country, quite teetotal and virtually chaste, and hated only by envious foreigners. In the first version the pathetic Tsarevich Alexei is opposed to his overriding father on personal grounds, but in the 1938 version (the year of the Munich crisis) it turns out he was planning to betray the country to the Germans. All this of course involved conscious distortions of history, which Tolstoy appears to have been happy to perpetrate. What mattered was not to relate his Peter to the Peter of history, but to his twentieth-century successor.[31]

Immediately after the first production of *On the Rack*, Alexei Tolstoy set to work on a massive novel on the same theme. Interrupted by his death, it was serialized in *Novy Mir* between 1929 and 1945.[32] Its immense length enabled him to devote far more space to the sort of crowded historical detail he loved, and it provides a brilliant panorama of the period, lovingly tricked out with a pageantry of historical material worthy in scope of the professional historian. At the same time its continuity suffered greatly from the changes of attitude already mentioned. Without any sense of natural development, Peter passes from a wild, cruel and irrational youth, through callous indifference caused by the furtherance of his schemes, to the majestic, far-seeing father of his country in whom the reader was clearly meant to see the victorious Stalin of World War II. However, Tolstoy took the trouble to rewrite much of the earlier portion in order to achieve consistency.[33]

Tolstoy's reward was commensurate with his efforts. He received the Stalin Prize of 100,000 roubles and was enabled to enjoy a lavish life-style. In Stalin's eyes to be the apotheosis of Peter the Great conferred enormous benefits. It exonerated the fearful sufferings inflicted by a Russian autocrat on his people, on the grounds that this was a necessary sacrifice on Russia's path to greatness. It required a man of gigantic courage, prepared if necessary to sink his arms to the elbows in blood, to drag this stagnant country forwards.

There was another significant aspect, one which in all probability accounts for Tolstoy's immunity from harm during the lopping of thousands of loyal heads in the late thirties. Tolstoy had been at pains in his novel to remind his readers that the Tsar's ablest servant had been another Count Tolstoy, Peter Andreevich. Peter Tolstoy had initially joined Tsar Peter's enemies, but after a stay in Western Europe returned to render his master brilliant services. But it was not so much this parallel which struck Stalin, but that with Count Leo Tolstoy. The greatest ornament of nineteenth-century Russian culture had been one Tolstoy, and now Stalin's Russia possessed another. The Leader's immortality was assured.

A curious fact appears to confirm that Soviet society in general lays great store by Alexei Tolstoy's aristocratic lineage, with its unique literary heritage. In view of the peculiar circumstances of Tolstoy's birth, it would be very easy for Soviet critics to argue that he was not the son of a noble cavalry officer, but enjoyed descent from his respectably Marxist stepfather, Bostrom. Rumours that he was illegitimate circulated in Soviet society,[34] but no one has ever been allowed to discuss even the possibility in print. Clearly there are advantages to being a Tolstoy in the Soviet Union.

The elevation of Stalin-Peter was far from being Alexei Tolstoy's only service to his master. It had not escaped his notice that a far more apt parallel was to be found in the person of Tsar-Ivan the Terrible, who had organized an effective predecessor of the NKVD, the *oprichniki*, with which he waged war on the Russian people. As his morbid suspicions grew, the savage Tsar massacred thousands of innocent people and made of Russia such a desert that the Crimean Tartars were enabled to sack and burn Moscow, thus closely anticipating Stalin's purges and Hitler's subsequent invasion. Another Alexei Tolstoy (Alexei Constantinovich, the poet) had been attracted to this theme. Whilst according the demented Tsar stature as a figure of tragedy, Alexei Constantinovich took care to present him as he really was: a bloody-minded tyrant whose cruelties did irreparable harm to Russia's development as a civilized nation.

This was not Alexei Nikolaevich's view. In 1942 he began work on two plays depicting Ivan the Terrible's heroic struggle to create a modern Russian state. Maybe he killed vast numbers of people, but this was necessary in order to overcome the fractious dissent of the boyars and the ignorance of the people. As for the *oprichniki*, well, they were a self-sacrificing group of warriors devoted to protecting the country. (Tolstoy's original version had them defending the *autocracy*, but Stalin himself intervened to suggest a more tactful version.) Most startling of all was the elevation to generous patriot of the sadistic chief of the *oprichniki*, Malyuta Skuratov. Clearly Stalin believed that Beria too deserved some credit.[35]

Finally, in his novel *Bread*, Alexei abandoned allegory and gave his public Stalin in person as hero. The theme was the siege of Tsaritsyn (afterwards Stalingrad) in 1918. Stalin's unbelievable heroism under fire and cool organization of victory is described in ecstatic terms, and contrasted with the unspeakable Trotsky's blackhearted treachery. The story (published in 1938) was so false and fawning as since to have embarrassed even Tolstoy's most ardent Soviet admirers; though at the time nervous reviewers naturally hailed it as his greatest achievement.[36]

Tolstoy's assistance to Stalin during this dangerous period was considerable. After the death of Gorky in 1936 he was considered Soviet Russia's greatest writer. His better works gained international respect as inspired literature. Sustained by his solid prestige, Tolstoy's historical novels underlined the inevitability of the Communist triumph and portrayed in vivid colours Stalin's two greatest predecessors, who like him had been reluctantly obliged to inflict colossal suffering on the people in order to achieve Russia's greatness. As propaganda for internal and external consumption it was superb. It touched precisely the chord that responded so effectively among impressionable foreigners. The egalitarian theory and idealism of Communism appealed strongly to guilt-ridden Western intellectuals, but its open savagery they found more embarrassing to swallow. But if it could be shewn that Russia had never known anything but brutality and hardship, and that it was an inescapable fact that her greatest advances had been made under rulers who employed those very qualities as tools of progress, then Stalin's terror could be seen in an acceptable context. "The Russians do not believe – and since the days of Kiev, never have believed – in individualism as we understand it. . . . Nor is the concept of Socialism worked out in the shadow of an autocrat in the least foreign to the Russian temperament . . ." wrote an English admirer, Edward Crankshaw, after a visit to the Soviet Union in the 1940s.[37]

Many of the themes and revisions of Tolstoy's writings were directly suggested to him by Stalin himself, and the author was at all times ready to oblige by some new convolution of ideas. His services did not pass unrewarded. From the moment of his return to Lenin's Russia in 1923, an appreciative government had seen to it that his needs were cared for. In emigration life had been bleak for Russian writers. Tolstoy himself recalled that "the French did not pay particularly well, and did not sell more than a book a year. For one book they paid 4,000 francs: and on that with very modest requirements a couple could only survive for two months."[38] He found, as he had guessed, that a grateful Socialism would provide a little more than that.

Not long after his return he and his wife settled down in "baronial style in a rambling, many-roomed old mansion stocked with rich antiques", by the Catherine Park at Detskoe Selo, outside Petrograd (soon afterwards Leningrad). It was surrounded by a cool garden, overlooked by a terrace, where the author loved to stroll of an evening and prune his roses. From inside floated out the limpid notes of a piano, where his younger son Dmitri was practising. Inside the front door was a spacious hall hung with portraits and filled with eighteenth-century furniture. A finely-carved balustraded staircase wound up to the private rooms. An eccentric touch was provided by several pairs of shoes and cleaning materials set out on the stairs, and an astonished visitor was informed that the

Count *for some reason liked to clean his own shoes.*

House and garden were generally crowded with visitors, laughing and chatting. Tolstoy was often out, strolling in nearby parks and palaces, or attending plays and concerts in Leningrad. Frequently he and a group of friends would call on acquaintances in the old capital, the unexpected visitors being welcomed with delight. In return, Tolstoy was hospitality itself.

"In the same way," recalled a friend, "he often came home to Detskoe Selo with a troop of unexpected guests. It could happen too that he would call out on coming home: 'In one hour twenty-five or thirty people are coming here in the train. It's been arranged for them to dine here.' And when Alexei Nikolaevich was asked 'Who is coming?' he would reply, 'Don't bother me now! I was strolling through town and invited I can't remember whom . . . but there's no question they're first-rate people! You'll see for yourselves.' The servants' faces, especially those in charge of the domestic offices expressed some trepidation, but things were always arranged to general satisfaction."

The servants were certainly kept on their toes. In January 1926, for example, after a visit to the theatre, Tolstoy invited back the entire cast and direction of the play. Despite the lack of warning the Count's kitchen supplied a superb dinner, whilst the cellar delivered up stores of good wine. The toasts, the laughter and the songs continued with such unabated delight that it seemed no time at all before the first grey light of dawn began to steal through the thick blinds. But joy continued unconstrained until to their surprise the guests saw servants clear one of the tables of its litter of bottles and plates and lay breakfast places. Next the Count's sons crept in to take their breakfast, gazing round-eyed at the revelling guests, and departed reluctantly for school. There was a momentary awkwardness, but Tolstoy called from the head of the table for the famous actor Vasily Kachalov to recite. Uproar broke out again, guitars appeared, songs followed recitations, and when the children returned from school they found the revellers still ensconced as they ate their tea. Servants trooped in and out, bearing coffee, cakes and liqueurs to the dinner tables. It was not until midnight that evening that the weary but happy visitors departed.[39]

"The October Revolution gave me everything," Alexei Tolstoy once wrote gratefully. He had much to be grateful for, and "everything" was not an exaggerated term. In 1935 he packed off his second wife and married a third, an attractive young singer named Ludmilla Ilinichna Krestinsky.[40] Then, in 1938, they moved to Moscow, staying in luxurious rooms at the Hotel Metropole whilst his town flat in Gorky Street and suburban mansion at Barvikha were being suitably prepared.[41] It was the year of the publication of his beatification of Stalin in the novel *Bread*, and now rewards heaped upon him in such profusion that he became as rich as any member of our family living before the Revolution. "He is supposed to have been so rich that Soviet bank accounts granted him an open account upon which he could draw without limitation."[42] Certainly there was nothing within the limits of material wealth that was outside his grasp. The country was starving, millions of people had been massacred, and some twenty million more toiled as slaves in the coalmines and goldfields of the Arctic and Siberia, but the privileges of the new ruling class now exceeded even Tolstoy's wildest dreams when assessing the situation in Berlin in 1923.

Alexei Tolstoy's house at Barvikha was the greatest draw for Moscow high society. High Party officials, actors, writers, and ballerinas vied with each other to obtain the entrée. The stout wife of an important NKVD official could feel a girlish uplift of excitement as she and her husband drew up at the gates. Their amiable host, large, broadshouldered, with blinking eyes peering from behind thick lenses, had all the old-world courtesy seen elsewhere only in films like *Glamorous Nights*. He was, after all, an internationally famous writer, bore one of the most famous names in Russian history, and was the only nobleman publicly surviving in the country.* Alexei's relations or other noblemen now in exile might have found the pose of *grand seigneur* rang a little false, for despite his ancestry Tolstoy had not been brought up or ever moved in aristocratic society. But they were far away, and with the Soviet elite he did very well.

Alexei and Ludmilla Tolstoy, spring 1941

For there is no question but that Tolstoy's title and lineage received homage in revolutionary Russia incomparably greater than he had ever known during the reign of Nicholas II. Stalin himself is said to have addressed him as "Count", and he lost no occasion of delighting his visitors with casual allusions to a heritage all present had worked so hard to destroy. His humble upbringing and childhood peasant companions had been long forgotten, and a friend could marvel at the man who felt so close to the people, "despite his title of Count, his education and youthful years, spent so far from ordinary folk". This was the impression Tolstoy himself sought to convey. Looking at a photograph of himself, he murmured good-humouredly, "and the Count was devilishly handsome"; hastily moving on, however, to praise heroic Russian man. And he would humour his auditors on occasion by referring in a mock-affected way to "dear Baron L," asking languidly after the health of "Countess Zh".[43]

* Actually, there was also a Count Ignatiev, but he was a rather pathetic creature, a sort of *petit-maître* given the daunting task of teaching Red Army officers table-manners.

In Moscow the Count lived even more sumptuously than at Leningrad. Conveniently close to a railway station, the manor at Barvikha stood on a hill amid rolling fields and pine-forests. With its handsome wooden pillared portico, and high, steep roof, massive but plain, it was a typical nobleman's house of the Moscow countryside. Over the year 1938–39, whilst stormclouds gathered over Europe and Stalin set about killing off the Red Army's officer corps, Count Alexei's gardeners toiled to make an exquisite garden around his new home, with a spacious veranda looking on cleverly designed paths weaving between shrubberies. In the spring of 1939, when Hitler's troops, at Stalin's invitation, were storming into what was left of Czechoslovakia, a visitor found the young Countess agitated by less intransigent problems.

"Here we'll have a rose-bush, and there a path . . . but would it be better if it went over here?"

The interior resembled a gorgeous stage setting for one of Tolstoy's more exotic historical plays. Dark, heavy furniture of Peter the Great's reign in the hall gave way to the light and airy satinwood of Catherine the Great in the drawing-room and salons. From the chaos and terror of purge-shattered Moscow, where no one knew in the morning what his fate would be that night, the house at Barvikha seemed a magical place. As the gong sounded in the hall, a deliciously attractive blonde maid blushingly invited parties of up to forty guests to assemble in the great dining-room, where a fire crackled in the open hearth, its flames burnishing bronze figurines, glittering in chandeliers and crystal goblets, and bringing marble statuary to momentary life. Priceless Flemish old masters and eighteenth-century portraits gazed down on a scene perfectly familiar to their aristocratic sitters.

With an apt quotation from Pushkin, the Count affably invited his friends to seat themselves. "We all took our places at the table," wrote one such guest. "Goblets and wine-glasses were filled (Alexei Nikolaevich always served the vodka from a finely-chased decanter of Peter the Great's time), as various pastries were being served on metal trays straight from the ovens, huge vessels containing buckwheat *kasha* with liver, mushrooms, and crackling, various fish and hot *zakuski* (hors d'oeuvres) in pans, warmed up over hot coals, spread out on salvers – and many other delicious and amusing dishes." The champagne and other wines were needless to say exquisite, as Tolstoy had long been a connoisseur.

After dinner he led his guests through folding doors into a softly-lit drawing-room, filled like the rest of the house with magnificent furniture, portraits and bric-à-brac. As the guests settled in sofas and armchairs, laughing and chattering, Dmitri Shostakovich would seat himself at the magnificent Bechstein piano, his fingers straying over the keys before launching into a piece by Tchaikovsky, Scriabin, or himself. One of the Count's little vanities was to claim a profound knowledge of musicology. Shostakovich smiled as his host expatiated on the art, but his private thoughts were less respectful.

"Count Alexei Tolstoy," he explained later, "wrote two major articles about my symphonies – the Fifth and the Seventh. Both articles are included in his collected works[44] and there are few people who know that actually the articles were written for him by musicologists. They were summoned to Tolstoi's *dacha* and they helped him through the morass of violins and oboes and other confusing things that a count couldn't possibly fathom."[45]

Privileged guests might be permitted to go upstairs to the great writer's library, its panelled walls displaying thousands of priceless books, and cabinets containing holograph manuscripts written by Peter the Great himself. As in all the other rooms, the servants had brightened the sombre effects of antique furniture and old oil-paintings with a profusion of flowers in cheerful vases. A gigantic polar-bear skin, symbol of the old Muscovite nobility, was stretched before the hearth. It was here that the great man penned his epic *Peter I*, after describing the heroism of an even greater ruler in *Bread*.[46]

Up to the darkest days of the war cars and chauffeurs waited to drive him where he wished. He might visit his club in Moscow, attend the ballet, and invite an attractive ballerina back to dinner. In peacetime, if he was sick, he set off for a cure at the German spa of Karlsbad. If he was bored, he went on a luxury cruise on the Baltic. Life was really very pleasant.[47]

Naturally all this wealth and elegance was purchased at a price. He was an extremely prolific writer, and he also worked hard on the political front, dedicating himself to advancing the cause of Communism at home and abroad. There was nothing he would not do for the Party to which he owed so much. What perhaps distinguished him from other enthusiasts was his capacity to display evident relish even for the most unpleasant tasks. In 1933 the Belomor Canal was opened, bearing the name "Stalin". 300,000 slave labourers, under the direction of the NKVD chief Yagoda, had toiled for two years on the project, during which tens of thousands had died of malnutrition, illness and harsh treatment. Alexei Tolstoy took a cruise on a pleasure-steamer down the canal, congratulating NKVD officers and haranguing the prisoners. Many of them would have been familiar with the great author's works, which were compulsory fare in the GULAG camps. Fortunately he was able to combine pleasure with business, picking up valuable old ikons cheap from persecuted Old Believers in villages near the camps.[48]

A. N. Tolstoy on his estate in Barvikha, 1939

Though the soul of hospitality and benignity in private life, he was as hard as nails towards those who opposed or betrayed Marxism-Leninism. When the purges began, he threw himself into the task of hunting down Trotskyite vermin with all the conviction of one whose name might well appear on the next list. When Kamenev and Zinoviev were accused in 1936 of conspiring with the exiled Trotsky to murder Stalin and overthrow the state, one of the most violent denunciations of their treachery came from Tolstoy's elegant library at Detskoe Selo. "But what could we expect from such people? Treachery! But imagination boggles at the extent of this treachery. And the reply to it can only be the ultimate punishment, and the execrations of Liberated Man to the end of recorded time." All went well at the trial, and both men were shot in their cells in the Lubianka Gaol. When Tolstoy's fellow-humanist Gorky, also a great admirer of the Belomor forced labour project, died in the same year, the Count's able pen proclaimed that once more it was Trotskyites who had perpetrated the dastardly act. Again, a number of people were indicted for the murder and subsequently executed.[49]

Alexei Tolstoy had already exhibited his skilful absorption of the new Socialist ethic in 1934. During a heated argument in the Leningrad Writers' Publishing House, the poet Osip Mandelstam (an acquaintance since 1906) had had the impertinence to slap him in the face. This could have aroused only one response in a Tolstoy under normal circumstances, but Alexei Nikolaevich was not like other Tolstoys. His customary equanimity quite shattered, he screamed with rage and left at once for Moscow. There he ran to Gorky to tell him of the outrage. The great humanist was highly indignant, declaring (it was reported) "We'll teach him to strike Russian writers" – the clear imputation being that Mandelstam was not only an impertinent commoner, but also a *Jew*. Strings were swiftly pulled (Gorky had in the previous year written particularly fulsomely about Yagoda, the NKVD chief), and on the night of 13 May 1934 NKVD agents called at the Mandelstams' flat and removed the poet. Four years later he died in the notorious forced-labour camp complex of Kolyma – frozen to death, according to the most likely story.[50]

In return for sterling services of this sort, which not everyone would wish to undertake, Alexei Tolstoy received extraordinary privileges. A rare boon was permission regularly accorded to travel abroad. Tolstoy, Gorky and Ilya Ehrenburg were particularly valuable to Stalin in presenting a genial image of the regime to foreigners. They were no mere unlettered and ill-mannered Party hacks, but internationally respected writers, sociable men of the world, and generally useful in persuading impressionable European intellectuals that Socialism has a human face.

Tolstoy and his successive wives (another important concession) were frequent participants at "peace" and "anti-fascist" congresses. In 1937 he attended the Paris Exhibition, and then went on to Spain for the Madrid International Congress of Writers for the Defence of Peace. The Civil War was raging at the time, and Soviet attitudes towards the Republic were highly ambivalent. Tolstoy found the martial atmosphere a little unnerving. He was obsessed with the idea that he was surrounded by Fascist agents, dismayed by Spanish inefficiency in tracking down "diversionists", and spent most of his time sulking because he thought his limelight was being taken by a French air ace serving with the Republicans. Tolstoy was even more afraid of Stalin's agents than Franco's, and took care not to speak French (at great inconvenience to himself and his delegation), lest it be reported that he engaged in conversations they could not understand.[51]

*A. N. Tolstoy with Gorky and
Chaliapin in Italy*

Still, life was good on the whole. In Paris he met on one of his trips an old friend, the Nobel prize-winning writer Ivan Bunin. Pressing him to return to the USSR, he explained: "You cannot imagine how you would live. Do you know how I live, for example? I have a whole estate in Tsarskoe Selo, I have three cars, I have such a valuable collection of English pipes that even the King of England has nothing like it."

But Bunin was not won over, and Tolstoy left for London, clearly unable to perceive there might be other considerations than cars and pipes.[52]

In the thirties Alexei was loud in his condemnation of Fascism, and even when he spoke of it, a Soviet memoirist tells us, "a grimace of hatred appeared on his normally goodnatured features, and his voice took on an unaccustomed note of acerbity."[53] During the war with Germany his was one of the loudest and angriest voices denouncing Nazi aggression and brutality. "We will be cowards," rang his stirring call in 1943, "if we do not write books about this war, in order that our grandchildren may know just what Fascism was!"[54] There was, however, a time when his hostility to Nazism vanished utterly; a time, indeed, when he found Hitler's war aims highly laudable. This was during the period 23 August 1939 to

22 June 1941, when it was discovered that Hitler and the Nazis were really very admirable people, and that the alliance signed in August 1939 served Soviet Russia's interests to perfection. On 17 September 1939 the Red Army invaded eastern Poland, having waited cautiously for over a fortnight until the Germans had crushed major Polish resistance. The next day in the Soviet newspaper *Izvestia* there appeared a long article by Tolstoy, exulting over the collapse of the Polish state, and explaining that the great-hearted Red Army had entered the country for one purpose only: to ensure that the inhabitants of eastern Poland ("yesterday's slaves") "may live in peace, prosperity and happiness". Germany was not mentioned in the article, whose whole tenor was that the Poles had brought disaster on their own heads. "Salvation is coming from the USSR," intoned the Stalin prizewinner smoothly; "grim, tough, unyielding and big-hearted – the workers' and peasants' Red Army is on its way."[55]

Amidst all this rhetoric it may appear small-minded to note that Tolstoy may have had a personal interest in the invasion. When Wilno was occupied by the Red Army in 1939–40, he sent an agent to buy up the cellar of the best hotel in the city for his own private use. Possibly it was a vintage burgundy expropriated at this time that the Count offered Ilya Ehrenburg, when receiving him at his Moscow mansion the following summer. "Do you know what you are drinking? It is Ro-ma-nea!"[56]

Alexei Tolstoy, like his master Stalin, had so far done well out of the Nazi alliance. When Hitler proffered peace to Britain and France in October 1939 in order to give him time to digest his Polish conquest, Stalin hastened to shew his gratitude by joining in the plea. Britain, however, rejected the offer and stepped up military preparations. On 7 November Tolstoy again sprang to print, this time in *Pravda*, to denounce French and British "factory-owners, bankers and speculators . . . preparing all the horrors of a bloody frontal attack" on the Siegfried Line, "under the slogan 'Democracies, save democracy!'" There was again no hint of German aggression, and it was stressed that eastern Poland had been occupied by the Red Army to protect its inhabitants, not from the Wehrmacht, but from Polish landowners and exploiters. "The people want peace," concluded Tolstoy's appeal, "and it is necessary before it is too late to seize with a firm hand the bridle of the steed of war."

Britain and France did not oblige, however, and on Christmas Day 1939 Tolstoy informed readers of *Pravda* that "England, placing itself at the head of World Reaction, is preparing the systematic, scientific destruction of humanity, in imitation of Rome's destruction of her rival, wealthy Carthage." Carthage here of course meant Nazi Germany, whose blockade by the Royal Navy had just been declared by Chamberlain and the British imperialists, and which was vigorously denounced by the writer. Next followed a long encomium on Stalin, "the hope of salvation from suffering and misery of those millions of people, whom Chamberlain drives into the trenches", and who would yet frustrate these hellish plans.[57]

This Stalin did very effectively by supplying all Hitler's major wants in the form of oil, cupro-nickel, guncotton, etc., and by enabling him to evade the British blockade by using routes through Siberia to the Far East. It came as a very nasty shock, therefore, to the Soviet Government when eighteen months later Hitler ungratefully launched his next attack against the Soviet Union itself. Everyone suddenly remembered how fervently anti-Fascist they had always been, and none more so than Alexei Tolstoy. If barrages of clichés could have saved the day, the German Army would never have crossed the Niemen. Everything was turned on its head overnight. By invading Poland and France, it turned out now that it was the *Germans* who had been committing frightful atrocities. As for the fiendish British who hitherto had been excoriated as the instigators of the war, *now* "every bomb dropped on London and other English cities is met with pain in our hearts." But before long the Red Army under Stalin's leadership would crush the vicious invader.[58]

Tolstoy's belligerent journalism grew ever more strident as he hastily removed himself hundreds of miles away from the front.[59] He settled firstly at Murom, a hundred and fifty miles east of Moscow. But by November the Germans were on the outskirts of the capital, and Tolstoy flew to Tashkent, nearly two thousand miles away amid the mountains of Central Asia. There he made his major contribution to the war effort, penning article after article urging the valiant Red Army to ever more heroic efforts and self-sacrifice. "Shame is worse than death," he declared, affirming that Russians should die rather than surrender. "Where will you go, coward, in what chink will you hide yourself from people, from your own self?"[60]

Count Tolstoy's own chink in Tashkent was a little more comfortable than those of the Russian prisoners in German hands. Denied by their own government the protection of the Geneva Convention and the assistance of the Red Cross, they were dying in millions in camps on the wintry steppe. Göring chuckled when he heard that they were reduced to licking lumps of coal, and Goebbels ordered film to be taken of cases of cannibalism among prisoners driven mad by hunger. Meanwhile Tolstoy in Tashkent "was living in the middle of the city, in a cheerful white house with big windows and high ceilings, standing in a shady garden." His Bechstein piano and other valuables had been installed, and he entertained just as at home in Barvikha. "We were given wines of Turkestan of strange taste and bouquet . . . a *shashlik* served by a genuine Circassian, perfumed with aromatic herbs and cooked over a special stove in one of the alleys of the garden. There was, too, a quantity of strange vegetables, and a course of many different kinds of sweet." Afterwards the Countess "sang a number of airs from Moussorgsky in a lovely mezzo voice"; while the Count commiserated with the émigré writer Bunin's uncomfortable life in occupied Paris, going on to explain that the formerly overlarge proportion of Jews among the Soviet intelligentsia had been corrected[61] . . . a readjustment, in the case of Mandelstam, to which he had lent personal assistance.

It is not easy to explain why Stalin chose to confer millionaire status on "the third Tolstoy" (his two great literary predecessors, of course, being Alexei Constantinovich and Lev Nikolaevich). None of the Soviet leaders from Lenin and Trotsky onwards had denied themselves any material luxury. All, without exception, appropriated the homes and any other property of the former ruling class to which they took a fancy. In the case of a few their revolutionary fervour was clearly a pretext for the "socialization" of the property of others. Mikoyan, for instance, simply seized the home of the industrialist whose employee he had been before 1917. Stalin himself possessed wealth so vast that a Soviet historian has suggested it exceeded that of the Tsar.[62] Successful actors, writers, musicians and other artists, whose work entertained their masters, kept the masses docile, and impressed foreigners with Soviet achievements, were also permitted to live very well.

316

But this does not quite account for Tolstoy's extraordinary wealth and privilege, nor the immunity with which he aired his aristocratic pretensions. It is true that, after Gorky, he was regarded as Soviet Russia's greatest writer. But the Soviet state could make and break great writers, as Pasternak, Mandelstam and others found to their cost. Perhaps the most likely explanation is that Stalin was in part cocking a snook at the people and Party he privately hated. Whenever it suited him he could turn history, science, tradition and the Soviet attitude to religion on their heads. He made Trotsky into a Fascist hireling, and Hitler into a noble ally. The logic of Marxism had conferred absolute power on him, and it was a power his terrible sense of insecurity led him to demonstrate in all sorts of contradictory or eccentric ways.

A touch of piquancy and variety was added to Soviet life, and Tolstoy's crawling and squirming added their own amusing touch. The Count was elected a member of the Supreme Soviet in 1936, whose order he flaunted on his double-breasted suit along with the Order of Lenin. A Western visitor is said to have been startled on calling at his Moscow house by the butler's courteous reply: "I regret, sir, that the Count is attending a session of the Supreme Soviet." He was indeed frequently present at court functions in the Kremlin, where he was believed to add a certain style.[63]

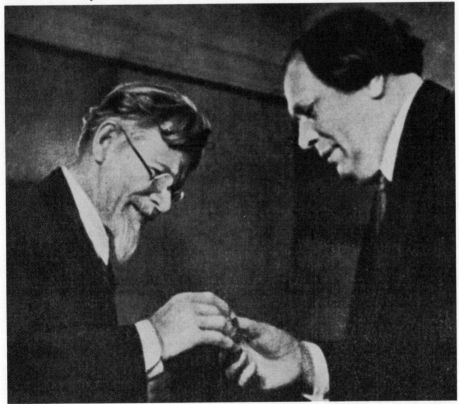

A. N. Tolstoy, decorated by President Kalinin, 1939

All this was quite harmless, if undignified. But if Stalin raised his pet Tolstoy to the heights, he also characteristically pressed him far down into the slime. In November 1942 the USSR's greatest author was appointed to the State Commission for the Investigation of Fascist War Crimes, of which he is said to have been one of the most active members. In December 1943 he attended in this capacity the trial of a number of alleged war criminals in liberated Kharkov. Afterwards occurred a scene as barbaric as those for which the accused were sentenced. Before a gloating crowd of thirty to forty thousand people, the victims were hanged by a process of slow strangulation, their sufferings being recorded on film for the delectation of other Party enthusiasts. The writer Ilya Ehrenburg, who was also present in the city, declined to attend the scene of torture but recorded later that Tolstoy insisted on being present for what he implied were artistic motives. One is reminded of his defence of Ivan the Terrible's cruelty, and of the endless scenes of torture described in his *Peter I*, in which more than one reader has noticed "the author's *full-blooded* delight (so obvious as one reads) in the cruel and savage atmosphere of the 17th century, so similar to that of the time in which we were living."[64]

Worse was to come. On 13 April 1943 Radio Berlin announced that local military units west of Smolensk had uncovered a mass grave at Katyn containing the bodies of thousands of Polish officers "murdered by the GPU" (Soviet political police). The Soviet Union hastily counter-claimed that they had been killed by the Germans, but when the Polish Government-in-exile pressed for an investigation the Soviets abruptly broke off diplomatic relations with them, and also declined to permit the International Red Cross to investigate the matter. In May the Germans arranged for a commission of international forensic experts to examine the graves, who established that the massacre took place in March and April 1940, when Katyn was occupied by the Soviets. Subsequent research has amply borne out the correctness of this verdict.

Soon after this, however, the Germans were driven back from the region by the advancing Red Army, and the Soviet Government despatched its own Commission to Katyn for the purpose of proving that it was the Germans who had perpetrated the crime. The ubiquitous Alexei Tolstoy was a senior member of this group, and was driven down by his chauffeur from Moscow to attend the investigation on 19 January 1944. He spent a week there, handling bones and interrogating "witnesses", and duly set his name to the report inculpating the Germans. It can scarcely be doubted, however, that he was aware of the true state of affairs.[65] By now there was no lie or crime of the Soviet Government to which Tolstoy was not prepared to lend his name.

But a life of unstinted moral and physical self-indulgence was taking its toll. He was only sixty-one, but the flesh hung loosely on his heavily-built frame. Within five months of his smiling and posing among the rotted corpses of the Polish officers he suffered attacks of sickness. Early in June he attended the exclusive Kremlin Hospital for a medical examination. A cancerous tumour was discovered under X-ray for which no operation was feasible, and the doctors estimated that he had only some six to eight months to live. The dire prognosis was concealed from the patient, but it could not be long before he became aware of the shortening hours.

He began to struggle desperately with his *Peter I*, which was very far from completion. Doubts as to whether his life achievement was as sublime as everyone told him perhaps obtruded themselves. His Stalin prize, membership of the Academy and a hundred other honours surely provided proof of his superlative abilities. But what was real and unreal in Stalin's Russia was hard to distinguish. He had always been an industrious writer, but now his energy seemed redoubled.

In September he suddenly began to plan a gigantic new work on the Great Patriotic War, then entering its decisive stages. Perhaps this at last would rival *War and Peace*, and he began to talk of a megalomaniac artistic conception "embracing the whole world and every nation". It may be, though, that a cold glimpse of reality intruded itself, for he also spoke nostalgically of *Nikita's Childhood*, the one work which suggests that under different circumstances he might have been a very different writer.

But time was galloping now. In the same month he entered a luxury sanatorium for the Party elite outside Moscow. In November the doctors concluded decisively that no hope of recovery was possible. All that could be done was to keep him comfortable. He returned home to the great mansion at Barvikha for the New Year, and on 10 January 1945 his family and friends gathered round his bedside for his sixty-second birthday. Six weeks later he was dead.[66]

The funeral rites contrasted sharply with those of Alexei Constantinovich in his little wooden church at Krasny Rog, and still more so with those of Leo Tolstoy in the birch-glade at Yasnaya Polyana. For the interment of "the third Tolstoy", the Soviet state arranged grandiose rites on a scale as lavish as anything the country had seen since the Revolution. Indeed, all that was lacking was any touch of aesthetic taste or spiritual uplift. Whether these deficiencies were in any way apt may be argued over as long as his books are read.

The ceremony followed an elaborate ritual process clearly resulting from much careful thought and planning. It fell into three parts, the lying in state, the cremation, and the funeral proper. On 25 February his body lay in state in the hall of the Trades Union House, where thousands of Muscovites were compelled to file through and pay their last respects to the great writer who had done so much to lighten their load and increase their awareness of the revolutionary achievement. A number of "people's artists", Ehrenburg and others, formed an unmilitary guard of honour as the masses shuffled obediently past. Next day at eleven o'clock the main ceremonial began. People's artists sang the author's favourite airs, and the USSR State Symphony Orchestra played the Finale from Tchaikovsky's *Pathetic Symphony*, while the urn containing Tolstoy's ashes stood waiting in isolated grandeur. When the violins had finished their last scraping, selected officials solemnly bore the urn out of the hall to where a military guard of honour was waiting in the street. An appropriate touch was the inclusion in this group of Andrei Vyshinsky, state prosecutor in the Purge Trials at which Tolstoy had also played a useful part.

The procession wound slowly through snowy streets to the Novodevichy monastery, where the Regent Sophia, patroness of the Tolstoy brothers, had been imprisoned by Tsar Peter in 1698. High Party officials delivered lengthy speeches into the frozen air, dwelling on the deceased's undeniably useful service to the state. His stirring wartime articles received high praise, as did his work at Kharkov and Katyn for the State Commission for the Investigation of German Atrocities. The urn was then lowered reverently into the hole prepared for it, and the icy earth closed over the last remains of a gifted man whose literary talents may be the subject of argument, but whose rôle as the pinnacle of Soviet social life is undeniable.

Finally, the Government published a decree on 28 February, ordering that the great author's name should be fittingly commemorated.

"1. To erect a monument to A. N. Tolstoy in Moscow;

2. To place a memorial tablet on house No. 2 in Spiridonevskaya Street where A. N. Tolstoy lived;

3. To rename Spiridonevskaya street Alexei Tolstoy Street;

4. To charge the State Publishing House of RSFSR with the publication of Tolstoy's complete works in 1945–46;

5. To establish the following scholarships in his honour,

    (a) At the Moscow State University two stipends of 400 roubles each for students of the philological faculty.

    (b) At the Literary Institute of the Writer's Union two stipends of 400 roubles each."[67]

It is not known whether it was choice or chance that led Tolstoy to live in a street named after his family's patron saint.

Alexei Nikolaevich Tolstoy's life remains in large part an enigma. The émigré Russian writer Ivan Bunin thought of him as "a man with many remarkable facets. He combined in a wonderful degree rare personal immorality . . . with rare gifts of nature, particularly in the form of great artistic talent."[68] Tolstoy himself believed that he owed everything to the Revolution. In a material sense this was very true, but as he expressed it a little naïvely in 1933: "My creative luggage for 10 years before October [1917] consisted of 4 volumes of prose, but in the 15 years since I have written 11 volumes of the most important of my works."[69]

The real question is whether he would have written better without the Revolution. All that can really be asserted with confidence is that he could have avoided the very worst of his writing: the black-and-white portrayals of characters in his political novels, the tedious and insincere political expositions, and the cliché-laden wartime propaganda. The sprawling historical novels which he mistakenly believed to be his forte probably sprang from incipient megalomania and a desire to emulate Leo Tolstoy's achievement.

It is hard not to believe that the degrading personal rôle he undertook in Soviet society exerted a damaging effect on his creative capacity. His personal character was without question beneath contempt, reflecting as it did the pitiful morality of many contemporary European intellectuals. His friend Ilya Ehrenburg wrote once that Tolstoy would do anything for a quiet life; and his personal philosophy rose no higher than this *confessio vitae*, uttered when an exile in Paris: "I only know this: the thing I loathe most of all is walking in town with empty pockets, looking in shop windows without the possibility of buying anything – that's real torture for me."[70]

There was no lie, betrayal or indignity which he would not hasten to commit in order to fill those pockets, and in Stalin he found a worthy master. Few families have produced a higher literary talent than that of Leo Tolstoy, but few have descended to one as degraded as that of Alexei Nikolaevich.

11
Epilogue: The Flight of the Tolstoys

F

or nearly six hundred years after the arrival of Indris in a Muscovy ravaged by plague and foreign invasion the Tolstoys lived in Russia, contributing not a little to the history and culture of their country. Then, in the present century, came another time of terror, when the land was once again torn apart by enemies within and without. Our family was dispersed over the face of the earth; a few remaining to survive within the Soviet Union, the rest scattered to places as far apart as Sweden and South America.

Of those who remained in the Soviet Union, Alexei Nikolaevich, the novelist, was the only one to display great talent. Most of the children and grandchildren of Leo Tolstoy wrote informatively about their recollections of the great man, and a granddaughter, Sophia Andreevna, was appointed in 1950 Director of the Tolstoy Museum. She had been the fourth wife of the Futurist poet Sergei Esenin. Ivan Ivanovich Tolstoy, grandson of Alexander II's Minister of Posts, was a Professor at Leningrad University and an authority on Classical Greece, and other collateral descendants occupied similar posts.

Ivan Matveevich Tolstoy,
Minister of Posts (1865–7)

Leo Tolstoy's favourite daughter Alexandra was a nurse in the Great War. When the Revolution came she was thrown for two months into the notorious Lubianka Prison in Moscow and then did a spell in a concentration camp. After the Civil War a decree was passed turning her father's home Yasnaya Polyana into a museum, and the estate into a collective farm. Alexandra, to her surprise, was appointed Custodian of the Museum and returned "home". But as a devout disciple of her father's philosophy she found the deprivation of liberty and persecution of religion more than she could stomach. Longing to escape, she was finally offered the chance when at the end of the summer of 1929 she received a telegram from Japan, inviting her to deliver lectures in Tokyo. "If you don't let me go," she told Lunacharsky (Commissar for the Arts), "I shall have to telegraph

Previous page: My grandmother, Eileen Tolstoy-Miloslavsky

Japan that you're frightened to let me go abroad." She received her passport and travelled to the East on the Trans-Siberian railway. After nearly two years in Japan, she emigrated and settled in the United States.[1]

Ten years later Alexandra Tolstoy, with Russian and American colleagues, established the famous Tolstoy Foundation, dedicated to assisting the resettlement of political refugees originating mostly, but far from exclusively, from the USSR. In 1941 a generous American lady, Mrs. Edward Harkness, gave a fine farm with seventy-five acres in New York State to the Foundation. Here Alexandra established the "American Yasnaya Polyana", with its farm, lodgings, chapel, hospital and library, which have provided a refuge for tens of thousands of helpless people driven by tyranny from their homes.[2] In 1979 she died there at the age of ninety-five, but her work lives on. I visited her shortly before she died, and was witness to the loyalty and devotion she inspired in all around her. Her mind was vigorous and alert to the end.

Serge Tolstoy, son of Leo Tolstoy's ninth child Mihail, is a well-known doctor

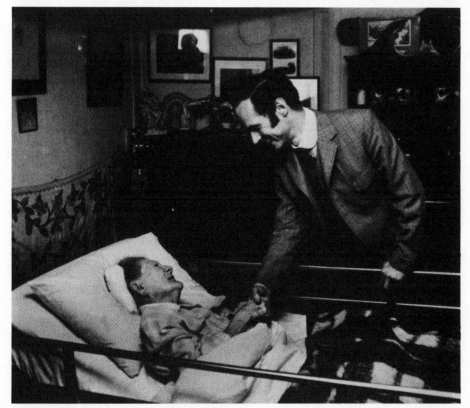

Myself with Alexandra Lvovna Tolstoy

in Paris, formerly Secretary-General of the *Société de Médicine* and recently author of an interesting monograph on his grandfather and his relations.[3] When I was at Trinity College, Dublin, I knew the late Mihail Pavlovich, last heir of the line of Golenishchev-Kutuzov-Tolstoy. He had led an adventurous existence at the end of World War II, dining at Red Army messes in Hungary before taking the sensible precaution of declining more pressing invitations, and settling for the tranquillity of the Irish countryside. He had miraculously preserved the magnificent dinner-service of his great ancestor, Marshal Kutuzov.

The genealogist Nicolas Ikonnikov lists just over a thousand members of our family in all, starting with Indris in the fourteenth century, and spreading over the subsequent six centuries. (Of these it should be remembered that roughly 50 per cent were women, who could not transmit the name, and that the list includes children dying at birth or soon after.) In the last two generations (*i.e.* those of my father and myself), he provides 35 and seven names respectively, but this is certainly incomplete – I have produced four more on my own account! It is not possible here to follow the fortunes of every member of the family since the Revolution, and I will confine myself to a concluding account of my immediate branch which, as the senior in descent, may perhaps stand here as representative.

We are scattered abroad, though close in spirit. My father, a Queen's Counsel, is retired and living in Spain, while his younger brothers Paul and Ivan live in Paris and Copenhagen. Cousin Vladimir is Professor of Russian at the United States Naval Academy at Annapolis. Another cousin, Michael, now alas no more, served with the British Fleet Air Arm in the War. He possessed boundless charm, which saw him through an endless succession of wild scrapes. There are many of his former fiancées around the world, I am sure, who retain fond memories of a dashing but very kindly personality. I believe he rose to dizzy heights, becoming an Air-Marshal in the Venezuelan Air Force, in which capacity he was last heard of selling old Dakotas to the late Emperor Haile Selassie of Ethiopia.

When I visited St. Petersburg in 1968 I paid a call at my great-grandfather's house at number 11, Mokhovaya Street. He lived there when staying at the capital, and performing his duties as a Chamberlain at the Court. It had become a block of flats, grey and dispiriting, like so much else in Soviet Russia. As I stood looking at its silent façade in the dusk, I could not help reflecting on the lively, colourful life it had known seventy years earlier when my great-grandfather was in residence. Pavel Sergeevich was born in 1848, and had seven children by his wife Nina. In 1876 she bore him twin boys, Sergei and Nikolai, who suffered the tragic fate so frequently endured then despite the best medical care. Within a few months both were dead. Unhappiness too awaited my great-grandparents with the next child. This was Dmitri, born in October 1877. He entered the Imperial Navy, and was commissioned as a lieutenant in 1904. It was not a propitious year for Russia's fleet. On 8 February of that year Japan launched a surprise attack on Russia's Far Eastern base at Port Arthur. The two countries were at war. On 15 October Admiral Rozhestvensky sailed with the Baltic Fleet around the world to attack the Japanese at sea. Uncle Dmitri was on board the ageing cruiser *Svetlana*. Six months later the fleet arrived in the China Sea, and Rozhestvensky attempted to force his way through to Vladivostock. In the Tsushima Straits the Russians were engaged by Admiral Togo's fleet, and Russia suffered the most appalling naval defeat in her history. On 28 May the *Svetlana*, acting as an advance scout vessel, was attacked by two Japanese cruisers and sunk. Dmitri was killed by a shell exploding in the deck beside him.[4]

The Tolstoys' fourth and only surviving son was my grandfather, Michael, born in 1884. Michael had two sisters, my very dear great-aunts Maroussia and Lily, born in 1881 and 1882, both now lying in Gunnersbury Cemetery, whom I shall remember with devotion to the end of my days. The last child, named Pavel after his father, suffered the fate of the twins, dying before the age of three. A

Michael Tolstoy-Miloslavsky (standing) and friend

photograph of the pathetic little body, surrounded by flowers on its bier, lies before me as I write.

When I visited our Petersburg home fourteen years ago, that lost world seemed very familiar to me. Aunts Maroussia and Lily lived on into their nineties, and many, many times did I talk to them of that magical country from which we are excluded, but where all our deepest roots lie. Aunt Maroussia settled in England just before the Russo-Japanese War. Temporarily deprived of funds at the out-

325

break of hostilities, she was befriended by an Admiral Nicholson and his wife. They became such close friends that Aunt Maroussia stayed permanently with the Nicholsons at Bude Castle in Cornwall. Admiral Nicholson was to become Sir Douglas, commander of the Home Fleet and ADC to King George, but I understand that Aunt Maroussia exercised firm control over the family and household. She had many endearing eccentricities, of which one was an extreme dislike of anybody discovering her age. To questioners she would reply "ninety-nine" or "a hundred". She told me in confidence that she was sixty-eight, and it was only when I was by chance looking in a Russian book of nobility that I discovered she was ninety-one. When our house in Wales was accidentally burned down, she told me she had overheard "Welsh Bolsheviks" plotting the deed, in the attic of the house where she lived. She held the Soviet Union in the greatest contempt and dislike, always referring to it as "Bolshevia". Aunt Maroussia was always very insistent I should marry and provide the family with an heir. She was greatly taken with my wife (with reason), and when our first child Alexandra was born she was as happy as I think I have ever seen anyone. "This is not a baby, this is an angel!" she kept exclaiming, as she hugged her ecstatically.

With her brothers and sister, Aunt Lily was brought up on the family estate at Murzikha, on the left bank of the great River Kama above Kazan. The village possessed about a thousand inhabitants, and was an important point of embarkation for the river traffic.[5] Many of the inhabitants were Tartars, and there was a mosque as well as an Orthodox church. The estate had been in our family for nearly two centuries before we were driven out by the Revolution. Vasily Borisovich, grandson of the celebrated Governor of Azov in Peter the Great's time, acquired it by marriage from his wife Darya Zmeev some time before 1730. She bequeathed it to their son Lev in 1772, and it remained the property of the Tolstoys until 1918.[6]

In Aunt Lily's childhood it was still the property of her grandfather, Major-General Sergei Pavlovich Tolstoy, who had fought against the Turks in 1877–78. His park bordered on the river, and from the house tugs and barges could be seen making their way downstream to Kazan, bearing timber, metals, grain and livestock from the Urals and Siberia, passing long flotillas steaming up to the great fair at Nizhny-Novgorod. A greater excitement derived from the fact that paddlesteamers discharged large numbers of passengers at Murzikha, who, if they were acquaintances or of consequence, invariably called at the General's house.

To Aunt Lily Murzikha was a paradise. I can hear her saying it now (literally: I am listening to a tape-recording), "Murzikha was something wonderful." The house was spacious and sunny, filled with uncles, aunts, cousins, visitors and servants. If the big house itself was full, as it often was, the young relations stayed in the *fligel*, a long wooden building adjacent to the house. I have never been there, and do not know even if it exists still. But it is easy to recapture those golden days, with the aid of Aunt Lily's memories and strings of photographs beside me here on my desk. There were stables and horses galore for riding in the park or in the fields and forests around. Visible from the house was the cupola of the village church, built by Aunt Lily's grandfather and where in 1894 he was to lie at rest. In the main hall of the house, which rose from ground floor to roof, was a special raised gallery built by the General's father, Pavel Lvovich (1784–1866), a veteran of Borodino and Dresden and a great lover of music, for which this stage was built. A nephew who called unexpectedly in 1838 found it was a gala night.

"The manor house was brilliantly illuminated: the orchestra's fortissimo could be heard even in the village street, and the inhabitants were listening to the music and gazing at the windows. Uncle Pavel Lvovich claimed to be a great music-lover, and had formed an excellent orchestra from his estate serfs. I was very friendly with my uncle, and my appearance aroused great jubilation.

"'How marvellous that you came,' said Pavel Lvovich, 'We've got a jolly evening ahead of us.'"[7]

This hall opened on to a broad terrace, where the household would dine in summer. Formerly they could also hear the orchestra there, but by Aunt Lily's time equal pleasure was to be derived from listening to the hooting of the paddle-steamers, wondering who might have arrived.

A favourite haunt of the General, who had an antiquarian bent, was the Murzikha muniment room. This contained charters, deeds, wills and letters of Tolstoys long dead. Perhaps the most precious archive was the correspondence between Peter the Great and Ivan Tolstoy at Azov. Fortunately it was not destroyed at the Revolution, and is among the historical archives at Kazan, preserved under the name "Tolstoy-Miloslavsky Collection".[8]

Among the snapshots are young men with guns and spaniels, cousins Seriozha and Leva trying out their new bicycles, girls in long skirts and trim waists sitting on the balcony, Aunt Lily setting out for a picnic on an estate *droshky*, a picnic in the woods with a silver samovar bubbling under the pines, trips on the Kama, walks by lakes . . . it is not difficult to see why Murzikha was "something wonder-

Family outing at Murzikha (Aunt Lily holding child)

full". Country life was never the lonely existence it can all too easily be today. Not only did scores of relations of all ages come to stay, and numerous visitors call all summer long, but all brought their own servants with them to swell the household. In Aunt Lily's time the estate comprised 11,184 hectares (27,635 acres). The family was devoted to the local peasants, formerly family serfs, and they equally adored the Tolstoys. Aunt Lily was particularly fond of them, and I have photographs of especial favourites, together with beautifully embroidered local peasant

Picnic in the Murzikha woods, 1903

Peasant girls at Murzikha

Opposite page: My grandfather, Aunt Maroussia and my grandmother in the Crimea

smocks Aunt Maroussia by a fortunate chance brought to England as fancy dress for children's theatricals.

My great-grandmother Nina (Aunt Lily's mother) never enjoyed good health, and when the girls were aged about ten the doctor told my great-grandfather she must live abroad for her health's sake. He decided to take her to the Riviera (she died at Cannes in 1895), and this meant that some provision must be made for the children, who would have to remain in Russia. Dmitri was still at the Naval Academy and my grandfather Michael would also undergo his schooling in St. Petersburg. He and his sisters had hitherto been in the care of an English governess whom they disliked, followed by a French one they loved. Now Maroussia was sent to school, and Lily received a government bursary to attend the famous Catherine Institute in St. Petersburg. The Institute's patroness was

the Dowager Empress Maria Feodorovna (widow of Alexander III), who frequently visited the girls. Even more popular visitors were (from 1896) the reigning Emperor Nicholas II and his consort Alexandra. Aunt Lily vividly recalled his kindliness and gentle good humour. When the time came for him to leave, the girls would clamour for him to stay. When they asked him to bring the little Grand Duchesses with him, he laughingly declined on the grounds that they might catch an infection among so many other children. Sometimes in turn the girls were taken to Court at the Winter Palace or Peterhof. The Tsar's affectionate personality made an indelible impression on Aunt Lily, who always regarded him as a saint (which in fact he now is in the Orthodox Church).

After his wife died at Cannes, my great-grandfather returned home and eventually married again. He appears to have been rather neglectful of his daughters, who saw little of him thereafter. Aunt Lily boarded at the Catherine Institute, and could if necessary live there all the year round. But a kind aunt, Maria Lvovna, offered to take care of her. Born in 1855, in 1872 she married Alexander Kazem-Bek. The Kazem-Beks came of distinguished Tartar origin, and had an estate at Novospasskoe near Murzikha. They spent the winter in St. Petersburg, where Kazem-Bek was Master of the Imperial Court and a Senator. Now that her father no longer maintained the house in Mokhovaya Street, Aunt Lily spent her leaves from school with her Aunt Maria, and the summer holidays at Murzikha. This arrangement continued after school-days finished, when Aunt Lily spent the winters with the Kazem-Beks.

So life moved tranquilly on. In 1894 General Sergei Tolstoy had died, and bequeathed the Murzikha estate to his second son Sergei. Sergei Tolstoy was appointed Marshal of the Nobility of Kazan, which made the house a hive of social activity. In 1905 came the tragedy of young Dmitri's death at Tsushima. Then in 1912 came a happy and romantic event. After their schooling had finished, Maroussia and Lily were sent to a finishing school at Dresden in the Kingdom of Saxony. Aunt Lily returned quite soon for some reason, but Aunt Maroussia stayed on. There she made friends with a beautiful English girl, Eileen Hamshaw, a fellow-student. This effected an introduction between the families, and Eileen came one summer to stay at Livadia in the Crimea. My grandfather Michael was also there, staying with a college friend. He and Eileen Hamshaw played tennis together, walked by the sea and strolled in the lovely gardens of Yalta. They fell in love, and on 25 January 1912 were married at the Russian Embassy chapel in London. The newly-wed couple returned to Russia immediately afterwards and went to live at Michael's house in Moscow, Sivtsev-Vrazhek 43.[9] There my father Dmitri was born on 26 October (8 November, New Style). The young couple joined the rest of the family for holidays at Murzikha, and Aunt Lily became very fond of her little nephew.

But clouds were looming on the horizon. Before two years had passed, Russia had mobilized and invaded Eastern Prussia. At the Masurian Lakes her armies were surrounded and destroyed, and the Empire was locked in a desperate struggle with the terrible German military machine. As in every other Russian household, high and low, young men left Murzikha to join the colours. Cousin Leva joined the cavalry, later winning two St. George's Crosses, Seriozha was also highly decorated, while my grandfather served with the Red Cross on the North-Western Front. In 1915 he returned to civil life, becoming administrator of one of the Imperial estates in the Province of Kazan. He could again be with his young wife and two-year-old Dmitri, but it was for a tragically short time. On 4 January 1916 my grandmother died, and father and baby were on their own. Little Dmitri was cared for by a devoted English nanny, Lucy Stark.

Events now gathered momentum. That year the Russian armies at last gained victories under the able General Brusilov, and as late as January 1917 achieved "a respectable success" with a surprise attack against the Germans by the Baltic.[10] But cracks had shivered the Russian monolith, the social structure was breaking up, and in February 1917 the community at Murzikha learned the stunning news of the Tsar's abdication. Horrifying as this appeared to the Tolstoys, several of whom were in the direct service of the Emperor in various capacities, life itself did not at first appear very different. The new Provisional Government was as resolved

Cousin Leva displays his St George's Crosses, 1915

as its predecessor to fight on until Germany was defeated, and proclaimed its adhesion to proper constitutional and legal forms. But rhetoric was no substitute for the sternly practical measures Russia needed so badly, and the notorious Order Number One virtually abolished discipline in Russia's more than 7,000,000-strong armed forces. In June the railway workers struck. In October Lenin and Trotsky staged their coup in the capital and proclaimed the world's first Workers' State.

Murzikha lay hundreds of miles to the east of the regions where these events were taking place, but little time elapsed before advancing ripples gave warning of the hurricane preparing in the centre. By midsummer large numbers of deserters from the front had arrived at Kazan, and as many dispersed home the infections of defeatism and revolution spread to every village. Kazan city was an important railway junction, and the railway workers formed an active Bolshevik cell. When the October Revolution broke out, they armed themselves from an army consignment of 40,000 rifles found in trucks waiting at the station.[11]

The Bolsheviks had not yet by any means established their subsequent iron

226—THE ILLUSTRATED LONDON NEWS, Feb. 17, 1912.

WITH CROWNS, CANDLES, RINGS, AND WINE: A WEDD

DRAWN BY O

1. ACCORDING TO THE RITUAL OF THE ORTHODOX GREEK CHURCH: CROWNS BORNE OVER THE HEADS OF THE BRIDE AND BRIDEGROOM WHILE THE POPE, HOLDING THEIR HANDS, LEADS THEM THRICE ROUND THE ALTAR.

2. A CEREMONY PERFORMED THRICE: THE BRIDE BRIDEGROOM EXCHANGE RINGS BEFORE CROWNS ARE HELD OVER THEIR HEADS.

Most picturesque scenes took place in the Russian Embassy Chapel in Welbeck Street the other day when Countess Tolstoi was married there according to rites of the Orthodox Greek Church. The bride and bridegroom stood in the heart of the chapel before a small altar. Then the door of the Sanctuary ope and the officiating pope or priest, accompanied by two others, all fully vested, came down the three steps to the sound of singing. The ceremony be when one of the clergy gave a candle to each of the bridal pair, and, after singing and prayers, placed a satin carpet in front of them. They then exchan

THE ILLUSTRATED LONDON NEWS, Feb. 17, 1912. - 237

THE RUSSIAN EMBASSY CHAPEL IN LONDON.

ÉDÉRIC DE HAENEN.

EMONY THRICE PERFORMED: THE BRIDE AND BRIDEGROOM
INK WINE FROM A SILVER CUP BEFORE BEING LED THRICE
UND THE ALTAR.

4. AT THE BIDDING OF THE OFFICIATING POPE: THE BRIDE AND BRIDE-
GROOM KISS ONE ANOTHER AFTER HAVING KISSED THE CRUCIFIX
PRESENTED BY THE PRIEST.

times: after which the officiating pope held over them crowns, which were afterwards borne by two gentlemen. Next, bride and bridegroom having
re from a silver cup, the pope took their hands and led them thrice round the altar. Later, they kissed the crucifix presented to them by the priest:
command, kissed one another. There ended the ceremony. Our Artist was able to make his drawings by courtesy of Countess Tolstoi. We ought,
point out that the Russian Embassy itself is in Chesham Place, not in Welbeck Street.

control over the country. However, life was swiftly becoming very harsh and difficult, and there seemed little choice but to bow one's head before the storm and survive as best as possible. Uncle Sergei spent the winter at his large town house in Kazan, on Letskaya Ulitsa. Most of the family moved in with him, including my father, grandfather and Aunt Lily. (My great-grandfather Pavel Sergeevich, who had married for the second time in 1912, was the only one to have escaped. He was in Yalta when the Revolution broke out, and he and his wife left at once for Paris. His wife, as a result of her previous marriage, possessed wealth abroad.)

It was an increasingly terrifying time for the family in Kazan. When they returned to Murzikha in the spring they found the house in a terrible state of disorder. Poor Aunt Liubov (Uncle Sergei's wife) went into hysterics over what she took to be bloodstains on a wall – fortunately it was only red paint!

It was hard to tell what to do. In May the Bolsheviks set up a branch of the dreaded Cheka, their new political police, in Kazan. They immediately began to round up political opponents in the city.[12] How long it would be before their final reckoning with the class enemy followed, no one knew. The night air was frequently punctuated by the sound of shots; in daylight truckloads of Bolsheviks moved threateningly along the streets, while agitators at street corners uttered lurid threats against White Guardist bandits and *bourjouis* exploiters. As for the news from the country outside, it was hard to know what to make of anything. The Empire seemed to be breaking up; the Germans occupied the Ukraine, British troops landed in Murmansk, and Czech legionaries in Siberia turned on the Bolsheviks after an attempt to disarm them by force. In the far south there was cautious cause for optimism: General Denikin and his anti-Bolshevik Volunteer Army was campaigning successfully in the Kuban, while the Don Cossack Ataman, General Krasnov, was bidding defiance to Bolshevism in the Don country. But that was hundreds of miles away; locally the Bolsheviks were all-powerful and, in any case, if they were attacked, what would happen to the defenceless people held virtual hostage in the city?

For Aunt Lily 1918 was a terrifying year. On 12 January her benefactress and friend Maria Kazem-Bek had died in her arms. About this time she had become engaged to a charming and intelligent young man she had known for some years. The night before the wedding was due to take place, a group of Bolsheviks broke into her fiancé's rooms and shot him dead on the spot. She wore mourning to the end of her days. Her nature was full of love, which henceforward she lavished on her family, particularly the young, but she was possessed by a deep pessimism. Almost as terrible a shock was the news in July that the Bolsheviks had murdered the Tsar at Ekaterinburg, together with his wife and children. The situation appeared grimmer every moment. Little Dimitry had gone down with scarlet fever, and Aunt Lily and the nurse Lucy had this anxiety to add to the predominating fear of being massacred by the Reds.

Then, very suddenly, things changed. The volunteer Czech Legion had become involved in fighting with the Bolsheviks and seized the Trans-Siberian Railway, along which they had originally been moving eastwards for evacuation at Vladivostok. Anti-Bolshevik Russians took the opportunity to set up a government at Samara and, believing that the British expeditionary force by the White Sea was advancing south from Archangel, adopted a forward policy. The local Soviet commander on the front before the newly-declared Samara Government hap-

Lucy Stark and little Dimitry. My father, grandfather and great-grandfather

pened to be a Social Revolutionary secretly opposed to Bolshevism. He seized control of Simbirsk and declared an alliance with the Czechs, but was in his turn overthrown and killed by local Bolsheviks. But the Samara Government saw its chance, and on 22 July a daring White officer, Colonel Vladimir Kappel, led a column of Samara levies into Simbirsk and seized it for the Whites. This success led the leaders in Samara to contemplate a still bolder stroke. On 6 August a force of Czechs and White Russians, advancing up the Volga from Simbirsk, captured not only Kazan itself but the entire Russian gold reserve, worth some hundred million pounds.

The joy of the Tolstoys in the beleaguered house on Letskaya Ulitsa can be imagined as the Communists pulled out westwards and Kappel's cavalry galloped in from the south. The tables were turned with a vengeance, and it was now the turn of their oppressors to be hunted. A leading Chekist chief, I. S. Sheinkman, was caught and shot two days after the Whites' arrival, and it seemed at last that night had lifted from over Kazan.[13] But the relief was short-lived. The Whites had over-extended themselves, and a massive Red counter-offensive was launched under Trotsky's guidance. On 10 September, a bare month after their arrival, the White troops were obliged to withdraw hurriedly from the city to fall back on Simbirsk. As the Czech infantry scrambled back into their armoured train, the thunder of Trotsky's guns could be heard approaching from Sviazhsk. By dawn they would be in Kazan, and no one nurtured any illusions as to what must follow.[14]

When the White commander informed Sergei Tolstoy of the decision, it was clear the Tolstoys had no choice but join the evacuation. As Marshal of the Nobility of the Province, Sergei Tolstoy-Miloslavsky was the leading figure in the city, and the house on Letskaya Ulitsa would be first on Trotsky's visiting-

335

list. It was unlikely to be a friendly call; on 2 September Lenin had ordered the massacre of five hundred hostages in Petrograd, killed solely on account of their class origins. Aunt Lily remembers how they spent that last evening burying precious ikons in the garden. "We thought we were going for a few days, but it was for all our lives," she recalled. Then came a sudden bombshell. My father, five-year-old Dimitry, was still very feverish and the family doctor announced that it was quite impossible for him to be moved. What was to be done? There was no question but that the Reds would massacre every adult male of the family they could lay hands on. It was then that Aunt Lily turned to her brother Michael, and declared firmly that she would stay and look after little Dima. It was a terrible moment, but what else could be done?

After brief and agonizing farewells, Uncle Sergei, his sons, my grandfather, and the other men of the Tolstoy family saddled their horses and rode or drove for Samara and safety. Uncle Sergei, who was sixty-nine, ultimately made his way across Siberia to Japan, ending his days in Italy. My grandfather, Michael Tolstoy-Miloslavsky, and his cousin Leva travelled south to join General Denikin's White Army which was achieving a series of striking victories over the Red Army in Southern Russia. A family photograph shows them with British officers on board a Royal Navy cruiser sailing down the Volga to join Denikin.[15] Both survived the Civil War, eventually settling in France.

Grandfather and Cousin Leva (on left) sail to join Denikin, 1918

Back in Kazan a time of terror had begun for Aunt Lily. The whole family was gone, leaving her with the sick child. She had one other companion, the English nanny Lucy Stark, who did not for a moment contemplate leaving her charge. Her courage never failed, though she had no idea at all of what was going on. The Revolutionary upheaval seemed to her the sort of wild aberration to which the otherwise charming Russians occasionally abandoned themselves. Of course there was no question of remaining in the deserted big house on Letskaya Ulitsa, and the trio took refuge in the home of a faithful family servant, who volunteered to protect them. Aunt Lily never forgot the terror of those days of concealment.

The fact that they were women with a small child was no protection at all. At the moment of the Red re-occupation of Kazan, Lenin had signalled to Trotsky: "I am confident that the suppression of the Kazan Czechs and White Guards, and likewise the bloodsucking *kulaks* who support them, will be a model of merciless-ness." The local Cheka Chairman, Karl Karlson, and his female Deputy, Vera Braude, needed no urging in their sanguinary task. There was no question of distinctions of age or sex, or of individuals' opposition to the Revolution. Latsis, acting head of the Cheka, laid down the policy to be observed that month: "We are not warring against individual bourgeois. We are out to destroy the bourgeoisie as a class. . . . Whenever a bourgeois is under examination the first step should be, not to endeavour to discover material proof that the accused has opposed the Soviet government verbally or actually, but to put to the accused these three questions: 'To what class does the accused belong?' 'What is his origin?' 'Describe his upbringing, education, and profession.' Solely in accordance with the answers to these three questions should his fate be decided. For this is what 'Red Terror' means, and what it implies."[16]

Daily people were disappearing in the streets of Kazan and from their homes. It was well-known that the Bolsheviks were particularly anxious to track down all the family of the Marshal of Nobility, and news reached Aunt Lily that someone had betrayed their refuge to Comrade Karlson's agents. The little party quickly moved to a friend's house, where they rented a couple of rooms. One day Aunt Lily underwent direct experience of the danger that menaced them. Always very devout, she eventually could not resist attending a church service. As everyone emerged at the end, a band of armed Chekists suddenly appeared and, surround-ing the whole congregation, drove them in a column along the streets to the city gaol. As the leading victims were already being herded through the entrance, Aunt Lily thought vividly of Lucy and Dima anxiously awaiting her return. Seizing her courage in both hands, she ducked past a guard and rushed among the crowd of bystanders lining the pavement. They let her through, immediately closing ranks around her. "Take off your hat!" cried several voices, and the incriminating headgear was whipped off by a friendly hand. Grim-faced Chekists pushed after, demanding the fugitive, but the crowd stolidly denied having seen her. Aunt Lily, who was small and neat in appearance, hid for a while among her protectors and then, when the coast was clear, ran all the way home. "For a long time," she told me, "my head swam and my hands trembled, and I was unable to move or speak properly."

Once again they had to move hastily, and took up quarters in a house on a corner, where Aunt Lily and my father slept in one room and Lucy had a bed at the end of the house in an alcove. So long months went by, not a single hour passing without the fear of heavy boots on the stair and a knocking at the door. Lucy, said Aunt Lily, "was wonderful". With true English aplomb she managed all their little household needs, her nationality imposing universal respect among the townspeople. She soon became as aware of the danger as the others, but betrayed no sign of fear and appeared to find the whole business a little ridiculous; certainly such things could never happen in England.

Meanwhile history was reshaping itself. The early victories of the White Armies gave way to defeat, and what was left of Denikin's army was being driven south to the Caucasus and the Black Sea. By the end of 1919 British intervention on the Whites' behalf had virtually ended, and Lloyd George's Government prepared to come to terms with the new masters of Russia. Cautious negotiations began, an important aspect of which was the return of the two countries' respective nationals to their homelands. As they were still in a state of undeclared war, the delegates meeting at the Hotel d'Angleterre in Copenhagen faced an extraordinarily delicate task. During the three months which they lasted talks broke down several times, the Bolsheviks tenaciously trying to retain certain grades of British prisoner, at one point even refusing to return any officers or civilians. Eventually on 12 February 1920, the Agreement was signed but not without strong British apprehensions that the Soviets would seek excuses not to comply in full.[17]

News of the Agreement filtered through to the fugitives in Kazan. It was said to apply to British subjects only, but as Lucy Stark was wholly and little Dmitri half British, Aunt Lily hoped this might prove an avenue of escape for her nephew. It was necessary to go to Moscow to register for repatriation, and with great difficulty the trio travelled there. As they were still being hunted by the Cheka, Aunt Lily took the ingenious precaution of despatching a telegram back to Kazan containing a report of her own death. The family still had friends in Moscow, eking out a precarious existence menaced by cold, hunger and the ubiquitous Cheka. Large numbers of the former ruling class were continually rounded up and placed in gaol, to be retained as hostages in case of anti-Soviet activity in the city. In September Anarchists had bombed Communist Party Headquarters. Without waiting to find out who was responsible, Dzerzhinsky, head of the Cheka, ordered *all* aristocrats and other class enemies held as hostages to be killed. Hundreds were massacred in consequence, some shot in prison basements, others herded into Petrovsky Park and gunned down *en masse* in the open air. As Aunt Lily must have heard only too often, it was common Cheka practice to torture and abuse women before shooting them; children too were frequently executed.[18]

Once settled in Moscow, Lucy Stark set off to find out about arrangements for the return home of English people in Russia. In the absence of a British diplomatic presence, registration of those entitled to return had been entrusted to the Rev. F. W. North, British Chaplain in Moscow, who had himself been held as a virtual prisoner for two years since the Revolution. Lucy explained who she was and asked if she could take Dimitry with her. Mr. North confirmed that all British subjects were permitted to return, but went on to regret that on no account could he include the boy, since he was allowed only to register British subjects. Lucy at once replied that Dimitry was a close relative of hers, and hence was British. He smiled: as British Chaplain in Moscow for the past fifteen years he had known my grandparents when they returned from their wedding in London in 1912, and remembered Dimitry's birth at the end of that year. It was a terrible moment for both these brave English people. Lucy saw the boy she loved being abandoned to the mercy of the Bolsheviks. Mr. North, should he accept Lucy's fiction, risked not only losing his own chance of leaving Russia but causing the breakdown of the entire delicate operation of the repatriation of prisoners. He himself had just emerged from a ruthless interrogation by the Cheka, who accused him of being an agent of the British and the Whites. They were plainly seeking a pretext to retain him, and now here was this Englishwoman seeking to embroil him in just such a pretext. But for such a man there could only be one decision. "I don't know anything about it," he murmured with a wink, as he enrolled my father as a British subject.

Greatly emboldened, Lucy next asked if Aunt Lily too could be included. But here the Chaplain had to draw the line. Aunt Lily was so clearly a Russian that it was impossible. There were countless Russians, with or without English connexions, who would have given anything to leave their stricken country at that time. That he knowingly included Dimitry must presumably be put down to the fact that he had known his English mother when she lived in Moscow. So poor Aunt Lily had to say goodbye to the nephew for whom she had risked everything, and stay behind in the wolf's maw. But just as she never dreamed of deserting him when the family fled Kazan in August 1918, so now she felt only relief that at last he seemed to be safe.

In fact the danger was not over. On the railway journey to the Finnish frontier Lucy repeatedly coached Dimitry in his role as an English boy. The Bolsheviks were morbidly suspicious that spies or class enemies would use this unique opportunity to escape (they even made a last-minute attempt to retain Mr. North), and sure enough there came a halt, when Red Guards entered the train and went through, compartment by compartment, until they came to where Lucy and Dimitry sat. Now came the most terrifying moment of the brave nanny's life. Each time she had instructed Dimitri on what to say and above all the necessity for giving an English name, he had replied with all the obstinacy of seven years, "I will *not* use that name. My name is Tolstoy." When the guards finally entered their compartment, Lucy was interrupted when she tried to answer for both of them and ordered out. Through the window she watched the interrogation proceed in dumb-show. What Dimitry had said she never fully discovered, but whatever it was satisfied the Bolsheviks and they were allowed to proceed.

On Friday 21 May 1920 the S.S. *Dongola* docked at Southampton with its cargo of freed British subjects – and one Russian boy.

Among the refugees and liberated prisoners from Russia who landed at Southampton on Saturday were: Left—Rev. F. W. North, Anglican chaplain in Moscow; centre—Dimitri de Tolstoy-Miloslavsky, whose English mother is dead and whose father is missing;

Daily Mail, *24 May 1920*

Back in Russia Aunt Lily moved to Petrograd, where she lived for a long time in the same danger as before. Then she too escaped. A former family maid who originated from the Baltic provinces had acquired a passport from the newly-founded Republic of Estonia. As loyal and self-sacrificing as the others, she changed passports with her former mistress. The Estonian Consul connived at the deception, and Aunt Lily travelled to Estonia, taking the precaution of crossing the Soviet frontier on foot through the woods. From Estonia she sailed to Copenhagen, where she visited the Dowager Empress Maria Feodorovna. After a brief visit to her sister Maroussia and nephew Dimitry in England, she joined the Russian community in Paris. Her brother (my grandfather) was still lost somewhere with the debris of the defeated White Army, but eventually he too escaped and went to live in Paris.

So it was that we came to Europe. I was born in England fifteen years after my father's arrival, when most émigrés still firmly believed that Stalin's terrible regime must soon collapse and the scattered émigrés return home. Today the generation which knew the old Russia has all but passed away, to be replaced by their sons and daughters who know the land of their ancestors only as visitors. But how well and nostalgically I recall that émigré world of thirty and forty years ago! Houses and flats in Kensington and Chiswick preserved the traditional Russia of the Romanovs; darkened rooms with heavy curtains, crowded with ikons, paintings, photographs of officers in jaunty uniforms and ladies with wonderfully narrow waists, and above all the ubiquitous photographs of the melancholy features of the murdered Tsar Nicholas II, and his beautiful children. Such homes still linger on, but soon it will be in fond memory that the dying echo of Imperial splendour lives on. Only in our Orthodox Church, where I was married and my children baptized, does the old faith burn steady and inextinguishable as the lamps before the ikons. The faith has survived the Tartar conquests, the Time of Troubles, and innumerable other persecutions and tribulations. It will certainly survive this present grim era.

So we have come full circle. In 1353 we arrived in Chernigov from the West in dreadful days of plague, war and desolation. 630 years later we are back in the West. What the future holds we do not know, but I hope this history will invoke a not discreditable past for the next generation, my four dear children Alexandra, Anastasia, Dmitri and Xenia. And may it supply them with that essentially noble virtue: the ability to judge an ephemeral present by the sonorous procession of a golden past.

The Tolstoy family today.
Left to right: Anastasia, Georgina, Xenia, Dmitri, Nikolai, Alexandra

Appendices
Acknowledgments

APPENDIX I

Note on Russian Titles

The only ancient title in Russia is that of *knyaz*, in English translated as "prince". Most princes were the descendants of former princely houses, native and foreign, absorbed into the Russian Empire. Under the law of 12 January 1682 all Russian nobles, regardless of title or ancestry, were defined as equal.[1] It was Peter the Great who introduced the titles of count (in 1706) and baron (in 1710) from Europe, as an inexpensive way of rewarding good service.

None of the hereditary titles provided the bearer with any privilege whatever, and they do not feature in the famous Table of Ranks of 1722 which stratified promotion within the Russian Empire. As every descendant of the original grantee bore the same title, hereditary titles became in themselves of very little significance. The value they bore varied greatly in differing historical periods and according to the name of the bearer, his wealth and personal status. The value was thus purely honorary, and not even an exclusive mark of the aristocrat, since many of the most famous families (such as the Naryshkins and the elder branch of the Sheremetevs) bore no title at all. Nevertheless, titles undoubtedly bore a cachet, prized to a variable and indefinable extent, particularly by the original grantee.[2]

On 7 May 1724 the title of Count was conferred by Peter the Great on Peter Andreevich Tolstoy for his services as Ambassador in Constantinople and afterwards. On 6 May 1727 he was stripped of the title, which was restored to his descendants by the Empress Elizabeth on 30 May 1760.

On 27 October 1796 Alexander Ivanovich Tolstoy was created Count Osterman-Tolstoy by Catherine the Great, a title which became extinct with his death in February 1857.

On 13 October 1863 Alexander Alexandrovich Dmitriev, grandson of the celebrated medallist Feodor Petrovich Tolstoy, was created Count by Alexander II, under the name of Alexander Tolstoy. This "line" is extinct.

On 16 April 1866 Ivan Matveevich Tolstoy, Minister of Posts and Grand Marshal of the Court, was created a Count by Alexander II.

After authorizing the addition of the surname Miloslavsky to Pavel Sergeevich Tolstoy in 1910, Nicholas II declared his intention of recognizing the title of count in the senior branch of the family, whose ancestor Ivan Andreevich Tolstoy had been on the point of receiving it when he died in 1713. Ratification of this intention was deferred by the gathering crisis which followed. The Emperor and his brother the Grand Duke Michael successively abdicated in 1917, when their cousin the Grand Duke Kyril Vladimirovich succeeded to the inheritance of imperial rights.[3] On 8 October 1930 he confirmed the former Chamberlain Pavel Sergeevich's right to the title, which had been recognized by the Dowager Empress and Grand Duchesses Xenia and Olga.[4]

The titles of Count and Countess have been omitted in the entries for the Tolstoy family in the index.

The arms of the Tolstoys are recorded anciently as "a shield with a blue field, on which are depicted a golden sword and a silver arrow which pass diagonally through the ring of a golden key, and on the right side above the key is a silver outstretched wing."[5]

The Tolstoy-Miloslavsky arms, as registered at the College of Arms

APPENDIX II
Note on Pedigree

This pedigree (which appears on the endpapers of this book), with minor corrections and additions, is based on the following works:

V. V. Rummel and V. V. Golubtsov, Родословный сборникъ русскихъ дворянскихъ фамилій (St. Petersburg, 1887), ii, pp. 487–533.

Count Alexander Bobrinskoy, Дворянскіе роды внесенные въ общій гербовникъ всероссійской имперій (St. Petersburg, 1890), i, pp.

Prince A. B. Lobanov-Rostovsky, Русская родословная книга (St. Petersburg, 1895), i, pp. 381–5.

V. G. Chertkov, (ed.), Л. Н. Толстой: полное собрание сочинений (Moscow-Leningrad, 1934), xlvi, pp. 479–514.

Nicolas Ikonnikov, *La Noblesse de Russie* (Paris, 1962), R.1, pp. r23–r193.

APPENDIX III
A Note on Transliteration

The system of transliteration of Russian names employed in this book is intended to accommodate the reader of English. The purist will note that I do not provide ladies' surnames with the feminine ending, and will doubtless detect many inconsistencies such as the use of the familiar "Nicholas I" alongside "Nikolai" Tolstoy etc. I have preferred familiar usages where they exist, and throughout my aim in this respect has been simplicity at the expense of pedantry.

Acknowledgments

I hope those kind people who have afforded me generous help and advice in the compilation of this book will not be disappointed with a text which owes much to their aid. They include Mrs. John Allen-Stevens, Mr. H. Graham Bower, Miss Margaret Dalton, the Rev. Martin Dimnik, Mr. Andrej Dzierzhinsky, Professor J. L. I. Fennell, Prince Emmanuel Galitzine, Mr. Michael Giedroić, Dr. Ronald Hingley, Madame Hélène Rehle, Professor Allen A. Sinel, Prince George Vassilchikoff, Mr. Igor Vinogradoff, Princess Catherine Volkonsky (of the Tolstoy Foundation), Professor Jackson Taylor, and Mr. Kyril Zinoviev.

Pushkin's description of Zaretsky (Feodor Ivanovich Tolstoy) is taken by kind permission from Sir Charles Johnston's admirable translation of *Eugene Onegin*.

It would be invidious to single out members of the staffs of the following institutions, whose help so often went much beyond the ordinary calls of duty: the Bodleian Library, the British Library, the Helsinki University Library, the Hermitage Museum, the London Library, the National Board of Antiquities in Helsinki, and the Slavonic and Greek Library of the Taylor Institution, Oxford.

Anthony Sheil, Penelope Hoare and Dr. Anthony Storr gave me continual encouragement and stimulating advice, even in those dark days when it seemed I would never get beyond the year 1700.

Writing a book of this sort is a remarkable experience, drawing as it does not only on conventional historical and literary researches, but also on the accumulated memories of my lifetime and those of relatives, many of whom have passed to a happier world. In particular, I owe more than I can say to my dear great-aunts Maroussia and Lily who preserved vivid memories extending back to the reign of the Emperor Alexander III. My grandfather devoted the latter part of his life to accumulating genealogical and other documentation of our family history. It is to my father, though, that I am indebted above all others for the fact that this book is freer from errors than it otherwise might have been. He read each chapter as I completed it, sifting the evidence, correcting my blunders, and adding much invaluable material from his own store of knowledge, personal and antiquarian. Occasionally we differed on minor matters of detail, but I hope that the final piece does not appear too rough-hewn an account of those who have passed before us.

Nikolai Tolstoy

Picture Credits

The author and publishers would like to thank the following for help with the assembling of illustrations: The British Library; the Bodleian Library, Oxford; the Hermitage Museum, Leningrad; The National Museum of Finland, Helsinki; the London Library; the Taylor Institution; V/O "Vneshtorgizdat".

Copyright of the British Library: Map of Azov (page 60); Kruzenstern at Petropavlovsk (page 129); Dmitri Andreevich Tolstoy (page 173); General Dmitri Bibikov (page 189); Dmitri Andreevich Tolstoy (page 201); General Loris-Melikov (page 203); Alexei Constantinovich Tolstoy (page 219); Ivan Matveevich Tolstoy (page 322).
Copyright of the Bodleian Library, Oxford: Maria Ilinichna Miloslavsky (page 19).
Copyright of the Hermitage Museum, Leningrad: Peter Tolstoy (page 79); General Osterman-Tolstoy (page 112); General Peter Alexandrovich Tolstoy (page 182).
Copyright of the National Museum of Finland, Helsinki: Bridge at Idensalm (page 131) and Dolgoruknov memorial (page 132).

The *Illustrated London News* (page 332).
The *Daily Mail* (page 336).
Map on pages 44–45: The Kirkham Studios.
The photograph on page 323: Henry Grossman.

Notes

Author's Preface

[1] Marc Raeff, *Origins of the Russian Intelligentsia: The Eighteenth-Century Nobility* (New York, 1966), pp. 18–20.

[2] Aylmer Maude, *The Life of Tolstoy: First Fifty Years* (London, 1911), p. 287. The two Tolstoys had dined together in 1856, but this seems to have been the virtual extent of their acquaintance (André Lirondelle, *Le poète Alexis Tolstoï: L'homme et l'oeuvre* (Paris, 1912), p. 138).

[3] Cf. S. Baring-Gould, *The Lives of the Saints* (London, 1898), xv, pp. 180–5.

[4] N. P. Pavlov-Silvansky, Очерки по русской историй XVII–XIX вв. (St. Petersburg, 1910), p. 9.

[5] Ibid., p. 4.

[6] 'Николай Васильевичъ Гоголь', Русская старина (1890), lxvii, p. 195.

[7] S. L. Tolstoy, Федор Толстой американец (Moscow, 1926), pp. 94–5.

[8] 'Воспоминанія М. Ѳ. Каменской', Историческій вѣстникъ (1894), lv, p. 303. In 1979 I heard from Mrs. Ida Seymour, daughter of the British Chaplain in Moscow before 1888, whose mother arranged to provide English girls for Russian families requiring governesses. "The Tolstoys were among those who applied", she wrote, "& were duly sent a girl who left after a short period & returned to my mother in considerable distress complaining of the very unruly behaviour of the male members of the family – so my parents had to explain why no other girls would be sent to them."

[9] Maude, op. cit., pp. 128, 173–4, 205, 367; Henri Troyat, *Tolstoï* (Paris, 1965), p. 801. All Leo Tolstoy's children inherited his exceptional physical strength (Tatyana Tolstoy, *Tolstoy Remembered* (London, 1977), pp. 37, 253–4).

1. Family Origins

[1] A. E. Pennington (ed.), *Grigorij Kotošixin: O Rossii v carstvovanie Alekseja Mixajloviča* (Oxford, 1980), p. 59.

[2] Cf. A. V. Artsikhovky (ed.), Очерки русской Культуры XVII века (Moscow, 1979), pp. 300–1; A. M. Kleimola, "Boris Godunov and the Politics of Mestnichestvo", *The Slavonic and East European Review* (London, 1975), liii, pp. 354–69.

[3] For the Indris depositions, cf. V. V. Rummel and V. V. Golubtsov, Родословный Сборникъ Русскихъ Дворянскихъ Фамилій (St. Petersburg, 1887), ii, p. 487; Alexander Bobrinskoy, Дворянскіе Роды внесенные въ Общій Гербовникъ Всероссійской Имперій (St. Petersburg, 1890), i, pp. 369–72; Pavel Stroev, 'Записки М. В. Данилова', Русскій Архивъ (St. Petersburg, 1883), ii, p. 4. A chronicler of 1353 would not of course have employed A.D. dating (introduced by Peter I), but that from the Creation: 6861. But both forms were in use by the late 17th century; cf. Полное Собрание Русскихъ Летописей (Moscow, 1968), xxxi, p. 88. It is significant that "although chronicles must have been kept at the courts of the Ol'govichi [Princes of Chernigov], none has survived" (Martin

Dimnik, *Mikhail, Prince of Chernigov and Grand Prince of Kiev 1224–1246* (Toronto, 1981), p. 1). The best genealogical authorities accept both the authenticity of the entry in the lost Chernigov chronicle and the implications of Indris's Lithuanian origins. Cf. Rummel and Golubtsov, op. cit., ii, p. 487; V. G. Chertkov (ed.), Л. Н. Толстой: полное собрание сочинений (Moscow-Leningrad, 1934), xlvi, p. 485.

[4] For a German named "Indrok", v. Полное Собрание Русских Летописей, xxxi, p. 136; cf. the name "Indrikh" (Лѣтопись по ипатоскому списку (St. Petersburg, 1871), pp. 268, 270, 614). The name "Leonti" assumed by Indris after his conversion is equivalent to the Western "Leo" (ibid., p. 79). The names "Indrikhovich" and "Zhimont" (the latter described as "a knight") occur in a charter of King Wladyslaw of Poland, dated 1378 (M. M. Peshchak (ed.), Грамоти XIV ст. (Kiev, 1974), pp. 59, 88, 89).

[5] J. L. I. Fennell, *The Emergence of Moscow 1304–1359* (London, 1968), pp. 145–7, 211–12.

[6] Ibid., pp. 204–7, 217.

[7] R. V. Zotov, О черниговскихъ князьяхъ по любецкому синодику и о Черниговскомъ Княжествъ въ татарское время (St. Petersburg, 1892), p. 255.

[8] Ibid., pp. 138–9, 145, 255; Henryk Paszkiewicz, *The Origin of Russia* (London, 1954), pp. 211, 216–17; Fennell, op. cit., pp. 122, 133.

[9] V. T. Pashuto, B. N. Florya and A. L. Khoroshkevich (eds.), Древнерусское наследие и исторические судьбы восточного славянства (Moscow, 1982), p. 32; Paszkiewicz, op. cit., pp. 215, 219, 249; Fennell, op. cit., pp. 256–8.

[10] Ibid., pp. 163–4; N. A. Kazakova, Русско-ливонские и русско-ганзейские отношения: Конец XIV-начало XVIb. (Leningrad, 1975), p. 134.

[11] Fennell, op. cit., p. 155. Olgerd's predecessor Mindaugas in the previous century had established an alliance with the Livonian Teutonic Knights (Eric Christiansen, *The Northern Crusades: The Baltic and the Catholic Frontier 1100–1525* (London, 1980), p. 134).

[12] M. Tikhomirov, *The Towns of Ancient Rus* (Moscow, 1959), pp. 357–71; B. A. Rybakov, Киевская Русь и русские княжества XII–XIIIвв. (Moscow, 1982), pp. 498–501.

[13] Robert Michell and Nevill Forbes (ed.), *The Chronicle of Novgorod 1016–1471* (London, 1914), pp. 120–37.

[14] Ibid., pp. 133, 145.

[15] Cf. the vivid images of the contemporary epic (M. N. Tikhomirov (ed.), Задонщина: похвала великому князю Дмитрию Ивановичу и брату его князю Владимиру Андреевичу (Moscow, 1980), p. 55).

[16] Cf. R. E. F. Smith, *Peasant Farming in Muscovy* (Cambridge, 1977), pp. 7, 16–21, 33–6, 57–79; K. G. Vasiliev and A. E. Segal, История эпидемии в России (Moscow, 1960), p. 31.

[17] Jerome Blum, *Lord and Peasant in Russia from the Ninth to the Nineteenth Centuiy* (Princeton, 1961), pp. 43–5, 80; Richard Hellie, *Enserfment and Military Change in Muscovy* (Chicago, 1971), pp. 25–7.

[18] Andrzej Walicki, *The Slavophile Controversy: History of a Conservative Utopia in Nineteenth-Century Russian Thought* (Oxford, 1975), p. 27.

[19] Задонщина, pp. 43, 97. The arms of Chernigov are illustrated and discussed in N. N. Speransov's handsome volume, Земельные гербы России (Moscow, 1974), pp. 80–1.

[20] For illustration, description and discussion of the Tolstoy coat-of-arms, see Общій Гербовникъ дворянскихъ родовъ Всероссійскія Имперій начашый въ 1797мъ году (1798), ii, pp. 12, 42; P. N. Petrov, Исторія родовъ русскаго дворянства (St. Petersburg, 1886), i, p. 310; Alexander Lakier, Русская Геральдика (St. Petersburg, 1855), pp. 556–9. Coats-of-arms developed in Russia at the end of the 16th century, under the influence of European heraldry (U.K. Lukomsky and N. A. Tipolt, Русская геральдика: руководство къ составленію и описанію гербовъ (Petrograd, 1915), pp. 1–2; cf. Pennington, op. cit., pp. 41–2). A mid-17th-century Western visitor found the Russians "very unskilled" at blazoning banners (A. Loviagin (ed.), Адамъ Олеарій: Описаніе путешествія въ Московію и черезъ Московію въ Персію и обратно (St. Petersburg, 1906), p. 41).

[21] *Lord and Peasant in Russia*, pp. 80–3; Marc Raeff, *Origins of the Russian Intelligentsia: The Eighteenth-Century Nobility* (New York, 1966), p. 16.

[22] Blum, op. cit., pp. 71–2, 172–4; Nancy Shields-Kollmann, "The Boyar Clan and Court Politics: The Founding of the Muscovite Political System", *Cahiers du Monde Russe et Sovietique* (Paris, 1982), xxiii, pp. 5–31.

[23] Rummel and Golubtsov, *op. cit.*, p. 488. The Emperor Nicholas I informed a Count Tolstoy that his surname was a translation from the German (Count M. Tolstoy, 'Краткое описаніе жизни графа Петра Андреевича Толстаго', Русскій Архивъ (1896), i, p. 21).

[24] Cf. B. O. Unbegaun, *Russian Surnames* (Oxford, 1972), p. 19.

[25] Cf. Prokofy Tolstoy's mission to Poland in 1584 (B. N. Florya, Русско-польские отношения и политическое развитие Восточной Европы во второй половине XVI—начале XVII в. (Moscow, 1978), p. 126.)

[26] V. I. Buganov (ed.), Разрядная книга 1559–1605гг. (Moscow, 1974), p. 73; idem, Разрядная кннга 1475–1598гг. (Moscow, 1966), pp. 240, 279, 308, 331, 487, 526; Боярские списки последней четверти XVI—начала XVII в. и роспись русского войска 1604г, pp. 138, 157, 171, 187, 190, 195, 202, 234, 241, 242, 292, 311, (part ii) 9, 13; M. N. Tikhomirov, Российское государство XV–XVII веков (Moscow, 1973), p. 252.

[27] V. Klyuchevsky, Курс русскои истории (Moscow, 1937), iii, p. 76.

2. The Tolstoys and the Miloslavskys

[1] Cf. Prince A. B. Lobanov-Rostovsky, Русская родословная книга (St. Petersburg, 1895), i, pp. 381–5.

[2] Сенатскіе Вѣдомости, (St. Petersburg, 1910), No. 97. Cf. G. de Morant and H. D'Angerville (eds.), *Annuaire de la Noblesse de France et d'Europe* (Paris, 1957), lxxxviii, p. 265.

[3] F. C. Belfour (ed.), *The Travels of Macarius, Patriarch of Antioch: written by his attendant Archdeacon Paul of Aleppo, in Arabic* (London, 1836), i, pp. 322, 379; ii, pp. 29–31, 45; A. M. Loviagin (ed.), Адамъ Олеарій: Описаніе путешествія въ Московію и черезъ Московію въ Персію и обратно (St. Petersburg, 1906), pp. 114, 116, 153, 155.

[4] Ibid., p. 257. In 1660 a diplomat was sentenced to be beaten with rods for omitting the word "lord" (*gosudar*) (A. E. Pennington (ed.), *Grigorij Kotošixin: O Rossii v carstvovanie Alekseja Mixajloviča* (Oxford, 1980), p. 1).

[5] Loviagin, op. cit., p. 153; Belfour, op. cit., ii. pp. 30, 113, 135.

[6] Ibid., i, pp. 342–6, 350; Loviagin, op. cit., p. 158; A. von Mayerburg, *Voyage en Moscovie d'un Ambassadeur, Conseiller de le Chambre Impèriale, Envoyé par l'Empereur Leopold au Czar Alexis Mihailowics, Grand Duc de Moscovie* (Leiden, 1688), p. 106.

[7] Guy Miège, *A Relation of Three Embassies From his Sacred Majestie Charles II to the Great Duke of Muscovie, The King of Sweden, and the King of Denmark* (London, 1669), pp. 44–5, 49–51.

[8] Ibid., p. 35; Loviagin, op. cit., pp. 198, 278–9; Belfour, op. cit., pp. 351. 399; Mayerburg, op. cit., pp. 101–2.

[9] The elaborate ceremonial of Tsar Alexei Mihailovich's wedding is described in great detail by Kotoshchikhin (pp. 19–29); Полное собрание русских летописей (Moscow, 1968), xxxi, pp. 164–8; Alexander Barsukov, Родъ Шереметевыхъ (St. Petersburg, 1883), iii, pp. 365–71. Contemporary Russian wedding ritual is to be found in Loviagin, op. cit., pp. 206, 210–17, 222, 262–3, 317; S. Collins, *The Present State of Russia, In a Letter to a Friend at London; Written by an Eminent Person residing at the Great Tzars Court at Mosco for the space of nine years* (London, 1671), pp. 6–11, 35–7; Count Macdonnell (ed.), *Diary of an Austrian Secretary of Legation at the Court of Czar Peter the Great* (London, 1863), ii, pp. 131–2, 212–16.

The absence of *skomorokhi*, minstrels, buffoons and other popular entertainers from the festivities made a marked contrast with previous royal weddings. The pious Alexei was to banish them altogether in later months (cf. Russell Zguta, *Russian Minstrels: A History of the Skomorokhi* (Oxford, 1978), pp. 57, 58–62, 106).

[10] Collins (op. cit.), pp. 103–4; Mayerburg (op. cit.), pp. 203–4; Loviagin, (op. cit.), pp. 262–3; Полное собрание русских летописей, xxxi, p. 168; Kotoshchikhin (op. cit.), pp. 19–20; N. I. Kostomarov, Русская исторія (n.d.), ii, p. 86; V. P. Semeonov, Россія: полное географическое онисаніе нашего отечества (St. Petersburg, 1899), i, p. 267; Ivan Zabelin, Домашній бытъ русскихъ царицъ въ XVI и XVII см. (Moscow, 1869), pp. 106–7, 252–3, 257–9.

[11] Lobanov-Rostovsky, op. cit., i, p. 381. The Rimsky-Korsakovs are descended from the same ancestor.

[12] V. P. Semeonov, op. cit., i, p. 267; 'Дневникъ И. М. Снѣгирева', Русскій Архивъ (1903), iii, p. 269. The Church of St. Nicholas is illustrated in M. Ilyin (ed.), Москва: Памятники архитектуры XIV–XVII веков (Moscow, 1973), plates 152–6.

[13] Cf. Боярские списки последней четверти XVI– начала XVIIв. и роспись русского войска 1604г. (?Moscow, n.d.), pp. 114, 116, 119 (1588–9 list of boyars), 188 (1598–9), 214, 231 (1602–3); V. I. Buganov (ed.), Разрядная книга 1559–1605гг. (Moscow, 1974), p. 80; idem, Разрядная книга 1475–1598гг. (Moscow, 1966), pp. 244, 260, 415, 492, 502, 511; A. N. Nasonov (ed.), Псковские летописи (Moscow, 1955), pp. 276–7, 278 (Mihail Miloslavsky, Voevod of Pskov in 1611–1613); "Списокъ воеводъ Яренскаго на выми городка", Русскій Архивъ (1906), iii, p. 611 (Iakov Mihailovich Miloslavksy, Voevod of Iarensk in 1629–1631). In 1634 B. E. Miloslavsky was on the list of nobles admitted to the Tsar's palace on grand occasions (Ikonnikov). For a complete list of Voevodships held by various Miloslavsky boyars between 1613 and 1679, cf. Alexander Barsukov, Списки городовыхъ воеводъ и другихъ лицъ воеводскаго управленія Московскаго государства (St. Petersburg, 1902), pp. 518–19.

[14] Collins, op. cit., pp. 57, 103–4; Miège, op. cit., p. 64; Barsukov, op. cit., p. 55. For Danilo Miloslavsky's relationship to Gramotin, for whom Collins alleges he "drew wine", cf. Lobanov-Rostovsky, op. cit., p. 382. Loviagin, op. cit., p. 263. For ways in which a noble family could lose its wealth, cf. Marc Raeff, Origins of the Russian Intelligentsia: The Eighteenth-Century Nobility (New York, 1966), p. 16. A folksong commemorated a Daniel Miloslavsky, who may have been Ilya's father, as one of Russia's military heroes (K. Waliszewski, Le Berceau d'une Dynastie: Les Premiers Romanov 1613–1682 (Paris, 1909), p. 182).

[15] Изъ писемъ И. Д. Бѣлаева къ А. Н. Попову, Русскій Архивъ (1886), iii, pp. 249–50.

[16] N. A. Smirnov, Россия и Турция в XVI–XVIIвв. (Moscow, 1946), i, p. 31; ii, pp. 87–9.

[17] Cf. Richard Hellie, Enserfment and Military Change in Muscovy (Chicago, 1971), p. 190; Русскій Архивъ (1912), ii, p. 8; Русская Старина (1909), cxl, p. 439; ibid. (1912), clii, p. 428; A. V. Artsikhovsky (ed.), Очерки русской культуры XVII века (Moscow, 1979), p. 268; Joseph T. Fuhrmann, Tsar Alexis: His Reign and his Russia (Gulf Breeze, 1981), p. 123.

[18] V. P. Semeonov, op. cit., i, p. 221; Loviagin, op. cit., p. 263; Collins, op. cit., p. 62; Русскій Архивъ (1893), iii, pp. 28–9; Zabelin, op. cit., p. 475; A. A. Novoselsky and N. V. Ustyug (ed.), Очерки истории СССР: период феодализма XVIIв. (Moscow, 1955), p. 92. An early 19th-century watercolour of the Miloslavsky Palace is reproduced by Ilyin, op. cit., p. 45. For the construction and magnificence of the Moscow magnates' houses at this time, cf. Belfour, op. cit., i, pp. 397–8. Olearius refers to a wedding arranged by Ilya Danilovich in his church (Loviagin, op. cit., p. 306).

[19] Passages from the Diary of General Patrick Gordon of Auchleuchries (Aberdeen, 1859), pp. 46, 61; N. B. Golikova, Политические процессы при Петре I (Moscow, 1957), p. 98. Cf. Macarius, i, p. 399.

[20] 'Записки М. В. Данилова', Русскій Архивъ (1883), ii, p. 5. Professor R. E. Smith has published a map including part of an estate of I. D. Miloslavsky at Anninskoe village near Moscow (Peasant Farming in Muscovy (Cambridge, 1977), plate 11).

[21] William Palmer, The Patriarch and the Tsar (London, 1876), v, p. 249 (2nd section); D. A. Rovinsky, Подробный словарь русскихъ гравированныхъ портретовъ (St. Petersburg, 1889), ii, p. 325. For church and state hostility to Western portraiture, cf. W. Bruce Lincoln, The Romanovs, Autocrats of All the Russias (London, 1981), p. 96; Belfour, op. cit., ii, p. 50. An interesting inscription in a prayer book commemorates Ivan Bogdanovich Miloslavsky's devotion to the memory of Ilya Danilovich and the latter's two successive wives (I. V. Pozdeeva, I. D. Kashkarova and M. M. Lerenman (ed.) Каталог книг кириллической печати XV–XVII в.в. (Moscow, 1980), pp. 80–1). The story of the Georgian Tsarevich is told by M. Rabinovich and G. Latysheva, Из жизни древней Москвы (Moscow, 1961), pp. 171–2). For painting at the Miloslavsky estate at Kirzhach, cf. Pierre Pascal, Avvakum et les Débuts du Raskol: La crise religieuse au XVIIᵉ siècle en Russie (Paris, 1938), p. 348. Their confessor was the famous Archimandrite Paul of Chudov (ibid., p. 357), and Anna Ilinichna's chaplain was a certain Dimitri (ibid., p. 331; cf. p. 334).

[22] Loviagin, op. cit., p. 263; Pennington, op. cit., p. 29. His silver, jewellery, sables, etc., are mentioned in Русскій Архивъ (1893), iii, pp. 15, 29; Zabelin, op. cit., pp. 94, 130, 135 (2nd pagination).

[23] Collins, op. cit., p. 31; Gordon, op. cit., p. 53; Mayerburg, op. cit., pp. 156–9, 297–8. In fact Miloslavsky had accompanied the Tsar at the siege of Riga in 1656 (Полное собрание русских летописей, xxxi, p. 170). For the campaign itself, cf. C. Bickford O'Brien, Muscovy and the Ukraine from the Pereiaslavl Agreement to the Truce of Andrusovo, 1654–1667 (Los Angeles, 1963), p. 40, and Ilya Miloslavsky's presence, Joseph T. Fuhrmann, op. cit., p. 74.

[24] S. A. Piontkovsky (ed.), Городские восстания в Московском государстве XVIIв. (Moscow, 1936), pp. 135–6. The Voevod of Ustyug generally had two or three secretaries under him (Pennington, op. cit., p. 121).

[25] The best general account of the 1662 copper riots is that of Richard Hellie, op. cit., pp. 55, 134–7. Cf. also W. Bruce Lincoln, op. cit., pp. 42–4; Loviagin, op. cit., pp. 264–73; Mayerberg, op. cit., pp. 205–6; Pennington, op. cit., pp. 113–18; Полное собрание русских летописей, xxxi, p. 168. For Ivan Mihailovich Miloslavsky's rôle, cf. A. A. Novoselsky and N. V. Ustyugov, op. cit., p. 260; N. N. Voronin and V. V. Kostochkin (ed.), Троице-Сергиева лавра: художественные памятники (Moscow, 1968), p. 138. Waliszewski remarked on the exceptional ability of the three leading Miloslavsky boyars, who were also, it is noted, "d'affreux coquins". (Waliszewski, op. cit., p. 529.) In 1654 Ilya ranked among the 29 great Muscovite boyars (Loviagin, op. cit., p. 276; cf. Pennington, op. cit., p. 37).

[26] Hellie, op. cit., pp. 141, 186–201, 222, 246–9, 254–5, 262–5, 370; Collins, op. cit., p. 105; Loviagin,

op. cit., p. 280; *Gordon Diary*, pp. 45–6, 52, 53. Ilya Danilovich was energetic in trying to convert foreign officers to Orthodoxy (Pascal, op. cit., pp. 177, 198).

[27] Loviagin, op. cit., pp. 282, 283–4; Collins, op. cit., p. 106; Mayerberg, op. cit., pp. 298–9. Apart from his public earnings and plunder, I. D. Miloslavsky invested largely in Russia's incipient industrialization, establishing factories, etc., on his estates (cf. A. A. Novoselsky and N. V. Ustyugov, op. cit., pp. 90, 91, 92, 343; Fuhrmann, op. cit., p. 110). For the purposes of the *prikazi* headed by him, cf. Pennington, op. cit., pp. 120–1, 122–3.

[28] Waliszewski, op. cit., pp. 82–6, 513; Hellie, op. cit., pp. 249–50; Pennington, op. cit., p. 113; Mayerberg, op. cit., pp. 298–9, 319, 348–51; Fuhrmann, op. cit., pp. 146, 150, 151. Ivan Andreevich Miloslavsky was head of the *Iamskoi prikaz* (Loviagin, op. cit., pp. 277, 281), for which see also Pennington, op. cit., p. 123.

[29] Zabelin, op. cit., pp. 350 (1st section), 94, 101, 102 (2nd section); Collins, op. cit., pp. 106–7; Mayerberg, op. cit., pp. 111, 114, 121; Palmer, op. cit., pp. 761–71. A curious piece of Muscovite etiquette prevented Ilya from publicly claiming relationship with his daughter the Tsaritsa (Collins, op. cit., p. 12; Mayerberg, op. cit., p. 297).

[30] Pascal, op. cit., pp. 229, 247, 331; Waliszewski, op. cit., pp. 491–2, 521; Zabelin, op. cit., pp. 159, 169, 294, 333–9, 348, 350–1, 356, 379, 416, 469, etc; Miège, op. cit., pp. 134, 144; Mayerberg, op. cit., pp. 304–5, 350; Pennington, op. cit., pp. 29, 46–9; Belfour, op. cit., ii, pp. 88, 107, 223–4, 249; Collins, op. cit., pp. 65, 112, 124; Fuhrmann, op. cit., pp. 189–92. The Tsaritsa lavishly endowed a monastery on the Miloslavsky estate at Alexandrov (Semeonov, op. cit., pp. 263, 267).

[31] Waliszewski, op. cit., pp. 156–7, 169–71; Bruce Lincoln, op. cit., p. 52; Novoselsky and Ustyugov, op. cit., pp. 303–8; Kostomarov, op. cit., ii, pp. 261, 266; Semeonov, op. cit., vi, pp. 389–90, 540; A. G. Mankov (ed.), Иностранные известия о восстании Степана Разина: Материалы и исследования (Leningrad, 1968), pp. 47, 71, 78, 116, 140, 149; Полное собрание русских летописей, xxxi, pp. 8, 217, 227–32; P. Martinov, Матеріалы историческіе и юридическіе района бывшаго приказа казанского дворца (Simbirsk, 1904), iv, p. 14. For contemporary accounts of Miloslavsky's capture of Astrakhan, *vide* A. A. Novoselsky (ed.), Крестьянская война под предводительством Степана Разина: сборник документов (Moscow, 1962), iii, pp. 181–90; Fuhrmann, op. cit., pp. 185, 186.

[32] Ivan Bogdanovich was present at his cousin's wedding to the Tsar, and the splendour of his subsequent life at court is frequently referred to. Cf. Полное собрание русских летописей, xxxi, p. 167; Zabelin, op. cit., pp. 351, 352, 386, 660 (1st section), 156 (2nd section); P. S. Sheremetev, 'О русскихъ художественныхъ промыслахъ', Русскій Архивъ (1913), ii, p. 456; Novoselsky and Ustyugov, op. cit., p. 72. In 1671 his Moscow house was at 12 Vozdvizhenka Street (Русскій Архивъ (1879), vi, p. 218); Fuhrmann, op. cit., p. 187.

[33] After Ilya Danilovich and Ivan Bogdanovich ranked Ivan Mihailovich Miloslavsky (cf. p. 38). In 1673 Feodor Iakovlevich Miloslavsky was sent as envoy to Persia (Novoselsky, op. cit., iii, p. 290).

[34] Nicolas Ikonnikov, *La Noblesse de Russia* (Paris, 1962), R.1. p. 41; Сборникъ русскаго историческаго общества, cxlii, p. 652; Nasonov, op. cit., pp. 289, 290; Zabelin, op. cit., pp. 28–30 (2nd section); L. M. Savelov, 'Страничка изъ исторіи смутнаго времени', Русскій Архивъ (1914), i, pp. 226, 228; Semeonov, op. cit., ii, p. 475; Разрядная книга 1475–1598, p. 487.

[35] Ikonnikov, op. cit., pp. 46–7; Zabelin, op. cit., p. 260 (1st section). A relation, Daria Ivanovna Tolstoy, was among the Tsaritsa's ladies-in-waiting (ibid., p. 499 (2nd section)).

[36] Belfour, op. cit., i, p. 265; Loviagin, op. cit., p. 194.

[37] Hellie, op. cit., p. 219.

[38] Kostomarov, op. cit., ii, pp. 352–53; Zabelin, op. cit., pp. 150–51, 496 (1st section). I. M. Miloslavsky was simultaneously Head of three Chancelleries: for Administration of Foreigners, Cavalry, and Artillery (V. I. Buganov (ed.), Восстание в Москве 1682 года: сборник документов (Moscow, 1976), p. 18); cf. L. V. Cherepnin and A. G. Mankov (ed.), Крестьянская война нод предводительством Степана Разина (Moscow, 1976), iv, pp. 190, 193; Zabelin, op. cit., p. 556.

[39] Cf. I. S. Bieliaev, 'Походъ боярина Петра Васильевича Большого Шереметева въ Малороссію въ 1679г', Русскій Архивъ (1915), ii, pp. 15–31.

[40] Kostomarov, op. cit., ii, p. 356; Bruce Lincoln, op. cit., p. 64. In January 1680 Ivan Miloslavsky was still high in royal favour (cf. A. G. Kuznetsov (ed.), Кунгурскіе акты XVII вѣка (1668–1699г.) (St. Petersburg, 1888), p. 43).

[41] Cf. Kostomarov, op. cit., ii, p. 391; N. B. Golikova, op. cit., p. 98. Ivan Mihailovich attended the funeral of Tsar Feodor (Полное собрание русских летописей, xxxi, p. 188).

[42] Kostomarov, op. cit., ii, pp. 352–81; Ernest Schuyler, *Peter the Great, Emperor of Russia* (London, 1884), i, pp. 38–119; Bruce Lincoln, op. cit., pp. 60–74; Robert K. Massie, *Peter the Great: His Life and World* (London, 1981), pp. 35–52; V. N. Smolianinov (ed.), Архивъ Кн. Ѳ. А. Куракина (St. Petersburg, 1890), i, pp. 44–9; Полное собрание русских летописей, xxxi, pp. 177–9; I. P. Sakharov (ed.), Записькихъ русскихъ людей (St. Petersburg, 1841), pp. 12–56; Buganov, op. cit., pp. 110–11; V. G. Chertkov (ed.), Л. Н. Толстой: полное собрание сочинений (Moscow, 1936), xvii, p. 423.

[43] Kostomarov, op. cit., ii, pp. 391, 393; Schuyler, op. cit., i, p. 340; Golikova, op. cit., p. 98. The letter itself is printed in Письма и бумаги Петра Великаго (St. Petersburg, 1887), i, p. 266.

[44] Bruce Lincoln, op. cit., p. 42; Waliszewski, op. cit., p. 201.

[45] G. de Morant and H. D'Angerville (ed.), *Annuaire de la Noblesse de France et D'Europe* (Paris, 1957), lxxxviii, p. 265. For the relative characters of the seventeenth-century Tolstoys and Miloslavskys, cf. the words of Constantin de Grunwald, *Peter the Great* (London, 1956), p. 62.

3. The Curse of the Tsarevich

[1] N. P. Pavlov-Silvansky, Очерки по русской истории XVIII–XIX вв. (St. Petersburg, 1910), pp. 7–9, 12; *Analecta Slavica: A Slavonic Miscellany Presented for his Seventieth Birthday to Bruno Becker* (Amsterdam, 1955), pp. 21–3; N. Popov, "Изъ жизни П. А. Толстаго", Русскій Вѣстникъ (Moscow, 1860), xxvii, pp. 320–1, 345; M. M. Bogoslovsky, Петр I: Материалы для биографии (Moscow, 1940), i, pp. 37, 388; R. Nisbet Bain, *The Pupils of Peter the Great: A History of the Russian Court and Empire from 1697 to 1740* (London, 1897), p. 37; V. Klyuchevsky, Курс русской истории (Moscow, 1937), iv, p. 267; 'Петр великій въ разсказахъ Нартова', Русская старина (1892) lxxiii, p. 124.

[2] Cf. Robert O. Crummey, 'Peter and the Boiar Aristocracy, 1689–1700', *Canadian–American Slavic Studies* (1974), viii, pp. 274–287; Count M. Tolstoy, 'Краткое описаніе жизни графа Петра Андреевича Толстаго'. Русскій Архивъ (1896) i, p. 20. For a list of Voevodships held by Tolstoys between 1621 and 1693, cf. Alexander Barsukov, Списки городовыхъ воеводъ и другихъ лицъ воеводскаго управленія Московскаго государства XVII столѣтія (St. Petersburg, 1902), p. 577).

[3] V. N. Smolianinov (ed.), Архивъ Кн. Ѳ. А. Куракина (St. Petersburg, 1893), iv, p. 74; Русскій Вѣстникъ, xxvii, pp. 320–1; V. I. Buganov (ed.), Восстание в Москве 1682 года (Moscow, 1976), pp. 16, 19, 262, 305; idem, Восстание московских стрельцов 1698г (Moscow, 1980), p. 288. For relatives in high places cf. A. A. Titov (ed.), Кингурскіе акты XVII вѣка (1668–1699г.) (St. Petersburg, 1888), p. 40; I. Zabelin, Домашній быть русскихъ царицъ въ XVI и XVII ст. (Moscow, 1869) pp. 499–500 (1st section); Bogoslovsky, op. cit., i, p. 179; Русскій Архивъ (1896), i, p. 21.

[4] Письма и бумаги императора Петра Великаго (St. Petersburg, 1887), i, pp. 133–5; Max J. Okenfuss, 'Russian Students in the Age of Peter the Great', *The Eighteenth Century in Russia* (ed. J. G. Garrard) (Oxford, 1973), pp. 133–6.

[5] Three Miloslavsky cousins accompanied Tolstoy (Письма и бумаги Петра Великаго, i, p. 610).

[6] The text of Peter Tolstoy's diary was edited by his descendant Count Dmitri Tolstoy: 'Путешествіе стольника П. А. Толстого', Русскій Архивъ (1888), i, pp. 161–204, 321–68, 505–52; ii, 5–62, 113–56, 225–64, 369–400. Cf. Pavlov-Silvansky, op. cit., ii, pp. 13–19; *Analecta Slavica*, p. 21; D. S. Likhachev, 'Повести русских послов как памятники литературы', Путешествия русских послов XVI-XVIIвв (Moscow, 1954) pp. 338–46; Klyuchevsky, op. cit., iv, p. 267; Русскій Вѣстникъ, xxvii, p. 322.

[7] Ivan Tolstoy was appointed Ambassador on 26 December 1700 (P. Martynov (ed.), Материалы историческіе и юридическіе района бывшаго приказа Казанскаго дворца (Simbirsk, 1904), iv, p. 355).

[8] Bogoslovsky, op. cit., i, p. 331; *Analecta Slavica*, p.

[9] Письма и бумаги Петра Великаго, ii, pp. 24–5, 98, 152, 169, 333, 384, 398, 421, 525, 532, 577–8, 580–1. For a contemporary plan of Azov, cf. B. B. Kaffengaus (ed.), Очерки истории СССР: период феодализма (Moscow, 1954), p. 443; Русская старина (1899), c, p. 261.

[10] Письма и бумаги Петра Великаго, ii, pp. 20–2, 30–8, 52–6, 321, 334–5; ibid., iii, pp. 79–80.

[11] Akdes Nimet Kurat (ed.), *The Despatches of Sir Robert Sutton, Ambassador in Constantinople (1710–1714)* (London, 1953), p. 2.

[12] N. Ustrialov, Исторія царствованія Петра великаго (St. Petersburg, 1863), iv (part 2), p. 399.

[13] The allegation by the French consul Villardeau that Tolstoy in fact poisoned his secretary to avert a revelation that the Ambassador had been embezzling Embassy funds (*Analectica Slavica*, pp. 22–3) appears to be a piece of contemporary slander. Tolstoy was receiving ample supplies of money and sables (cf. Письма и бумаги Петра Великаго, v, pp. 585–6), and a little malversation of funds would have been unlikely to agitate the Tsar overmuch. (Русскій Вѣстникъ, xxvii, pp. 326–9).

[14] A. V. Cherepnin and A. G. Mankov (ed.), Крестьянская война под предводительство Степана Разина (Moscow, 1976), iv, p. 216); cf. Письма и бумаги Петра Великаго, iii, pp. 392–4, 859–60, 865, 873, 876, 1019–21.

[15] Письма и бумаги Петра Великаго, vii, p. 649.

[16] Ibid., p. 837. For the codes, cf. pp. 734–5.

[17] For Ivan Andreeich Tolstoy and Bulavin, cf. Major-General P. S. Tolstoy, 'Иванъ Андреевичъ Толстой †1713г. Письма къ нему Петра Великаго', Русская старина (1879), x, pp. 144–7; Собраніе сочиненій Н. И. Костомарова (St. Petersburg, 1905), vi, p. 581; Kaffengaus, op. cit., pp. 262–4. Ivan Tolstoy's report of his victory is printed in Письма и бумаги Петра Великаго, viii, p. 478, and his reply to the Tsar's letter of thanks in ibid, p. 481; ibid., x, pp. 502–3; xii, (pt. 1). pp. 271, 343–5; xii (pt. 2), p. 351; A. Karasev, 'Бумаги относящіяся къ Булавинскому бунту', Русскій Архивъ (1894), iii, pp. 299–305.

[18] Ibid., x (pt. 1), p. 186.

[19] Русская старина, x, pp. 252–4. Ivan Tolstoy replied on 3 July (Письма и бумаги Петра Великаго, ix, pp. 1001–2); he also passed on the significant news to his brother Peter in Constantinople and the Khan of the Crimea (ibid., pp. 996–7).

[20] Kurat, op. cit., pp. 13–35.

[21] Cf. ibid., pp. 17, 47, 170–1.

[22] Ibid., pp. 72, 90–1; V. V. Rummel and V. V. Golubtsov, Родословный сборникъ русскихъ дворянскихъ фамилій (St. Petersburg, 1887), ii, pp. 493–4.

[23] Martynov, op. cit., pp. 585–8.

[24] Kurat, op. cit., pp. 144–6.

[25] For Peter Tolstoy's embassy to Turkey, cf. Pavlov-Silvansky, op. cit., pp. 19–26; Русскій Вѣстникъ, xxvii, pp. 323–9; Kaffengaus, op. cit., pp. 514, 522; Smolianov, op. cit., ii, pp. 232–4; iv, pp. 174–5,

202–3, 211–12, 218–19, 295–6; v, p. 211.

[26] *Analecta Slavica*, p. 23.

[27] L. A. Nikiforov, Русско-англичанские отношения при Петре I (Moscow, 1950), pp. 144–8.

[28] Eugene Schuyler, *Peter the Great, Emperor of Russia: A Study of Historical Biography* (London, 1884), ii, p. 386; Robert K. Massie, *Peter the Great: His Life and Times* (London, 1981), p. 654; Vicomte de Guichen, *Pierre le Grand et le Premier Traité Franco-Russe* (Paris, 1908), p. 189.

[29] The account of the flight, abduction and death of the Tsarevich is chiefly based on the staple source: the magnificent collection of documents edited by Ustryalov in Volume Six of his *History of Peter the Great* ('Царевичъ Алексѣй Петровичъ'). Cf. also Русскій Архивъ (1912), iii, pp. 44–9; Русская старина, lxxiii, pp. 122–3; Schuyler, op. cit., ii, pp. 406–36; Massie, op. cit., pp. 668–710; *Analecta Slavica*, pp. 24–5; Kaffengaus, op. cit., pp. 425–7.

[30] Pavlov-Silvansky, op. cit., p. 9.

[31] Русскій Вѣстникъ, xxvii, pp. 333–4, 336; Ustryalov, op. cit., vi, p. 578; Русская старина, x, pp. 261–2; Schuyler, op. cit., ii, pp. 441, 474; Pavlov-Silvansky, op. cit., pp. 31–2; *Analecta Slavica*, p. 33; Klyuchevsky, op. cit., p. 122.

[32] Pavlov-Silvansky, op. cit., pp. 30–1.

[33] Ibid., pp. 32–3; Nikiforov, op. cit., p. 211; Schuyler, op. cit., ii, pp. 524–7. A fine portrait of Tolstoy at this time by Tannauer is reproduced in the anniversary volume, S. M. Borisov, Ясная Поляна (Moscow, 1978), p. 50. For other portraits, cf. A Wassiltschikoff, *Liste Alphabétique de Portraits Russes* (St. Petersburg, 1875), ii, pp. 472–3.

[34] Schuyler, op. cit., pp. 587–96; Pavlov-Silvansky, op. cit., pp. 32–3; Kaffengaus, op. cit., p. 609; L. Maikov, 'Княжна Марія Кантемирова', Русская старина (1897), lxxxix, pp. 67–8.

[35] Pavlov-Silvansky, op. cit., pp. 33–4; Русскій Архивъ (1896), i, p. 20; *Analecta Slavica*, p. 34.

[36] Pavlov-Silvansky, op. cit., pp. 29–30; Constantin de Grunwald, *Peter the Great* (London, 1956), pp. 198–9; Сборникъ русскаго историческаго общества (1868), iii, pp. 333, 394, 481; ibid., xxxiv, pp. 309, 397.

[37] Schuyler, op. cit., i, pp. 533, 537; ii, p. 549.

[38] *Analecta Slavica*, pp. 25–6.

[39] Cf. 'Указъ по поводу смерти Петра Великаго', Русская старина (1890), lxvii, p. 876 and facsimile.

[40] *Anecdotes Originales de Pierre le Grand . . . par M. de Staehlin* (Strasbourg, 1787), pp. 59–60.

[41] For Tolstoy's latter years, cf. Pavlov-Silvansky, op. cit., pp. 29–38; Русскій Вѣстникъ, xxvii, pp. 337–44; *Analecta Slavica*, pp. 25–30; 'Обозрѣніе историческихъ журналовъ', Русская старина (1894), lxxxi, pp. 249–55; Nisbet Bain, op. cit., pp. 80–111; Klyuchevsky, op. cit., pp. 274, 286–7.

[42] S. A. Malsagoff, *An Island Hell: A Soviet Prison in the Far North* (London, 1926), p. 74.

[43] Pavlov-Silvansky, op. cit., pp. 38–9; 'Историческія замѣтки профес. В. С. Иконикова', Русская старина (1888), lviii, p. 603. The title of Count was restored to Peter Tolstoy's descendants on 26 May 1760. His coat-of-arms added to the Tolstoy device quarterings displaying the

Seven Towers (in which he had been imprisoned at Constantinople), the Russian Imperial Eagle, and the Cross of St. Andrew (Общій Гербовникъ дворянскихъ родовъ Всероссійскія Имперіи начашый въ 1797мъ году (St. Petersburg, 1798), pp. 11–12).

4. The General and the Three Bears

[1] V. A. Bilbasov, Исторія Екатерины второй (Berlin, 1900), ii, pp. 187–91; Русскій Архивъ (1912), ii, p. 482; Русская старина (1876), xv, p. 747; Laurence Kelly, *St. Petersburg: A Travellers' Companion* (London, 1981), p. 67. For the conspiracy of Khrushchev and Guryev, cf. Isabel de Madariaga, *Russia in the Age of Catherine the Great* (London, 1981), pp. 33–4. The Tolstoy to whom the Tsaritsa referred could equally have been Count Peter Andreevich, of whom and whose children she was fond (see Chapter VI).

[2] The principal sources for Osterman-Tolstoy's career are A. A. Polovtsov, Русскій біографическій словарь (St. Petersburg, 1905), pp. 420–3; Dmitry Zavalishin, 'Воспоминаніе о графѣ А. И. Остерманъ-Толстомъ', Историческій вѣстникъ (1880), ii, pp. 92–9; 'Изъ старой записной книжки, начатой въ 1813 году', Русскій Архивъ (1875), i, pp. 196–200; 'Графъ Остерманъ-Толстой', ibid. (1878), i, pp. 360–4; Сочиненія И. Лажечникова (St. Petersburg, 1884), xii, pp. 319–47.

[3] P. Karatygin, 'Семейныя отношенія Графа А. И. Остермана', Историческій вѣстникъ (1884), xvii, pp. 603–23.

[4] V. V. Rummel and V. V. Golubtsov, Родословный Сборникъ Руссихъ дворянскихъ фамилій (St. Petersburg, 1887), ii, p. 517.

[5] General A. I. Mikhailovsky-Danilievsky, Описаніе первой войны Императора Александра съ Наполеономъ въ 1805-мъ году (St. Petersburg, 1844), pp. 256–67.

[6] Michael and Diana Josselson, *The Commander: A Life of Barclay de Tolly* (Oxford, 1980), p. 30.

[7] Denis Davydov provides a glimpse of Bennigsen and Tolstoy before Eylau, crawling over their maps and discussing battle-plans before a crowd of staff-officers (V. Orlov (ed.), Денис Давыдов: Военные Записки (Moscow, 1940), p. 74; cf. pp. 74, 100). Immediately after Friedland Bennigsen instructed Tolstoy to protect the Russian frontier against any further French advance (General A. I. Mikhailovsky-Danilievsky, Описаніе второй войны Императора Александра съ Наполеономъ въ 1806 и 1807 годахъ (St. Petersburg, 1846), p. 344). For Tolstoy's escape at Eylau, see Lazhechnikov, op. cit., p. 337.

[8] Leonid I. Strakhovsky, *Alexander I of Russia: The Man Who Defeated Napoleon* (London, 1949), p. 78; Русскій Архивъ (1901), iii (supplement), p. 347. A fine portrait of Nikolai Tolstoy by Angelica Kaufman is reproduced in N. K. Schilder, Императоръ Александръ Первый (St. Petersburg, 1897), ii, p. 57. His armorial bookplate is reproduced by S. G. Ivensky, Книжный знак: история, теория, прак-

тика художественного развития (Moscow, 1980), p. 34.

[9] Once in Paris, however, French politeness struck a chivalrous response in the old soldier's breast. On one occasion Marshal Macdonald spoke to him disarmingly of Russia's great military hero: "Although the Emperor Napoleon does not allow himself to deny Suvorov's achievement in Italy [in 1799], nevertheless he does not like to speak of it. I was very young at the Battle of the Trebbia; that misfortune could have had a harmful effect on my career, and I was only protected by the fact that my conqueror was Suvorov." For Count Peter Tolstoy's embassy to Paris, cf. vols. lxxiv, lxxxviii, lxxxix of the Сборникъ Императорскаго Русскаго Историческаго Общества, where many of his despatches are collected; 'Россія въ ея отношеніяхъ къ Европѣ', Русская старина (1890), lxv, pp. 143–221; ibid., cxxii, pp. 316–20; V. Orlov, op. cit., p. 48. Prince Dolgorouky described him as "generally venerated for the loyalty of his character; he is a chevalier sans peur et sans reproche" (Prince Pierre Dolgorouky, Notice sur les Principales Familles de la Russie (Brussels, 1843), p. 89). For a reproduction of the portrait by Henry Dawe, cf. Schilder, op. cit., ii, p. 201. The philosopher La Harpe reported in 1808 to Alexander I that "the Count Tolstoy is an excellent man, very attached to your person, loyal, loved for his good nature, and, so far as I can judge, incapable of being deceived nor of suffering wrong in his duty." (Jean Charles Biaudet and Françoise Nicod, (ed.) Correspondance de Frédéric-César de La Harpe et Alexandre Ier (Neuchâtel, 1979), ii, p. 313; cf. p. 409.)

[10] Josselin, op. cit., p. 61.

[11] Ibid., pp. 96, 99–100; Русскій Архивъ (1878), i, p. 361; P. A. Zhilin, Гибель Наполеоновской армии в России (Moscow, 1974), p. 105.

[12] Ibid., p. 110; Josselin, op. cit., pp. 108–11; David G. Chandler, The Campaigns of Napoleon (London, 1967), p. 779.

[13] Ibid., pp. 794–808; Josselin, op. cit., pp. 134–46; Rev. Herbert Randolph (ed.), Narrative of Events during the Invasion of Russia . . . . . . by General Sir Robert Wilson (London, 1860), pp. 141, 147, 153, 163; L. G. Beskrovny and G. P. Meshcheryakov (ed.), Бородино:Документы, письма, воспоминания (Moscow, 1962), pp. 319–20, 325, 327, 333, 336, 352, 356, 364, 365, 386.

[14] Zhilin, op. cit., pp. 226, 231; A. M. Savelov, Московское Дворянство въ 1812 году (Moscow, 1912), p. 31. Cf. Governor Rostopchin's interesting correspondence with P. A. Tolstoy. 'Четыре письма графа Ө. В. Растопчина къ графу П. А. Толстому. 1812 года', Русскій Архивъ (1885), iii, pp. 409–14.

[15] Josselin, op. cit., pp. 148–51; Polovtsov, op. cit., p. 421.

[16] 'Записки князя Николая Ворисовича Голицына', Русскій Архивъ (1884), ii, pp. 346–7.

[17] For the battle of Kulm and its aftermath, vide General A. I. Mikhailovsky-Danilievsky, Описаніе войны 1813 года (St. Petersburg, 1840), i, pp. 338–80; idem, Записки о походѣ 1813 года (St. Petersburg, 1836), pp. 237–68; Chandler, op. cit., pp. 911–12; Josselin, op. cit., pp. 179–80; The Memoirs of the Baron de Marbot (London, 1892), ii, pp. 373–6; Randolph, op. cit., p. 236. For the decorations awarded to the army by the Allied sovereigns, see the scholarly account by V. G. von Richter, Собрание трудов по русской военной медалистикѣ и истории (Paris, 1972), pp. 293–303. In 1823 Osterman-Tolstoy's talented relative Count Feodor Petrovich Tolstoy struck a handsome medal commemorating the victory (E. V. Kuznetsova, федор Петрович Толстой (Moscow, 1977), pp. 68, 71, 312).

[18] Antony Brett-James (ed.), Europe against Napoleon: The Leipzig Campaign, 1813 from eyewitness accounts (London, 1970), pp. 255–6.

[19] Lazhechnikov, op. cit., p. 322. For the Grand Duchess Catherine's stay at Weimar in 1814, see I. N. Bozheryanov, Великая Княгиня Екатерина Павловна (St. Petersburg, 1888), p. 74.

[20] A. B. Granville, St. Petersburgh. A Journal of Travels to and from that Capital (London, 1828), ii, p. 714. The paper rouble was in practice worth only a quarter of the silver (ibid., p. 329). For the English Quay, cf. ibid., i, pp. 434, 442–3, and the view by Feodor Alexeev reproduced in V. Pushkyarov, The Neva Symphony: Leningrad in Graphic Works of Art and Painting (Leningrad, 1975), plate 39.

[21] Clifford Musgrave, The Royal Pavilion (Brighton, 1958), p. 25.

[22] Историческій Вѣстникъ (1880), ii, pp. 95–6. For the Bolshoi Theatre, cf. the description in Granville op. cit., ii, pp. 376–81, and illustrations in V. Pushkyarov, op. cit., plates 63 and 117. The statue of Countess Osterman-Tolstoy was modelled by Thorwaldsen during a visit to Rome in 1815 (Eugene Plon, Thorvaldsen: His Life and Works (London, 1874), p. 282; Adolf Rosenberg, Thorwaldsen (Bielefeld and Leipzig, 1896), p. 49).

[23] Hugh Seton-Watson, The Russian Empire 1801–1917 (Oxford, 1967), p. 211.

[24] Granville, op. cit., i, p. 354.

[25] The medal is illustrated by von Richter, op. cit., p. 303.

[26] Русская старина (1880), xxvii, p. 642; Русскій Архивъ (1875), i, p. 199; ibid. (1884), ii, p. 253; Lazhechnikov, op. cit., p. 332.

[27] D. A. Rovinsky, Подробный словарь русскихъ гравированныхъ портретовъ (St. Petersburg, 1889), i, p. 1201. Osterman-Tolstoy's house in Florence was that afterwards occupied by his compatriot, the celebrated sculptor Prince Yury Trubetskoy (M. D. Buturlin, 'Записки графа М. Д. Бутурлина', Русскій архивъ (1898), iii, p. 436).

[28] John Murray, A Hand-Book for Travellers in Switzerland (London, 1846), p. 152.

[29] For engravings of Osterman-Tolstoy, cf. Rovinsky, op. cit., i, pp. 1199–1201. His relative Feodor Petrovich Tolstoy made a fine wax bas-relief head-and-shoulders of him in his general's uniform some time before his temporary retirement in 1810 (Kuznetsova, op. cit., p. 307).

5. "The American"

[1] Andrew Steinmetz, *The Romance of Duelling in all Times and Countries* (London, 1868) ii, pp. 291–2.
[2] S. L. Tolstoy, Федор Толстой американец (Moscow, 1926), p. 7; G. V. Krasnov (ed.), Л. Н. Толстой в воспоминаниях современников (Moscow, 1978), i, p. 91. In these notes I avoid pointless repetition of references to Sergei Tolstoy's authoritative monograph, an essential source for any study of F. I. Tolstoy. Cf. also V. I. Saitov (ed.), Остафьевскій архивъ князей Вяземскихъ (St. Petersburg, 1899), i, pp. 518–21.
[3] N. Arnold, С. Н. Марин (1776–1813): полное собрание сочиненій (Moscow, 1948), pp. 311, 377.
[4] S. L. Tolstoy, op. cit., p. 14; cf. E. V. Kuznetsova, Федор Петрович Толстой 1783–1873 (Moscow, 1977), p. 15.
[5] K. T. Khlebnikova (ed.) Русская Америка в неопубликованных записках (Leningrad, 1979), p. 267.
[6] S. L. Tolstoy, op. cit., pp. 15–26; Русская старина (1876), xv, pp. 539–40; Литературный Вѣстникъ (1904), vii, p. 43; Русскій Архивъ (1873), xi, pp. 1102–4; P. A. Tikhmenev, *A History of the Russian-American Company* (Washington, 1978), pp. 65–74; Richard Belgrave Hoppner (tr.), *Voyage Round the World, in the years 1803, 1804, 1805, & 1806 . . . under the Command of Captain A. J. von Krusenstern . . .* (London, 1813), p. 212.

It is worth noting that the foregoing account of Feodor Ivanovich's adventures in the Far East contains minor discrepancies impossible wholly satisfactorily to reconcile. The anecdotes themselves and Tolstoy's sojourn in the wilds are well attested by friends and relations to whom he recounted them. But when Kruzenstern sailed to Kamchatka he did not visit a desert island, on which most accounts place Tolstoy's disembarkation. Moreover, the epithet "the American" which Tolstoy received and the fact that he lived among the Tlingit people of Alaska indicate that his stay was far from Kamchatka, and must have been on Kodiak, Sitka or another adjacent island. The most likely explanation is that Feodor Ivanovich was deposited on a lonely stretch of seashore near the port of Petropavlovsk in Kamchatka, and thence made his way for motives unknown across the Aleutians to the island off the coast of Russian Alaska where he passed the winter. There are other possibilities suggested by Sergei Tolstoy, but it is essentially only the geography that is in question and not the history.

[7] N. Arnold, op. cit., p. 376; Русскій Архивъ, xi, p. 1103.
[8] 'Изъ записокъ И. П. Липранди', ibid. (1871), viii, pp. 339–47. The poet Marin sent Tolstoy an amusingly sympathetic ode to his place of exile at Nyslott (N. Arnold, op. cit., pp. 103–6; cf. p. 290) in reply to an ironical appeal from Tolstoy of 7 August 1805 (pp. 374, 375–6).
[9] Ibid., pp. 348–9; V. Orlov (ed.), Денис Давыдов: Военные записки (Moscow, 1940), p. 199.
[10] Русская старина, xv, pp. 538–9.
[11] 'Записки графа П. Х. Граббе', Русскій Архивъ (1873), xi, pp. 839, 1046; T. G. Tsiavlovskaia, Рисунки Пушкина (Moscow, 1980), p. 140;

Русская старина (1878), ii, p. 335. The English Club building still exists, its magnificent classical exterior now alas housing the "Museum of the Revolution of the USSR" (M. Ilyin, Москва: Памятники архитектуры XVIII-первой трети XIX века (Moscow, 1975), pp. 273–6).
[12] Литературный Вѣстникъ, vii, pp. 42–3; V. Veresaev, Спутники Пушкина (Moscow, 1937), p. 35. The full text of the Knights of the Corks' anthem was published by T. A. Martemianov in Историческій вѣстникъ (1903), xcii, pp. 210–11.

An interesting point, not taken up by Sergei Tolstoy in his monograph, is the statement in the verse that Feodor Ivanovich had been set down at Kamchatka and afterwards journeyed to the Aleutians. Tolstoy's placid reception of this version provides likely confirmation that that was indeed the order of his travels.

[13] Cf. the good-humoured exchange of poems between Tolstoy and S. N. Marin (N. Arnold, op. cit., pp. 103–6, 375–6).
[14] For Tolstoy's relationship with Pushkin, cf. S. L. Tolstoy, op. cit., pp. 49–56; Tsiavloskaia, op. cit., pp. 141–3; L. A. Chereisky, Пушкин и его Окружение (Leningrad, 1975), p. 415; V. Veresaev, op. cit., pp. 36–7; 'Г. В.', 'Эпиграмма Толстова-Американца на А. Пушкина', Литературная мысль: альманах (Petrograd, 1923), ii, pp. 237–9; Пушкин: Письма последних лет 1834–1837 (Leningrad, 1969), pp. 473–4; N. Lerner, 'Съ кого Пушкинъ списалъ Зарѣцкаго', Русская старина (1908), cxxxiii, pp. 422–4.
[15] Cf. Русскій Архивъ (1901), i, p. 89.
[16] N. Arnold, op. cit., pp. 367, 368.
[17] T. G. Tsiavlovskaia, op. cit., pp. 143–4.
[18] 'Воспоминанія М. О. Каменской', Историческій вѣстникъ (1894), lvii, pp. 41–2.
[19] Русскій Архивъ (1873), xi, p. 838; ibid. (1871), viii, pp. 349–50.
[20] Nikolai Varsukov, Жизнь и труди М. П. Погодина (St. Petersburg, 1892), v, p. 360.
[21] M. A. Shchepkin, Михаилъ Семеновичъ Щепкинъ 1788–1863г. (St. Petersburg, 1914), p. 219.
[22] Veresaev, op. cit., p. 35.
[23] Русскій Архивъ (1876), ii, p. 218.
[24] Русская старина, cxxxiii, pp. 426–7.
[25] *The Half-Mad Lord: Thomas Pitt 2nd Baron Camelford* (London, 1978).
[26] R. F. Christian, *Tolstoy's Letters* (New York, 1978), p. 202.

6. "The Embodiment of an entire Academy"

[1] 'Воспоминанія М. Ѳ. Каменской', Историческій вѣстникъ (1894), lv, pp. 48–58. Madame Kamensky's memoirs remain the prime source for Feodor Petrovich's personal life. With a few exceptions, no references or bibliography will be provided in this chapter, as all available sources are listed in the recent admirable biography by E. G. Kuznetsova, Федор Петрович Толстой (Moscow, 1977).

[2] Cf. Max J. Okenfuss, 'The Jesuit Origins of Petrine Education', in J. G. Garrard (ed.), *The Eighteenth Century in Russia* (Oxford, 1973), pp. 106–30.

[3] For the Academy, cf. Kuznetsova, op. cit., pp. 16–17; A. B. Granville, *St. Petersburgh. A Journal of Travels to and from that Capital* (London, 1828), ii, pp. 138–44.

[4] A self-portrait in 1804 shows Tolstoy in his naval uniform, with dirk and cocked hat (Kuznetsova, op. cit., p. 109).

[5] Reproduced in ibid., p. 27.

[6] Историческій вѣстникъ, lv, p. 315. For the exchange rate, cf. Granville, op. cit., ii, pp. 329–31, 714.

[7] Kuznetsova, op. cit., pp. 32. 307.

[8] Cf. Harold B. Segel, 'Classicism and Classical Antiquity in Eighteenth- and Early-Nineteenth-Century Russian Literature', Garrard, op. cit., pp. 48–71.

[9] Cf. A. Strycek, *La Russie des Lumières: Denis Fonvizine* (Paris, 1976), pp. 344–69.

7. Two Reactionaries

[1] Count M. Tolstoy, 'Краткое описаніе жизни Петра Андреевича Толстаго', Русскій Архивъ (1896), i, p. 20. The Count's devotion to Bishop Tikhon (*vide infra*) was recalled years later by Dmitri Andreevich Tolstoy when Minister of Education (P. D. Shestakov, 'Графъ Дмитрій Андреевичъ Толстой: министръ народнаго просвѣщенія', Русская старина (1891), lxx, p. 200). A Count N. S. Tolstoy travelled about the same time on similar journeys with 10 carriages drawn by 45 horses, accompanied by 45 servants 'Русская жизнь въ началѣ XIX вѣка', ibid. (1899), xcvii, p. 35).

[2] The practice was certainly as old as the twelfth century (cf. Russell Zguta, *Russian Minstrels: A History of the Skomorokhi* (Oxford, 1978), p. 98). For Count Feodor Tolstoy's library, cf. Friedrich Otto, *The History of Russian Literature* (Oxford, 1839), p. 384. He died in 1849 aged 90 (Vladimir Saitov, Петербургскій Некрополь (Moscow, 1883), p. 132).

[3] Dmitri Tolstoy's cousin, the poet Alexei Constantinovich, began his service contentedly enough in the Archives, but later chafed strongly against the golden chains that bound him to the Court (André Lirondelle, *Le Poète Alexis Tolstoi: l'homme et l'oeuvre* (Paris, 1912), pp. 28, 191–4). The best discussion of the Table of Ranks is that by Helju Aulik Bennett, 'Evolution of the Meanings of Chin', *California Slavic Studies* (1977), x, pp. 1–43.

[4] Cf. M. V. Nechkin (ed.), Возстаніе Декабристовъ: Документы (Moscow, 1980), xvii, pp. 126, 233.

[5] M. D. Buturlin, 'Записки графа М. Д. Бутурлина', Русскій Архивъ (1898), iii, pp. 424–41, 522–79; L. A. Chereysky, Пушкин и его окруженіе (Leningrad, 1975), p. 416.

[6] Cf. Daniel T. Orlovsky, *The Limits of Reform: The Ministry of Internal Affairs in Imperial Russia, 1802–1881* (Harvard, 1981), pp. 72, 117, 148.

[7] 'Изъ памятныхъ замѣтокъ П. М. Голенищева-Кутузова-Толстаго', Русскій Архивъ (1883), i, pp. 221–2.

[8] D. N. Tolstoy's autobiography up to 1861 was published as 'Записки графа Дмитрія Николаевича Толстаго', ibid. (1885), ii, pp. 5–70.

[9] E. M. Feoktistov, Воспоминанія за кулисами политики и литературы (Leningrad, 1929), p. 163.

[10] For the Lyceum in D. A. Tolstoy's time, cf. Allen Sinel, *The Classroom and the Chancellery: State Educational Reform in Russia under Count Dmitry Tolstoi* (Harvard, 1973), pp. 37–44; idem, 'The Socialization of the Russian Bureaucratic Elite, 1811–1917: Life of the Tsarskoe Selo Lyceum and the School of Jurisprudence', *Russian History* (1976), iii, pp. 1–31. I am indebted to Professor Sinel for helpful advice in compiling this section.

[11] 'Воспоминанія князя А. В. Мещерскаго', Русскій Архивъ (1901), i, pp. 497–500; Feoktistov, op. cit., p. 166.

[12] Orlovsky, op. cit., pp. 35–6, 224.

[13] Hugh Seton-Watson, *The Russian Empire 1801–1917* (Oxford, 1967), p. 380.

[14] Cf. Lyman H. Legters (ed.), *Russia: Essays in History and Literature* (Leiden, 1972), pp. 27–32; R. E. F. Smith, *The Enserfment of the Russian Peasantry* (Cambridge, 1968), p. 26.

[15] Robert K. Massie, *Peter the Great: His Life and World* (London, 1981), pp. 781–2; Isabel de Madariaga, *Russia in the Age of Catherine the Great* (London, 1981), pp. 298–9.

[16] Terence Emmons, *The Russian Landed Gentry and the Peasant Emancipation of 1861* (Cambridge, 1968), p. 310.

[17] Aylmer Maude, *The Life of Tolstoy: First Fifty Years* (London, 1911), p. 299.

[18] I. Listovsky, 'Письмо графа Д. А. Толстого къ дядѣ его графу Д. Н. Толстому', Русскій Архивъ (1905), i, p. 688. For the elder Tolstoy's influence over the younger, cf. Sinel, op. cit., pp. 47, 49, 275. According to Feoktistov (op. cit., p. 167), D. N. Tolstoy's unequal marriage and the subsequent birth of an unexpected heir to the Znamenskoe estate caused Dmitri Andreevich to break off relations with his uncle.

[19] Sinel, op. cit., pp. 49–52.

[20] W. Bruce Lincoln, *The Romanovs: Autocrats of All the Russias* (London, 1981), pp. 437–40.

[21] James C. McClelland, *Autocrats and Academics: Education, Culture, and Society in Tsarist Russia* (Chicago, 1979), pp. 58–60, 95–6.

[22] Nicholas V. Riasanovsky, *A Parting of Ways: Government and the Educated Public in Russia 1801–1855* (Oxford, 1976), p. 275.

[23] Sinel, op. cit., pp. 57–8; Feoktistov, op. cit., pp. 169–70.

[24] Sergei Manassein, 'Графъ Д. А. Толстой въ Казани', Русская старина (1905), cxxii, pp. 572–7; P. D. Shestakov, 'Графъ Дмитрій Андреевичъ Толстой какъ министръ народнаго просвѣщенія', ibid. (1891), lxix, pp. 387–405; N. Bekkarevich, 'Оренбургская гимназія стараго времени', ibid. (1903), cxvi, pp. 408–10.

[25] McClelland, op. cit., pp. 11, 40.

[26] 'И. И. Пироговъ', Русская старина (1881),

xxx, pp. 631–3.

27 McClelland, op. cit., p. xi.

28 Sinel, op. cit., pp. 130–1.

29 E. Lampert, *Studies in Rebellion* (London, 1957), pp. 151–4.

30 Allen Sinel, 'Educating the Russian Peasantry: The Elementary School Reforms of Count Dmitrii Tolstoi', *Slavic Review* (New York, 1960), xxvii, p. 70.

31 Idem, 'Count Dmitrii Tolstoi and the Preparation of Russian School Teachers', *Canadian Slavic Studies* (Montreal, 1969), iii, pp. 261–2.

32 McClelland, op. cit., pp. 14, 22.

33 Sinel, op. cit., p. 53.

34 Orlovsky, op. cit., pp. 170–96.

35 Roger Fulford (ed.), *Beloved Mama: Private Correspondence of Queen Victoria and the German Crown Princess 1878–1885* (London, 1981), p. 97.

36 W. Bruce Lincoln, op. cit., p. 592.

37 Cf. Hans Rogger, 'The Jewish Policy of Late Tsarism: A Reappraisal', *The Wiener Library Bulletin* (1971), xxv, pp. 44–5; idem, 'Tsarist Policy on Jewish Emigration', *Soviet Jewish Affairs* (1973), iii, pp. 28–9; idem, 'Government, Jews, Peasants, and Land in Post-Emancipation Russia', *Cahiers du Monde russe et soviétique* (1976), xvii, pp. 171–85; Sylvain Bensidoun, *L'agitation paysanne en Russie de 1881 à 1902* (Paris, 1975), pp. 292–6.

38 Русскій Архивъ (1905), i, pp. 688–9. For Mihail Vladimirovich Tolstoy, cf. 'Путевые очерки, замѣтки и наброски Троице-Сергіева лавра, 1882г.', Русская старина (1889), lxii, pp. 508–9.

39 Stephen Lukashevich, 'The Holy Brotherhood: 1881–1883', *The American Slavic and East European Review* (1959), xviii, pp. 491–509.

40 *Soviet Jewish Affairs*, ii, p. 29.

41 'М. Н. Катков и Александр III в 1886–1887гг.', Красный архив (1933), lviii, pp. 74–5.

42 Cf. Seton-Watson, op. cit., pp. 569–74. Tolstoy's personal feelings were strongly patriotic and hostile to the overbearing power of Germany (Edmond Toutain, *Alexandre III et la République Française 1885–1888* (Paris, 1929), pp. 62, 216).

43 My summary account of Dmitri Tolstoy's period as Minister of the Interior draws extensively on Professor Jackson Taylor's unpublished Ph.D. dissertation submitted at New York University in 1970 under the title *Dmitrii Andreevich Tolstoi and the Ministry of the Interior, 1882–1889*. I am greatly obliged to Professor Taylor for further comments and information in correspondence.

44 Cf. Jac L. Williams, 'The Turn of the Tide: Some Thoughts on the Welsh Language in Education', *Transactions of the Honourable Society of Cymmrodorion* (1963), i, p. 51.

45 *Bernhard Fürst von Bülow: Denkwürdigkeiten* (Berlin, 1931), iv, pp. 572–4. I am indebted to Professor Jackson Taylor for pointing out to me this important reference.

46 A. Walicki, *The Controversy over Capitalism: Studies in the Social Philosophy of the Russian Populists* (Oxford, 1969), pp. 132–65; Seton-Watson, op. cit., pp. 530–1; Leszek Kolakowski, *Main Currents of Marxism* (Oxford, 1978), ii, pp. 329–44.

47 Ibid., p. 331.

48 D. Mackenzie Wallace, *Russia* (London, 1877), i, pp. 167–8.

49 Cf. Richard Jefferies, *Hodge and his Masters* (London, 1880), ii, pp. 231–58.

50 Bensidoun, op. cit., pp. 201–301; cf. Красный архив (1938), lxxxix–xc, pp. 208–57.

51 Th. G. Terner, 'Воспоминанія жизни Ѳ. Т. Тернера', Русская старина (1911), cxlv, pp. 394–6.

52 Professor Jackson Taylor has pointed out to me the detailed accounts of Tolstoy's illnesses to be found in the British Embassy reports (PRO: FO.65/1216, 1295, 1329, 1333).

53 FO. 65/1361.

54 Русская старина, lxx, p. 208.

56 V. P. Semeonov (ed.), Россія: полное географическое описаніе нашего отечества (St. Petersburg, 1902), ii, p. 402.

8. Quentin Durward in a Frock Coat

1 Cf. Tolstoy's friend Prince A. V. Meshchersky's account ('Воспоминанія князя А. В. Мещерскаго', Русскій Архивъ (1900), ii, pp. 370–4).

2 For Alexander Petrovich Tolstoy's friendship with Gogol, cf. Henri Troyat, *Gogol* (Paris, 1971), pp. 429–31, 507–9, 518, 560–1; N. D. Brodsky et al. (ed.), Гоголь в воспоминаниях современников (Moscow, 1952), pp. 122, 311, 405, 414, 428, 435, 445, 496, 504, 509, 517, 519–20, 546, 549, 552–3; Русская старина (1902), cx, pp. 441–7. David Magarshack weaves a conspiracy theory around Gogol's last days which is not borne out by the first-hand evidence (*Gogol: A Life* (London, 1957), pp. 303–7; cf. pp. 226, 235, 237, 248, 251, 261–3, 269).

3 I am indebted to my old friend Mr. H. Graham Bower for drawing this unpublished correspondence to my attention.

4 In view of the superb biography by André Lirondelle, *Le Poète Alexis Tolstoï: l'homme et l'œuvre* (Paris, 1912), of which I have made extensive use, I do not append here the usual apparatus of notes. More up-to-date bibliographies are to be found in D. S. Likhachev et al. (ed.), Русские Писатели: Библиографический словарь (Moscow, 1971), pp. 620–4; and in the excellent literary study by A. K. Dalton, *A. K. Tolstoy* (New York, 1972).

9. The Pursuit of Innocence

1 I am indebted to Bezirksleiter Willi Moser, who was stationed at Yasnaya Polyana in the medical corps in 1942, who has supplied me with photographs and an account of the house during the occupation.

2 R. F. Christian, *Tolstoy: A Critical Introduction* (Cambridge, 1969), pp. 28–9; cf. E. B. Greenwood, *Tolstoy: The Comprehensive Vision* (London, 1975), p. 23. In view of the extraordinary number of books written about L. N. Tolstoy, I have confined references in this chapter to occasional specific points of interest. The richest biographical source (up to 1892) is N. N. Gusev's Лев Николаевич Толстой (Moscow, 1954–79); probably the best-written and

most perceptive remains Aylmer Maude's *The Life of Tolstoy* (London, 1911). A lengthy picturesque version for the general reader is that of Henri Troyat, *Tolstoï* (Paris, 1965), who, astonishingly enough, does not appear to have read Maude's work. Quotations from Tolstoy's letters are generally in the translation by R. F. Christian, *Tolstoy's Letters* (New York, 1978).

[3] Cf. *Oeuvres de J. J. Rousseau* (Paris, 1819), iii, pp. 221–3, 228; H. Kohn, *The Mind of Germany* (London, 1965), p. 50.

[4] Greenwood, op. cit., pp. 57–81.

[5] Alfred Adler, *The Practice and Theory of Individual Psychology* (London, 1929), pp. 280–5.

[6] Idem, *Problems of Neurosis: A Book of Case-Histories* (London, 1929), p. 146.

[7] Gusev, op. cit., iv, p. 209.

[8] Troyat, op. cit., p. 650.

[9] S. M. Borisov, Ясная Поляна (Moscow, 1978), pp. 52–3.

[10] V. G. Chertkov (ed.), Л. Н. Толстой: Полное собрание сочинений (Moscow, 1936), xvii, pp. 402, 407, 423–4, 628.

[11] Quoted by R. F. Christian, *Tolstoy's "War and Peace": A Study* (Oxford, 1962), pp. 102–3.

[12] Л. Н. Толстой: Переписка с русскими писателями (Moscow, 1978), i, p. 203.

[13] Greenwood, op. cit., pp. 148–9.

[14] Cf. Troyat, op. cit., pp. 804–5.

[15] Gusev, op. cit., iv, pp. 329–31.

[16] 'Николай Васильевичъ Гоголь: Письма къ нему А. О. Смирновой. рожд. Россетъ', Русская старина (1890), lxvii, p. 195. The reference is to Sophia Petrovna Apraxin (1800–1886), daughter of Peter Alexandrovich Tolstoy, Ambassador to Napoleon in 1807.

[17] S. A. Makashin (ed.), Л. Н. Толстой в воспоминаниях современников (Moscow, 1978), ii, p. 448.

10. "The Third Tolstoy"

This chapter draws extensively on the following books, and precise references will only be made where the point is of specific interest.

A. V. Alpatov, Алексей Николаевич Толстой (Moscow, 1955); Алексей Толстой—Мастер исторического романа (Moscow, 1958).

A. V. Alpatov and L. M. Poliak (ed.), Творчество А. Н. Толстой: сборник статей (Moscow, 1957).

Vadim Baranov, Революция и судьба художника: А. Толстой и его путь к социалистическому реализму (Moscow, 1967).

I. I. Veksler, Алексей Николаевич Толстой: жизненный и творческий путь (Moscow, 1948).

P. A. Borozdina, А. Н. Толстой и Театр (Voronezh, 1974).

V. A. Zapadov, Алексей Николаевич Толстой: биография (Leningrad, 1969).

Y. A. Krestinsky, А. Н. Толстой: жизнь и творчество (Краткий очерк) (Moscow, 1960).

Alexei Naldeev, Революция и родина в творчестве А. Н. Толстого (Moscow, 1968);

Алексей Толстой (Moscow, 1974).

Z. A. Nikitina and L. I. Tolstoy (ed.), Воспоминания об А. Н. Толстом: сборник (Moscow, 1973).

L. M. Poliak, Алексей Толстой—художник: проза (Moscow, 1964).

I. S. Rozhdestvenskaya and A. G. Khodyuk, А. Н. Толстой: семинарий (Leningrad, 1962).

G. Smirnova, Трилогия А. Н. Толстого "Хождение по мукам" (Leningrad, 1976).

M. Charny, Путь Алексея Толстого: очерк творчества (Moscow, 1961).

These Soviet works, though in most cases scholarly and valuable, suffer seriously from not being permitted to utilize works published outside the Soviet Union. Of these Ivan Bunin's memoirs are the most indispensable. A convenient English bibliography of Tolstoy's own works is published by Heinrich E. Schulz *et al.* (ed.), *Who was Who in the USSR* (Metuchen, N. J., 1972), p. 545.

[1] Nikitina and Tolstoy, op. cit., pp. 250–2, 293–4.

[2] Ernst Fischer and Franz Marek, *Lenin in His Own Words* (London, 1972), p. 89.

[3] Cf. *Encounter* (April, 1979), lii, p. 94.

[4] L. D. Opulskaya, Лев Николаевич Толстой: Материалы к биографии с 1886 по 1892 год (Moscow, 1979), p. 268.

[5] Gleb Struve, *Russian Literature under Lenin and Stalin 1917–1953* (Oklahoma, 1971), pp. 142–3.

[6] Nikitina and Tolstoy, op. cit., pp. 22–3.

[7] For a full, though perhaps biased account of the quarrel between Tolstoy's parents, cf. ibid., pp. 70–3.

[8] Cf. Richard G. Robbins, Jr., *Famine in Russia 1891–1892* (New York, 1975).

[10] Zapadov, op. cit., p. 47; Nikitina and Tolstoy, op. cit., p. 116. Tolstoy's appearance and "ancestors" are described by Ivan Bunin, Воспоминанія (Paris, 1950), pp. 210–12.

[11] R. H. Bruce Lockhart, *Memoirs of a British Agent* (London, 1933), p. 145.

[12] Nikitina and Tolstoy, op. cit., pp. 113–14. For the Zemstvos, cf. George Katkov, *Russia 1917: The February Revolution* (London, 1967), pp. 3–11.

[13] A. S. Miasnikov, A. N. Tikhonov and L. I. Tolstoy (ed.), А. Н. Толстой: Полное собрание сочинений (Moscow, 1949), xiii, p. 557.

[14] Countess Tolstoy's account is in Nikitina and Tolstoy, op. cit., pp. 124–5; but cf. Bunin, op. cit., p. 234.

[15] Guy Verret, 'Maxime Gor'kij et Alexis Tolstoj à la Croisée des Chemins', *Revue des Études Slaves* (Paris, 1975), xxxiv, pp. 144–50.

[16] D. Fedotoff White, 'An Aristocrat at Stalin's Court', *The American Slavic and East European Review* (New York, 1950), ix, pp. 209–10.

[17] Ibid., p. 216. Cf. Bunin's pointed comments about Tolstoy's attitude to his life in exile (op. cit., pp. 205–7, 234).

[18] Nikitina and Tolstoy, op. cit., pp. 41–2.

[19] Struve, op. cit., pp. 270–1.

[20] Nikitina and Tolstoy, op. cit., p. 131.

[21] Cf. G. Nivat, 'La genèse d'un roman historique soviétique: Pierre le Grand d'Alexis Tolstoï', *Cahiers du Monde Russe et Soviétique* (The Hague, 1961), ii, pp. 40–2.

22 J. P. T. Bury and J. C. Barry (ed.), *An Englishman in Paris: 1803; The Journal of Bertie Greatheed* (London, 1953), p. 46.

23 Cf. my *Stalin's Secret War* (London, 1981), pp. 35–49. Edward J. Brown shrewdly remarks that "if Tolstoy could upon his return live as a kind of 'workers' and peasants' Count', what was even more important for him was that he could remain a Russian 'Count' " (*Russian Literature Since the Revolution* (London, 1969), p. 255).

24 Struve, op. cit., p. 83; George Reavey, *Soviet Literature To-day* (London, 1946), p. 46.

25 Spencer E. Roberts, *Soviet Historical Melodrama: Its Role in the Development of a National Mythology* (The Hague, 1965), pp. 46–86.

26 Cf. Peter Reddaway, 'Literature, the Arts and the Personality of Lenin' in Leonard Schapiro and Peter Reddaway (ed.), *Lenin: The Man, the Theorist, the Leader* (New York, 1967), pp. 37–70.

27 Roberts, op. cit., pp. 86–91.

28 Cf. Rozhdestvenskaya and Khodyuk (ed.), p. 274.

29 Roberts, op. cit., p. 4.

30 Alexander Barmine, *One Who Survived: The Life Story of a Russian under the Soviets* (New York, 1945), pp. 298–9; Nikitina and Tolstoy, p. 367.

31 Cf. Roberts, op. cit., pp. 95–126.

32 Cf. Rozhdestvenskaya and Khodyuk (ed.), pp. 274–5.

33 Cf. *Cahiers du Monde Russe et Soviétique*, ii, pp. 37–55. For an evaluation of the literary and historical value of Tolstoy's portrayal of Peter, cf. Professor Xenia Gasiorowska's *The Image of Peter the Great in Russian Fiction* (Wisconsin, 1979).

34 Barmine, op. cit., p. 298.

35 Roberts, op. cit., pp. 144–51.

36 Cf. Rozhdestvenskaya and Khodyuk, op. cit., p. 60.

37 Edward Crankshaw, *Russia and Britain* (London, n.d. ?1944), p. 110.

38 Полное собрание сочинений, xiii, p. 491.

39 Eugene Lyons, *Assignment in Utopia* (London, ?1937), p. 587; Nikitina and Tolstoy, op. cit., pp. 140–1, 194, 241–3, 291, 300–3.

40 Ibid., p. 243; Rozhdestvenskaya and Khodyuk, p. 164.

41 Nikitina and Tolstoy, op. cit., pp. 244, 342.

42 Brown, op. cit., p. 257.

43 Ibid., pp. 159–60, 259, 272, 446; Adam B. Ulam, *Stalin: The Man and his Era* (London, 1974), p. 436.

44 Полное собрание сочинений, xiii, pp. 474–6; ibid, xiv, pp. 360–2.

45 Solomon Volkov (ed.), *Testimony: The Memoirs of Dmitri Shostakovich* (London, 1979), pp. 172–3.

46 Nikitina and Tolstoy, op. cit., pp. 248–50, 322–3, 360–3, 422–4, 430.

47 Ibid., pp. 179, 193–4, 283, 291–2, 364.

48 Ibid., p. 270; Alexander Solzhenitsyn, *The Gulag Archipelago 1918–1956: An Experiment in Literary Investigation* (London, 1978), iii, p. 487.

49 Полное собрание сочинений, xiii, pp. 146–8; Robert Conquest, *The Great Terror: Stalin's Purge of the Thirties* (London, 1968), p. 330; Struve, op. cit., p. 63. Tolstoy must have been aware that the NKVD had a dossier for him too, if necessary (Nadezhda Mandelstam, Воспоминания (New York, 1970), p. 336).

50 Ibid., pp. 7, 15, 25, 96, 236, 378; Nikitina and Tolstoy, op. cit., p. 239.

51 Ibid., pp. 261, 306–20.

52 Bunin, op. cit., p. 235.

53 Nikitina and Tolstoy, op. cit., p. 261.

54 Ibid., p. 165.

55 Полное собрание сочинений, xiii, pp. 249–50.

56 Joseph Czapski, *The Inhuman Land* (London, 1951), p. 187; Nikitina and Tolstoy, p. 97.

57 Полное собрание сочинений, xiii, pp. 250–5, 262–6.

58 Ibid., xiv, p. 87.

59 Cf. the booklet of collected articles, Статьи (1942–1943) (Moscow, 1944), which is said to have had an inspiring effect on front-line troops.

60 Полное собрание сочинений, xiv, pp. 111–17.

61 Czapski, op. cit., pp. 187–91.

62 Cf. Nikolai Tolstoy, op. cit., pp. 35–49, and the sources quoted there.

63 Rozhdestvenskaya and Khodyuk, op. cit., p. 167; Nikitina and Tolstoy op. cit., pp. 177, 244–5, 262, 289, 364, 367, 369–70.

64 Zapadov, op. cit., p. 124; Czapski, op. cit., p. 188; Arthur Koestler, *The Yogi and the Commissar and other Essays* (London, 1945), p. 152; Ilya Ehrenburg, 'Люди, годы, жизнь', Литературная газета (1960), 4 June. Molotov provided a welcoming speech at Tolstoy's first appearance in the Supreme Soviet (Bunin, op. cit., p. 202).

65 Rozhdestvenskaya and Khodyuk, op. cit., pp. 26, 182, 186–7, 393, 438; Louis FitzGibbon, *Katyn: a crime without parallel* (London, 1971), p. 164; idem, *Unpitied and Unknown: Katyn ... Bologoye ... Dergachi* (London, 1975), pp. 60, 83, 183, 191.

66 Rozhdestvenskaya and Khodyuk, op. cit., pp. 188–91; Nikitina and Tolstoy, op. cit., pp. 295–8; Zapadov, op. cit., pp. 125–6. Tolstoy was exceptional in being allowed a car in wartime. (Reavey, op. cit., p. 31.)

67 Ibid., pp. 37–8.

68 Bunin, op. cit., p. 201.

69 Полное собрание сочинений, xiii, p. 494.

70 Ilya Ehrenburg, 'Люди, годы, жизнь', Новый Мир (April, 1962), xxxviii, p. 61; Bunin, op. cit., pp. 229–30.

11. Epilogue

1 Alexandra Tolstoy, Дочь (London, Ontario, 1979), pp. 69–409.

2 Cf. Paul B. Anderson, 'The Tolstoy Foundation', *The Russian Review* (1958), xvii, pp. 60–6.

3 Serge Tolstoï, *Tolstoï et les Tolstoï* (Paris, 1980).

4 Cf. Vladimir Semenoff, *The Battle of Tsushima* (London, 1907), p. 65; A. S. Novikov-Priboi, Цусима (Moscow, 1958), p. 765.

5 V. P. Semenov (ed.), Россия. Полное географическое описаніе нашего отечества (St. Petersburg, 1901), vi, p. 362.

6 P. Martynov (ed.), Матеріалы историческіе и юридическіе района бывшаго приказа Казанскаго дворца (Simbirsk, 1904), iv, pp. 365, 590.

7 G. M. Tolstoy, 'Поѣздка въ Туринскъ къ декабристу Вас. Петр. Ивашеву', Русская старина (1890), lxviii, p. 334.

[8] Письма и бумаги императора Петра Великого (Moscow, 1946), vii (part 2), p. 844.

[9] Cf. Вся Москва: адресная и справочная книга на 1915 годъ (Moscow, 1915), p. 493.

[10] Cf. Norman Stone, *The Eastern Front 1914–1917* (London, 1975), pp. 280–1.

[11] Roger Pethybridge, *The Spread of the Russian Revolution: Essays on 1917* (London, 1972), pp. 43, 50, 67, 174.

[12] George Leggett, *The Cheka: Lenin's Political Police* (Oxford, 1981), pp. 37, 280.

[13] Ibid., p. 77.

[14] John Silverlight, *The Victors' Dilemma: Allied Intervention in the Russian Civil War* (London, 1970), pp. 61–2, 78–9.

[15] The picture found its way somehow into the massive history edited by H. W. Wilson and J. A. Hammerton, *The Great War* (London, 1919), xiii, p. 377).

[16] Leggett, op. cit., pp. 119, 261, 451; Lennard D. Gerson, *The Secret Police in Lenin's Russia* (Philadelphia, 1976), p. 137.

[17] Richard H. Ullman, *Britain and the Russian Civil War: November 1918–February 1920* (Princeton, 1968), pp. 339–43.

[18] Leggett, op. cit., pp. 198–9.

[19] Cf. *The Times* for 19, 29 and 30 April and 18, 22 and 24 May 1920.

Appendix I

[1] Prince Pierre Dolgorouky, *Notice sur les Principales Familles de la Russie* (Brussels, 1843), p. 5.

[2] Cf., for two exceptionally clear accounts of the nature of the Russian nobility, Marc Raeff, *Origins of the Russian Intelligentsia: The Eighteenth-Century Nobility* (New York, 1966), pp. 38–9, 181–2; Kyril Fitzlyon and Tatiana Browning, *Before the Revolution: A View of Russia under the Last Tsar* (London, 1977), pp. 21–5.

[3] Nicholas II abdicated on behalf of himself and his son the Tsarevich on 2 March 1917; his brother, the Grand Duke Michael, reigned as Emperor for precisely one day until he too abdicated on 3 March 1917. According to the law of succession the Grand Duke Kyril automatically succeeded to his rights, though of course the *de facto* monarchy was now at an end, being abolished some time later by an unconstitutional act of the Provisional Government (cf. George Katkov, *Russia 1917: The February Revolution* (London, 1967), p. 413). He asserted his hereditary rights in August 1924, when it was clear that the late Tsar, Tsarevich, and Grand Duke Michael were no more.

[4] The *Gramota* of 8 October 1930 in favour of Pavel Sergeevich Tolstoy-Miloslavsky was confirmed to his descendents by a further authorization on 18 December 1930. Cf. comte Georges de Morant and comte d'Angerville (ed.), *Annuaire de la Noblesse de France et d'Europe* (Paris, 1957), lxviii, p. 265. For the legal position of grants conferred by non-regnant heads of dynasties, see Ronald E. Prosser, *The Royal Prerogative* (Iowa City, 1981), pp. 51–3, and the remarks of the Marquis de Ruvigny in his preface to *The Jacobite Peerage* (Edinburgh, 1904), p. xiii.

[5] Общій Гербовникъ дворянскихъ родовъ Всероссійскія Имперій начашый въ 1797мъ году (1798), ii, p. 42.

Index